W9-CUH-586

Windows NT® 4.0 Connectivity Guide

Windows NT® 4.0 Connectivity Guide

Rich Grace

IDG Books Worldwide, Inc.
An International Data Group Company

Foster City, CA ◆ Chicago, IL ◆ Indianapolis, IN ◆ Southlake, TX

IDG
BOOKS
WORLDWIDE

Windows NT®4.0 Connectivity Guide

Published by
IDG Books Worldwide, Inc.
An International Data Group Company
919 E. Hillsdale Blvd.
Suite 400
Foster City, CA 94404
www.idgbooks.com

Library of Congress Catalog Card No.: 97-77220
ISBN: 0-7645-3160-3
Printed in the United States of America

10 9 8 7 6 5 4 3 2 1

1E/QZ/QR/ZY/FC

Distributed in the United States by IDG Books Worldwide, Inc.

Distributed by Macmillan Canada for Canada; by Contemporanea de Ediciones for Venezuela; by Distribuidora Cuspide for Argentina; by CITEC for Brazil; by Ediciones ZETA S.C.R. Ltda. for Peru; by Editorial Limusa SA for Mexico; by Transworld Publishers Limited in the United Kingdom and Europe; by Academic Bookshop for Egypt; by Levant Distributors S.A.R.L. for Lebanon; by Al Jassim for Saudi Arabia; by Simron Pty. Ltd. for South Africa; by Pustak Mahal for India; by The Computer Bookshop for India; by Toppan Company Ltd. for Japan; by Addison Wesley Publishing Company for Korea; by Longman Singapore Publishers Ltd. for Singapore, Malaysia, Thailand, and Indonesia; by Unalis Corporation for Taiwan; by WS Computer Publishing Company, Inc. for the Philippines; by WoodsLane Pty. Ltd. for Australia; by WoodsLane Enterprises Ltd. for New Zealand. Authorized Sales Agent: Anthony Rudkin Associates for the Middle East and North Africa.

For general information on IDG Books Worldwide's books in the U.S., please call our Consumer Customer Service department at 800-762-2974. For reseller information, including discounts and premium sales, please call our Reseller Customer Service department at 800-434-3422.

For information on where to purchase IDG Books Worldwide's books outside the U.S., please contact our International Sales department at 415-655-3172 or fax 415-655-3295.

For information on foreign language translations, please contact our Foreign & Subsidiary Rights department at 415-655-3021 or fax 415-655-3281.

For sales inquiries and special prices for bulk quantities, please contact our Sales department at 415-655-3200 or write to the address above.

For information on using IDG Books Worldwide's books in the classroom or for ordering examination copies, please contact our Educational Sales department at 800-434-2086 or fax 817-251-8174.

For authorization to photocopy items for corporate, personal, or educational use, please contact Copyright Clearance Center, 222 Rosewood Drive, Danvers, MA 01923, or fax 508-750-4470.

The IDG Books Worldwide logo is a trademark under exclusive license to IDG Books Worldwide, Inc., from International Data Group, Inc.

ABOUT IDG BOOKS WORLDWIDE

Welcome to the world of IDG Books Worldwide.

IDG Books Worldwide, Inc., is a subsidiary of International Data Group, the world's largest publisher of computer-related information and the leading global provider of information services on information technology. IDG was founded more than 25 years ago and now employs more than 8,500 people worldwide. IDG publishes more than 275 computer publications in over 75 countries (see listing below). More than 60 million people read one or more IDG publications each month.

Launched in 1990, IDG Books Worldwide is today the #1 publisher of best-selling computer books in the United States. We are proud to have received eight awards from the Computer Press Association in recognition of editorial excellence and three from *Computer Currents'* First Annual Readers' Choice Awards. Our best-selling ...For Dummies® series has more than 30 million copies in print with translations in 30 languages. IDG Books Worldwide, through a joint venture with IDG's Hi-Tech Beijing, became the first U.S. publisher to publish a computer book in the People's Republic of China. In record time, IDG Books Worldwide has become the first choice for millions of readers around the world who want to learn how to better manage their businesses.

Our mission is simple: Every one of our books is designed to bring extra value and skill-building instructions to the reader. Our books are written by experts who understand and care about our readers. The knowledge base of our editorial staff comes from years of experience in publishing, education, and journalism — experience we use to produce books for the '90s. In short, we care about books, so we attract the best people. We devote special attention to details such as audience, interior design, use of icons, and illustrations. And because we use an efficient process of authoring, editing, and desktop publishing our books electronically, we can spend more time ensuring superior content and spend less time on the technicalities of making books.

You can count on our commitment to deliver high-quality books at competitive prices on topics you want to read about. At IDG Books Worldwide, we continue in the IDG tradition of delivering quality for more than 25 years. You'll find no better book on a subject than one from IDG Books Worldwide.

IDG BOOKS WORLDWIDE

John Kilcullen
CEO
IDG Books Worldwide, Inc.

Steven Berkowitz
President and Publisher
IDG Books Worldwide, Inc.

*Eighth Annual
Computer Press
Awards ≥1992*

*Ninth Annual
Computer Press
Awards ≥1993*

*Tenth Annual
Computer Press
Awards ≥1994*

*Eleventh Annual
Computer Press
Awards ≥1995*

Credits

ACQUISITIONS EDITOR
Anne Hamilton

DEVELOPMENT EDITOR
Janet Andrews

TECHNICAL EDITOR
Bruce McFarland

COPY EDITORS
Nate Holdread
Timothy Borek
Paul McBrearty

PRODUCTION COORDINATOR
Katy German

BOOK DESIGNER
Jim Donohue

GRAPHICS AND PRODUCTION SPECIALISTS
Stephanie Hollier
Shannon Miller
Linda Marousek

QUALITY CONTROL SPECIALISTS
Mick Arellano
Mark Schumann

PROOFREADER
David Wise

INDEXER
Donald Glassman

About the Author

Rich Grace is author of a number of computing titles, including *The Lingo Handbook for Director 6*, *The Sound & Music Workshop for Windows 95*, several best-selling books on Microsoft PowerPoint, and co-author of *Dummies 101: Windows NT 4* (with Andy Rathbone). A technical journalist for over 10 years, Rich has also tinkered with multimedia, networks, and telecommunications for that period of time. He is a frequent contributor to InfoWorld and other computing publications, and lives in San Francisco with his wife, fellow IDG author Elisabeth Parker Grace.

This book is dedicated to my wife, Elisabeth Parker Grace.

Preface

Welcome to *Windows NT 4.0 Connectivity Guide*. You hold in your hands the first book that describes Windows NT networking in functional, approachable terms. This is a concise, direct, task-oriented, no-nonsense book about tying your office network together using the fastest-growing network operating system (NOS) in the computer business: Windows NT. *Windows NT 4.0 Connectivity Guide* gives you the meat-and-potatoes stuff for connecting your office's mainstream client computers to Windows NT Server. Theory isn't discussed in this book; at least, not at any length. Getting the job done is the subject.

Who Should Read this Book

When you pick up this book, you're not expected to be a networking genius. With Windows NT you really don't have to be a genius to build a decent network. All you need to be is a computer-savvy person who wants to learn more about Windows NT and about setting up a small network. Despite the groaning shelves of Windows NT books, no book aims at the mid-range computer user who already knows how to use a word processor, has considerable computing knowledge, probably reads *InfoWorld* or *PCWeek*, and doesn't necessarily need an MCSE or a CNE certificate to build a small- or medium-size network. Unique among network operating systems, Windows NT 4.0 makes many things simpler and more approachable for a reasonably sophisticated computer user. None of the "encyclopedic" Windows NT books on the market reflect this fact. Many are written by committee. None are written with the reader in mind. None are written to be *read*.

This book is for you, my friend.

Windows NT 4.0 Connectivity Guide is not aimed primarily at those persons trying to use Windows NT 4.0 in enterprise networks. (If you're in that position, you'll still find great value in this book.) Users building and configuring small networks for 2-100 clients are the audience for this book. But this book also takes a more catholic approach, recognizing that many offices include Windows NT Workstation, Windows 95, Windows 3.*x*, NetWare, and even Macintosh computers. Don't throw out all those perfectly good machines! You'll find out exactly how all those different systems can gracefully fit into a Windows NT-based LAN.

What if you don't have a server and want to go the peer-to-peer route? Full attention is also paid to those users who have a few Windows NT Workstation and Windows 95 systems and want to peer-network them in their office. You'll find out exactly how peer-to-peer networks operate and what their limitations are.

Who Are You?

Imagine these scenarios: You're a mid-level manager on a limited office budget. Suddenly your supervisor tells you that you need to set up a small server for your department using Windows NT. Or maybe you're running your own business and have chosen to add Windows NT application serving to your old Novell NetWare network. Perhaps you're a new IS technician who needs a clearly worded, quick reference to Windows NT networking and communications – one that helps you put out most of the fires in the office network. What if your laptop-owning boss needs to connect to the server from his or her hotel room? What if you have field personnel who connect to the server over phone lines, and your boss demands that you find a way to cut down on those exorbitant long-distance phone costs? *Windows NT 4.0 Connectivity Guide* helps you do all these things, and much, much more.

The previous situations apply to individuals. In the bigger picture, organizations that will want this book include smaller stock brokerages, insurance companies and brokers, software and hardware developers, school administrative offices and education departments, accounting houses, magazine and book publishers, bank branch offices, and just about any other business or non-profit organization that doesn't want to hire an expensive consultant to hook up and integrate a Windows NT Server-based network.

Another core audience for this book is the small-business or home-based entrepreneur who wants to build a Windows NT network to organize their business. NT is a powerful business tool, and its rapidly growing market share is a sign of its accessibility, utility, and increased power. Just about any reasonably experienced computer user can build a Windows NT-based network. This is the first book about Windows NT that makes it real.

What won't you find here? This book does not cover intranets and Internet services in great detail. By the time you finish this book, you'll be ready to tackle an intranet, having gained a great deal of accessible advance preparation. Despite the tremendous hype surrounding intranets and their associated buzzwords (*extranets*, *ultranets*, and so on), they are not too complicated, and their missions are not revolutionary. Many companies with working, existing networks realistically have no need for intranets, sexy as they currently are. The amount of value intranets add to an existing network is still in serious doubt.

The amount of value this book brings to you is not in doubt. No other Windows NT book brings so many applied networking tasks to you in such compressed, direct, and honest terms. *Windows NT 4.0 Connectivity Guide* provides twice the amount of networking solutions compared to any competing title on the market. The same result is accomplished with half the page count. If you need to find the solution to a problem in 60 seconds or less, no other book delivers what you need in quite the way this book does.

Bigger does not necessarily mean better. Strike a blow for yourself and your business. If you need to build a Windows NT network, look no further than *Windows NT 4.0 Connectivity Guide.*

Difficulty Level

The difficulty level of this book is moderate. Many of the procedures described here stretch over fifteen to twenty discrete steps. For example, to gain a solid under-standing of how to set up a user account and connect a Windows 95 system to the network, you need to read all of Chapter 2. Unlike any other book in its field, *Windows NT 4 Connectivity Guide* provides painstaking, step-by-step procedures for every key connectivity task in this book. Nothing of importance is left to chance. This is the most straightforward Windows NT Server book you'll ever find because it's written from *your* perspective.

Inevitably, as in any networking book, some basic computing knowledge is assumed. You should know how to navigate dialog boxes and use pull-down menus, use the command-line interface once in awhile, and follow clear, concise instructions. That's pretty much it. Nothing in this book is rocket science. When you run across a confusing feature or element during an exercise, I explain it in understandable terms and discuss what to do about it. Broad-based networking skills are *not* necessary for getting the most out of this book. Requiring only aver-age computer knowledge and an ability to follow directions, this book is accessible to any knowledgeable computer user.

How This Book Is Organized

Windows NT 4.0 Connectivity Guide is organized into four sections, plus an intro-ductory chapter.

Part 1: Networking Tasks

A large number of Windows NT users will spend a lot of time in the six chapters of this section. These chapters take you through all the key areas of mainstream Windows NT LAN building: Building and installing your server, defining user accounts, connecting Windows 95 and a Windows NT Workstation clients to a Windows NT Server, connecting Windows 3.*x* and Macintosh clients, peer-to-peer networking, and finally setting up a print server.

Perhaps the most important part of this book comes in Chapter 3, which pro-vides a rare discussion of TCP/IP networking and its Windows NT services: WINS, DNS, and DHCP. It's rare because you're actually able to read, understand, and apply TCP/IP in less than forty pages. TCP/IP is the foundation of modern network-ing. This book is the first to explain it in concise, approachable terms.

CHAPTER 1: THE DIGITAL GAUNTLET: SETTING UP WINDOWS NT

This first chapter takes you through two important topics. First there's an intensive discussion of the type of hardware you need if you're going to run Windows NT. No, NT won't run on just any old PC. Particularly if you run a business, you need to make the right equipment investments. I tell you how to do so in painstaking detail.

When you have the right hardware, you must set up Windows NT. The second part of Chapter 1 focuses on the arduous process of setting up Windows NT. You literally run a gauntlet when you install NT. Potential errors and problems abound. I guide you between the Scylla and Charybdis of hardware problems and setup crashes, to bring you safely to your goal — getting a functional Windows NT Server up and running. Windows NT Workstation setup is also described in detail.

CHAPTER 2: SETTING UP MAINSTREAM MICROSOFT NETWORKS

In this chapter you learn the nuts and bolts of connecting and networking a Windows NT workstation and Windows 95 clients to a Windows NT server. The basic assumption is that you're using a Windows NT domain server, which provides most of the key security and management features you need to create an efficient working network. A key area discussed here is the process of creating user accounts and defining share-level permissions and access rights for each client. The default networking protocol used in this chapter is NetBEUI, but the methods described here are mostly protocol-invisible and apply for any networking protocol.

CHAPTER 3: LAN-BASED TCP/IP NETWORKING

This is perhaps the most important chapter. It discusses, in concrete, real-world terms, how to build, configure, and activate a TCP/IP-based LAN under Windows NT. By itself this task is the most all-encompassing one you'll find in this book. Every major Windows NT service has a role to play in such a network, but you'll concentrate on three: WINS (Windows Internet Naming Service), DNS (Domain Naming Service) and DHCP (Dynamic Host Control Protocol). Although many Windows NT books spend 100 pages or more describing the technical ins and outs of TCP/IP networking, you get the core information you need in *four* pages. Then you apply that information in a practical, understandable way. You set up each key TCP/IP-related Windows NT service in ways that make sense for your network, and in each case determine whether or not the service is needed for your application.

CHAPTER 4: CONNECTING ALTERNATIVE NETWORK CLIENTS

Chapter 4 describes how to network and integrate three different types of client computers to a Windows NT server: Windows for Workgroups, Macintosh System 7, and Macintosh System 8. Windows for Workgroups is really the only 16-bit Windows client OS usable on a Windows network, and it's the version I endorse for that purpose. Windows NT also provides solid AppleTalk/Macintosh networking support, using the AppleTalk protocol, and it receives a full discussion here.

CHAPTER 5: PEER-TO-PEER NETWORKING

Chapter 5 discusses the important topic of connecting and networking peer network clients. Because peer-to-peer networking is composed of a bunch of equal partners in the network, the issues you have to deal with are markedly different from the client-server model. You learn how to set up multiple Windows NT Workstation clients with the proper user accounts for peer resource sharing, and how to include Windows 95 systems in the same scheme. You also find out about the real complexities and limits involved in using peer networks.

CHAPTER 6: PRINT SERVING FROM WINDOWS NT

This chapter describes how to set up print services from Windows NT Server and how to set up print sharing in a peer-to-peer network of Windows clients. It's simple, but a few minor tricks are needed to run print sharing properly.

Part II: Windows NT to Novell NetWare Connectivity

Novell NetWare is a longtime standard in business computing, and no one expects it to go away anytime soon. Just because you're going to Windows NT, there is no reason to discard your existing investment. Microsoft has done a good job making Windows NT capable of coexisting with legacy network operating systems. Novell also provides a large library of free software for efficiently interfacing NetWare to Windows NT. You focus on linking Windows NT with NetWare 4.11 and 3.12 in the two chapters from this section, using both Microsoft and Novell solutions. You'll be surprised at how straightforward the process really is in either case.

CHAPTER 7: WINDOWS NT TO NOVELL NETWARE 4.11 CONNECTIONS

Chapter 7 discusses the important topic of how to make Windows NT communicate with Novell NetWare 4.11 (also called *IntranetWare*). Most critically, you find out how to use Windows NT's various Gateway and Client Services for NetWare to share Novell-based resources through the Windows NT server, and set up Novell's free software programs on a Windows NT workstation to perform comprehensive NetWare system management.

CHAPTER 8: WINDOWS NT TO NOVELL NETWARE 3.12 CONNECTIONS

In Chapter 8 you learn how to connect a Windows NT server to a Novell NetWare 3.12 (or 3.x) file server, and how to share a NetWare print server through a Windows NT server with the various users on your network. You also find out how to use a Windows NT workstation as a primary connection to the NetWare 3.x server.

Part III: Internet and Online Connectivity Tasks

Key online connectivity applications are discussed in Part III. Two main tasks are discussed: setting up Remote Access for dial-up network use by Windows clients, and setting up Windows NT for use with simple Internet browsing, mail, and news applications. Remote Access is a powerful and inexpensive tool for creating LAN connections over phone lines, and you discover exactly how it works. You also find out how to use Remote Access in conjunction with the Internet to create a closely related but different connection – a Virtual Private Network. Finally, you're given a quick tour of Microsoft's new Routing and Remote Access Service upgrade for Windows NT, and I explain why you really need it.

Windows NT Server provides Microsoft Exchange as a key electronic mail service. Unfortunately, using Exchange can be a real pain. Its setup is difficult and poorly documented, particularly for the version most Windows NT Server owners have – Exchange 4.0. The final chapter in this section describes how to set up Exchange and use it without tears. You're also introduced to Exchange 5.0, whose availability shows that Microsoft has gotten serious about competing in the messaging and groupware markets. You find out about the Exchange 5.0 applications, its setup, and why it's important to you.

CHAPTER 9: SETTING UP REMOTE ACCESS ON WINDOWS NT SERVER

Chapter 9 describes how to set up and use Dial-Up Networking connections with Remote Access Service, including both NetBEUI and TCP/IP protocols. In this chapter, the RAS mission is to create a true LAN connection through dial-up, and not for an Internet connection. You find out how to set up Remote Access Service (RAS) on the server to use either protocol, and how to set up a client for a dial-up RAS connection.

CHAPTER 10: INTERNET CONNECTIONS AND RAS UPGRADES

Remote access connectivity is taken to the next level in Chapter 10. You start off with a fairly simple application – setting up a Windows NT server or workstation to use a dial-up connection to the Internet. Building on this topic, you learn how to create Virtual Private Networks using the new Windows NT 4.0 Point-to-Point Tunneling Protocol (PPTP) capabilities. Finally, you learn about Routing and Remote Access Service, Microsoft's vital upgrade to your Windows NT server's RAS capabilities.

CHAPTER 11: SETTING UP MICROSOFT EXCHANGE FOR ELECTRONIC MAIL

In Chapter 11 you discover how to set up and use Microsoft Exchange 4.0, Windows NT's built-in office messaging application. It's not the most efficient or well-presented feature in Windows NT, but it's free, and it can be made to work effectively in a Windows network for both Internet e-mail and LAN-based mail. Unlike version 4.0, Exchange 5.0 is an expensive BackOffice add-on to Windows NT server, offering expanded messaging standards support and powerful groupware capabilities. Although a comprehensive discussion of Exchange 5.0 is far beyond the scope of this book, you receive a good introduction to it in this chapter.

Part IV: User Management and System Maintenance

The final section of this book talks about the key things you need to do to keep everything running merrily along. Many crucial areas of user account management are discussed in Chapter 12, including user rights and account policies, defining roaming user profiles, and working with the System Policy Editor. Chapter 13 describes server maintenance tasks, such as keeping multiple generations of Emergency Repair disks, setting up a Backup Domain Controller and synchronizing it with the Primary, upgrading a Windows NT server from single- to dual-processor while keeping your user accounts, building a Windows NT boot floppy, and many other useful jobs on your server.

CHAPTER 12: GENERAL SYSTEM MANAGEMENT

In this chapter you find a collection of vital networking tasks valuable to you as the administrator of an established and growing network. You learn how to make Windows NT domain servers communicate with each other, using a mechanism called trust relationships. You also discover how the trust relationships mechanism is used to design different types of larger Windows NT networks. You find out what a system policy is, how it relates to your system's Registry, and what a policy can do to help you control and create customized desktops across your network. You painstakingly discover how home directories work in Windows NT, how to create them, and what their strengths and weaknesses are. Finally, you encounter the Holy Grail of network management – Windows NT's roaming user profiles – and what they can do for you and your users.

CHAPTER 13: TYPICAL TASKS YOU NEED TO DO

This chapter provides a grab-bag of more or less unrelated Windows NT topics that didn't really fit anywhere else. A number of quotidian yet quite important items are discussed here, including creating logon scripts under Windows NT and enabling their execution during client bootup over the network. Various backup tasks and techniques are discussed here. You take a look at Windows NT's Performance Monitor, a surprisingly powerful program for monitoring a huge collection of networking and throughput characteristics in your system. You learn how to create a Windows NT boot floppy disk, which allows you to bypass the frequent problem of losing a boot track on a hard disk.

As the last key task in this book, you find out how to create and use a Backup Domain Controller, and why you should always have one in your network.

Appendix A of this book sends you off with two useful sections: an introduction to the absolute basics of networking, and a collection of last-minute tips and useful information that filtered in across my transom during the production process of this book.

Finally, a glossary of terms and acronyms is provided at the end of this book.

Notes on the CD-ROM

A CD-ROM is provided with this book. Although none of the software contained therein is actually used in any of the exercises or processes within this book, it contains a large number of Windows NT utilities and applications that may be quite useful to you in the future. The software is provided as a convenience to the reader. Some programs are usable without immediately paying a fee; some are fully functional except for lack of printing capabilities or the ability to save file. Several programs are even freeware and can be used immediately if desired. Details of the CD-ROM contents are provided in an appendix of this book.

Conventions and Features Used in This Book

Other than the subject matter, there is little complexity in this book. However, several conventions and features are used consistently, particularly typical Windows NT/Windows 95 interface features. Windows NT 4.0 and Windows 95 share the same user interface and similar methods of doing things, so if you've used Windows 95 to any extent, you'll be right at home. Windows NT uses a system of multitabbed dialog boxes, clickable buttons, options, and check boxes for most of its networking settings. Figure 1 shows an example of a dialog box showing several of these elements:

Mutually exclusive option buttons

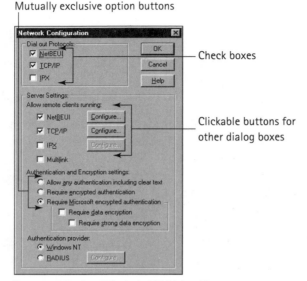

Check boxes

Clickable buttons for
other dialog boxes

Figure 1: Viewing Windows NT Dialog Elements

Figure 1 shows a collections of check boxes that can be enabled or disabled by the user. Check boxes come in groups of one or more and can be combined to add or enable an operating system or program feature. Sometimes check boxes are tristate: enabled, disabled or *empty,* and grayed out. In most cases the enabled or disabled states are the only ones relevant to your work. Option buttons can also be selected, but when you see a group of them, as shown in Figure 1, each option is mutually exclusive to the others. If one option is selected, the other option buttons cannot be activated.

Clickable buttons, such as the Configure button in Figure 1, indicate other program functions that can be displayed in the form of another dialog box. You can go several levels deep in many feature areas of Windows NT by clicking these buttons. When this occurs, as it will many times in this book, the process is often called *drilling down.* I won't be using that term too often in this book, but it does come up a couple of times.

Windows NT and Windows 95 make heavy use of multi-tabbed dialog boxes, which combine the functions of many different dialog boxes into a single window. Each of the tabs contains a set of functions that often bears some relationship to other tabs of the same dialog box. Figure 2 shows an example of a multi-tabbed dialog box.

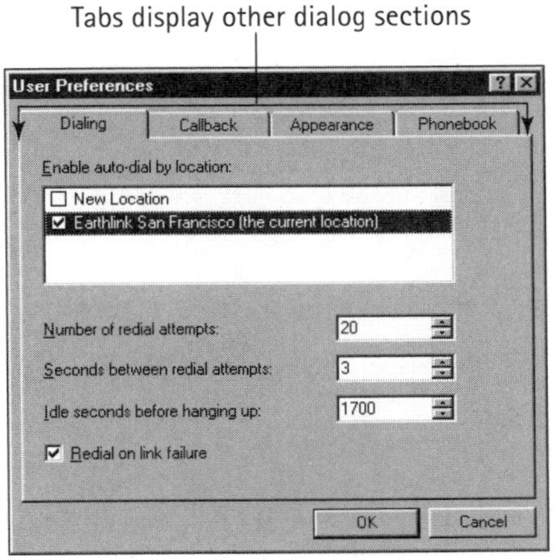

Tabs display other dialog sections

Figure 2: A Multi-Tabbed Dialog Box

In Figure 2, four tabs are shown at the top of the dialog box. Each tab can be clicked to display a new set of functions. For the most part in this book, I assume that you know the basics of navigation through all the basic screen tools displayed in Windows NT.

Here are some more conventions used throughout this book:

◆ The terms *click* and *double-click*. Click indicates that you need to click the mouse over an object on the screen, such as:

1. Click Next.

Frequently, a step of this type indicates that you're meant to click a button in a dialog box to continue performing a procedure.

Click is the mouse action you perform the majority of the time throughout this book. When the term *click* is used, it indicates that you're pressing down the left mouse button — the most common mouse-related action under Windows.

Clicking can also indicate selecting an item on the screen, such as one item in a list from a dialog box or an icon on the screen. Again, the left mouse button is used.

◆ A *double-click* is used when you select a screen item with the first click and immediately commit it to an action with the second click, such as:

2. Double-click the Guests group name in the Not member of pane.

Programs are also frequently started by double-clicking their icon.

◆ When the term *open* is used in a step, it means to double-click an icon on the desktop or in a program group, or to select an easily locatable program from the Start menu. In all cases, *open* means to open a new window in the desktop.

◆ *Right-click* means to click the right mouse button. In many Windows NT screen elements, clicking the right mouse button on an object displays a special menu, often called the *shortcut menu*. It's not just a convenience feature — shortcut menus are often the fastest and most efficient means of launching and locating features in a Windows software program. For example:

 3. Right-click the (C:) icon in My Computer, as shown in Figure 2-17. The shortcut menu appears.

◆ *Enabling* a check box means to click in a previously empty check box to place a check mark inside of it, thereby enabling that feature in the program. For example:

 4. Enable the Wired to the network check box.

> For many networking tasks, you run into unfamiliar terms and alien concepts that can interrupt the flow of a particular job or inject an element of confusion. Some writers dedicate chapters to explaining things such as SNMP or LDAP, for example. (See the glossary for definitions of these user-hostile acronyms.) Whenever needed, I created two- or three-paragraph sidebars in gray boxes that explain things like this, but they are broken out in a way that enables you to ignore them if desired.

Whenever appropriate, I provide a Web site link where readers can get more information about a topic, locate software updates, or otherwise obtain information beyond the scope of this book. Web links are provided in monospace font, such as `http://www.matrox.com`.

TIP

In many cases I telescope a key point in the text to a Tip. This enables a reader to locate important information rapidly without reading a lot of expository text (which I've tried to keep to a minimum anyway).

Troubleshooting sections occupy the end of each chapter. They're culled from my own experiences and from many other users of Windows NT Server and Workstation, and sometimes from my explorations of Windows NT newsgroups. Microsoft's Web site (`http://www.microsoft.com/support`) provides the base-point from which you can discover this valuable resource for yourself. While you're at it, you may want to think about converting to Microsoft's Web browser (Internet Explorer) and especially its News and Mail programs, which are currently best-of-breed. (This can change at any time, given the fluid nature of the Web.)

Author's Note

A huge amount of information is crammed into the pages of *Windows NT 4.0 Connectivity Guide*. I've made every possible effort to make each word of this book essential and approachable for anyone who needs to learn about Windows NT networking. My hope in writing this book is not to get a fancy column in some networking magazine, or to schmooze with the heavyweights in the networking industry. (Ok, maybe just a little.) My primary aim in writing this is to make Windows NT networking as approachable as possible to a broad audience of computer users. (An aim that no one else has yet achieved, in my humble opinion.) I believe that for all its warts, and there are quite a few, Windows NT 4.0 is the most approachable and downright friendliest networking OS in a field where ease-of-use traditionally takes a back seat to utility. Although Windows NT 4.0 is quite approachable compared to its competition (or its previous versions), its relative ease doesn't imply a lack of power. Quite the contrary. Windows NT 4.0 is the first version of NT considered mature enough for mainstream use, and the market affirms this claim. You owe it to yourself to consider it, particularly if you're running a small shop and need to tie your clients together. The benefits are many. Using this book as your guide, you'll discover those benefits, and the pitfalls will also be few and far between.

I welcome feedback on my work. Please send me e-mail at `rgrace1@earth-link.net`. If you can, use the header "About your NT Book . . ." to let me know what it's about. It's important to me to always have a sense of what people want in the books they buy. When you open your wallet or checkbook and shell out $40-$50 for a book, you expect to be able to *use* it. To get your money's worth. To know that in this sometimes cold, distant world of computing, someone out there actually knows what you're going through and addresses it. If you have ideas for improvement or stories to share, please offer them to me. When I revise this book, your comments and questions will be taken into full consideration. And whenever I possibly can, I'll answer them.

Acknowledgments

First, I'd like to acknowledge all the production people and editors at IDG. In particular, I'd like to thank my front-line Development Editor, Janet Andrews. We have had a rather efficient process during this book, and a large part of that result is due to her work. This is particularly true considering that I had to fly to the east coast for a month for the process of getting married, and I had to juggle technical editing and other production aspects at the same time. Janet managed every minor crisis, and every stress-ridden phone call (and there were a few), and consistently helped me to come through. I want to also thank the initial Development Editor for this book, Michael Koch, who was able to house-train me to IDG's Microsoft Word style sheet, gave me a huge amount of insight into how IDG works as a company, and gave me highly useful advice about editorial content, outline construction, and document formatting. It was due to his work that many potential pitfalls were avoided during the writing of this book. Susannah Pfalzer is the managing editor for this project, and her work is greatly appreciated.

I would also like especially to thank IDG Books Worldwide and my acquisitions editor, Anne Hamilton, who seized upon my proposal almost before I could rip it out of my laser printer. Both have been very enthusiastic about this project. Most important, they carried on a consistent dialog with me and enabled me to write exactly the type of book I wanted to write. This is a rare thing in any publishing field. Lisa Sontag also managed the process of obtaining permissions for distributing the shareware, freeware, and demo programs that populate the CD-ROM for this book. If you don't think that's a tough job, try it sometime.

I also want to thank Bruce McFarland for tech editing this book. We've worked together before in the "outside" world, and it's been good to rope him in on this project.

I'd also like to thank Marc Busch, who is the key enabler for helping me build the Novell NetWare 3.12 and 4.11 network servers I used in Chapters 7 and 8 of this book.

A huge number of Windows NT experts, users, technicians, and aficionados were very open with their time and their help during the process of writing this book. I encountered many of them in Microsoft's Usenet mailgroups, which themselves were a great source of help and information. Among those experts I'd like to single out for appreciation are:

Arvin Meyer
Robert Bruce Thompson
Jerrold Schulman
Jason Tehaney
Charlie Russel and Sharon Crawford
Ralf Morgenstern
Gerald A. Cloud, a.k.a. Thunder

and many others whose names I can't locate on the Usenet groups.

Contents at a Glance

Table of Contents

Part IV   User Management and System Maintenance

Part 1

Networking Tasks

Chapter 1 of this book, "The Digital Gauntlet: Setting Up Windows NT," helps you build the hardware foundation for your server. You find out what kind of hardware you need to run a Windows NT server effectively, and see into the process of installing the operating system. It doesn't sound like a big deal, does it? It is. If you're just getting started with Windows NT or even just thinking about it, don't miss this chapter!

Chapter 2 is where your exploration of Windows NT begins in earnest. A wide variety of networking applications are discussed in several chapters within this section. Chapter 2, "Setting Up Mainstream Microsoft Networks," provides a bite-size chunk of the most important things to know about building Microsoft Networks around Windows NT Server. If you're creating a simple network without a lot of extra services, this chapter gives most of what you need to know. Chapter 2 focuses on the use of the simple NetBEUI protocol for building a network fast. You also find a lengthy discussion of how to create user accounts, apply share permissions, and understand the basic levels of network management in Windows NT.

Chapter 3, "LAN-Based TCP/IP Networking," takes you to the next level of knowledge. In its server edition, Windows NT 4.0 takes Microsoft's support for TCP/IP to a much higher level. TCP/IP, a sophisticated, powerful networking protocol, is the standard on the Internet and on corporate and enterprise networks. It is the prohibitive favorite throughout the computing industry. Starting with version 4.0, Windows NT embraces all key aspects of TCP/IP networking, and you owe it to yourself to become thoroughly acquainted with it. Chapter 3 starts off a brief, tightly compressed five-page discussion of how TCP/IP works, defining such key terms as *default gateway* and *subnet mask*, and how TCP/IP addressing is defined in networks. With these critical concepts in mind, you fit them into the context of Windows NT by installing the TCP/IP protocol and setting it up for networking on your Windows NT Server. Then you proceed to brief, directly worded explanations of the critical NT services – WINS, DNS, and DHCP – and fit them into the context of Windows NT networking. Finally, you layer in each of these services while assessing whether each service is required for your network.

If you do nothing else except read Chapters 2 and 3 of this book, you will have learned 90 percent of what you need to know to build a functional Windows NT network.

Chapters 4 through 6 focus on a more diverse group of networking tasks. Chapter 4, "Connecting Alternative Network Clients," describes how to include 16-bit Windows 3.11, Macintosh System 7, and Macintosh System 8 clients within a Windows NT Server-based network. Chapter 5, "Peer-to-Peer Networking," tells you everything you need to create a peer-to-peer network using Windows NT Workstation and Windows 95 clients. You also discover why peer networking has its limitations. Finally, Chapter 6, "Print Serving From Windows NT," describes the important process of sharing printers across the network.

Chapter 1

The Digital Gauntlet:
Setting Up Windows NT

IN THIS CHAPTER
This chapter covers two main topics:

- ◆ Buying and configuring Windows NT hardware: How to buy it, what to look for, and what to stay away from

- ◆ Setting up Windows NT: The Grand Tour

WINDOWS NT SETUP IS a difficult and demanding obstacle course of an operating-system installation. By simply installing NT Server, you get a grasp of almost every key networking feature the system has to offer. If you know what you're doing, all you need to do after finishing NT Setup is set up shared folders and devices and define your user accounts (described in Chapter 2). Then all your network users can log on to the server and begin sharing the resources you have allocated to them. At that point you'll have built a basic network.

Of course, you can perform many other tasks as well after Setup is complete, including the following:

- ◆ Designate some of the Windows NT Server's resources to be shared among network users

- ◆ Add Macintosh users to the network

- ◆ Connect your Windows NT system to a Novell NetWare server

- ◆ Create a print server

- ◆ Add other services later that you overlooked or didn't need when you originally set up Windows NT

- ◆ Create a Dial-Up Networking connection for an Windows NT user so that he or she can use the Internet

- ◆ Build an intranet

3

As complicated as some of these tasks may be, none of the operations can compare to the single act of setting up Windows NT, particularly the server flavor. When you or your company decide to make an investment in NT, you're not just buying a piece of software. You're also making an investment in changing the way your business works.

Compared to any other network operating system (NOS) available, Windows NT 4.0 is far more low-maintenance and furnishes more bases for the users in your company. NT provides both file and print serving as well as application serving. It's also a powerful and evolving intranet platform. Of course, NT has its bugs and glitches (which are noted as you go through this book). No major application or operating system exists that does not have its share of problems. You must ask yourself whether those problems prevent you from relying on your system, day in and day out, to get your work done. I think you'll find NT to be a highly reliable, robust operating system that your company can safely rely on for every conceivable mainstream business application.

Now it's time for the hard stuff. Setting up NT isn't a bed of roses — it's the most time-consuming task you'll find in this book. The more you know before you start, and the more advance preparations you make, the smoother the process will be.

The first step in setting up NT is to decide on your hardware. Particularly if you're setting up a server, this decision is absolutely critical.

Choosing Windows NT Hardware

In this section, you discover some of the painful realities involved in buying and using hardware for running Windows NT. If there's one statement you can take to heart and that sums up everything, it's this: If something *can* go wrong with the hardware on which you install and run Windows NT, it *will* go wrong. If just one component is bad, NT Setup will blow up in your face by simply locking up or freezing or by displaying an extremely cryptic *Blue Screen of Death* with a huge hex dump of incomprehensible data.

A hardware-compatibility list is available from Microsoft for Windows NT. The list is updated consistently and is worth a look. Also, consider this rule of thumb: Using only name-brand components that have Windows NT 4.0 drivers will eliminate most of the problems.

Buying hardware for Windows NT is surprisingly difficult, down to the merest memory component. As a systems integrator, I have run the gamut regarding hardware problems and NT. Almost everything you read about in the first section of this chapter derives from my traumatic experiences choosing and building hardware for my NT servers. In doing so, I've often felt like the proverbial pioneer with the arrows in his back. Here you can get the benefits from my experience. I've learned to make conservative choices.

If you buy the right components for your Windows NT server, things should go quite smoothly. Although NT 4.0 is not plug-and-play, it does a good job sensing components in your system during installation.

Wherever possible in this section, I've mentioned company Web sites. If a product you've bought for Windows NT has a new or updated driver, you'll usually find it on that company's Web site. You should also check them to make sure a product supports Windows NT before you make the purchase. Checking company Web sites is one area where the World Wide Web really makes users' lives much easier.

Microprocessors

Microprocessor technology changes constantly. By the time you read this book, Pentium *Classic* chips will probably be either off the market or incredibly cheap. Sixth-generation processors from AMD and Cyrix are popping up to challenge Intel's stranglehold on the microprocessor market. I'm not going to editorialize here; this discussion is an assessment of the market and what is widely considered best for various applications.

"Classic" Pentiums are fading fast. Nevertheless, if you have some around, don't throw them away. Classic Pentiums are still extremely useful for Windows NT, Windows 95, or UNIX clients, and they are powerful microprocessors in their own right. Pentium CPUs can also be used in a dual-processing system with minimal expense. (I used two P-133s in my test server for this book.) For budget NT workstations, a non-MMX Pentium of any clock speed costs virtually nothing. For a real step up, MMX Pentiums offer a significant performance boost for Windows NT even without direct use of MMX. (This was a big surprise in my testing.) Performance improves because MMX Pentiums offer other enhancements, such as a larger Level 1 cache and more efficient execution algorithms. If you don't have applications that take advantage of MMX capabilities, then you won't get any direct benefit from them. Nevertheless, when it's properly configured, running an NT Workstation on a 200MHz MMX Pentium system can yield stunning performance for a very reasonable price.

Intel's Pentium Pro processor is highly scaleable, which is always desirable in a server. The Pro scales to four, six, or eight processors for high-capacity servers, which are typically built and sold by HP, Compaq, and ALR, along with a few others. Offered with built-in Level II memory caches of 256K, 512K, and a mind-boggling 1MB, the Pentium Pro is widely considered the best match for NT. The Pro runs other operating systems such as Windows 95 at disappointing speeds. Conversely, NT sings on a Pentium Pro (or two or four). You can build a blindingly fast NT Workstation around a single-or dual-processor Pentium Pro desktop.

The big changes for the Pentium II are its packaging, its inclusion of MMX, and its use at clock speeds between 233MHz and 300MHz. Starting with the Pentium II, Intel changed the form factor of system boards by eliminating the processor socket. (The processor socket is commonly called Socket 7. There are several socket types, however: Socket 5 is used for the Pentium classic up to 166MHz; Socket 7 for Pentium Classic/MMX's up to 233MHz, and Socket 8 for the Pentium Pro up to 200MHz.) Instead of sockets, Intel uses a new scheme called *Single Edge Cartridge* or *Slot 1*, which places the processor on a small circuit board with an edge-connector that plugs into the motherboard. According to published reports, the Pentium II isn't a good option for NT Servers. The Pentium II isn't too scaleable; you can't use more than two Pentium IIs in a multiprocessing system. (Scalability doesn't matter much in workstations, but it's very important in servers.) Now, existing Pentium II owners will be annoyed to learn that Intel produces (or will soon produce) a revised Pentium II chip with heavy modifications for improved multiprocessing, faster memory access, and lower power consumption. This revised chip is meant to provide four-way SMP capabilities for higher-end workgroup servers in the Wintel market. What's the problem? The revised chips are physically incompatible with existing Pentium II systems because their advances required a larger Single Edge connector. Thus, they plug into a new Slot 2 motherboard connector, which is incompatible with Slot 1. The chips are also much more expensive than the *regular* Pentium II and run at a minimum clock speed of 333MHz. They may also have a larger built-in cache.

The Pentium II uses similar core logic to the Pentium Pro, uses a 512K Level II cache that is built into the cartridge's circuit board (but not into the actual chip die), running at half the clock speed as the processor (the cache of a 266MHz Pentium II runs at 133MHz, for example). The initial reviews of this chip are mixed, but the Pentium II does represent part of the next generation. Don't jump into this platform unless you're sure it will meet your needs. Based on Windows NT benchmark tests I've run, a well-built 200MHz MMX Pentium roughly equals many 233MHz Pentium II systems. System bottlenecks in the first Pentium IIs are a major factor. Pay particular attention to the motherboard and chip set, and have a look at Intel's Web site (`http://www.intel.com/PentiumII`) for the latest information. Also, read the forthcoming section "About Chip Sets" for more on this issue.

Processors, Bus Speeds, and the Law of Diminishing Returns

Most current Pentium and Pentium Pro systems run the main system bus (the bus between the processor/level II cache and the main system memory) at 60 or 66MHz, (PCI card buses usually run at 33MHz.) Design improvements are expected to boost the system bus speed to 75, 83, or even 100MHz, particularly in next-generation Pentium II machines. In many ways, this change will benefit users more than a mere processor-speed boost, because overall system throughput is much greater with a faster bus speed. Those improvements will be integrated into Pentium II-based systems as new chip sets come out but will not benefit current Pentium or Pentium Pro users.

continued

Owing to the relatively slow bus speeds in most current systems (and other unavoidable system bottlenecks), you'll find that a law of diminishing returns occurs with many high-speed computers. As an example, there's little real-world difference between a 166MHz Pentium and a 200MHz Pentium (or a 233MHz/266MHz Pentium II). The higher a computer's processor speed becomes, the less impact a 33MHz or even 66MHz boost in processor clock speed provides. Consider the enormous price premium you'll often pay for those speed bumps, and how much that extra speed will really benefit you.

Third-party Pentium clone chips are common. The two most prominent are Cyrix and AMD. Their basic Pentium chips (the Cyrix 6x86 and the AMD K5) are relegated to the low end of the market. AMD has a faster, higher-end processor called the K6 that is gathering glowing reviews, reportedly equals a Pentium Pro in NT performance at the same speed, and fits into a conventional Pentium socket. Cyrix produces a chip called the 6x86MX that is intended as another Pentium II competitor. Again, a key difficulty is motherboard compatibility with Windows NT. Typically, offshore motherboard makers are the first ones to support clone processors, which is good but can present problems. Normally, AMD makes a fine processor. Neither the K6 nor the Cyrix chips can run in a multiprocessor system, which makes them more suitable for workstations than servers. Proceed carefully but don't rule out the K6 as an option.

Third party x86 processors can be very complicated. For multiprocessor NT servers, the Pentium Pro is still definitely the way to go. MMX-enabled processors are basically irrelevant in a server role unless you plan to do a lot of video serving. MMX is more useful for Windows 95 client systems and is startlingly strong for NT workstations. (Check my Web site, `http://www.byteit.com/rgrace`, for details.) The Pentium II is a definite contender, but not for a high-end server environment. Also, Pentium II represents the first entry in a huge wave of new improvements in PC architecture, including faster memory, bus speed, and hard disk access support. Check system architecture specs carefully before you buy.

Motherboard Wars

If you like to build your own systems, congratulations and welcome to the loony bin. The motherboard is probably the most sensitive part of the whole computer when you're building a Windows NT system. A huge number of manufacturers compete in this market. Many boards are capable of running under Windows 95 but choke under Windows NT, even failing to run the setup program.

Relatively few motherboards run reliably under Windows NT. Many current boards are manufactured offshore. Do not touch them! You will be wasting your money. A frequent problem with offshore motherboards involves the use of poor-quality capacitors, which wear out over time and can eventually fry your processor in its socket. Although most boards use Intel chip sets, you should view board sellers' claims with a suspicious eye. Is their board NT-certified? Do they have a demonstration system running NT with it? If you're building a server, you need guarantees that the product you buy is going to work. In many cases, you may find it not worth the trouble, and you'll want to buy a complete, fully-integrated system from a top-tier manufacturer such as Dell, Compaq, or IBM. Some other manufacturers, such as SAG Electronics and Gateway 2000, also build highly reliable computers. As you move down the vendor food chain, things get riskier.

I've found Tyan (http://www.tyan.com/) and Intel boards to be quite reliable under Windows NT for both Pentiums and Pentium Pros. (Other manufacturers, such as Mylex and Micronics, also manufacture boards domestically and have good reputations, but I have not used them. Abit and Asus are clone motherboard manufacturers that consistently get good reviews are Abit and Asus; again, I haven't used any of their products and so can't comment.) Intel boards have one drawback: many are offered with built-in features such as a video controller or sound chip. These features are rather pointless in a server and only slightly less so in an NT Workstation, where multimedia performance is apt to be poor.

Some Intel Pentium Pro and Pentium II boards provide an Adaptec Ultra-Wide SCSI-III controller (based on the Adaptec 7880 SCSI chip) that can prove very handy for a server. For a detailed overview of Intel motherboards, the best place to go is the Intel Motherboard Web site at http://www.intel.com/design/motherbd/ (see Figure 1-1). In general, you're better off using domestically-manufactured system boards — or computers that use them — simply because NT is so sensitive to hardware.

ABOUT CHIP SETS

Pay close attention to the chip set on your server's board. Intel releases a steady stream of revised chip sets that offer different features, depending on the age and generation of the chip set. The first Pentium-class chip set, now obsolete, is the 430FX or *Triton* chip set present on most older Pentium motherboards. The Triton set does not support multiprocessing and allows only 128MB of RAM. Don't buy any Windows NT-intended machine that still uses the 430FX chip set.

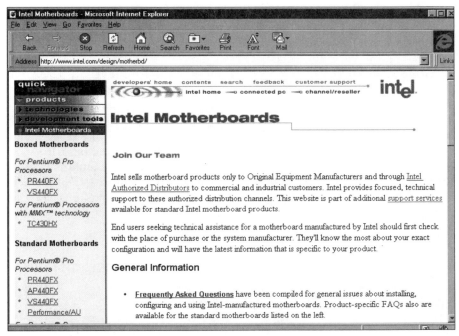

Figure 1-1: The Intel Motherboard Web Site

Reproduced by permission of Intel Corporation, copyright 1988 Intel Corporation.

The 430HX chip set, also called *Triton II,* provides a much higher RAM limit (512MB), faster memory performance, and dual-processor support. The Triton II is common in dual-processor Pentium boards and higher-quality boards that support Pentium MMX. This is the baseline chip set you should look for in a current Windows NT system. A newer chip set, called 430VX, also supports Pentium MMX.

Intel also offers special chip sets for Pentium Pro systems, the most prominent being the 440FX. Both offer support for large quantities of RAM and dual processors. 44FX is also used in the first generation of Pentium II Motherboards. The new 440LX chip set is designed to work with Pentium II processors, offering support for higher-speed SDRAM, the Accelerated Graphics Port (AGP), and a 33MB/s EIDE hard disk interface (called Ultra-DMA). Any Pentium II system is apt to be fast, but buying 440LX-based motherboards ensures that everything else you buy that surrounds the processor – disk and memory I/O, bus speed, and so on – runs at its maximum potential for the current state of technology.

ABOUT MEMORY – SIMMS VERSUS DIMMS AND OTHER ISSUES

Memory is another area where things can get technical very quickly, so only the key points will be discussed. First, for a normal NT server, 64MB of RAM is absolutely crucial. Don't skimp on RAM to meet the department budget. The more networking protocols and layers you add to the system, the more memory those additions occupy. You're better off buying a slower processor for less money than shorting your server on memory. For database servers, the sky's the limit regarding RAM. A file server or Internet/intranet server can get by with 96-128MB of memory, but more never hurts. NT workstations should start with 32MB of RAM and go on from there, depending on what you're doing with them. (Even at 32MB, NT Workstation is a bit sluggish.)

Second, if there's anything that Windows NT is more picky about than motherboards and hard disks, it's memory. Whichever type of RAM you buy, make sure it's *major-brand* memory, and make sure you buy it from a reputable seller. Major brands of memory include Siemens, Samsung, Micron, Toshiba, and Intel. If you're offered memory manufactured by anyone else, you probably shouldn't buy it. (Resellers such as Kingston and VisionTek are also a good option.) One of the best major-brand mail-order memory resellers is The Chip Merchant in San Diego, CA, which can be found on the Internet at http://www.thechipmerchant.com/ (see Figure 1-2).

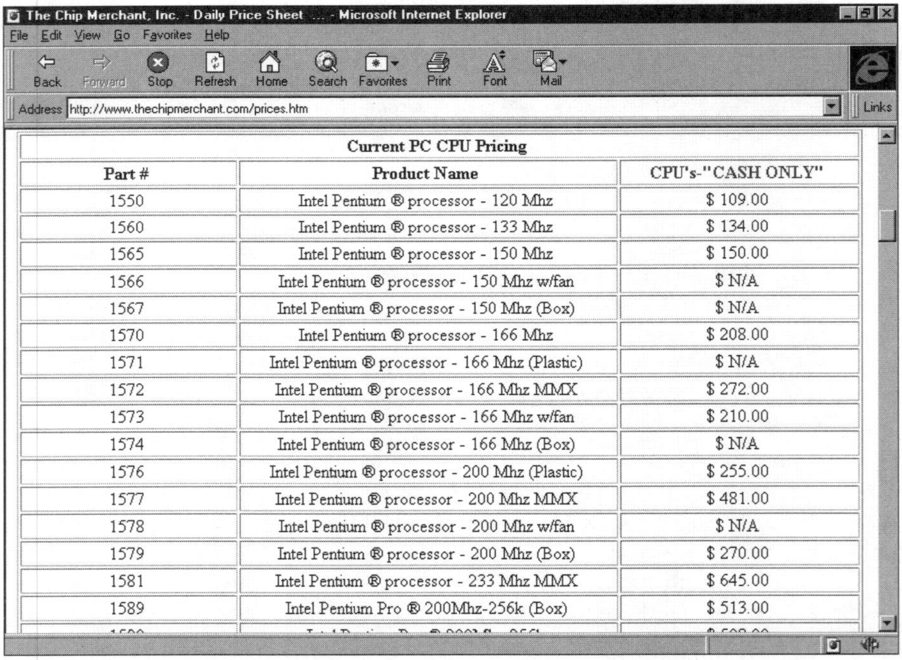

The Chip Merchant, Inc. - Daily Price Sheet ... - Microsoft Internet Explorer

File Edit View Go Favorites Help

Back Forward Stop Refresh Home Search Favorites Print Font Mail

Address http://www.thechipmerchant.com/prices.htm

Current PC CPU Pricing		
Part #	**Product Name**	**CPU's-"CASH ONLY"**
1550	Intel Pentium ® processor - 120 Mhz	$ 109.00
1560	Intel Pentium ® processor - 133 Mhz	$ 134.00
1565	Intel Pentium ® processor - 150 Mhz	$ 150.00
1566	Intel Pentium ® processor - 150 Mhz w/fan	$ N/A
1567	Intel Pentium ® processor - 150 Mhz (Box)	$ N/A
1570	Intel Pentium ® processor - 166 Mhz	$ 208.00
1571	Intel Pentium ® processor - 166 Mhz (Plastic)	$ N/A
1572	Intel Pentium ® processor - 166 Mhz MMX	$ 272.00
1573	Intel Pentium ® processor - 166 Mhz w/fan	$ 210.00
1574	Intel Pentium ® processor - 166 Mhz (Box)	$ N/A
1576	Intel Pentium ® processor - 200 Mhz (Plastic)	$ 255.00
1577	Intel Pentium ® processor - 200 Mhz MMX	$ 481.00
1578	Intel Pentium ® processor - 200 Mhz w/fan	$ N/A
1579	Intel Pentium ® processor - 200 Mhz (Box)	$ 270.00
1581	Intel Pentium ® processor - 233 Mhz MMX	$ 645.00
1589	Intel Pentium Pro ® 200Mhz-256k (Box)	$ 513.00

Figure 1-2: Rock-Bottom Price Listings Are Provided on The Chip Merchant's Web Site

RAM capacity is crucial for an NT system. As memory gets cheaper, it becomes much easier to pack an NT computer with 128MB or 256MB of RAM for a department's server. Buy all your RAM from the same dealer and, if possible, the same manufacturer, or you may run into problems. Try to avoid boards and computer systems that provide only four SIMM sockets. Many of them are older and support only 128MB of RAM, which can be eaten up pretty fast in a busy server environment. (Motherboards that use DIMMs are an exception to this rule, as you'll see.)

There are two factors to keep track of for memory:

◆ Type of package (SIMM, DIMM)

◆ Type of memory (EDO, SDRAM, Burst EDO, Parity, and so on)

Typically, memory comes on a small circuit board that you snap into a socket on your motherboard. The most common type of memory package is called a SIMM, *Single In-Line Memory Module*. SIMMs require installation in pairs of the same type (a 32MB SIMM with a 32MB SIMM, for example) and thus limit flexibility. A DIMM (*Double In-line Memory Module*) is a newer memory package that offers the advantage of requiring only one of each type for the memory to work in your system. You can't mix DIMMs and SIMMs — they have different form factors. (Some boards, many of doubtful provenance, do provide both SIMM and DIMM sockets.) The newest motherboards use DIMMs, the memory package of the future.

The type of memory your computer uses can have a major bearing on performance. One current standard is EDO (Extended Data Out) memory, which offers some performance boosts over other types, at a lower cost. EDO is what you will probably wind up with if you buy a complete system as a server or workstation. (There are other types, such as Fast-Page-Mode DRAM and non-parity RAM, but they're not worth considering, even in terms of cost, because of their incompatibility with newer NT systems.) EDO RAM can be had on both SIMMs and DIMMs.

In the long run you'll probably want to buy systems that use SDRAM (Synchronous DRAM), because SDRAM is designed to run at bus speeds higher than 66MHz. SDRAM is usually sold in DIMM packages. It offers some performance boosts over other types of memory besides bus speed, primarily in the number of clock cycles the memory requires to access data.

Another system element is Level II cache memory, which is usually built into the motherboard. (It is called Level II because current microprocessors use smaller, extremely high-speed Level 1 memory caches built directly into the processor.) Figure 1-3 shows the basic memory schemes commonly used in PCs. The most common type of cache RAM is pipeline-burst cache; Pentium-class systems have a minimum of 256K installed. 512K is becoming the norm with faster machines, because larger caches are required to offset the increasing throughput problems that RAM experiences at high speeds. Increasingly, you'll find 1MB caches becoming the standard. Pentium Pro chips already have the Level II cache built in (up to 1MB), but every other Pentium-class chip, including the Pentium MMX, Pentium II, Cyrix M2 and 6x86, and the AMD K5 and K6 processors, does not. (Intel has announced that their next generation of server-level chips, currently code-named Deschutes, will have 2MB of internal Level II cache.) Fortunately, no manufacturer worth its cab fare tries to sell a computer without pipeline-burst Level II cache. If one does, go elsewhere.

PC Processor/Memory Archives

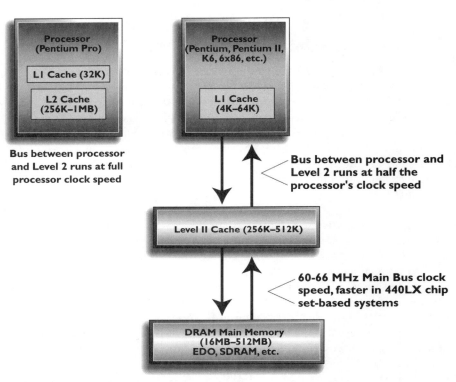

Figure 1-3: System Memory Architectures

SCSI Versus EIDE

These hard disks are pretty much in a dead heat. Despite what SCSI loyalists say, current EIDE hard drives often match SCSI hard disks in speed and throughput. Except for SCSI hard disks that use a 7,200-rpm spin rate (or Seagate's new 10,000-rpm hard drives), there is little functional difference. Even capacity levels are more or less the same, with 6-8GB EIDE drives becoming common (and more to come). One thing can be guaranteed, however: as CPUs become faster, drive subsystems are hard-pressed to keep up, and fast SCSI hard disks are still the speed king.

Hard disks are obviously a critical component of your system. Unfortunately, few brands of hard drives are actually certified to work with Windows NT. Most will work fine with Windows 95, including all those multigigabyte EIDE hard disks that are now so popular. Unfortunately, you have to be extremely careful with NT. It simply refuses to install on a hard disk that doesn't meet its stringent (and undocumented) requirements. If you're pressed for a budget and must use EIDE drives, I have found that Western Digital (http://www.wdc.com) hard disks (see Figure 1-4) *always* work for me when other brands fail. (I won't mention any other names. You can check my Web site, http://www.byteit.com/rgrace, for that.)

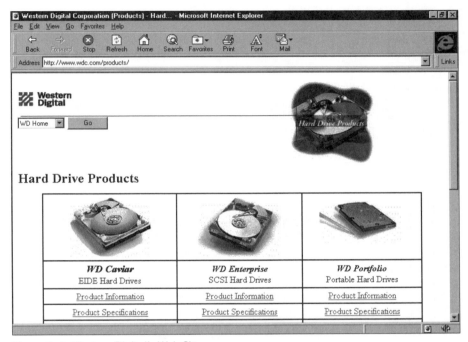

Figure 1-4: Western Digital's Web Site

If you buy EIDE hard drives, make sure you buy them from a reputable reseller. Some fly-by-night PC clone shops will not exchange a hard disk for another model if it doesn't run with NT. Make sure they will stand behind their products. For a Windows NT Workstation, a high-capacity EIDE disk should be just fine, unless you plan to run high-end applications.

SCSI DRIVES AND CONTROLLERS

Particularly for NT Servers, SCSI is definitely a better idea. SCSI controller cards have come a long way in the last few years, becoming easier to install and more reliable. Several manufacturers, including QLogic, BusLogic, and especially Adaptec — make solid, compatible cards. Many other SCSI card makers are around, but unless they bundle a Windows NT driver with their card, do *not* buy it. Spend a little more and get an industry-standard card.

If you plan to use SCSI, the task of finding compatible hard drives gets a bit easier, though more expensive. Although SCSI can be a bit of an alphabet soup (SCSI-II, Ultra SCSI, Wide SCSI, Ultra-Wide SCSI, Fast-Wide SCSI, Ultra-Wide SCSI, *ad nauseum*), Windows NT tends to be more compatible with SCSI hard disks than with run-of-the-mill EIDE devices.

With the fastest NT systems, you'll notice that EIDE drives may become a bottleneck. Using a 7,200-rpm SCSI hard disk (which usually come in Ultra SCSI or Ultra-Wide SCSI types from Quantum, Micropolis, Western Digital, and Seagate) will guarantee the best possible disk performance, at a price premium. (Seagate makes a 10,000-rpm hard disk that is the current speed champion, but I've also heard you can fry an egg on its case.)

Tape drives are a key conundrum for NT users. It's unlikely, even at this late date, that you'll find a high-capacity EIDE tape drive compatible with Windows NT. NT does a much better job of supporting SCSI tape devices such as high-capacity DAT (Digital Audio Tape) drives. They're more expensive but also a must in a hard-working server environment.

REMOVABLE SCSI DRIVES

SCSI also provides a wider array of choices for removable media, such as the 1GB/2GB Iomega Jaz drive, the 1.5GB SyQuest SyJet, and optical drives such as the 4.6GB Pinnacle Micro Apex. You must also have a SCSI controller in order to use read-write CD-ROM drives or the new DVD-ROM drives. Rewritable CD-ROM (often called CD-RWs) are also becoming common and are an excellent option for disk mastering and backup.

For Windows NT installation, a SCSI CD-ROM drive is the most reliable solution. TEAC and Toshiba make solid, reliable SCSI CD-ROM drives. Although it's hard to find it in the documentation, NT also requires a SCSI-II controller to make proper use of a SCSI CD-ROM drive. If you decide to use an IDE CD-ROM, make sure it's a current model.

Assessing Additional Hardware Needs

Now you can take a quick glance at the other categories of hardware typically found in better PCs. Among the key types are Network Interface Cards (NICs), video display cards, and networking support hardware including routers and bridges. In the late' 90s, I've found that as long as you spend a little more to get quality components, you'll normally experience few problems getting your systems up and running. Although it's still far from perfect (and may never achieve that state), PC hardware really has come a long way. It's much more reliable, easier to set up, yields better performance, and is far more sophisticated all the way around.

NETWORK CARDS AND CABLING

A network card is another vital component of your NT system. Without a NIC (Network Interface Card) in your server, it's obviously useless. Choose carefully, grasshopper!

Where all other cards have caused problems, I've found that Novell Eagle 16-Bit ISA and 32-Bit PCI Ethernet cards have always worked reliably on all networking platforms I've used, including Windows for Workgroups, NT 3.5, NT 4.0, and Novell NetWare 3.12 and 4.11. Hands down, I think these cards are the best ones available. Generally, you shouldn't have trouble with 3Com, SMC, and Intel networking cards; beyond that, you really can't afford to buy cards from second-tier or unknown/clone manufacturers. Why take a chance on this critical component to save twenty bucks? Also, *make sure* to get network cards that offer a software utility to set the interrupt and I/O Port address. (It's all too easy to have the card set to one set of addresses and have the OS expecting to find the card at another set of addresses, which means your network won't work, of course.) Again, all Novell Eagle/Microdyne cards offer this feature.

Unless you have a bunch of 486s to integrate into your network, buy PCI Fast Ethernet network cards. These cards are typically called 10/100 Fast Ethernet, and they provide autosensing features that enable them to detect whether they are connected to a 10Mbps hub or a 100Mbps hub. The initial investment will be well spent and will take you into the turn of the century. Particularly on the server side, a PCI Fast Ethernet card is an absolute must. If you need to buy 16-bit cards to keep costs down, the same rule holds: Buy major-brand networking cards. The expense will be repaid in terms of reliability and easy configuration.

When you install your network card, make sure to keep careful track of its IRQ (Interrupt Request) and I/O Port memory address. For 16-bit NICs, you can often use IRQ 5 and address 300h, but this will not always be true. PCI devices generally use higher interrupt numbers between 9 and 14. In newer systems, the network card should be detected automatically during installation. You should also be able to use more than one card if desired, particularly if you have enough PCI slots available. (This is called a *multi-homed* server.)

If network cabling doesn't already exist, you should have it built into the walls or cubicle enclosures of your office. In a small office this may not be a problem, but for a department it's almost imperative. If you don't have network cabling, you'll encounter terrible cable clutter as you build up your network. When you plan your installation, you may need to take this into account. Obviously, cabling quality is also crucial — 90 percent of LAN networking problems are usually cable-related. Immediately after you install your cabling, make sure it works. This can save huge amounts of troubleshooting from the start. Also, if you plan to use Fast Ethernet, you will have no choice but to use Category 5 100BaseTX cabling, which resembles phone cabling with a slightly wider RJ-45 connector.

One final tip: If you plan to use two or more Network Interface Cards in your NT server, do yourself a favor and get the same cards for each slot. I've seen people on mailing lists wonder why they can't get their multi-homed server to work and then mention that they have network cards from two different manufacturers in their system.

HUBS, ROUTERS, AND SWITCHES

This is a broad and complex area that, for the most part, isn't germane to this discussion of basic NT networking. If you're running a small network of less than 10 users, a good-quality, inexpensive 10Base-T hub will set you back around $100. Fast Ethernet hubs cost more. You'll spend more on a hub that supports Fast

Ethernet, but the addtional expense is worth it. You can spend enormous amounts of money on network support hardware, so make sure what you're buying is what you need.

Switches are another broad area. One application with direct interest to you is switching connections between 10BaseT and 100BaseT networks. If you have both types of networks or expect to have both, and you want to make sure they communicate properly, you need a 10/100 switch. This is not a hub — it's a device that allows you to hook a 10BaseT network segment to a 100BaseT segment and have them communicate. Most Fast Ethernet hubs will not work with stations running 10BaseT; Fast Ethernet hubs are not backwards-compatible, unlike the Fast Ethernet network cards discussed earlier.

Routers are needed (and, potentially, much more than that) if you're working with multiple LANs in your company. An interesting development for Windows NT 4 users is Microsoft's recent release of software-based routing technology. Titled *Routing and RAS,* the theory behind it is to eliminate some of the administrative costs and headaches involved in integrating and maintaining hardware routers in an office network. In practice, Routing and RAS emulates a small Cisco-type router within the NT operating system, which is particularly useful in a multi-homed NT server. Keep an eye out for this upgrade, which Microsoft makes available for NT 4 servers on their Web site (`http://www.microsoft.com/NTServer`).

WIDE-AREA INTERFACES

Online communications are one of your most important NT applications. Particularly if you plan to use Remote Access services, you have to decide what types of transmissions you plan to support. The choices are many and bewildering, and some are even deceptive.

DIGITAL CONNECTIONS   First you have the high-end dedicated-line services, such as T1 and Fractional T1. T1s provide a 1.544 Mbps data stream (called a DS1) that can be split into separate channels of 56K/64K each (called a DS0) using a multiplexer. To use the full capability of a dedicated T1 line, you need expensive hardware, the coverage of which is way beyond the scope of this book. Many other options are available that also require expensive relationships with your telephone company.

You have two commonly available options for digital modems: ISDN and 56K. ISDN is a highly useful, reliable, fully digital communications standard that provides many capabilities. First, ISDN provides two separate 64K connections (called *B-channels*). These connections can be combined for a fast 128K digital data link or run separately — one dedicated for data and the other for simultaneous voice transmissions (phone calls). Internal ISDN adapters are as cheap as modems nowadays. ISDN lines provide an almost instantaneous hookup — you get none of the obnoxious handshaking modem squawking that you hear with regular analog modems on a phone line. ISDN is a beautiful technology.

The biggest problem? Setup. You must obtain an ISDN connection from your Regional Bell Operating Company (RBOC). Some are most decidedly better than others, and even the better ones can be difficult to deal with. Depending on where you live, you may not be able to get it at all. If you can get an ISDN connection, prepare for a significant hit on your pocketbook. RBOCs are unpredictable regarding ISDN provisioning rates, and monthly charges add up even for occasional use. If you can afford it and can get it with a reasonable degree of efficiency, ISDN is definitely an option.

If you get an ISDN line, try to squeeze some room in your budget for an Ascend Pipeline bridge/router. You can hook it up to your network through Ethernet and thus provide all your systems with access to the ISDN line when they need it. I won't go into all the various capabilities and features of the Pipeline series; just be assured that if you think you might need it, you should probably have had it yesterday. Ascend can be located at `http://www.ascend.com/`.

The 56K Con

As far as I'm concerned, 56K modems are more trouble than they're worth and grossly overhyped. Modem companies are squabbling over whose product will be the standard. The two major modems are the U.S. Robotics 56K, or X2, and the Rockwell K56Flex, based on a Rockwell modem chip set. The two modems are incompatible, and there's a big fight going on as to which one is going to prevail. By the time a decision is reached, something else will come along.

Even without this problem, neither X2 nor K56Flex are long-term contenders. That's because they only use high-speed connections for incoming data (in a manner of speaking) and a 33.6K connection for outgoing data traffic. If you send many files, you get no benefit from 56K modems. They also require digital termination at the other end (usually the ISP), which makes them sort of pointless for anything except making Web browsing a little faster than it is now.

No phone line in this country can support full 56K transmission rates. Most regions in the United States can't even hit 45K. In many urban areas on the East coast, you can't even get a full 28.8K connection. In this area, anecdotal evidence is meaningless. In practice, the 33.6 modem is the realistic limit for analog transmission over our existing POTS (Plain Old Telephone Service) network. Meanwhile, our supposedly deregulated phone companies continue to drag their feet offering digital alternatives, and the modem companies continue to publish deceptive advertising implying twice the transmission rates of other modems.

There is hope, however. Another option just emerging is the *sixty-seven* modem. This new modem architecture, created by the Brazilian communications company Digitel Corp. and marketed in this country by a company called Transend (`http://www.transend.com`), appears to be an exciting development. Sixty-seven modems are so-called because they operate at a top *analog* transmission speed of 67.2Kbps. Essentially, they combine two 33.6 modems on the chip level. Each 33.6 connection uses a phone line, so you have two phone lines connected to the device, and their signals are multiplexed internally. Unlike 56K modems, you get 67.2K going both ways. No digital termination is required at the ISP end. The modem combines the two 33.6 signals internally, uses any transmission protocol, and can hook up to your serial port. Theoretically, all you should have to do is buy another phone line, configure the modem, and blast off. Other clever devices are popping up that allow you to combine as many as three separate modem connections.

The only particular disadvantage I can see with sixty-seven modems is that you need to hook up two phone lines. Considering the headaches involved with ISDN and 56K modems, the need for two phone lines to support this architecture may be one that many people can live with. (I can't wait to get my hands on one.) Keep an eye out for these devices. Start bugging modem manufacturers to adopt this standard. Make a statement by not buying 56K modems. Wait until something better comes along or go straight to ISDN.

VIDEO CARDS

For NT servers, the choice of a video card isn't important. Any basic VGA card will do, because an NT server shouldn't normally be used as a high-resolution workstation. Any card that can display a decent 640x480 or 800x600 screen will do. Of course, a good card doesn't *hurt*, but it can add costs that could be better spent elsewhere. NT's basic VGA driver is the best choice for running video on a server screen, but if NT loads the drivers for your particular card, there's no reason not to stick with them.

For NT workstations, the issue is more complex. A bewildering array of cards are available from many different manufacturers. As a rule, I've found only a few major manufacturers worth bothering with: Diamond (`http://www.Diamondmm.com`), Number Nine (`http://www.nine.com`), Hercules (`http://www.hercules.com`), Matrox (`http://www.matrox.com`), and a few others. (Of course, they're all domestic card makers.) I've tested cards from all of these companies at one time or another in NT, and their mainstream offerings all work fine. (I use Number Nine Imagine 128 and Matrox cards for my main systems.)

Windows NT 4.0 also directly supports a substantial list of the most common high-quality video cards, including the Number Nine Imagine 128, the Diamond Stealth 2000 series, Matrox Millennium, and a host of others. The better card manufacturers all have Web sites, as noted in the previous paragraph.

3D is now the big selling point in video cards. Unless you have a specific application for 3D, it isn't that big a deal for an NT workstation. 3D is primarily meant for games, most of which don't run efficiently under Windows NT, and which you really shouldn't be playing at work (admonishing finger waved here). Because almost every current video card actually uses a 3D-capable chip, it's not really a big deal. The key rule is obvious: Don't buy the card for your NT workstation if it doesn't bundle NT video driver software in the box. Also, do a little research on the Web. Each card maker worth considering has Web sites offering its latest drivers.

An entirely separate, high-end area of NT workstation video performance exists at the high end. If you're interested in this area and want to perform a lot of CAD or 3D modeling, you'll want the fastest system you can buy. Higher-end video cards typically have a $3,000 price tag but also provide a mind-boggling 32-40MB of RAM for high-end video tasks. Intergraph (`http://www.intergraph.com/`

`ics/tdzext/tdz.htm`) manufactures $20,000 NT workstations for this market, and they're widely considered the best systems of their kind. Many other PC manufacturers are entering this market, including Compaq and Gateway.

Now that I've managed to bore you with a drawn-out discussion of hardware, it's time to get down to cases. When your hardware's squared away, you still have to set up NT. That, as you'll see, is not a trivial task.

Installing and Configuring Windows NT

Setting up Windows NT is the true test of your hardware. By that simple act, you're also subjecting your computer to a thorough compatibility test. This is true whether you're setting up NT Workstation or NT Server. The processes of setting up Server and Workstation start off almost identically, until it's time to install networking features. I'll note any key differences during the procedure.

Windows NT 4.0 comes with a CD-ROM and three floppy diskettes. The normal and expected method for installing NT is to boot your system off the first installation floppy, with the NT CD disc in the CD-ROM drive. Then you simply follow the instructions on the screen. (NT's Setup usually automatically detects the CD during the process.) Unfortunately, the floppy-based installation of Windows NT can be painful. There are numerous situations where the installation simply will not work no matter what you do. I begin by describing the standard floppy-based installation, and then I show you a somewhat more economical way to approach setting up NT.

When you set up an NT Server, you have many decisions to make, particularly when installing networking features. NT's networking setup adds another layer of complexity to the process, but given what it does for you, it is actually quite straightforward. By the time you finish setting up the server, all you'll need to do to get your network up and running is to define your user accounts and have them log on. Installation and account setup are 90 percent of the battle with NT. (User account setup is discussed at length in Chapter 2.)

The only assumption made throughout this section is that you are performing a fresh installation of Windows NT onto a new or reformatted hard drive. If so, you install Windows NT onto a hard disk initially formatted with the FAT (File Allocation Table) file system, which is used in MS-DOS and Windows 95. (Do *not* try to use FAT-32, which is a new addition to Windows 95.) You can start the installation using a boot floppy with a proper set of batch files, DOS programs, and device drivers configured for your system. For details on that topic, see the section titled "Constructing a Boot Floppy for Installation and other Emergencies." If you have already done this, simply go to the sections that follow.

A Note About Windows NT Upgrades

If you are installing Windows NT 4.0 over an existing NT 3.5 or 3.51 system, you're in luck. The upgrade should be seamless, and NT 4.0 will automatically use all your previous desktop and networking settings.

If you want to upgrade a Windows 95 or Windows 3.*x* system, forget it. It can't be done. This is true for both NT Workstation and NT Server. No meaningful transition can be made from Win95/Win3.1 to NT. NT Setup will blow all your previous settings away, and you will have to reinstall your applications. A dual-boot system is a possibility, but what's the point, especially if you're building a server? Unless you're upgrading from an older version of NT or are planning to install NT on a separate disk partition for a dual-boot scenario, just back up all your data and programs, scrape the hard drive clean (in other words, partition and format it), and start over.

File Systems: FAT Versus NTFS

FAT stands for *File Allocation Table*. What is it? It's an ancient 16-bit file system originally used in MS-DOS. It is also used in Windows 95 and has a file cluster size of 64K, which partially explains why Windows 95 applications often eat up so much disk space. (A newer version of Windows 95, called Windows 95B and available only to hardware OEMs who resell it with their systems, partially alleviates this problem by using an updated version for FAT with smaller cluster sizes. Unfortunately, that new file system won't work for an NT installation, as you'll see later.)

NTFS stands for *NT File System*. It is the standard file system used for Windows NT, whose security features require it. NTFS uses a file cluster size of 16K. For NT users, the FAT file system should remain largely irrelevant. The FAT file system should not be used on an NT server. Period. You will lose many of your server's security features if you decide not to use NTFS. Also, NTFS file cluster sizes are smaller than for FAT, thereby saving you considerable amounts of disk space. During Windows NT setup, you're offered the chance to change a FAT-formatted hard disk to NTFS.

You can choose to use FAT to install Windows NT, but you're not permanently committed to it. After you get NT up and running, you can use Disk Administrator to change the hard disk's file system from FAT to NTFS *while NT is running*. (To view Disk Administrator in NT, select Start ➪ Programs ➪ Administrative Tools ➪ Disk Administrator.) Changing the file system does *not* damage any data you already have on your hard disk. You'll get slightly better performance and enable all of the Windows NT file and directory security capabilities.

Running a Floppy-Based Installation

Windows NT begins with a DOS-based installation screen. When you perform a fresh installation, you place Setup floppy #1 into your floppy disk drive and continue from there. The classic Windows NT blue screen appears, and the setup program slowly loads each of the device drivers it requires. Follow these steps:

1. You're prompted to exchange floppies, and the Welcome to Setup screen appears. It offers four options:

```
To learn more about Windows NT Setup before continuing, press F1.
To set up Windows NT now, press ENTER.
To repair a damaged Windows NT version 4.0 installation, press R.
To quit Setup without installing Windows NT, press F3.
```

2. To continue with NT Setup, press Enter. You learn about making and updating emergency repair disks at the end of this chapter in "Making Emergency Repairs."

   The next screen provides a key message that installers must heed during the Setup:

```
"Setup automatically detects floppy disk controllers and standard ESDI/IDE hard
 disks without user intervention. However on some computers detection of certain
 other mass storage devices, such as SCSI adapters and CD-ROM drives, can cause
 the computer to become unresponsive or to malfunction temporarily.
"For this reason, you can bypass Setup's mass storage device detection and
 manually select SCSI adapters, CD-ROM drives, and special disk controllers
 (such as drive arrays) for installation."
 ◆ To continue, Press ENTER.
    Setup will attempt to detect mass storage devices in your computer.
 ◆ To skip mass storage device detection, press S.
    Setup will allow you to manually select SCSI adapters, CD-ROM drives,
    and special disk controllers for installation.
```

3. Pressing Enter is the best option here, whether or not you have additional devices to install. Setup detects the EIDE controller built into the motherboard of your computer. Many NT systems still have an EIDE hard disk built into their system, even if they have SCSI, so you should press Enter in any case. Later in the process, you're asked again if you want manual installation of special devices.

4. The Setup program asks you to insert the Setup floppy #3. Do so and press Enter.

Setup goes through the process of detecting the EIDE disk controller. A large number of SCSI device drivers are also loaded, and Setup uses them to detect any industry-standard SCSI controllers installed in the computer, including a large collection of Adaptec, BusLogic, Future Domain, and QLogic disk controllers. If your system has an Intel motherboard that contains a built-in Adaptec controller, it will also be detected automatically. When Setup finishes detecting, the following screen appears:

```
Setup has recognized the following mass storage devices in your computer:

IDE CD-ROM (ATAPI 1.2)/PCI IDE Controller

To specify additional SCSI adapters, CD-ROM drives, or special disk
controllers for use with Windows NT, including those for which you have a
device support disk from a mass storage device manufacturer, press S.
If you do not have any device support disks from a mass storage device
manufacturer, or do not want to specify additional mass storage devices for
use with Windows NT, press ENTER.
```

If a SCSI controller is detected by Setup, it is also listed here.

5. If you have a SCSI controller and it doesn't show up here, press S. The next screen prompts you to insert the floppy disk with your SCSI card's driver software, or the driver for any other SCSI device, such as a RAID drive array.

   After the driver is loaded, you are returned to the previous screen.

6. To continue Setup without detecting any other devices, press Enter.

   The Setup program continues to load device drivers from the floppy drive. If you are installing Windows NT on a brand new system or hard disk, the following screen appears:

```
Setup has determined that your computer's startup hard disk is new or has been
erased, or that an operating system is installed on your computer with which
Windows NT cannot coexist.
If such an operating system is installed on your computer, continuing Setup may
damage or destroy it.
If the hard disk is new or has been erased, or you want to discard its current
contents, you can choose to continue Setup.

◆ To continue Setup, press C. WARNING: Any data currently on your
  computer's startup hard disk will be permanently lost.
  To exit Setup, press F3.
```

7. Press C.

   Setup displays a screen showing the basic configuration of the computer it has detected.

8. To continue, press Enter.

   The setup routine passes to the next phase, setting up the system's hard disk as a temporary cache for a huge collection of compressed files laboriously copied from the CD-ROM. It doesn't matter how fast your CD-ROM drive is; this file copy will cost you 45 minutes to an hour. A bar graph appears on the screen along with the percentage of the completed copy. After copying is finished, you have to reboot. Setup prompts you to do this and automatically continues after restarting the computer. After Setup comes back, you're greeted by the Windows NT licensing agreement. (It's quite long, so I won't reproduce it here.)

9. Press the Page Down key until the end of the agreement appears, and then press the F8 key. (You can also read the agreement, if desired. There is some useful information in it.)

   The Windows NT Setup continues and displays the available disk partitions on which NT can be installed.

10. Select the desired partition and press Enter. A screen similar to the following appears:

```
Setup will install Windows NT on partition.
C: FAT 2047 MB (2038 MB free)@sron 2047 MB Disk 0 at Id 0 on bus 0 on atapi.
Select the type of file system you want on this partition from the list below.
 Use the UP and DOWN ARROW keys to move the highlight to the selection you
want. Then press ENTER.

If you want to select a different partition for Windows NT, press ESC.

 Convert the partition to NTFS
 Leave the current file system intact (no changes)
```

   The drive size, letter, and type may differ depending on your system. More drives may show up on this screen depending on your system. Here, Setup also offers the chance to reformat a disk partition to the NTFS file system. If you're running an NT Server, you should definitely choose this option.

Debating File Systems in Windows NT

Many of Windows NT's security features are disabled unless you use NTFS. You also get better disk performance and smaller file cluster sizes, which saves space. You can also choose to bypass this option until you finish installing NT. Afterwards, when you have NT running, run NT's Disk Administrator to change any FAT partition to NTFS. (The reverse is not true: You can't change an NTFS partition back to FAT without reformatting it.)

For an NT server installation, I mildly recommend opting for NTFS during setup because it makes the process more inclusive. All your security features will be enabled from the beginning. It doesn't matter, however, if you do it then or afterwards.

11. Select the Convert the partition to NTFS option, and press Enter.

    NT Setup issues the following warning:

```
WARNING: Converting this drive to NTFS will render it inaccessible to operating
 systems other than Windows NT.

Do not convert the drive to NTFS if you require access to the drive when using
 other operating systems such as MS-DOS, Windows, or OS/2.

Please confirm that you want to convert
C: FAT 2047 MB (2038 MB free)on 2047 MB Disk 0
at Id 0 on bus 0 on atapi.

 To convert the drive to NTFS, press C.
 To select a different partition for Windows NT, press ESC.
```

As the screen states, NTFS disk partitions cannot be accessed by other operating systems common in the PC world. You're also offered a way to backtrack to the previous screen to select another disk partition if you want.

12. Press C. This converts the drive partition's file system to NTFS.

    Setup next prompts you to enter the directory in which you want the operating system to be installed.

    The default directory is \WINNT, and I recommend accepting it.

13. Press Enter.

    Setup displays the following screen:

```
Setup will now examine your hard disk(s) for corruption.
In addition to a basic examination, Setup can perform a more exhaustive
secondary examination on some drives. This can be a time consuming operation,
especially on very large or very full drives.

To allow Setup to perform an exhaustive secondary examination of your hard
disk(s), press ENTER.
To skip the exhaustive examination, press ESC.
```

If you want to be cautious, the exhaustive examination never hurts. I encourage using the exhaustive exam, even on brand-new drives, because it doesn't add much time to the process. Also, because a server installation is apt to be sensitive and highly important, every measure needs to be taken.

14. Press Enter to perform the exhaustive disk exam.

    The system pauses for the disk examination and then begins copying files to the WINNT directory. A bar graph appears, files are decompressed from the temporary directory, and after a couple of minutes Setup prompts you to restart your computer again.

15. Press Enter to restart your system.

After the reboot, the famous Windows NT blue screen appears and an NT version of CHKDSK runs. This is where NT converts the FAT file system on the hard disk to NTFS. (It doesn't run if you're just installing to a FAT partition.)

Then the system reboots yet again and goes through the process of starting up NT. Don't be concerned with this additional reboot; it's part of the normal setup procedure.

NT starts and displays its first actual GUI (Graphical User Interface) screen. You're through the obstacle course and entering a new phase of Setup that enables you to install and configure the functional parts of the operating system.

Setup displays a dialog box that lists the next three parts of the process:

```
Gathering information about your computer
Installing Windows NT Networking
Finishing Setup
```

You'll perform a lot of work in the second phase, Installing Windows NT Networking:

1. Click Next.

   After a moment of preparation, Setup presents four choices for setting up your NT system: Typical, Portable, Compact, and Custom.

2. Select Typical (which is the default) and click Next.

3. Enter your name and organization in the dialog provided.

   Setup then displays the registration dialog box, in which you enter a 10-digit CD Key number. (This can be found on the jewel box for your Installation CD.)

4. Enter the 10-digit number and click Next.

   The next screen requests a name for your computer.

5. Enter a preferred name for the computer and click Next.

   The name you enter *must* be unique within the network.

 At this point, if you're running a Windows NT Server installation, please jump ahead to the sub-section titled "Installing Networking for NT Server." If you're setting up a workstation system, simply continue through this section.

6. Setup asks if you want to create an Emergency Repair Disk. To do so, simply click the Next button. If you want to save it for later, select the No option and click Next. (For more information on this topic, go to the section titled "Making Emergency Repairs" later in this chapter).

   The Select Components screen appears. The next step is to select software components for installation.

7. In the Typical install option, most of the more important applications are already selected. Make sure the Windows Messaging check box is selected (and the *really* important part – Games), and then click Next.

   Setup passes on to the second phase of the graphical-based installation (and the most important one), which is "Installing Windows NT Networking."

INSTALLING NETWORKING FOR WINDOWS NT WORKSTATION

When the Setup program enters its networking phase, you're installing the key software components to hook your computer up to the network and to otherwise communicate with other systems. It is assumed that you already have a network card installed in your system and that its IRQ and I/O port addresses are set correctly. NT automatically detects the card and its settings during this process. In case NT makes a mistake, which has been known to happen, make sure you know the NIC's settings so you can enter them.

Read This if You're Installing Windows NT Server

NT Server provides a much broader range of networking services than NT Workstation. There are many networking tasks Server can do that the Workstation simply doesn't allow for (Services for Macintosh, full Remote Access, the various TCP/IP networking services and Routing and Remote Access Service, for example). NT Server networking setup is described in a separate section titled "Installing Networking for NT Server." If you're setting up NT Server, please go to that section.

To start, bear in mind that it's easy to add further networking services and features after your server or workstation is up and running. If you find yourself missing something important when you run the system, you can easily add it through the Network applet in the Control Panel. This includes Remote Access and many other features.

The first dialog box that appears lets you specify how the system will be connected:

1. Select the This computer will participate on a network option.

    Two check boxes are also offered that are not mutually exclusive.

2. Select the Wired to the network check box.

3. If you have a modem connected to the system, select the Remote access to the network check box.

    You need to select this check box even if you're only planning to use dial-up Internet connections on the NT Workstation system. NT's Remote Access is used for dial-up accounts to Internet service providers (ISPs) as well as dial-up access to the NT Server. (Remote Access is discussed in Chapter 8.)

4. Click Next.

    A new screen appears labeled *To have setup start searching for a Network Adapter, click the Start Search button.* Although you can also select your own driver from a list (or load your own driver) by clicking the Select from list button, you're better off letting Windows NT do its thing first.

5. Click the Start Search button.

Installing Device Drivers for Network Devices

When you click the Select from list button, a Select Network Adapter dialog box appears. You can scroll through the rather long list to find the adapter that matches your hardware, or you can click the Have disk button. Some new network interface cards, such as the Novell NE5500, may also need to be installed using this method.

If your network card is installed correctly, it will appear in the window within a couple of seconds. The NT system makes its own choice of the driver that best matches the installed device. If you have something more specific in mind, you can always install it using the Select from list method.

After you run the adapter search, the Start Search button changes to read Find Next. This applies only if you have more than one networking card installed in your system. If that's the case, click *Find Next* one or more times to have NT search for the other networking devices.

If you selected Remote Access to the network back in Step 3, then Setup passes on to the phase in which Remote Access is installed. The Remote Access Setup windows appears, displaying the following message:

> There are no RAS capable devices to add. Do you want RAS setup to invoke the Modem installer to enable you to add a modem?

6. Click Yes. The Install New Modem dialog box appears.

7. Click Next to allow NT to detect your modem.

    NT polls the serial ports on your computer, searching for a modem. If it detects one, it goes through a short series of handshaking operations.

8. If NT doesn't successfully detect your modem, select the Don't detect my modem; I will select it from a list check box.

9. Click Next.

    If an ISDN modem card or external ISDN device is hooked up to your system, the Install New Modem screen is where it can be detected and installed. Otherwise, the computer searches for any modems connected to external serial ports and for an internal modem card. If you have any of those devices installed, and NT isn't finding them, you either have to load them from Windows NT's list or insert the device's NT Drivers disk.

If you have an ISDN adapter installed and it provides NT drivers, you will probably need to load the drivers from the provided floppy. Most popular ISDN cards, which have suddenly become affordable, were not yet available when Windows NT 4.0 was released. ISDN adapters are likely to provide NT drivers in the box, unlike modems, which are a more general-purpose consumer item.

Also, if you've bought a modem in the period of time after Windows NT 4.0 was released, there's a good chance that it won't be auto-detected by NT. This is particularly true if you've bought one of the new 56K models that have just come out. Even if you've just bought a normal 28.8 or 33.6Kbps modem, its particular model may not be directly supported. Modem manufacturers are also not in the habit of providing NT driver disks with their products, particularly if you buy the most popular brands. If your driver isn't listed, and you have no disk, you still have an alternative that should work:

10. In the Manufacturer list, select the company whose modem you're installing.

11. Select the model from the Models list.

12. Click Next.

    The system then asks you on which port the modem should be installed.

13. Click the Selected ports option. If your modem is connected to COM1 or COM2, select either port.

14. Click Next.

    After a moment, NT returns the following message: *Your modem has been set up successfully.*

15. Click Finish.

    The Remote Access Setup dialog box reappears, listing the modem or other device that you're using.

16. Click the Configure button. The Configure Port Usage dialog box appears.

    The next step, although small, is important.

If you're planning to dial out, don't miss this step! If you plan to use your Windows NT Workstation to perform any Internet dial-up for software updates, e-mail, or plain old Web browsing, make sure you select the Dial out and Receive calls option in Remote Access Setup's Configure Port Usage dialog box. If you don't, RAS will not be able to dial out. This is one of those silly little problems that you can tear out your hair over.

17. Select the Dial out and Receive calls option.

18. Click Continue.

    NT will take a moment to finish installing files. The next step is to install the networking protocols that your system uses.

19. Click each check box to enable support for NetBEUI and TCP/IP. You need both of them throughout this book. (You'll install the IPX/SPX Compatible Transport in a later chapter of this book.)

20. Click Next.

21. Click Next again to install your selected components and network protocols.

INTRODUCING NETWORKING PROTOCOLS

A *networking protocol* is a package of low-level software drivers that set up a method by which computers talk back and forth. Although this book is not intended to be a comprehensive discussion of what protocols are and how they work (the bookstore shelves are groaning with books that do exactly that), you should spend a little bit of time on them as an introduction. Windows NT Workstation offers three networking protocols, any or all of which you can install at the start of your NT experience: TCP/IP, NWLink IPX/SPX, and NetBEUI. These protocols are the three most commonly used in Windows NT computing. Each has an important role to play in a workstation, and even more so in a server, depending on what you're planning to do.

NT Server offers the same three protocols as NT Workstation, plus quite a few more. For the moment I'll stick to the three key ones, because you'll get well acquainted with using them in the course of this book:

◆ **TCP/IP protocol.** Used for a diverse number of networking tasks, TCP/IP is the versatility champ (and the complexity champ) of networking protocols. It provides your system with the capability to dial up the Internet, the capability to use a Web server program such as Internet Information Server on an NT Server machine and with routable networking connections between computers on separate LANs.

◆ **NWLink IPX/SPX compatible transport.** Used to set up NT machines to communicate with Novell NetWare file and print servers. Don't install this protocol unless you plan to connect your NT system to a Novell NetWare server. When IPX/SPX is loaded by the operating system, it occupies memory and adds overhead. (NT-to-Novell networking is discussed in Chapters 6 and 7 of this book.) IPX clients can use NT's Remote Access to dial up and connect to Novell servers on the LAN.

◆ **NetBEUI protocol.** Microsoft's standard protocol used to connect Windows computers to each other — NT, Win95, and Win3.1. If you're doing nothing else with your server besides hooking Windows machines together, you *must* have this protocol running. You can also use NetBEUI to have Windows clients dial up Remote Access. Using NetBEUI is the simplest way to enable Remote Access for clients in the field.

At this point you've finished Windows NT Workstation setup. Congratulations! After going over a huge number of potential pitfalls, you now have Windows NT Workstation up and running. The computer takes a couple minutes to finish installing files, and then it asks you to reboot. When you log on to your new system for the first time, use the Administrator user name and give it a password you can easily remember. The system asks you to verify the password entry, and then it logs you on to the system for your first working session. After that, you can read Chapters 2 and 4 of this book!

INSTALLING NETWORKING FOR NT SERVER

If you're setting up Windows NT Server and you're reading this section, you've reached the point where the server setup differs from NT Workstation. You've also reached the most demanding and rewarding phase of the installation process. All your networking components, including Remote Access dial-up and selecting from a laundry list of networking protocols and services, must be cautiously plodded through. After you're finished with this phase, much of your work is actually done.

NT SERVER: DOMAIN CONTROLLER OR STAND-ALONE?

At this point, NT Server Setup provides three mutually exclusive options for how the computer will be used:

◆ As a Primary Domain Controller (PDC)

◆ As a Backup Domain Controller (BDC)

◆ As a Stand-Alone Server

Note on Windows NT Domains

What exactly is a domain? (It sounds like one of those intensely intimidating computer terms.)

A *domain* is a group of Windows NT systems that designate all their security tasks to a central computer (or more than one) set up as the *domain controller*. Essentially, domains are a security measure. Windows 95 and Windows 3.*x* systems can log on to a domain and use the shared resources provided to them, just as they would to a stand-alone server.

A domain can be considered an *ultimate* workgroup because it centralizes control of network security and user accounts in one place. This centralized control is one of the key elements of Windows NT 4.0.

At this point, another question needs to be asked: What are you going to do with the server?

INTRODUCING DOMAINS   For Microsoft Windows NT, domains are used to help manage large collections of users — up into the thousands. They're also used to help manage larger multiple-server networks. Domains are a security measure, but they're also a convenience feature. In a typical small network, you must log on to every individual resource you want to use: someone's shared hard disk, a printer hooked up to a server or to someone else's machine, or several different folders in different locations on the network. Logging on to every resource can be time-consuming, and you don't actually get anything done.

If all those network resources are set up as part of a domain, all you have to do is log on to the domain, and all those resources are automatically made available to you. In a domain, whatever resources are set up to be shared *to* the domain are available to all users *in* that domain. This availability can be handy if you have dozens or hundreds of users in a domain, because all they have to do is log in once, and everything they need is there.

Domains also offer greater flexibility for managing networks and user accounts than stand-alone servers can provide. For example, with a domain you can determine the hours during the day that a particular user has access to the network (with the Hours button). Stand-alone servers don't provide this feature. (I discuss this topic in Chapter 11.)

If you're only going to hook up a few Windows 95 or NT Workstation machines to your NT server, you can choose to set up your server as a Stand-Alone Server. Nevertheless, even for the small networks used in my office, I've become convinced that using NT Server as a Primary Domain Controller is the way to go. It's a little more trouble to set up (not that much more, however), but the rewards are greater in terms of ease of administration and less confusion for your users. Here are a few key points:

◆ A Primary Domain Controller can work just as well on your server as a Stand-Alone setup. When you set up your network stations to log on, it's easier and more bulletproof to have them log on to a Windows NT Domain. (Both Windows 95 and NT Workstation allow for this, as you'll see in Chapter 2. There are advantages and disadvantages, as described in that chapter.)

◆ If you're running a Primary Domain Controller, I urge you *also* to build a Backup Domain Controller. Once a domain controller goes down, you may lose everything and have to rebuild from scratch. (Chapter 12 discusses this topic in greater detail.)

◆ A domain can have a *collection* of NT servers gathered within it or added to it, simplifying administration of larger networks. Thus, a domain gives you room to grow as your needs change. This is a major application for NT domains.

◆ Stand-Alone Servers are good for a small office environment in which you don't plan to have many Remote Access dial-in accounts, don't plan to have a significant Internet presence based on the server you're currently setting up, and have a limited user base.

◆ If you set up your server as stand-alone, you will not be able to change it to a domain server unless you reinstall Windows NT from scratch. (An Upgrade installation will not work.) So, this decision does have consequences. You may grow to the point where a domain becomes a necessity, and you may be forced to wipe out your previous installation and rebuild all your user accounts.

◆ Domain controllers don't normally add too much overhead to the system, but they're one reason you're better off investing in as much memory as possible when you build your server.

Continue with Windows NT Server Setup as follows:

1. Select the As a Primary Domain Controller option.

2. Click Next.

3. Enter an administrative password.

   Make sure the password can't be easily guessed by outside users (*please* make a written record of it). As an example, don't use your first or last name, or a word such as *guest* or *admin* or anything of that sort. If you're creating a Primary Domain Controller, your administrative password gives you access to the entire domain, no matter how many servers and workstations eventually participate in that domain.

4. Now you're prompted to make an Emergency Repair Disk. Select the Yes option and click Next. (Setup creates the disk later.)

   Setup provides a list of check boxes for selecting the components you want to install into your server.

5. Select the software components you want to install.

   Again, you may want to make sure Windows Messaging is included. (Don't worry; if you miss something, you can always install it later using the Add/Remove Programs applet in the Control Panel.)

6. Click Next.

   Now Setup asks "How the computer will participate in the network"?

7. Select the option "This computer will participate on a network."

8. Select the check boxes *Wired to the Network* and (if you have an installed a modem or ISDN card or other high-speed connection device) *Remote Access to the network.*

9. Click Next.

   The next screen is about installing the Internet Information Server (IIS). If the reader so chooses to install IIS, then the screen can be left alone and he or she can click Next. Otherwise, the reader needs to uncheck the box.

   The next screen appears, labeled *To have setup start searching for a Network Adapter, click Start Search button.* You can load your own driver from a disk or have Windows NT detect the device for you. This step applies only to network cards and *not* to modems or other communication devices.

10. Click the Start Search button.

If your network card is installed correctly in its slot, it will appear in the window within a couple of seconds. The NT system makes its own choice of the driver that best matches the installed device. If you have something more specific in mind, you can always install it using the Select from list button.

After you run the adapter search, the Start Search button changes to read Find Next. There's a good chance, particularly in a server, that you'll have more than one network card installed in the computer. (If you do, make sure the cards are the same type from the same manufacturer!) If you do have more than one network card, click Find Next one or more times to have NT search for those other devices.

CHOOSING NT LICENSING MODES   Setup makes a sharp turn away from domain configuration for the time being and passes on to other phases of the installation. (No, it's not terribly logical, but that's the way it is.) The next question asked by Setup is how you want your Licensing Modes defined.

Windows NT 4.0 offers two licensing modes:

◆ **Per Server.** Also called *per connection,* in this mode each log-on from a workstation to the domain uses up a license *for each server* to which they're connected. If a user logs on to a domain that has eight servers on it and then logs on to all eight servers (for whatever reason), that user takes up *eight* licenses! If a user logs on to a domain and then has connections to two servers during the course of the day, that user takes up two licenses.

◆ **Per Seat.** This mode is a simpler method of tracking user licenses. Each user logged on to the domain occupies a license, whether there are six, eight, or 10 servers in the domain or just one, as in our current example. In larger networks, this is definitely the way to go. Then a user in the domain can log on to as many servers as needed, and the license count remains at one for that user.

In this case, you're setting up just a single server, so either method is fine. If you plan to use more than one server in your domain in the future, use the Per Seat mode.

Per Server licensing is quite stringent because it ensures that the server is only allowed to service as many client connections on the network as its licensing provides for. Its advantage is that it allows you to purchase a license for the number of clients that will connect at any particular time rather than for the total number of clients on the network. Microsoft actually suggests that Per Server licensing be used for small, single-server networks.

If you're running a Primary Domain Controller with a Backup Domain Controller, plus another server to handle Microsoft Exchange or application serving, and you're still running a relatively small network, then you're somewhat in the middle ground. Since the plan for this book is to gradually build up to a network of this type, Per Seat licensing offers the advantage of being able to purchase individual seat licenses for around $40 each, while providing for each connection to have full access to all the servers in the domain. In other words, Per Seat allows you to purchase network licenses for each client. In effect, I recommend using Per Seat licensing for the networking applications in this book, because although you'll start off building a single Primary Domain Controller, that will expand as you proceed through this book.

Interestingly, Windows NT also allows you to convert a collection of Per Server licenses to Per Seat licenses. You can do this one time only. The feature is made available if you expand your network beyond one server (such as adding a Backup Domain Controller, an Exchange or Internet/intranet server, and so on). You can't perform the opposite function (converting from Per Seat to Per Server), however.

1. Select Per Seat and then click Next.

A dialog box pops up and asks: If there is a DHCP Server on your network, Setup can configure TCP/IP to use a dynamic address. Do you wish to use DHCP?

2. Click No. (DHCP is discussed in Chapter 3.)

   Because your current application is for a single server running a Primary Domain Controller, and you're not running huge TCP/IP-based enterprise networked systems, there is no immediate need for this additional TCP/IP service.

3. Windows NT Server displays a list of the networking services you've decided to install. They should include the following:

   ◆ NetBIOS Interface

   ◆ Computer Browser

   ◆ RPC Configuration

   ◆ Remote Access Service

   ◆ Server

   ◆ Workstation

   Setup may also ask if you want to install Internet Information Server 2.0. Although this adds another step or two to the setup process, it's pretty simple. Internet Information Server is not be discussed here; that particular topic is far beyond the scope of this book.

4. Click Next.

   Setup now passes on to another important phase – installing Remote Access Services (RAS) for your server.

INSTALLING REMOTE ACCESS SERVICES (RAS)   Whether you're running NT Server or Workstation, you should definitely install Remote Access into your computer. On Workstation, RAS enables the system to use a modem, dial in to a server, and connect to it as though the station were wired in on the network. Of course, if you're using a modem, the access is likely to be a bit slow. On NT Server, RAS services enable the server to receive incoming calls from user accounts, allow normal log-on, and participate in normal network use without physically being in the office. (Note: a firewall never hurts.) NT Server can also be set up to call back users if they're calling long-distance, to save toll-call charges.

The Remote Access Setup window appears and displays the following message:

There are no RAS capable devices to add. Do you want RAS setup to invoke the Modem installer to enable you to add a modem?

After reading the message, follow these steps:

1. Click Yes. The Install New Modem dialog box appears as shown in Figure 1-5.

2. Click Next to allow NT to detect your modem.

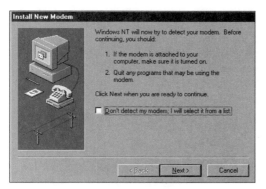

Figure 1-5: Installing a New Modem During RAS Setup

If an ISDN modem card or internal ISDN device is hooked up to your system, now is when it can be detected. Otherwise, the computer will search for any modems that are connected to external serial ports and for an internal modem card. (External ISDN devices are usually hooked up through a serial port.) If you have any of those devices installed and NT isn't finding them, you'll have to load them from Windows NT's list or insert the device's NT Drivers disk.

3. If the modem isn't detected, and you have a major-brand modem, click Next.

4. Scroll through the Manufacturers list shown in Figure 1-6 until you locate your modem's maker and select your modem's model if it's listed.

   If you have a standard 28.8 modem, but its particular name doesn't show up in any of the driver lists, and an NT-specific driver floppy disk isn't provided to you, you still have an option.

5. Under the Standard Modem Types category in the Manufacturers list, select Standard 28800 bps Modem, as shown in Figure 1-7.

6. Click Next.

   Install New Modem asks you on which port the modem should be installed.

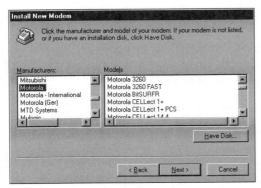

Figure 1-6: Selecting a Modem Mode

7. Click the Selected ports option. If your modem is connected to COM1 or COM2, select either one.

8. Click Next.

9. You're prompted to enter the area code and dialing mode (Tone or Pulse) and an outside line dialing sequence. Type in your entries accordingly.

    After a moment, NT returns a message reading "Your modem has been set up successfully." You're also asked to provide an area code and an outside line dialing sequence, if necessary.

10. Click Finish.

    The Add RAS Device dialog box reappears, listing the modem or other device you're using.

11. Click OK.

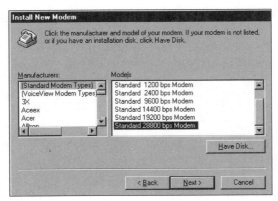

Figure 1-7: Select the Standard 28800 bps Modem
Setting if NT Cannot Detect Your Modem

The Remote Access Setup dialog box appears, listing the installed modem. See Figure 1-8.

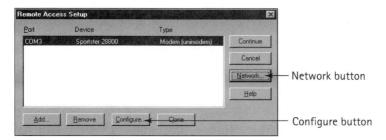

Figure 1-8: The Modem Is Shown as Installed by Remote Access Setup; Your Modem May Differ from That Shown

12. Click the Configure button. The Configure Port Usage dialog box appears.

    The next step, though small, is important.

If you're planning to dial out, don't miss this next step! If you plan to use NT Server to perform any Internet dial-up for software updates, e-mail, or plain old Web browsing, or you want RAS to be able to call long-distance users back, make sure you select the Dial out and Receive calls option in Remote Access Setup's Configure Port Usage dialog box. If you don't, RAS will not be able to dial out. Again, this is one of those silly little problems that you can tear out your hair over. This also applies to NT Workstation users.

13. Select the Dial out and Receive calls option and click OK.

    The next step is also important.

14. Click the Network button (refer to Figure 1-8).

    The Network Configuration dialog box appears as shown in Figure 1-9.

Dial out protocols

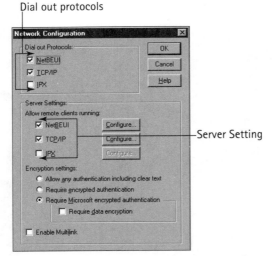

Server Setting

Figure 1-9: The Network Configuration Dialog Box

This dialog box is the key decision-making place for NT online networking.

◆ To dial up the Internet to browse the Web and check e-mail (which you can do with your NT server, and may need to do to get software updates), your dial-out protocol should be TCP/IP. This is true for both NT Server and Workstation. If you plan to have your RAS Service call users back in long-distance calls (for example, your boss with his laptop in Newark, New Jersey, who will appreciate it), add NetBEUI here. (Any proocol will work for this purpose, but Net BEUI is simpler.)

◆ For any Windows-based remote clients who need to dial *into* your server from an outside location in the field, check e-mail, and get files off the LAN, use NetBEUI. Nothing else is needed. You can use TCP/IP (or even IPX), but it is slower and more complicated to set up. You can easily add TCP/IP later if and when it becomes necessary. Chapter 3 discusses TCP/IP networking topics in greater detail.

15. In the Network Configuration dialog box, select the TCP/IP and NetBEUI check boxes in the Dial out Protocols section.

As noted, you'll also want NetBEUI as a dial-out protocol so that Windows-based remote access clients can be called back by the server.

16. In the Network Configuration dialog box, enable the NetBEUI check box in the Server Settings section. Disable all other check boxes. See Figure 1-10.

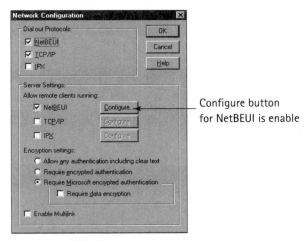

Configure button
for NetBEUI is enable

Figure 1-10: The Network
Configuration Dialog Box

The NetBEUI protocol allows your Windows-based network users to log in to the network and use it as though they were still in the office. They do not require TCP/IP to do this. If you plan to run just Windows clients on a small local-area network, you can use NetBEUI as your Remote Access Dial-out protocol. It's faster and more economical.

I recommend using NetBEUI if your clients in the field will simply be Windows 95/Windows NT users dialing in to your server and browsing on the local LAN segment. You *don't need* TCP/IP for that purpose, and you add complexity if you do so. If you plan to use your new server or client on a larger network, you'll need to use TCP/IP, whose installation and configuration are described in Chapter 3. Its use for Remote Access and other online applications is described in Chapters 9 and 10.

17. In the Server Settings section of Network Configuration, click the Configure button next to the NetBEUI check box option. (It's labeled in Figure 1-10.)

A new dialog box appears (RAS Server NetBEUI Configuration). You have two choices:

 ◆ **This computer only.** Clients can access only the server that logs them in.

 ◆ **Entire network.** Clients can access the whole network across the communications link just as though they were a client computer in the office.

18. Select the Entire network option.

If you're more concerned about security, choose the This computer only option. Unfortunately, a Remote Access NetBEUI client may need to get at a file from its own computer on the network. Plan to use shared folders for your users' work files on the server, for your users' sake and for system security. (Running an application across a modem is not workable.)

19 .Click OK.

20. Click OK.

21. Click Continue.

You can also use the IPX/SPX protocol for Remote Access services natively under NT, even without a Novell NetWare server on the LAN. Windows NT employs IPX/SPX as just another protocol that its clients can make use of to participate on the network.

As I've mentioned, you don't need to use TCP/IP in every networking application. NetBEUI is a very suitable protocol for small, simple networks and works very well in a remote access connection between a laptop client and the server. It also makes things simpler for the laptop user.

22. Finally, click Next to start the network.

The TCP/IP settings are shown on the screen. (TCP/IP is the default protocol for NT.) After the last step is completed, NT Server Setup will *then* appear with a screen that reads:

```
You have requested that Windows NT create a Primary Domain Controller.
You must supply the name of the domain that this Primary Domain Controller will
  manage.
```

A pair of fields is displayed:

◆ **Computer name.** The name of the computer (in my case, it's called RICH'S_BOX) that you created at the beginning of Setup, which is automatically displayed here.

◆ **Domain.** The domain name you must now decide on (in my case, I've called my Primary Domain Controller for this book MAIN_SERVER)

23. Enter a logical and *brief* domain name, under 12 characters, and click Next.

NT Setup goes away again for a minute or so. Then the following dialog box displays:

```
Setup is almost finished. After you answer a few more questions, Setup will
  complete installation.
To continue, click Finish.
```

24. Naturally, click Finish.

If you chose to install IIS earlier in the installation, then IIS services (WWW, FTP, and Gopher) and the appropriate directories are the next set of screens that would appear here in the sequence.

You have battled through the most difficult part of using NT Server — installing it on your computer. As complicated as it was, it can get much more difficult. If you decide you simply must have TCP/IP as your dial-in protocol to your servers instead of or along with NetBEUI, then you need to deal with a lot of TCP/IP network configuration issues. Chapter 9 goes into that topic in greater detail.

Over time I think you'll be quite amazed at the variety of things you can do with NT Server with remarkably little trouble, after you get the system up and running. The machine configuration, DOS-based installation, and networking setup are the real killers. Speaking of which, you really should take the time to read the next section.

BYPASSING WINDOWS NT INSTALLATION PROBLEMS

All too often, Windows NT Setup fails for no apparent reason. This can be quite frustrating, because running the normal three-floppy installation takes 10 to 15 minutes. Failure almost always occurs in the DOS-based portion of NT Setup. Setup usually fails because it can't *detect* the hard drive on which you intended to install the operating system's temporary files. This is a situation in which you can beat your head against a brick wall, because there is likely nothing wrong with your computer. As I've noted, NT's Setup program is primitive compared to the rest of the operating system. (There may be lots of good reasons for it. Nevertheless, it is what it is — a pain.)

When you administer computers in a network, one article of faith in the business is to keep a boot floppy around for every system. Because Windows NT doesn't automatically create boot floppies, this means creating one from DOS/Windows or, most preferably, Windows 95. In fact, you should keep boot floppies around for *all* your networked systems. This stuff can get rather complicated, but you must deal with it even if you're administering small networks, and you'll need all the tools you can get to smooth the process. Boot floppies, tailored for all your systems, are part of your front line of defense against crippling system problems. The next section describes what the boot floppy should contain. It is not as simple as you think! (This is a separate issue from having an NT Emergency Rescue disk, so bear that in mind. There is also a way to set up a special NT boot floppy for a specific purpose. Which is described in Chapter 13.)

Another key issue is the process of creating an actual Windows NT boot floppy. This process has nothing to do with installation. Windows NT boot floppies are created to bypass and help fix startup problems with an existing Windows NT installation. Unlike a DOS or Windows 95 boot floppy, a Windows NT boot floppy can detect the presence of an NTFS-formatted hard disk.

 If you already have such a boot floppy for your NT installation computer and are still having serious problems getting out of the DOS-based portion of NT Setup, simply pass by the following section and continue from the section titled "Using the WINNT Program to Set Up Windows NT."

CONSTRUCTING A BOOT FLOPPY FOR INSTALLATION AND OTHER EMERGENCIES
Keeping a boot floppy for each of your NT systems is a must. However, Windows NT does not directly support the creation of boot floppies, so you must make one from another operating system. The best choice is Windows 95, because you're more likely to have updated drivers for that operating system for all the needed devices in your system.

A lot goes into building a Windows 95 boot floppy. Although all your computers may have differing configurations, each boot floppy should have the following things on it:

◆ The basic Windows 95 operating system (created on a floppy disk by running the **format a: /s** command)

◆ All the necessary CD-ROM startup and driver files

◆ The DOS programs FDISK.EXE, FORMAT.COM, CHKDSK.EXE, HIMEM.SYS, SMARTDRV.EXE, and EDIT.COM from the C:\Windows\Command directory of a Windows 95 machine

   FDISK.EXE enables you to set up disk partitions.

   FORMAT.COM is a command-line utility for formatting disks.

   CHKDSK.EXE is a program that enables you to check the current state of your hard drive.

   EDIT.COM is a small text editor that I keep on the boot floppy to edit the AUTOEXEC and CONFIG files, if that ever becomes necessary.

   HIMEM.SYS is a memory driver for extended memory in MS-DOS that enables programs to use memory above the 640K barrier. Windows 95 provides a version of the program. It's used here to allow SMARTDRV.EXE to execute.

   For config.sys, add the line **device=himem.sys.**

◆ Microsoft's standard CD-ROM driver, MSCDEX.EXE

◆ For systems that have SCSI with the CD-ROM drive connected to it, all the needed SCSI support files must also be on the floppy, either in the root or in a separate directory.

◆ Properly configured AUTOEXEC.BAT and CONFIG.SYS files, sitting on the root directory of the floppy (Yes, the horrid old AUTOEXEC and CONFIG.SYS files still live in my office, and I still have to mess with them once in a while.)

Windows 95 has a directory called C:\WINDOWS\COMMAND that contains a complete set of MS-DOS commands (FDISK, FORMAT, etc.) that are rewritten for Windows 95 but function exactly the same way as in the bad old MS-DOS days. You'd be amazed how handy they can be in certain situations, such as a scratch NT installation.

AUTOEXEC.BAT and CONFIG.SYS are used to start up the CD-ROM drivers and initialize the CD so that it can be accessed after you boot from the floppy. Here's a sample CONFIG.SYS statement that loads the CD-ROM driver for one of the systems in my network:

```
DEVICE=A:\CDROM12X\CD1200.SYS /D:CD003
```

In this case, because the statement is for an EIDE-based CD-ROM, one statement is all you need. If you're running a SCSI card with a CD-ROM, remember that you'll need several DEVICE= statements in the CONFIG.SYS file to start up programs for the SCSI card. Check your SCSI card's documentation for details.

As an example, the following three lines are a listing of a CONFIG.SYS file with a set of SCSI initialization commands from the boot floppy for my dual-Pentium NT Server:

```
DEVICE=A:\QLOGIC\QL10DOS.SYS
DEVICE=A:\QLOGIC\QL00ASPI.SYS
DEVICE=A:\QLOGIC\QL00CDRM.SYS /D:MSCD000
```

All three statements enable SCSI drivers for a QLogic card. If you're running a different SCSI controller in your system, your statements will differ somewhat but should be quite similar. Bear in mind that these statements are not used in Windows NT — just on a Windows 95 boot floppy. (Again, if you're running a standard IDE CD-ROM, this is not necessary.)

Here's a typical AUTOEXEC batch statement that runs Microsoft's MSCDEX driver to start up the CD-ROM drive:

```
A:\MSCDEX /V /D:CD003 /M:10
```

Your own CD-ROM initialization will be different depending on the type of drive you have, but you will always need to run MSCDEX, whether it's an IDE or SCSI CD-ROM.

Enforcing Consistency for Users' Boot Floppies

If you have a lot of control over how your users' networked computers are configured, try to get them the same CD-ROM drives (whether IDE or SCSI), the same SCSI cards, and the same network cards (or even the same machines!). If you can do this, you have a good chance of being able to make a generic boot floppy with all the right drivers, utilities, and batch files for most of the systems in your care. Troubleshooting is also simplified. This is another aspect of planning ahead.

It's also easy to have a generic boot floppy around that just has the basic operating system and batch files, but things are made more difficult by the fact that you also need CD-ROM drivers, which may differ between systems. If your CD-ROM is a SCSI device, that makes things a little more complicated. Swallow hard and deal with it, because if you have a library of boot floppies and something goes wrong with someone's system, you'll thank yourself for having them. Check SCSI controller documentation, which almost always has instructions for the proper statements to put into those boot files.

It's ironic that, although you're planning to use a highly advanced operating system like Windows NT, you still have to reckon with legacy MS-DOS command-line techniques to help you get around installation problems. Nevertheless, because NT's Setup program is so balky, you need to use all the tricks in your trade to get the job done.

CAN YOU USE WINDOWS 95B'S FAT-32 FILE SYSTEM FOR AN NT SETUP?

As I noted earlier in this chapter, a newer version of Windows 95 (called Windows 95B or OSR2) offers a new file system called FAT-32. It provides support for hard disk partitions over 2GB in size and smaller file cluster sizes. When you create a boot floppy using this version of Win95, the FDISK and FORMAT programs also are compliant with this feature. Unfortunately, Windows NT Setup *cannot* recognize FAT-32 formatted hard drives. If you use a boot floppy to reformat a hard disk with FAT-32 (for example, if you have a 4GB IDE hard disk that you want to use as one big C:\ NT partition), NT Setup will not see it and will fail. In that case, use FDISK to change the file system by disabling support for larger hard drives (the program asks if you want to do this when you start it up), redefine your partitions, reformat the drive, and then start Setup yet again.

What does all this mean? Basically, your Windows NT boot disk can't be more than 2GB in size. For a boot drive this is fine. Any other hard disks you install into your NT system (including RAID devices) can be handled within NT using Disk Administrator, up to any size possible for hard drives. Thus NT is still haunted in this small way by the MS-DOS legacy.

USING THE WINNT PROGRAM TO SET UP WINDOWS NT   Note that the hard disk partion has to be formatted with the FAT file system for the temporary installation directory. (If the drive was previously formatted NTFS, then NT Setup will not see it, so the issue is important.)

After you boot the computer off your floppy disk and the CD-ROM is initialized, you can partition and format the hard disk if needed, or simply start the NT Setup process again from scratch, right off the CD-ROM. How do you do this? By using the WINNT program, which is on the Windows NT Server or NT Workstation CD in the D:\i386 directory (assuming that your CD-ROM drive is initialized as drive D).

There are many ways to run WINNT. If you run into glitches by simply starting Setup from booting off the NT Setup Floppy #1, WINNT provides workarounds that enable you to have a successful installation. WINNT provides a number of command-line options:

◆ WINNT /B: Enables installation of NT off the CD-ROM drive without using the three Setup floppies. (Recommended)

◆ WINNT /X: Prevents the WINNT program from automatically creating the three Setup floppies. This can be done if you already have a set.

◆ WINNT /I:[Drive name]: Forces NT Setup to install its Temp files directory onto the drive letter you specify. (For the C drive, an example is WINNT /I:C.)

◆ WINNT /U: Updates an existing Windows NT Setup in unattended mode. All the previous user and network settings are taken from the existing installation without requiring prompts from the user.

There are other options, but these are the most commonly used. You can use more than one option in the same command line.

WINNT and the LOCK Command

Sometimes when you try to start WINNT, it will also refuse to run. If this happens, before you run WINNT again, enter the LOCK command from the DOS prompt:

D:\i386\:\> LOCK

This fixes the problem. You can then run WINNT.

To install Windows NT directly from the CD, follow these steps:

1. Boot your system from the previously described boot floppy (*not* from the Windows NT Setup disk).

2. Type the following command at the DOS prompt and press Enter:

   ```
   CD D:\i386
   ```

3. Type the following command and press Enter:

   ```
   WINNT /B
   ```

   Windows NT Setup appears. It displays a screen requesting the directory in which the NT installation files can be found. The screen automatically displays the correct directory, which should be D:\i386 (assuming your CD-ROM is drive D).

4. Press Enter.

   Setup commences the hour-long copy of temporary installation files to your hard drive. A bar graph is displayed showing the copy's progress.

5. When the system asks you to do so, restart.

   If you simply start Setup by typing **WINNT**, you're eventually greeted by the following screen before restarting:

```
The MS-DOS-based portion of Setup is complete. Setup will now restart your
computer. After your computer restarts, Windows NT Setup will continue.
Ensure that the floppy you provided as "Windows NT Workstation Setup Boot Disk"
is inserted into Drive A: before continuing.
Press ENTER to restart your computer and continue using Windows NT Setup.
```

   Setup resumes after reboot and goes through the process of loading device drivers and detecting any devices such as SCSI controllers and CD-ROMs. (It will do so much faster than in the floppy-based install, however.)

6. Press Enter.

   Setup displays the License Agreement screen.

7. Press Page Down to get to the bottom of the agreement, and press F8 to signal your acceptance of its terms. Setup then continues.

   At this point, you're home free and on your way to a successful installation. Setup displays the list of hardware components that it has detected (Computer, Display, Keyboard, and so on).

8. Press Enter.

   NT Setup displays the following screen:

```
The list below shows existing partitions and spaces available for creating new
 partitions.
Use the UP and DOWN ARROW keys to move the highlight to an item in the list.

 To install Windows NT on the highlighted partition or unpartitioned space,
 press ENTER.
 To create a partition in the unpartitioned space, press C.
 To delete the highlighted partition, press D.
```

A list of partitions and available drives is displayed. If you have a SCSI hard disk installed in your system, it is displayed on this screen.

9. If necessary, select the desired disk partition and press Enter.

From this point on, the installation process is the same as described previously. At this point, you should be on your way (unless you have a more severe hardware incompatibility problem).

KEEP A COPY OF THE I386 DIRECTORY ON YOUR HARD DRIVE   There will no doubt be occasions when you'll need to install new services or device drivers on your NT system, whether it's a server or a workstation. One handy trick to speed the process up is to keep a complete copy of the i386 directory (and its subdirectories) of the Windows NT CD-ROM on your hard disk. When the Control Panel asks you for the location of the needed files, simply give it the drive letter and the directory. If your hard disk is big enough, this shouldn't be a problem. If ever necessary, you can also run the WINNT program from this directory. This is more handy on a server than on an NT Workstation, where users' disk space may be at more of a premium.

Here's another trick: If you have a totally new hard disk for use with NT, go ahead and copy the i386 directory and all its contents from the CD-ROM over to the hard disk before you run WINNT. Then enter WINNT /B from that directory on the hard disk, and you should be on your way.

Also remember the trick about using HIMEM.SYS and SMARTDRV.EXE as previously mentioned. That advice also applies if you're using a DOS 6.22/Windows 3.1 boot floppy to do your installations.

WINDOWS NT'S INSTALLATION LIMITS

When you buy a copy of Windows NT Server, you have a minimum five-client limit — the ability to network at least five other computer systems to use Windows NT's server capabilities on a *per-seat* basis. If you get NT Server through a direct dealer and not a typical "computer superstore," the number of licenses you have available can be much greater. When you purchase and use Windows NT Server, just make sure you have an installation that provides enough client licenses out of the box, and hopefully leaves some room to grow without coughing up fees for more clients.

When you install NT Server, you're prompted for the number of clients for which your copy of the software is enabled. Simply be aware that you may need to use the License Manager to set yourself up with more clients when that becomes necessary.

MAKING EMERGENCY REPAIRS

During your Windows NT installation, you're asked by Setup if you want to make an Emergency Repair diskette. I strongly recommend doing so. It has saved my bacon more than once. In fact, after you have NT up and running, you can make an Emergency Repair floppy at any time by running a special program called RDISK.EXE, which is located in your WINNT\SYSTEM32 directory. You can also use this little program as an update for an existing Repair disk when your server's configuration becomes more complicated than it is during installation. Annoyingly enough, you won't find this handy program on your Start menu or in the Control Panel.

If you have an existing Emergency Repair Disk, it will be wiped out and reformatted, and then your current system configuration will be saved in the new Emergency Repair diskette. You can also keep several generations of repair disks by date.

You use the Emergency Repair disk in NT Setup's DOS-based portion. You're offered the option to do this when the Setup program asks if you want to set up NT. Be sure to make regular updates to your Emergency Repair disks.

A Final Word

Exhaustively, you've covered the following topics in this chapter:

◆ Installing Windows NT Workstation

◆ Installing Windows NT Server

The next chapter allows you to start getting acquainted with many of the most basic networking features of Windows NT. Chapter 2 describes how to use Windows NT's basic user account creation features, what they mean, and how to apply that knowledge to build basic networking connections between Windows NT Server and Windows NT Workstation and Windows 95 client computers.

Troubleshooting

Why do I keep getting the following error message when I try to install Windows NT?

```
Setup is unable to locate the hard drive partition prepared by the MS-DOS
  portion of Setup.
When you run the MS-DOS Windows NT Setup program, you must specify a temporary
  drive that is supported by Windows NT. See your System Guide for more
  information.

Setup cannot continue. Press F3 to exit.
```

You may be using a set of installation floppies created by the WINNT program off the CD-ROM. Irritatingly, they are actually somewhat different from the sets of original three-disk installation floppies bundled with most copies of NT. Run the command WINNT /B from the CD-ROM's i386 directory to avoid this problem.

Why does Setup keep freezing the system when I try to install Windows NT?
   There are three things to look at:

   ◆ **The system board.** As noted earlier in this chapter, the system board is extremely important. NT is notoriously picky about hardware, and the system board is the foundation for everything else. Based on my research on the World Wide Web, the following manufacturers can usually be relied on to build reliable system boards: Intel, Tyan, Asus, Abit, Micronics, and Mylex. If your board isn't one of these, or if it's a 486-based system board, I recommend replacing it. A huge number of no-name manufacturers produce motherboards in this market. Most work under Windows 95 but inevitably choke under Windows NT, even during Setup.

   ◆ **Memory.** Even if your system board is a known good product, take a close look at your RAM. If it isn't major-brand memory, this might be your problem. At the least, make sure that each pair of SIMMs you buy is a matched pair. SIMMs must be bought in pairs to work properly. Also, be careful who you buy memory from. Many smaller places resell *gray-market* components of doubtful quality and do not accept returns or exchanges. Though DIMMs don't have to be installed in pairs to work properly, the major-brand rule should still apply.

◆ **Hard disk.** Many EIDE hard disks won't work reliably under Windows NT. This includes an older line of three-platter Western Digital hard disks (model numbers Caviar 31000, 31200, 31600, and up) that have been replaced by a line of two-platter drives (Caviar 11200, 22100, 22500 and so on). For EIDE, I recommend the two-platter Western Digital and comparable drives from other manufacturers. The new Quantum 3.8GB EIDE drives are also getting a good reputation. SCSI is also something you should consider.

Windows NT Setup just crashed during the Windows part of the installation, and I got a *Blue Screen of Death*! What's wrong?

There's a chance that this may not be a big deal. Every once in awhile on some systems, at certain phases of Setup, you may experience a system hang. If that happens, simply press the Reset button. Setup may resume from the place where it hung and continue without a murmur. If this isn't the case, you need to start over from scratch. Check the network card installed in your system. Strip your system down to its bare essentials (CD, RAM, hard disk, and video card) and perform a reinstall. Then if you get NT up and running this way, layer in each device. Follow the hardware guidelines earlier in this chapter, and problems of this sort should disappear.

I've installed a Windows NT Primary Domain Controller (PDC) and it runs fine, but it takes forever to reboot!

NT normally takes a few minutes to start itself. Unless you have the fastest system (a dual Pentium Pro or maybe a Pentium II system), an NT Server has many services to start up, especially with a PDC. When the administrator logs on to a PDC system during start up, he or she generally sees a *Logon in Progress* message that will persist for a minute or so. This is normal. If things take more than a few minutes, or the NT system takes forever to shut itself down, try turning off the Spooler in the Control Panel's Services applet and then restart.

Chapter 2

Setting Up Mainstream Microsoft Networks

IN THIS CHAPTER
This chapter describes the following tasks:

◆ Creating user accounts and groups

◆ Networking Windows NT workstations to Windows NT Server

◆ Networking Windows 95 clients to Windows NT Server

FOR MANY NT USERS, the next few chapters describe the most important features of their operating system. Hooking up Windows workstations to an NT server, and sharing files, folders, and disks among them, is perhaps the most accessible and popular NT application. Windows NT 4.0 makes this process easier and more productive than ever. Only a few years ago you needed comprehensive training, costing thousands of dollars, to be able to string together a functional LAN (local area network) for a small company. Because of the efficiency of NT 4.0, the need for comprehensive training is no longer the case. You can still get Microsoft Certified Systems Engineer (MCSE) and Master Certified Novell Engineer (MCNE) certifications if you want to service huge Fortune 500 networks, but if you just want to build a network for your office, you have come to the right place.

Before diving into the mechanics of building your Windows NT LAN, there are some key aspects of the operating system you need to get under your belt. These aspects include defining user accounts, understanding permissions and user rights, and knowing why security is so important in an NT networked environment.

Understanding Windows NT's Basic Network Building Blocks

Although the main theme of this chapter is how to hook up Windows NT and Windows 95 clients to a Windows NT server, you're also going on an extremely brief grand tour of the operating system. A number of important factors that go into setting up users to participate on your LAN. You need to know about user rights, permission levels, groups, and a number of other NT networking features before you can navigate the process of connecting your users.

User accounts are the foundation for every networking function you'll perform with Windows NT Server. When you finish Setup, the user accounts are the most important part of the operating system. Everything else is just a tool.

If you want anyone else's computer to use the resources on your server, Windows NT needs to know who those people are. After that, sharing devices such as hard disks, folders, and printers must be set up from both ends (the Server end and the Client end) so that users and administrators have the proper levels of access.

NT is quite flexible with its sharing features. (So flexible, in fact, that sharing can be a bit confusing.) You can share as few or as many resources as you want with any user on your network. Printers, single folders, and entire hard disks can be mounted on a networked system for their use. Permissions can be set for several escalating levels of access. Before you build your network and connect the clients, you need to gather a certain amount of information about your users:

- The passwords the users prefer to use (if you aren't simply assigning them)
- The user names they want to use (if, again, you aren't assigning them)
- What *groups* you plan to place your users in
- The types of resources the user will need
- The permissions and access types the users will

If you're organized about this at the start, things will come together faster, and there's a real possibility that you'll have a small but functional LAN up and running in the span of a working day (the hardware gods willing). Yes, it is possible to do this using Windows NT.

User Accounts, Permissions, User Rights, and User Names

User names and passwords are pretty self-evident. A *user name* is the name your connected worker uses to log on and use the network. The names should be crafted according to common sense and reasonable security requirements. There are some basic rules that can be followed when you assign them:

- No passwords such as *Administrator, guest,* or *user.*
- No users' first or last names.
- No passwords indicating a profession.
- Make passwords as long as possible, up to 14 characters.

◆ Gather and assign your user names and passwords in advance. Keep a written or printed log of that information in a *very* safe (locked) place.

◆ Skip using names from figures of Greek mythology.

◆ Use numbers as part of the password if at all possible. It makes it harder for intruders to crack them.

All of these factors are especially important if some of your users will be dialing into the network with a modem, using Remote Access.

If you're running a small LAN without meaningful Internet connections beyond the usual dial-ups for e-mail and browsing, following these basic rules should be sufficient to maintain the integrity of your system. If you have a system with Internet gateways, are using NT's Domain Naming Service (DNS), and have heavy dial-in traffic, your security requirements go up exponentially. To begin with, you already know that Windows NT creates a user account called *administrator* that provides unrestricted access to the system. Do yourself a favor: Change the name of your administrator account. This falls under the same rules just mentioned: Don't use any obvious names or passwords for user accounts or key administrator accounts.

A trend among system managers is to use catchy names to signify administrative accounts. Greek mythology names are popular: Zeus, Apollo, Athena, Hermes, and so on. As pleasing or witty as it may be, try to resist doing this. If your server or domain has or will have a gateway to the Internet, or even commonly used dial-in links, an obvious name of this type can easily be hacked. Sniffer programs exist with which crackers can bombard a server's dial-in connections with thousands of likely password combinations. Odds are high that *someone's* account will have such a name, after all.

To get to know NT Server a bit better, you need to know the definition of a few more terms: permissions, access type, and groups.

A *group* is a collection of user accounts gathered into a convenient set and labeled something like "Domain Users," "Administrators," or any other name you deem appropriate ("GenXers," "Accounting," "R&D," and so on). You'll learn how to create and manage groups later in this chapter.

You use an *access type* to determine how individual users and groups interact with a network device. In Figure 2-1 the Administrators group has Full Control access to the shared resource, the Domain Users group has the Change access type, and the Everyone group has the Read access type.

Windows NT, has four different access types for shared resources, as shown in Table 2-1:

TABLE 2-1 WINDOWS NT'S ACCESS TYPES FOR SHARED DEVICES ON THE NETWORK

Access Type	Capability
No Access	Locks the user(s) or group away from the resource, rendering it invisible to that user.
Read	Allows the user or group to read files from the resource. The user can then modify the information at his or her own workstation but cannot write the information back to the resource.
Change	Enables normal read/write privileges for users and groups. Files can be read, modified, and saved out to the resource, which is usually a shared drive or folder on the network.
Full Control	Allows full access to the shared resource for the user account. User rights, share settings, and other administrative tasks can be managed through the network. Use this access level sparingly!

Figure 2-1 shows these three elements in a single place: a permission list showing three groups and the drop-down list of the access types available for network resources under NT.

In NT, *permissions* are used to determine how groups and individual network users can work with a shared network resource. For example, you might have a hard disk on your server called "Server D Drive" to which the user group "GenXers" can read and write files. Another group, called "Management," might also have read/write privileges. Another group, "Accounting," might have read-only privileges. Those three groups, taken together, comprise a *permission list* for that resource.

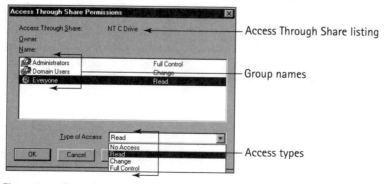

Figure 2-1: Share Permissions List for a Shared Hard Disk

Figure 2-1 shows three group names: Administrator, Domain Users, and Everyone. (Any number of other groups can be added to this.) All three are collected under the permission list for the NT C Drive. You'll create permission lists for every resource shared on your NT network.

Working with user accounts, groups, access types, and permissions is the key way to set up your users to access the resources on your NT server. The next section applies those basic concepts to an important piece of software: NT's User Manager.

Introducing the Windows NT User Manager for Domains

The Windows NT *User Manager* is the central utility program where you manage nearly every key aspect of your server's user base. If you're running a Primary Domain Controller (which I recommend, as discussed in Chapter 1), the User Manager is simply titled User Manager for Domains.

User Manager for Domains is a handy and surprisingly approachable program, considering what it does. You'll start by taking a brief tour and move on to creating a test user account that you'll use for later exercises in this chapter.

For brevity, throughout this chapter I refer to the User Manager for Domains as *UMD*. At times I also refer to it as the User Manager for convenience.

Share-Level Versus Directory Permissions

Windows NT actually provides two major types of permissions. The more conventional type, *share-level permissions*, is the type I'm discussing in this chapter. *Directory & File permissions* are a bit more confusing. They offer a larger selection of access types, and they can be heavily customized for each user or group in your system, and specified all the way down to individual files. I discuss a specific application for Directory permissions in Chapter 12, where you learn how to use Home Directories. Otherwise, this chapter focuses mainly on Share-level directories, which allow the sharing of resources across the network.

What if You're Running a Stand-Alone Server?

Throughout this section, the assumption is made that you've created an NT Server using a Primary Domain Controller, specifically as described in Chapter 1. Consequently, you'll be using the program User Manager for Domains to create and manage your user accounts. If you've created a stand-alone server, you can still carry out most of the key elements in this chapter by opening the program User Manager by clicking the Start button, pointing to Programs, and then pointing to Administrative Tools. NT Workstation also has a version of User Manager that contains most of the features described here.

The stand-alone User Manager program provides many, but not all, of the same functions as the User Manager for Domains. User Manager for Domains is a bit more specialized because it is actually located where you create and administer domains on your Windows NT Server. (It isn't provided with Windows NT Workstation, which uses the more generic User Manager.) I discuss the care and feeding of Windows NT domains in Chapter 12, and I introduced them earlier in Chapter 1. User Manager for NT Workstation is described in Chapter 5.

The UMD is part of the NT Administrative Tools group. It can be launched by clicking Start, Programs, Administrative Tools, and finally User Manager for Domains. The User Manager is shown in Figure 2-2.

User Manager is split into two parts: the User pane and the Groups pane. The User pane, on top, lists all the individual user accounts on the system. New individual accounts are created in the User pane. When you open User Manager for the first time, a couple of basic user accounts are provided: Administrator and Guest. In Figure 2-2, a few other accounts are listed ("Laptop" and "Rich" and so on), which were created in my in-house network for this book.

A much larger list is shown in the bottom pane, the Groups pane.

Understanding Local and Global Groups

The Groups pane enables you to create new groups and add users to them, arranging them as you want. (In networking parlance, these groups are often called *workgroups*.)

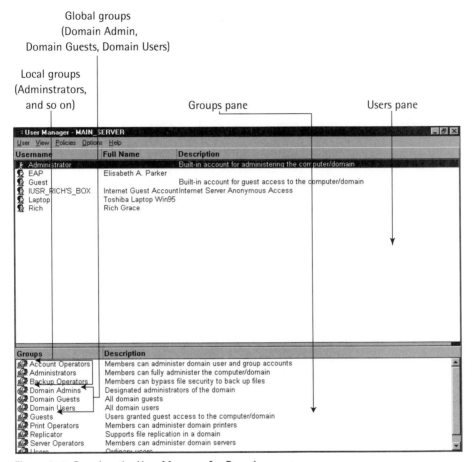

Figure 2-2: Running the User Manager for Domains

What are the advantages of User Manager groups? They're easier to administer. Groups function like little minidomains. When a user becomes part of a networked group under Windows NT, the administrator can issue Share-level permissions and user rights for those groups to networked devices, and all users in that group will automatically have those user rights. By using groups, you don't have to laboriously assign the rights for each network resource to every individual user.

There are two categories of groups: local and global. *Local* groups function exclusively inside their own domain and aren't able to access any other LANs or resources in other domains. (In a small network this doesn't have much meaning, but it does in a multidomain enterprise network.)

Global groups are created when one Windows NT domain (like the one you may have created in Chapter 1, which we dubbed MAIN_SERVER) needs to establish accounts that can cross domain boundaries and connect with other resources in another domain. This can be handy, for example, if you have a user in your domain that needs to send a graphics file to be printed on the high-end color laser printer in the NT domain administered in the graphics department. Global groups also can use special characteristics assigned by the administrator, using a special program called the System Policy Editor, which is discussed in Chapter 12.

Approximately a dozen local groups are built into the Groups pane, including Administrators, Users, Power Users, and Guests. Additional groups may be in your system already, depending on how you've set up your server. If you run a Primary Domain Controller, three other Global groups are automatically created: Domain Admins, Domain Guests, and Domain Users. You can pick them out in Figure 2-2 (and in your User Manager for Domains) by their distinctive icon.

Another special "group" bears mentioning: the Everyone group. No, it doesn't ever show up in the User Manager, but it will always appear when you try to set up permissions for a shared device on the network. "Everyone" is not actually a group; it's a catchall that automatically contains every user account you create in your server/domain.

Understanding User Rights

Another important feature in the User Manager is user rights. User rights are a more complex list of access capabilities that can be applied to groups and individual user accounts. They're separate and distinct from the Access Types that we discussed earlier. Though you can apply them to individual accounts, they're typically used with groups.

To view user rights, open the User Manager for Domains, click the Policies menu, and select User Rights. The User Rights Policy dialog box appears as shown in Figure 2-3.

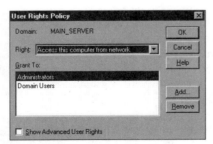

Figure 2-3: Inspecting User Rights

A considerable list of rights types is offered. Selecting each one from the drop-down list displays a list of the groups that have access to them. Selecting the Show Advanced User Rights check box increases the list to show capabilities usually reserved for system programmers and application developers.

When you create new groups, you apply the desired user rights to them. Then, when you add users to those groups, they automatically have those capabilities on the network. Applying user rights to groups is a good application for this feature, because it is more convenient than applying them to each individual account. Table 2-2 lists a brief account of the NT user rights and their privileges.

TABLE 2-2 USER RIGHTS IN WINDOWS NT

User Right	Privilege
Access this computer from network	Enables the user account to connect to the system over the network.
Add workstations to domain	Allows users to add their system or others to a Windows NT domain.
Back up files and directories	Enables the user (or group of users) to run backup utilities on the server or computer in question.
Change the system time	Allows the user to change the system time and date.
Force shutdown from a remote system	Allows the user account to shut down or reboot the server from a connected workstation. *Guard this right carefully.*
Load and unload device drivers	Enables the user account, or group accounts, to load and disable device drivers on the server or workstation. Administrators can do this for primary and backup domain controllers in an NT domain. For any other NT system, the right only applies to the system that runs the user right locally.
Log on locally	Enables the user account to log on directly to the physical server. Administrators can do this for primary and backup domain controllers in an NT domain. For any other NT system, the right only applies to the system that runs the user right locally.

continued

TABLE 2-2 USER RIGHTS IN WINDOWS NT *(Continued)*

User Right	Privilege
Manage auditing and security log	Enables the user, typically administrators, to monitor audits of file and directory usage, and security. Audits are a handy feature for administrators to study access patterns on their server and general patterns of user activity. The Audit feature on the Policies menu provides the basic capabilities to enable system auditing. The Event Viewer program is used to view and audit events.
Restore files and directories	Allows the user to restore files and directories on a server or a local workstation.
Shut down the system	Allows the user to shut the computer down locally.
Take ownership of files or other objects	Allows user accounts to change ownership of files and directories on the system.
Bypass traverse checking (advanced right)	Enables users to navigate through directory trees on system drives, even if the user has no other permissions therein.

Working with user rights is not particularly diff0icult, but if you create your own groups, you need to deal with this issue and make decisions about which rights each group should have. Study the groups created by NT and check the rights listings applied to them. Unfortunately, those default groups can't be used as templates for new ones, copying and creating one from an existing template won't copy the assigned user rights to the new one. Any existing user accounts in the original group are copied over, however.

A close relationship exists between users and groups in the User Manager. When you create new users, you can easily add them to an existing group or create a new group from scratch for that user. Then user rights can be applied to amplify or restrict the group's privileges in the system.

Creating Users, Accounts, and Permissions

Now you are armed with the information you need to take action. To start with, you'll create a new user in the User Manager so that you get a full introduction to that process.

Creating a New User

After you get the hang of creating new user accounts in the User Manager, you'll begin to appreciate the simplicity of NT 4.0 networking.

A final point must be mentioned. When users log on to their system, user names are not case-sensitive, but *passwords* definitely are. As long as the name is spelled correctly, users can type it in however they prefer; if a password is not typed in exactly as its case is (caps in the right place, and so forth), then users will not be able to log on.

To create a new user, follow these steps:

1. Start the User Manager program. The program window appears (refer to Figure 2-2).

2. From the User menu, select the New User command. The New User dialog box appears as shown in Figure 2-4. It contains five fields that require the administrator's input

   ◆ The Username is the agreed-upon name that the user logs on to the system with. That user name must be defined on the server side but can be used by the user account from any client computer. Of course, the client computer must be able to access the network and the domain first. (You will learn how to do this for a Windows NT Workstation system and a Windows 95 system a bit later.)

   ◆ The Full Name is simply the name of the computer user.

   ◆ The Description field provides a place to add a brief description of the user account or the computer user.

   ◆ The Password and Confirm Password fields are where the client's password is defined and then confirmed by the administrator.

   The New User dialog box provides four check boxes that determine how the user interacts with the account password. (For an existing account, this dialog box's title changes to "User Properties" but is otherwise the same.) Table 2-3 lists the password settings and their functions.

TABLE 2-3 PASSWORD SETTINGS IN WINDOWS NT

Password Setting	Function
User Must Change Password at Next Logon	Enables the user to define their own password the first time they begin to use their network account. This can be handy in small networks when the user is in a more informal situation and wants to do things with a little more freedom. Nevertheless, make sure you keep accurate records of all the passwords used in the network!
User Cannot Change Password	Disables any ability to change passwords from the client system.
Password Never Expires	Ensures that the defined password can be used as long as the user account is active. This setting can be changed at any time by an administrator.
Account Disabled	Clicking this check box disables the user account. This setting can be handy when a user goes on vacation, for example.

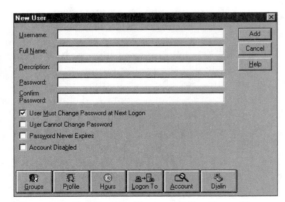

Figure 2-4: Starting the Process of Creating a New User on the Network

Do not enable the User Must Change Password at Next Logon and User Cannot Change Password check boxes together. If you enable both of these check boxes in the User Manager, the user account will not be able to change the password, even though the system requires them to do so. This will result in a lockout (and one very annoyed user).

3. For our new user account's Username, enter in the phrase **Test User**.

4. In the Full Name and Description fields, add the appropriate information. Figure 2-5 shows an example.

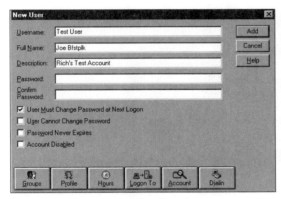

Figure 2-5: Entering the New User Account

Next you enter and confirm passwords. Password entries can contain up to 14 alphanumeric characters. Here's where a little advance work can pay off, as you'll soon see.

5. In the Password text box, enter the password for the new user account. It can be any alphanumeric phrase of up to 14 characters.

   Make sure you enter the password correctly, because Windows NT encrypts an 'x' for each character onscreen. You can backspace over and try again if necessary.

6. Type the same password in the Confirm Password text box.

7. Leave the check boxes in their current defaults for the moment, because I'll demonstrate their use a bit later.

8. Close the New Users dialog box. Then reopen it, with the new account still selected in the User Manager. You will see some subtle changes to the dialog box for the new account, as shown in Figure 2-6.

Groups button
Profile button   Hours button

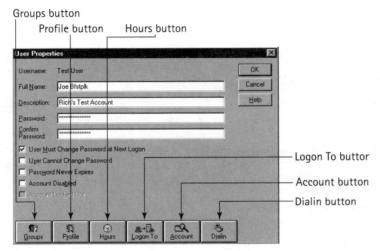

Logon To buttor
Account button
Dialin button

Figure 2-6: Inspecting the New Account

The *Username* is now a permanent record in the NT database (until you delete it from the User Manager).

The password fields have also changed. In Figure 2-6 you can see how a series of fourteen *x*s have been inserted in the Password and Confirm Password fields. No, NT has *not* changed the passwords on you, although that's how it appears. NT automatically masks the passwords you've entered with *x*s, and also *masks the exact number of characters* you use in your passwords by placing fourteen *x*s in the fields, regardless of how long your password is. This is why advance gathering and recording of passwords is so important. After passwords are entered into user accounts, it's not easy to determine what they are!

Adding an Account to a Group

Creating a user account is just the beginning. Figure 2-6 shows six important buttons in the User Properties dialog box: Groups, Profile, Hours, Logon To, Account, and Dialin. They add another level of complexity, but they govern key aspects of your users' access to the network. Because you'll heavy use of these features in other parts of this book, it's time to start having a good look at them.

For now you'll concentrate on three buttons and their features: Groups, Profile, and Dialin. The three buttons are used to set *group assignments*, *user profiles*, and *dialin permissions*, respectively. All three feature areas are vital for setting up basic NT network functions for your clients.

If you're running a *stand-alone* server and not a Primary Domain Controller, the Groups, Profile, and Dialin buttons will be the only buttons you see in the User Properties window. The assumption throughout this chapter is that your NT server is a domain controller. To add an account to a group, follow these steps:

1. In the User Manager for Domains (or User Manager), double-click the new user account you just created, called Test User. The User Properties dialog box appears.

2. Click the Groups button in the User Properties dialog box. The Group Memberships dialog box appears, as shown in Figure 2-7.

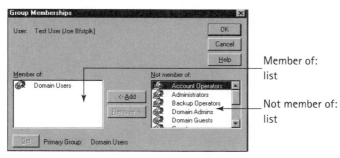

Figure 2-7: Assigning Your New User Account to a Group with the Group Memberships Feature

After a new user account is created, it's automatically added to NT's prebuilt Domain Users group. (In the User Manager for stand-alone Servers or workstations, it's automatically placed into the Users group.)

You can double-click in the Not member of list to place the new account in another group, or select the desired group from the Not member of list and then click Add.

3. Double-click the Users group name in the Not member of list. The Users group will display in the Member of list.

4. Click OK. The user account is now officially a member of the Users group.

Any available group in the Not member of list can be double-clicked for participation by the new account. You can also select the group name and click the Add button.

Similarly, if you want to remove the user account from a group, simply double-click the group in the Member of list or select it and click the Remove button. Nothing to it. Adding a new member to one of the existing NT groups also gives it the same user rights assigned to all the members in that group, as noted above.

Creating Permissions for a System Resource

In this section you inspect and change a permissions list for a resource, such as a hard disk, on your NT system. When I mention a system *resource*, I'll normally be referring to a folder, hard disk, removable disk drive, printer, or CD-ROM, because those devices of drives can be shared across the network. The term *resource* is meant generically here, and sharing them works similarly in all cases. It's easy to relate to the idea of sharing a hard disk across the network, so I use that as a prominent example.

When you decide to share hard disks and other resources across the network, you'll encounter a strange thing: a *C$* or *D$* share designation, depending on the drive letter (which can go up to *Z*). This is called a default or *hidden* drive share. The dollar sign is the giveaway, as labeled in Figure 2-8. You're not meant to use those default shares for anything — NT sets them up as *placeholders*, if you will. Here's how to set up a disk drive to be shared across the network:

1. Open My Computer.

2. Right-click the C drive of your Windows NT computer. The shortcut menu appears.

3. Select Sharing from the shortcut menu. The drive's Properties sheet appears, as shown in Figure 2-8.

4. To test your existing setup, click the Permissions button. A message is displayed.

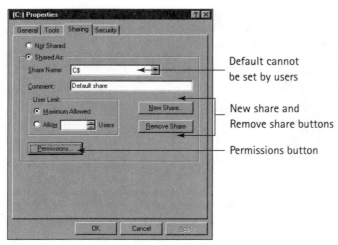

Figure 2-8: The Properties Sheet for an NT System's C Drive

If you click the button, what happens? You'll see the Sharing dialog box. Don't worry, nothing's wrong with your computer. Nor is the system locking you out, even though you're the administrator. What this means (although NT doesn't *say* it) is that the "C$" share is a basic, uneditable default share that you can't make special settings for. You *must* create a new share. Every hard disk you install in your NT system has a default share defined for it by the operating system.

The Windows NT default drive shares don't lock you out of being able to access the drive across the network. If the user has permission to access a disk, they can do so through the default share. Simply open Windows NT Explorer, click the Tools menu, and select Map Network Drive. In the Path text box, enter **\\computer_name\C$** and the desired user name. You may also have to give a password if the desired account isn't the same as the current one. It's that easy. But it's also not meant to be used this way, and I don't recommend it for your users. This is basically an administrative *back door* to systems on the network.

5. From the Properties sheet, click the New Share button. The New Share dialog box appears, as shown in Figure 2-9.

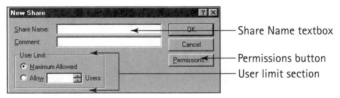

— Share Name textbox
— Permissions button
— User limit section

Figure 2-9: Setting Up a New Share for a
Network Resource

6. In the Share Name text box, enter the phrase **NT C Drive**. It should appear as shown in Figure 2-10.

Figure 2-10: Entering a New Share Name

6. Click OK. A warning message appears because you are naming a share that has more than eight characters. MS-DOS/Windows 3.1-based systems will not be able to use it. For now we're not concerned about that.

7. Click Yes. (You can always change it or delete it later.)

8. Now click the Permissions button. This opens up the permissions for the new share. The Access Through Share Permissions window reappears, but this time it's for the new share that you've created. Notice how the Everyone group appears again, like a bad penny. The Everyone group is a default user group created by Windows NT that automatically collects every user account you create.

9. Click OK.

10. Click OK to close the Properties sheet. A new share has been created.

Typically, permissions to access a resource, like the one you just created, are assigned to *groups* of users, like the Everyone group you've just seen, rather than individual users. As discussed earlier, groups are easier to administer and allow you to set permissions for a networked device for a bunch of users at once, although individual user accounts and shares can also be set.

Sharing Resources with Network Users

After you create a user account, the account needs to be set up to share resources. You begin by sharing an NT server's C drive with the new account you created, called Test User.

Remember that you need to log on using the administrator account, or another account with administrator privileges, in order to perform the following steps:

1. On your NT Server, double-click My Computer.

2. Right-click the C: icon in My Computer. The shortcut menu appears.

3. From the shortcut menu, select Sharing. The drive's Properties sheet appears, as shown in Figure 2-11.

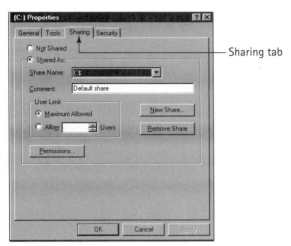

Figure 2-11: The [C:] Properties Sheet,
Displaying the Default Drive Share

Remember the *NT C Drive* share you created earlier in the section of this
chapter titled "Creating a New System Resource?" Here is where you build
upon your previous work.

4. Display the Share Name list by clicking its down arrow.

5. Select the share titled NT C Drive, or whatever share you created in the
   previous exercise.

6. Click the Permissions button.

The drive's Access Through Share Permissions dialog box appears, as
shown in Figure 2-12.

As seen in Figure 2-12, the Everyone group is added as a default to every
resource you share on a domain-based network. When a new share is
created for a system resource, it provides NT's Everyone group as a user
group share. Its Type of Access is automatically set to Full Control.

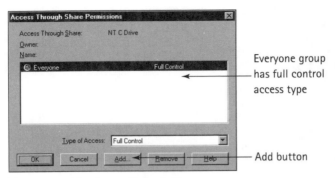

Everyone group
has full control
access type

Add button

Figure 2-12: The Access Through Share
Permissions Dialog Box for a Hard Disk

Understanding the Everyone Group

Everyone isn't actually a group, and it doesn't show up in the User Manager. It's considered a *placeholder*, a catchall storage for all the individual user accounts you create in your NT domain. You can't remove or add user accounts from the Everyone "group." By default, Everyone accounts can use shared folders and printers.

When you administer disks as a system administrator, having an Everyone group share with an access level of Full Control is not a good idea. Anyone on the network can mess around with any piece of data, and change any directory or folder on any drive that has been shared in this manner.

Conversely, do not use the No Access option.

If you change user rights for the Everyone group to No Access, or delete it entirely from the Access Through Share Permissions dialog box, Windows NT displays a message:

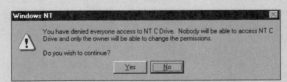

A System Notice Warning You That Access to a Device
by "Everyone" Is About To Be Removed

continued

Understanding the Everyone Group *(Continued)*

This message is as dire as it sounds. The warning serves notice that once the Everyone group loses its access, only the owner of the device will be able to change its permissions. What it *doesn't* say is that if you remove or disable access for the Everyone group, *none* of your user accounts will work with that device, including administrator accounts.

What is the problem with this? What can you do to ensure that any user accounts, can't muck about in the server whenever they feel like it?

The best solution is to assign the Read access type to Everyone. Why? If you add other groups to the Permissions list for a share, they'll contain some of the same user accounts that Everyone does. Assigned user accounts, and local and global groups, always take precedence in a share over Everyone; the user rights for other groups will be activated in higher priority than those assigned to Everyone.

7. Select the Everyone group if it isn't already highlighted in the Access Through Share Permissions dialog box.

8. In the Type of Access list, select Read.

   This step prevents *every* user account from being able to make changes to this network resource. The resource can be viewed, but all the user accounts in the default Everyone group won't be able to write to the shared resource. Any user accounts placed in other groups, or functioning separately, override their copies in the Everyone group.

   Now, you can craft nonredundant access for other groups and users, tailored to their specific needs.

9. In the Access Through Share Permissions dialog box, click Add.

   The Add Users and Groups dialog box appears, as shown in Figure 2-13. In this dialog box you add groups or user accounts for access to the drive over the network. (Again, this requires administrative privileges.)

Names list

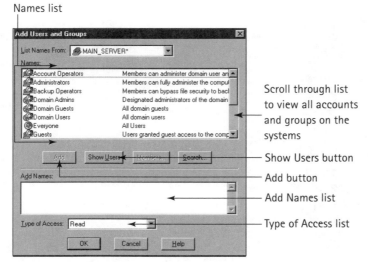

Scroll through list
to view all accounts
and groups on the
systems

Show Users button

Add button

Add Names list

Type of Access list

Figure 2–13: The Add Users and Groups Dialog
Box, Applied to Setting Up Shares for a Hard Disk

10. Click the Show Users button. This displays any individual user accounts in the Names list. If you don't click the Show Users button, only groups are shown.

11. Scroll down the list in the Names pane until you locate the Test User account.

12. Select the Test User account listing and click the Add button.

    You can easily add any group you want. Add the Administrators group to the list.

13. Scroll up the Names pane and select the Administrators group. (The Test User account should *not* presently be part of that group.) Click Add to add it to the list.

14. Click OK. The Access Through Share Permissions dialog box reappears with the two new entries shown in Figure 2-14.

    In this dialog box you change the all-important access levels for the two new entries. (You can't do that as easily in Add Users and Groups, because if you have more than one user or group added, changing the Type of Access level changes it for all of them. It's a brute-force method and doesn't offer enough control.)

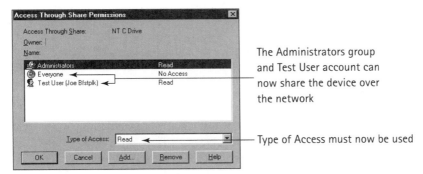

The Administrators group
and Test User account can
now share the device over
the network

Type of Access must now be used

Figure 2-14: New Shares Have Been Added

15. Select the Administrators group entry if it isn't already highlighted.

16. In the Type of Access list, select Full Control.

17. Select the Test User listing.

18. In the Type of Access list, select Change.

19. Click OK.

20. Click Yes. The system goes through the process of creating and verifying ownership of the contents of the hard disk, including all directories and subdirectories.

21. Finally, in the C: Properties sheet, click Apply.

To successfully commit the permission changes to the server or sharing system, the Apply button must be clicked. The device's permission settings are then changed, and the next time the Test User logs on, they'll have access to the resource labeled NT C Drive.

You may have more than one hard disk on your NT server. If that's the case, you can follow the same procedure for them. The same is true for individual folders or directories — they can be shared or networked in the same fashion. The later section "Sharing a Folder with a Windows NT Workstation User" discusses that topic.

Now take a look at how all these new permission settings can be used on a workstation, for the Test User account on the network.

Networking a Windows NT Workstation to Windows NT Server

Whenever you or your company's budget can justify it, using NT Workstation for your clients should be done. You get the tightest fit between the clients and server and the highest degree of central control. An administrator can have complete control of the server by logging on through NT Workstation. Windows 95 clients also have a high degree of basic network integration with Windows NT (as you might expect, given that they share the same interface). You work with them in the next section.

After reading this section and the next on Windows 95 systems, you'll understand why you spent so much time on user accounts, groups, and permissions before getting to the meaty stuff. Windows NT networking is built on those basic things, and you can't go anywhere without them. Follow these steps:

1. Boot up NT Workstation if it isn't already running. If your NT station is already running, you simply log on as a different user by clicking the Start button, choosing Shut Down, and then selecting the option Close all programs and log on as a Different User. Windows NT Workstation's Logon Information window appears.

2. Enter the desired user name and the account's assigned password. If you're running a Primary Domain Controller as described in Chapter 1, make sure it is selected in the Domain list, which will also be shown in Logon Information.

3. Press Enter. After a moment the NT workstation displays a Welcome splash screen.

   There are a few things left to do before the new user account can do anything meaningful on the network.

4. To begin exploring on the network, double-click Network Neighborhood on the Windows NT Workstation desktop.

   When your workstation accesses the network for the first time, the system may pause for a moment. If, for example, you have a single server called *Rich's_box* and the single workstation called *Nt_station*, system icons will appear in Network Neighborhood similar to those shown in Figure 2-15.

Figure 2-15: Opening Network Neighborhood in Windows
NT Workstation Using the New User Account

The names of your systems on the network will be different.

5. Double-click the icon named for the server in Network Neighborhood.
(Note how it is not listed as the domain — just by the computer name of
the server.) A list of its available resources is displayed in another
window, as shown in Figure 2-16.

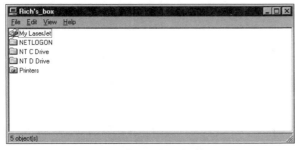

Figure 2-16: Opening a Server Icon in Network
Neighborhood Displays a List of Resources.

As seen in Figure 2-16, several items are displayed, including a networked
printer, a shared hard disk (NT C Drive), a Printers folder, and a special
NETLOGON folder that appears whenever a networked system opens up a
domain server, which in this case is *Rich's_box*.

6. Double-click the hard disk folder icon labeled NT C Drive. If your
permissions are set properly, which you learned to do in the previous
exercise, the C drive's window on the server opens on your workstation
screen.

At this point you should be able to browse the contents of the shared resource. This depends, of course, on the permissions and share privileges provided to the user account that you've used on the workstation.

 On a small network consisting of trusted colleagues, sharing a server's hard disk can be a useful way of maximizing everyone's capabilities on the network. An administrator should minimize the number of users allowed to browse entire networked hard disks from their workstations. If you have more than a few users, the possibilities for confusion and damage to your system are endless.

Normally, to open a shared resource you need to start with Network Neighborhood. A handy shortcut is provided by NT so that you don't have to open up four or five windows in succession to open a networked hard disk on your system. It's called *mapping a network drive.*

MAPPING A NETWORKED HARD DISK ON WINDOWS NT WORKSTATION

Mapping network drives is another good solution for small networks, departments with a few trusted employees, or a private LAN of one's own. When you map a hard disk, you place a networked drive icon into My Computer. Its window can then be opened just like any other drive (user rights and permissions willing, of course) and browsed with Windows NT Explorer. Here's how to map a networked drive, based on the previous exercise:

1. Open Network Neighborhood.

2. Double-click the system icon for the drive you want to map.

3. Right-click the desired drive's folder. The shortcut menu appears.

4. From the shortcut menu, select Map Network Drive.

    The Map Network Drive dialog box appears, as shown in Figure 2-17.

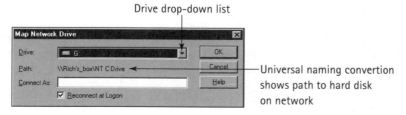

Figure 2-17: Mapping a Network Drive to a Local Drive Letter

There are a few things of interest here. One thing you should note is the Path shown in the dialog box. In Figure 2-17, the path is `\\Rich's_box\NT C Drive`. The use of a double back-slash (\\) denotes a name based on the Universal Naming Convention. Each system, drive, and directory level is separated by another backslash.

Of more immediate interest is the Drive drop-down list.

5. Click the down arrow in the Drive list.

6. Select the first available drive letter from the Drive list.

7. Click OK. After a second or so the system comes back and displays a new window showing the mapped drive's contents.

NT allows you to map up to 23 other devices into the system, depending on how many drives you already have installed in the computer doing the mapping. Assuming you have a floppy drive, one hard disk, and a CD-ROM, those drives are mapped to A, C, and D in most typical systems.

Because you're mapping a server's hard disk to be displayed in My Computer on a workstation, you should take the first available drive letter in the sequence above the local drives. (In my test system's case, it's drive G.)

The newly mapped hard disk's icon appears in the My Computer window, as shown in Figure 2-18.

Network drive icon

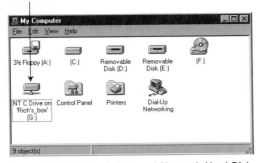

Figure 2-18: A Newly Mapped Network Hard Disk

Notice how the new drive icon bears a subtly different appearance from other hard disk icons such as C. Namely, it shows a little pipe connected to the drive. Isn't it cute?

After you map the drive, you can also place a shortcut on the screen by dragging the drive icon onto the desktop. A message appears stating that you cannot copy the drive to the desktop; do you want to create a shortcut? Click Yes and the new drive icon appears on the desktop. With a double-click you can open the hard disk's window. You can also edit the shortcut's caption. You cannot create the shortcut unless you map the network drive first.

The mapped network hard disk can also be accessed in NT Explorer, as shown in Figure 2-19.

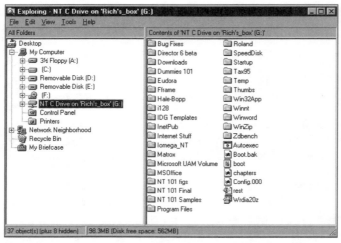

Figure 2-19: Viewing a Network Hard Disk's Contents in Explorer

SHARING A FOLDER WITH A WINDOWS NT WORKSTATION USER

What do you do when you don't want to share an entire hard disk with a user, but do want to share some of its contents? This is a common connectivity application in all but the smallest LANs, because it's impractical to share an entire hard disk with dozens or hundreds of users. Sharing with numerous users can create an administrative nightmare, and a *very* slow server. Here's how to set up a folder to be shared with a user or group without sharing an entire disk. For this exercise you'll continue using the Test User account as an example, but any account or group can be used.

1. If you have a hard disk on the NT Server that is *not* shared, open it from My Computer on the server. (In this example it is drive D)

2. Select a folder in the unshared drive for use. (In this example it is *Hypersnap*.)

3. Right-click the folder to bring up its shortcut menu.

4. From the shortcut menu, select Sharing.

   The Properties sheet for the folder appears as shown in Figure 2-20.

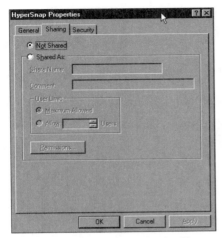

Figure 2-20: A Folder's Properties Sheet

5. To activate sharing, click the Shared As option.

6. Edit the Share Name as desired.

7. Click the Permissions button. The Access through Share Permissions dialog box appears.

8. Delete the Everyone group from the Permissions list by clicking Remove.

Unlike sharing a hard disk, you can safely delete the Everyone group from a folder share between NT systems. You may have a collection of folders on your server drive, each of which can be specially allocated to an individual user. By taking the Everyone group off a folder share, you prevent any users *except* those you designate from accessing the folder. (The administrator can still access the folder from the server.)

9. Click the Add button.

   The Add Users and Groups window appears.

10. Click the Show Users button to display the individual user accounts.

11. In the Names pane, double-click the Test User account.

If you have created another account, you can use that instead. You can select a group if desired; the methods here apply for any account or group.

12. In the Type of Access drop-down list, select Change. Figure 2-21 shows the results.

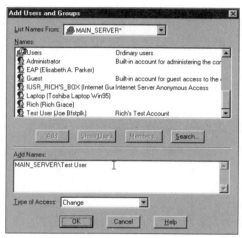

Figure 2-21: Adding a Single User for Access to the Shared Folder.

13. Click OK.

14. Click OK in the Access Through Share Permissions dialog box.

15. Click Apply in the folder's Properties sheet to activate the share.

16. Click OK to close the Properties sheet. You may receive a message saying that your share name is not accessible from some MS-DOS workstations. Click OK if this isn't an issue on your network. If this may be a problem, you need to either rename the folder or make sure your naming conventions don't exceed eight characters.

Note how the folder icon changes its appearance, as shown in Figure 2-22.

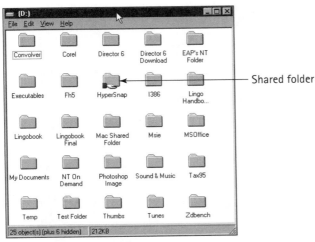

Shared folder

Figure 2-22: The Shared Folder Acquires
a New Icon

You don't need to restart the server or the user's workstation to use the shared folder. If the user account is already logged on to NT Workstation, all the users to do is open the NT server icon in Network Neighborhood.

The shared folder's icon has appears as shown in Figure 2-23.

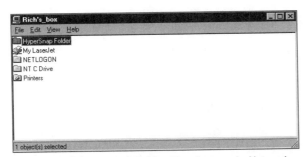

Figure 2-23: The Shared Folder Also Appears in Network
Neighborhood

Double-click the folder to open it on the workstation.

Although the process seems to take quite a few steps, the key part is knowing the basics about sharing and permissions. That's why so much attention was given to them at the beginning of this chapter. If you have the basics mastered, you can rapidly create a collection of shared folders for each of your users on the network. You can give them complete and exclusive access on the network to those folders, without endangering the contents of your hard disk.

If you have a large collection of users, set up a single folder off the root of the hard disk, and then create a series of folders or subdirectories, one for each networked user. Any number of folders can be shared this way. Users can have access to as many folders as they need. Folder permissions are fully separate from drive permissions.

You can also run applications off a shared folder. Simply designate the folder containing the application and follow the same process shown previously. Or, shortcuts can be dragged from the application's directory into a user's shared folder. You need to pay attention to the type of application: does it require DLL libraries to be installed on the client system? If so, you may receive error messages or the program may refuse to run. (Fortunately, this doesn't happen too often. Windows NT makes a very useful application server.) You also need to pay close attention to licensing issues. If you have a copy of Microsoft Word on your server and designate it for use in a shared folder, you might actually be breaking the license agreement if more than one user accesses the program at a time. Contact your software vendor for information on buying a multistation license for your programs.

Directory and NTFS Permissions

Referring back to Figure 2-20, you may notice a Security tab next to the Sharing tab. Clicking the Security tab reveals another Permissions button. If you click that Permissions button, you'll see another list of permissions for the same resource. They seem quite similar to the Share permissions you've already looked at, but they are a very different element in your system. That list of permissions is called Directory Permissions, also frequently called NTFS Permissions (the two terms are synonymous). They are a separate and distinctly different set of permissions from Share permissions. They're usually called NTFS Permissions because they apply to shared directories only if they are on an NTFS-formatted disk drive. They provide a more exacting selection of access rights to users and groups, and are a key feature of Windows NT file security on the network. If you use FAT-formatted drives, you'll never see Directory/NTFS permissions on your system. They have a number of characteristics that I won't describe here; NTFS permissions become increasingly important as your network grows, and you'll definitely need to know about them. Chapter 12 discusses NTFS permissions in greater detail, within the context of creating home directories.

Networking a Windows 95 Workstation to Windows NT Server

When you set up a Windows 95-NT connection, you'll find that Windows 95's networking features are quite similar to those for Windows NT. The dialog boxes offer many of the same features and settings, and look very much alike. The Network Neighborhoods are functionally identical.

Nevertheless, there are some differences. Here's a key one. If you have a Primary Domain Controller, you must set up the Windows 95 system to log on properly to the Windows NT domain. (If you're logging on to a stand-alone server, this doesn't apply to you.) You may also have to navigate through different levels of Network Neighborhood to locate the shared resources. Fortunately, it's simple.

To start with, you need to make sure that Client for Microsoft Networks is installed in the Windows 95 system. The assumption made here is that you've already done so. If not, open the Control Panel, double-click the Network applet, and click the Add button if Client for Microsoft Networks does not appear on the list. Follow the instructions from there. Client for Microsoft Networks must be installed on the Windows 95 clients for proper networking. Also, Network Neighborhood won't appear on the Windows 95 desktop unless the Client for Microsoft Networks is installed.

When Client for Microsoft Networks is installed in your Windows 95 machine, you can open the Network applet and set its logon properties. Here's how:

1. On the Windows 95 client, open the Control Panel.

2. Open the Network applet.

3. Select Client for Microsoft Networks, as shown in Figure 2-24.

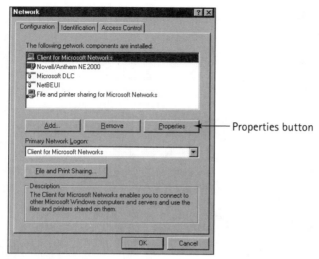

Properties button

Figure 2-24: Selecting the Client for
Microsoft Networks Service in the Windows
95 Network Control Panel

4. Click the Properties button.

   The Client for Microsoft Networks Properties sheet appears.

5. Click in the Log on to Windows NT domain check box. The Windows NT
   Domain text box will be enabled.

6. Enter the name of the Primary Domain for your network. As originally
   created in Chapter 1 and depicted in Figure 2-25, it is called
   MAIN_SERVER, but yours may differ.

7. For a faster logon, you can select the Quick logon option button.

   If you prefer to have all your networked resources available when the
   system finishes logging on, select the Logon and restore network
   connections option, as shown in Figure 2-25. If you choose this
   option, whatever network resources are running when you log on
   automatically made available without further password access. In many
   cases, this will add very little time to the startup.

8. Click OK.

9. Click OK again to set the new network settings. The Win95 client requests
   a restarts to enable the changes.

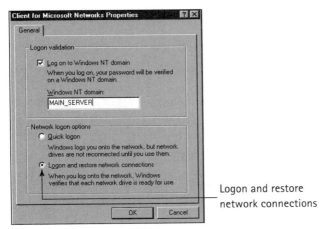

Logon and restore
network connections

Figure 2-25: Adding a Domain for the
Win95 Client.

10. Restart the client by clicking Yes.

The system reboots. When its logon screen appears, a third field listing the
Windows NT domain will be displayed.

11. Enter your user name and password and press Enter.

For the most part, browsing and using network resources under Windows 95 are
the same as when using NT Workstation, described in the previous section. Simply
open Network Neighborhood and browse through the available servers and network resources.

MOUNTING A WINDOWS NT HARD DISK ON A WINDOWS 95 CLIENT
Here's how to locate and mount an entire shared Windows NT hard disk so that it
appears on the Windows 95 desktop:

1. Enable sharing for a hard disk on the NT system, and define the
   permissions in the same way described in the earlier section "Sharing
   Resources with a Network User." Use the Administrative group and the
   Test User individual account, if desired.

For this example, continue using the Test User account we've been working with
throughout this chapter.

2. Log on to the network at the Windows 95 client as Test User with the
   appropriate password.

3. Open Network Neighborhood. It appears similar to Figure 2-26.

Entire Network is where you browse for the Domain server

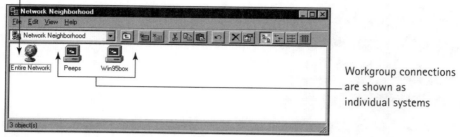

Workgroup connections
are shown as
individual systems

Figure 2-26: Opening Network Neighborhood in a Windows 95
Network Client

When you have other Win95 systems on the network, you may see them
as other stations. By default, servers and domains are placed in the Entire
Network group, shown as globe icons. If you want more detail in your
Network Neighborhood display, select Toolbar from the Network
Neighborhood View menu.

4. To locate the NT server, double-click the Entire Network icon. The Entire
   Network group opens as shown in Figure 2-27, displaying any
   workgroups or domain servers in the network. (Windows 95 usually
   doesn't display NT Domain servers immediately upon opening Network
   Neighborhood, but NT workstations do unless there's a network problem.)

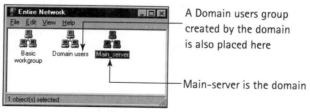

A Domain users group
created by the domain
is also placed here

Main-server is the domain

Figure 2-27: Opening the Entire
Network Group

Notice how the Domain Users group, originally created by the NT Server
domain, shows up here. This indicates, among other things, that the
Win95 client is successfully participating in the domain. The Primary
Domain Controller, in this case titled "Main_server," also appears. This is
the actual Windows NT domain that your Win95 client logged on to.

5. Double-click the domain icon, which in this case is "Main_server" but will be different in your system's case.

   The domain's Network Neighborhood window opens, as shown in Figure 2-28.

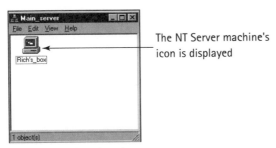

The NT Server machine's icon is displayed

Figure 2-28: Opening the Primary Domain in Network Neighborhood

   Finally, after opening so many windows that it has started to feel like a Russian eggshell doll, the actual server machine comes into view. In our example it's called "Rich's_box," which should sound familiar at this point. Your actual system, of course, may be different.

6. Double-click the server icon. The server's shared contents appear. Notice how the shares appear just as they do in an NT workstation network browse, including a networked printer, a folder, and a hard disk share.

   Printer sharing and setting up a print server are described in Chapter 5.

7. Right-click the shared hard disk icon (which defaults to a folder) and select Map Network Drive. Windows 95's Map Network Drive window appears. It's quite similar to that of Windows NT, showing a drop-down list and the universal name for the path to the network drive. The first available drive letter is shown.

8. If you want the user's Win95 client to automatically connect to the hard disk every time they log on, click in the Reconnect at logon check box.

9. Click OK. The drive's window automatically opens. The drive is mapped into My Computer and can be browsed with Explorer or through an MS-DOS window.

As you can see, the methods for integrating a Windows 95 system closely resemble those for NT. Most of the operations are not a big deal.

Folders can be shared in the same way as described earlier for an NT workstation.

FOLDER SHARES ON A WINDOWS 95 CLIENT

There is one subtle difference in folder shares on a Win95 client that can be confusing: the use of the Everyone group. Unlike sharing a folder with an NT workstation, where you can delete the Everyone group entirely from the share, you *can't* delete it when the share is connected to a Windows 95 client.

Table 2-4 lists the various ways in which the Everyone group can be interacted with for various client types and shares.

TABLE 2-4 BEHAVIOR OF THE EVERYONE GROUP IN CLIENT
        SHARES WITH A SERVER

Client Type	Share Type	Everyone Group Behavior
Windows NT client	Drive share	Everyone group must be part of the share.
	Folder share	Everyone group can be removed entirely from the share.
Windows 95 client	Drive share	Everyone group must be part of the share.
	Folder share	Everyone group must be part of the share.

The table points up a key advantage of using Windows NT Workstation in a company network: better security for shared folders. Folders are what most LAN users will be using anyway.

The rule of thumb: Set the Everyone listing in any share to Read access type. This ensures that all your users and groups have proper access, and that no stray user accounts can delete or modify files in the server. For folders shared with an NT workstation or server client, you can remove Everyone entirely from the Permissions list.

Other User Account Considerations

After you create user accounts for your 32-bit Windows workstations and they're happy campers on the LAN, you may have some more decisions to make. Will the user account have a home directory on your server? Do they need Remote Access dial-up capabilities? Do they need a user profile in case they move around between machines?

Now I turn to another important (and more complicated) part of your user accounts: the User Environment Profile. All the operations carried out in this section are performed in Windows NT Server.

INTRODUCING USER PROFILES AND HOME DIRECTORIES

There are two more areas of server management to which you should be introduced. user profiles and home directories have already been mentioned earlier in this chapter. Now you'll have a closer look at them. To begin inspecting, user profiles and home directories, open the User Manager, double-click a user account, and click the Profiles button. Figure 2-29 shows an example of a blank user profile for a just-created account.

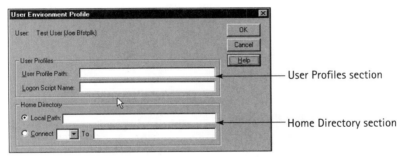

Figure 2-29: Displaying a Blank User Profile for a
User Account

User Environment Profiles have a variety of purposes:

◆ Ensure that a user moving around between different client computers can have a consistent interface to the server — the same user rights, program groups, and network connections. This is called a *roaming* profile.

◆ Define a logon script that the client can execute when they log in to the server, which can be a batch file (shades of MS-DOS!) or an executable program of any usable type.

◆ Automatically set up the client's computer screen with the user's cosmetic preferences, such as wallpaper, screen saver, and color scheme.

◆ Define a *home directory* that the user's system defaults to for saving and opening files.

The Windows NT user profiles cannot be used with Windows 95 client computers. They are only compatible with Windows NT Workstation clients or other

NT servers. This includes NT features such as home directories. If you have a large collection of Win95 systems on your network, you can't use NT profiles, and users must work with the individual settings for each geographically distant client. All the features to be discussed in this subsection apply only to Windows NT systems. If your company wants all your Win95 clients to use the same appearance and desktop arrangements, you've got some extra work ahead of you. (Or you can just issue a memo and make your users do the work!) Despite bearing the same user interface, Windows 95 is not a fully integrated client type with Windows NT – something that causes administrators many problems. I discuss this topic further in Chapter 12 and Appendix A.)

The User Environment Profile dialog box is one of the more difficult areas of Windows NT for an administrator to muck around in. Nevertheless, there's much power here, and it combines a number of features that are even more difficult to configure in many other networking operating systems. Features are divided into two key areas, as shown in Figure 2-30: User Profiles and Home Directory.

What is a user profile? For an example, you need only open the System applet in the Control Panel on the NT workstation where the user account is active, and click the User Profiles tab. Figure 2-30 shows an example.

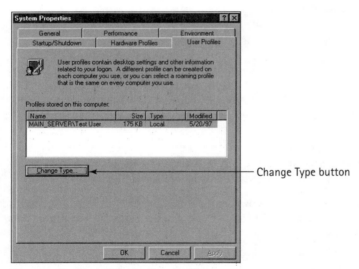

Figure 2-30: Displaying the User Profile on the Workstation

Typically, the Profiles contain the user's preferences for their desktop wallpaper, screen saver, color scheme, and other cosmetic elements. The file is fairly beefy, running to almost 200K, as shown in Figure 2-30. You can't directly edit it using any of Windows NT's utilities, because the operating system automatically saves it out with the user's preferences or those the administrator defines.

To set a roaming profile, click the Change Type button. Then, if the user logs on to another station in the network, his or her screen settings will appear there. User profiles are discussed at further length in Chapter 12.

Home directories (as shown in Figure 2-29) are a useful tool for system administrators, because a user's computer can use it for its defaults in File Open and File Save operations in application programs. All the user's data files can be stored here, ensuring easy and predictable data backups and user account deletion.

If your users have a shared folder on the server, you can define that folder as their home directory. After that, any time the user wants to save or open a file for an application, that default path is displayed in the dialog boxes for their programs. All their data can be stored in a safe and convenient place, and things are much more manageable for you.

A local path can also be defined, which is a bit tricky. The local path for a client should not be on the server's main hard disk; it's located on the C drive *on the client system*. (If the client has other hard disks, those could also be used.) The text Connect To box shown in Figure 2-29 allows you to select any networked hard disk (such as your server's) and specify a directory path to that hard disk to serve as a user's home directory, which *could* be located on the server.

Whenever you define a path using the Connect To box, you must use the UNC (Uniform Naming Convention). For example:

```
\\RICH'S_BOX\USERS\CAROL
```

where RICH'S_BOX is the name of the server, USERS is the directory off the root, and CAROL is the subdirectory. The case is not important.

This feature is worth playing around with a little bit to see what you can accomplish. But home directories and user profiles are important tools for general network management, and they get much more complicated. Chapter 12, "General System Management," provides the information you need to effectively use these features.

Elsewhere in the User Properties dialog box, a simple but important setting lurks: the Dialin button. If your user accounts need remote access to dial in to the server, you need to know about this feature. You can find out more about how to create home directories in Chapter 12.

ENABLING DIALIN AND REMOTE ACCESS FEATURES FOR A USER ACCOUNT

Using a modem, ISDN connection, or other high-speed link, a user can dial up an NT server in their office, and the server will behave just as though the remote user was connected to the local area network. It's a commonly used tool for telecommuting, and workers and executives rely on it to stay in touch with home, gather e-mail, and send files efficiently.

I've already discussed how to set up Remote Access, in Chapter 1. This section shows you how to set up a user account to actually *use* it. It's not at all difficult compared to the process of setting up the service, especially with TCP/IP.

Remember that if all your users are running Windows machines for remote access, TCP/IP is not always required. Although it's the most practical networking protocol for office and corporate use, you may not need it if you're running a small network. Remote Access clients can use any networking protocol supported by NT, including TCP/IP, IPX, and NetBEUI. TCP/IP networking is discussed in considerable detail in Chapter 3, and Remote Access connections for both NetBEUI and TCP/IP are described in Chapter 9.

The Windows NT Remote Access features are managed through two areas: the Dialin feature in User Properties and the Dial-Up Networking applet in My Computer. You can open a user account's Dialin settings by clicking the Dialin button in the User Properties sheet:

1. From the Start menu, select Programs, Administrative Tools, and then User Manager for Domains.

2. Double-click a user account.

   The User Properties sheet appears.

3. Click the Dialin button. The Dialin Information dialog box appears, as shown in Figure 2-31.

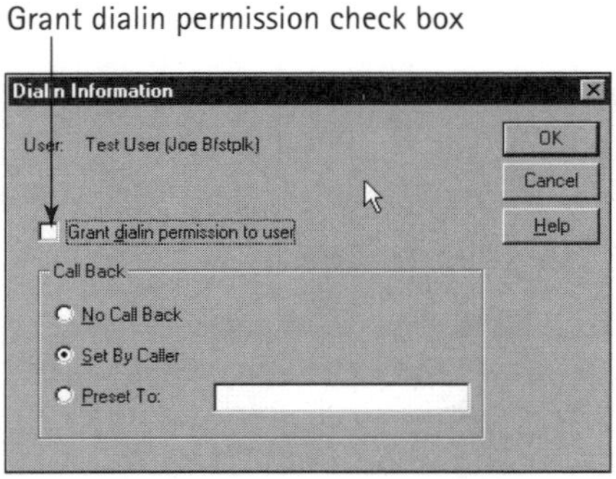

Grant dialin permission check box

Figure 2-31: Dialin Information dialog box for a New User Account.

4. To enable dialin capabilities for the user account, click in the Grant dialin permission to user check box, as shown in Figure 2-31.

5. In many cases the user will want to provide the server with a callback number, particularly if they're a laptop user roaming around through a series of locations. Click the Set by Caller option button if that's the case, so the user can provide the numbers whenever necessary.

6. If the user is expected to call from a single location, click the Preset To option button and enter the callback phone number in the box.

7. Click OK to close the Dialin Information dialog box.

The user account can now be used to access the server from a remote location. That's all it takes!

If they're using NT Workstation, the remote user can also set the callback number in their Dial-Up Networking (DUN) program. Here's where to locate this feature:

1. Open My Computer on the Windows NT Desktop and double-click Dial-Up Networking. (This step applies equally to NT Server and NT Workstation.)

    The Dial-Up Networking window appears, as shown in Figure 2-32.

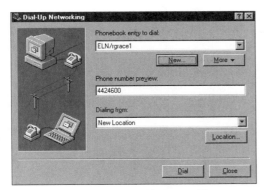

Figure 2–32: Opening Dial-Up Networking

2. Click the More button. A menu drops down.

3. From the More menu, select User Preferences. The User Preferences dialog box appears. Four tabs are offered: Dialing, Callback, Appearance, and Phonebook.

4. Click the Callback tab. Figure 2-33 shows its contents.

Option buttons

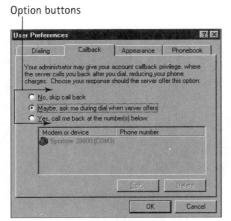

Figure 2-33: The Callback Tab Offers Several
Options for Server-assisted Remote Access.

Remember the check box you enabled in Figure 2-31? Here is where your clients'
dial-up capabilities tie in with it. Anyone who is running a Windows NT
Workstation client remotely can use Dial-Up Networking's User Preferences dialog
box to determine how their dial-up account behaves.

The default, as shown in Figure 2-33, leaves the Maybe, ask me during dial when
server offers option button selected and enabled. If your user's account on the NT
Server has its check box enabled in User Properties, the server will do precisely that —
ask the user if they want a callback when they dial up and log on. The user is then
prompted to enter the callback phone number.

If your client has a more or less permanent callback phone number, you can
select the Yes, call me back at the number(s) below option button and click the Edit
button to enter the callback phone number. When the user calls up, the server logs
them on, breaks the connection, and calls them back. In either case, all the user's
permissions, user rights, and networked resources are used in the same way as if
they were back at the office LAN.

A more complete account of Remote Access setup for your server and for your
clients is described in Chapter 9.

A Final Word

You're finished with this chapter. That concludes your grand tour of Windows NT's key user account features. You've learned how to perform the following basic actions:

◆ Create a new user account with the User Manager for Domains

◆ Add that user account to a group

◆ Set user permissions for a shared device on the network

◆ Log on a Windows NT Workstation to an NT-based domain

◆ Log on a Windows 95 system on to a Windows NT domain

◆ Share a hard disk from the server and map it onto a Windows NT Workstation client and a Windows 95 client

◆ Share a folder on the server for exclusive use with a client's user account

◆ Learn what a user account's home directory and user profiles are

◆ How to set up a user account to use Remote Access dialin services

This chapter covered many of the most important and common connectivity applications you'll perform with Windows NT. However, there are many other useful functions that you haven't even gotten to yet, such as system policies and trust relationships. For the most part they are peripheral issues to the key task of hooking up clients to your LAN and sharing resources with them. Chapter 12 discusses all these topics in greater detail.

The next chapter, "LAN-Based TCP/IP Connectivity," guides you through the all-important realm of TCP/IP networking in Windows NT. TCP/IP is not just used when you access the Internet — you can also use it to tie your entire network together. It's a powerful, but more complex, networking protocol used in larger corporate and enterprise networks, and NT provides a panoply of features for supporting it in your LAN. You're introduced to the use of TCP/IP in the context of Windows NT and how the protocol works on a basic level, and you find out exactly how Windows NT's key TCP/IP networking services (WINS, DNS, and DHCP) really work and how to use them in your network.

Chapter 4, "Connecting Alternative Network Clients," focuses on simpler methods for networking Windows 3.x and Macintosh computers to a Windows NT LAN. You find out how Services for Macintosh works, how to print from a Macintosh to an NT print server, how to network System 8 Macintoshes to Windows NT, and how to gracefully integrate legacy Windows 3.x systems.

Troubleshooting

My Windows NT system doesn't see my Windows 95 clients. They show up in Network Neighborhood, but they don't have any drives or folders there.

You need to set up your Windows 95 client's devices to be shared. The methods are the same as those described earlier: Right-click the drive or folder you want to share and select the Sharing menu option. The device's Properties sheet appears, displaying the Sharing tab. Click Shared As and give it a desired name in the Share Name field.

What is really fascinating is the way the Windows 95 client can see parts of the Windows NT Server domain that it's logged in to, as shown in Figure 2-34.

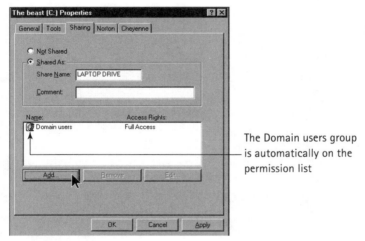

The Domain users group is automatically on the permission list

Figure 2-34: Setting Up a Share on a
Windows 95 Client to an NT Domain

Click Add to place more NT Server groups on the Windows 95 drive's Sharing list, and you'll see another interesting dialog box, shown in Figure 2-35.

The Windows 95 client obtains its list of possible permissions from the NT domain. This can also be done by Win95 machines with stand-alone NT Servers and even NT Workstations, as you'll discover in Chapter 5.

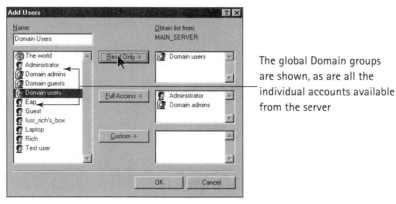

The global Domain groups
are shown, as are all the
individual accounts available
from the server

Figure 2–37: Adding Users and Groups on a
Windows 95 Shared Device

Select a group or user and click the Read Only, Full Access, or Custom buttons
to set an access type for them. In Figure 2-35, the Administrator account and the
Domain admins group have full access, and Domain users has read-only access. If
you add a user or group to Custom access, click OK. Windows 95's Change Access
Rights dialog appears, as shown in Figure 2-36.

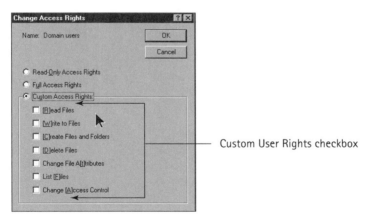

Custom User Rights checkbox

Figure 2–36: Setting Custom User
Rights from a Windows 95 Client
for Its Shared Device

The Windows 95 capabilities in this area are actually pretty impressive. When you're finished making your choices (which are pretty self-evident here), click OK, and then finally click OK to set your share on the client. You should then be able to access that resource using the Windows NT system and the proper account without rebooting.

Chapter 3

LAN-Based TCP/IP Networking

IN THIS CHAPTER

In Chapter 3 the following Windows NT networking topics are discussed:

◆ Providing a brief description of the core basics of TCP/IP networking as it relates to Windows NT.

◆ Introducing and explaining Windows NT's key networking features, including DNS, DHCP, and WINS.

◆ Configuring and employing LAN connections using TCP/IP the WINS and static IP addresses.

◆ Setting up DNS for expanded TCP/IP connections across the LAN and WAN.

◆ Adding DHCP as a graceful substitute for static IP addressing in a TCP/IP-based LAN.

◆ Using the NT Command Prompt to check TCP/IP network connections.

FOR MAINSTREAM BUSINESS CONNECTIVITY, this chapter is the most important one in the book. The permutations of using TCP/IP on your Windows NT-based network are vast, spanning almost every important service and connection type Windows NT Server has to offer. You can approach it in many different ways, and you can mess up in just as many different ways, particularly in a company environment where consistent availability is a requirement. If you're not too experienced in TCP/IP networking, you can run into many pitfalls I will discuss many key topics in this short chapter. When I've finished, you'll have a guaranteed recipe for TCP/IP network connectivity without tears or pink slips.

Because TCP/IP is the current state of the art in networking protocols and is fully routable, it's the prohibitive favorite in corporate networks. Unfortunately, this doesn't mean it's simple. In this chapter I stick to the most crucial basics of TCP/IP knowledge and do it *briefly*. Key elements such as default gateways, subnet masks, and IP address schemes are defined and placed in the larger context of Windows NT networking.

You also get a quick introduction to some of Windows NT's most important TCP/IP support services, primarily DNS (Domain Naming Service), DHCP (Dynamic Host Control Protocol), and WINS (Windows Internet Naming Service). Depending on your situation, your TCP/IP solutions for general networking may be simple or fiendishly complicated. I'll eschew lengthy discussions of theory and mechanics (some books spend 80 to 100 pages discussing the nuts and bolts of TCP/IP) and focus mainly on what *works*, in specific and exacting detail.

Even if you use only Windows 95 and Windows NT Workstation clients on your network with your Windows NT Server (which is the assumption here), networking with TCP/IP is loaded with pitfalls and potential problems. Nevertheless, compared to other widely used network operating systems that use TCP/IP, NT does a good job making this key networking methodology reasonably approachable for knowledgeable users. When things go wrong, it's a good practice to use the Windows NT command line with a few special commands to perform basic connection troubleshooting. The final section of this chapter provides an overview of command-line troubleshooting techniques.

Introducing Windows NT and TCP/IP Networking

In Chapter 1 I mentioned that for your local-area network server to connect and manage clients, you do *not* always need TCP/IP.

If you are building a Windows NT server that you know is going to need connections to other discrete LANs in different locations, however, and that you'll be using routing to do so (as is almost certain), you definitely need TCP/IP to be fully installed and configured on your Windows NT server as your networking protocol. This goes way beyond simply using TCP/IP to dial up the Internet with your modem for Web browsing and e-mail. When you connect to the Internet for the fun stuff, your Internet service provider dynamically allocates you an address on the network, and you never (or seldom) have to worry about it. It's a different story, however, when you're setting up your *own* TCP/IP networking scheme for your internal network.

When you start hooking up multiple LANs together, you start having to deal with things such as wide-area networks (WANs), which require high-speed pipes or connections between them. These are 56K or faster connections that use TCP/IP for communications between them because it is the most widely supported routable protocol. The alternative would be bridging between LANs, which adds enormous overhead to the interconnection. ISPs normally won't deal with bridging at all, and you definitely don't want to bridge across the Internet!

A comprehensive discussion, or even a lengthy overview, of the ins and outs of TCP/IP is beyond the scope of this chapter and of this book. The next several paragraphs are meant to introduce you to what is really required to understand even the basic elements for setting up TCP/IP services for general Windows NT networking. If you are already a highly experienced network technician, you probably shouldn't bother reading this section.

No matter who you are, one annoyance you'll rapidly become acquainted with is the propensity of Windows NT to restart after even the smallest tweaks and adjustments in the Network applet.

If things start going wrong during the setup process, you'll spend more time rebooting than you do making the actual changes in the Network applet.

About IP Addresses, C-Classes, Subnets, and Routing

Do you plan to use TCP/IP in your LAN or remote access dialins to your server? Do you expect to have your network participate in a much larger network down the road? There are some critical pieces of information you need to know, such as the following items:

◆ IP address

◆ Subnet

◆ Subnet mask

◆ Class C network

◆ Default gateway

An *IP address* is a station's address on the network. IP addresses are a 32-bit number that can contain up to 12 digits, a unique code assigned to every network card. An example is 225.225.225.224. Another example is 1.1.1.1, which is obviously not a 12-digit value but fits the address format. It is also called *dotted quad* notation, because periods are used to break up the address. Without IP addresses, connections between machines on the Internet or in wide-area networks (WANs) would be nearly impossible, and some other equally difficult scheme would have to be used. In TCP/IP, every system on the network must have an IP address, which is typically assigned to the computer's network card.

The current 32-bit IP addressing scheme allows for over four billion individual addresses — nearly one for every human individual on Earth. (Many more than there are computer users at this point, anyway.) In practice, not quite so many addresses can be used. As you'll see later, TCP/IP based networking hardware, such as routers, occupies IP addresses by itself. The total address space for computer clients on the Internet or on company LANs isn't as great as it first appears. It's not feasible to have every single networking device in the world possess its own special 32-bit IP address, because that makes the task of simply networking them next to impossible. For that reason, IP addresses are split into two parts: the *network* address and the *node* address. They are set up according to how many of the four bytes of the IP address are assigned to each of the two. Class A networks use one byte, Class B networks occupy two bytes of the IP address, and Class C networks occupy three bytes of the IP address. The remaining bytes specify the actual network client. Table 3-1 provides a little more indication of what this looks like.

TABLE 3-1 A CLASS, B CLASS, AND C CLASS NETWORK ADDRESSING

Type of Network	Sample Address	# of Possible Networks	Characteristics
A Class	122.x.x.x	127	Node addresses occupy *three* bytes of the IP address, for 16.7 million possible unique client addresses per network.
B Class	122.122.x.x	16,384	Node addresses occupy *two* bytes of the IP address. Because the first and last bit of Class B node addresses are reserved, a total of 16,384 possible unique Class B networks are available. Each of those networks can contain up to 65,534 clients, in theory.
C Class	122.122.122.x	Approximately 2.1 million. (The first three bits of any Class C network are reserved for a specified value.)	Node addresses occupy *one* byte of the IP address, providing a maximum of 253 IPs for clients on each of those 2.1 million Class C networks. (It's not 256 IP addresses — a few addresses are reserved.)

Say you had an IP address assigned to you from a Class A network. If that address was 122.32.46.230, the network address is simply 122, and the node or station address is 32.46.230.

If you had the same 122.32.46.230 IP address assigned to you from a *Class B* network, the network address would be 122.32, and the node or station address is 46.230.

For the same address numbering in a Class C network, the network address would be 122.32.46, and the node's address is simply 230.

This area can get quite complicated. Within this book you're presumed to be using a Class C network. All the little tricks mentioned in Table 3-1 (reserved bits and so on) are elements in the actual design of TCP/IP by the people who created it in the first place. The key to understanding how IP addressing works involves mastery of some binary mathematics and a lot of persistence, neither of which I'll discuss here.

In practice, a Class C network is a contiguous group of 256 IP addresses. An example is IP addresses 128.92.3.0 to 128.92.3.255, or 205.205.205.0 to 205.205.205.255. If you're going to have a more or less permanent link to the Internet, and your LAN is going to participate in a larger network or WAN (using, say, a high-speed link such as a T1 line) with other company networks, your ISP or corporate-wide IS manager must assign you the IP network or *subnet* of IP addresses that you will use.

A *subnet* is a portion of a network assigned so that its addresses can be routed by the customer to its own or other sites for client TCP/IP connections. For example, you can break out 4, 8, 16, 32, or 64 IP addresses from a C-Class for use as a subnet. This collection of IP addresses can be assigned to clients as needed, either by you through hand-coding or dynamically assigned by the server. If you had a full C-Class allocated to you, you can use more routers to break out those subnets for use in your departments.

In a subnet of any size, the first IP address provided is assigned to the *network*. The last address is allocated as the *broadcast* IP. The broadcast IP is used to transmit information that you designate to be transmitted across the network to every single user or client within that C-Class *or* subnet. (TCP/IP is therefore a broadcast-type network protocol, but there are ways to alleviate that.)

Here's where the concept of routing comes into play. Essentially, routers are used to connect subnets to larger networks. Routers can be small networking devices designed to handle small subnets or share an IP connection between several machines, or huge electronic devices capable of handling thousands of connections at a time. In any subnet an IP address is occupied by the router that maintains the subnet's communications to the larger network. Typically, the router's IP address is the first address available in the subnet after the network IP. (This is also called the default gateway address.) In other words, out of a subnet three addresses are automatically subtracted from the collection of IP addresses that you can use. What I'm talking about is the basic mechanism of how routers work (and which addresses are usable in your subnet), but it can get much more complicated than I describe here.

Here's an example of how network IPs and broadcast IPs work. Say you have a full 256 IP-address C-Class whose addresses started at 128.92.3.0 and ended at 128.92.3.255. The first address, 128.92.3.0, is allocated to the network. The last address in the C-Class, 128.92.3.255, is allocated as the broadcast address. The second address in the C-Class, 128.92.3.1, is occupied by the router. All the other IP addresses, from 128.92.3.2 to 128.92.3.254, are usable by clients, for a total of 253 usable IPs.

Now, with a smaller subnet it works similarly. If you have a small subnet of four IP addresses in that C-Class (from 128.92.3.4 to 128.92.3.7), the IP address 128.92.3.4 is assigned to the network. The ending address of the subnet, 128.92.3.7, is the broadcast address. Since one of those two remaining addresses is usually taken up by a router, only one IP address is actually available for clients. This kind of setup is relatively rare. (Home office ISDN adapters, such as the Motorola BitSURFER or the USR Courier iModem, are ISDN devices that plug directly into the serial port, require no IP, and don't possess routing functions. You can buy small routers, such as the Ascend Pipeline, that can be used to share an ISDN connection between several computers.

A *subnet mask* simply tells the computer how big your subnet is, and, thus, how big your immediate network is. It tells you and the system whether you have a full C-Class or a subnet available for your TCP/IP settings in the server. There is a standard set of subnet masks used to indicate the size of a subnet.

Here's a breakdown of how subnet masks work in our sample C-Class (128.92.3.0 to 128.92.3.255). A subnet mask for any full C-Class is 255.255.255.0. (The B-Class subnet mask is 255.255.0.0.) If you know you have a full C-Class to work with in your TCP/IP setup, this is the value you should enter in the Subnet Mask field of the TCP/IP Properties sheet. Table 3-2 shows the subnet masks for the normally used address ranges of subnets.

TABLE **3-2 STANDARD SUBNET MASKS AND SUBNET SIZE MATCHUPS**

Subnet Mask	IP Address Subnet Size
255.255.255.0	full C-Class
255.255.255.192	64-IP-address subnet (64 = /26)
255.255.255.224	32-IP-address subnet (32 = /27)
255.255.255.240	16-IP-address subnet (16 = /28)
255.255.255.248	8-IP-address subnet (8 = /29)
255.255.255.252	4-IP-address subnet (4 = /30)

Your subnet mask will be one of these values. Figure 3-1 graphically shows how a C-Class and a typical subnet are broken down:

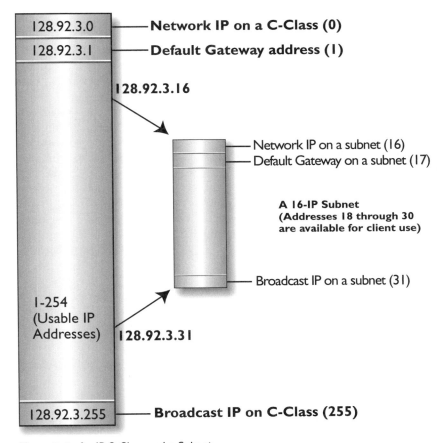

Figure 3-1: An IP C-Class and a Subnet

When you set up a subnet, the first IP address in the C-Class will be divisible with no remainder *by the number of IP addresses assigned.*

For example, if you had a full C-Class and wanted to break out a 16-IP-address subnet (64-IP-address subnets are the largest size subnet you can feasibly route out of a C-Class), the starting IP address in the subnet is calculated by being divisible by 16 with no remainder.

In a full C-Class, subnets can be broken out at 128.92.3.16, 128.92.3.32, 128.92.3.48, 128.92.3.64, and so on. Each of the initial addresses is divisible by 16 in the C -Class.

It gets better. Say your ISP (Internet service provider) routes a subnet from a C-Class over to you. You can then split that subnet into *smaller* subnets and then route them internally for use in separate LANs in your office. If your provider assigns you a 64-address subnet from a C-Class, you can then route parts of that subnet as other 4-, 8-, 16-, or 32-address subnets for use by other departments' LANs in your company. This does make your network planning more complicated.

Again, you must allow for the network and broadcast IP addresses not being usable by clients, and the first usable IP address being occupied by your router. Also, subnet assignments follow the same rule of addresses being divisible with no remainder. (A deep discussion of this whole thing goes far beyond the scope of this book. Ph.D.'s write books on this stuff, and IP addressing and routing can get much more extensive than what is discussed here.)

If you want to set up your computer to simply dial up the Internet for Web browsing, you need TCP/IP for dialout, as shown earlier in this chapter. However, you don't have to go through all these gyrations, or need a C-Class or subnet assignment or a subnet mask. When you dial up Earthlink or Netcom or some other service provider to browse the Web or build a Virtual Private Network (both discussed in Chapter 10), your ISP dynamically assigns an IP address to your system, and you never (or rarely) have to think about it. (Well, with VPNs you might.)

Connecting your server using RAS to browse the Web or check e-mail isn't a big deal. Setting up dial-up or LAN connections to your *server* using TCP/IP can be. You need to make sure you can get the following pieces of information to perform an effective TCP/IP setup in that case:

◆ The IP address for your client or server system, which is assigned out of the IPs made available to you (or chosen from a reasonably safe A-, B-, or C-Class if you don't have an Internet presence and still want to use TCP/IP).

◆ Your subnet mask. (If you know the size of your subnet, the subnet mask can be taken from the table above unless you have a much larger network. If you do, you probably don't need this book!)

◆ The *default gateway* address, which is usually the address assigned to the device used to route your connections within or outside your LAN. Customarily, it's placed on the first available usable IP address in your C-Class or subnet. If you're just using an NT server for RAS dialup, the server itself is doing the TCP/IP routing inside your network, so it takes that default gateway address. This is not the same as the IP address for your server.

As an example, if you have a subnet of 16 that begins at 128.92.3.16, the address 128.92.3.16 is taken as your network's assigned address, and 128.92.3.17 is occupied by your router to your LAN. *That* is the default gateway for the subnet. As an example, Figure 3-2 shows the TCP/IP Properties sheet, displaying the fields for those values to be entered.

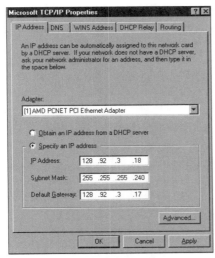

Figure 3–2: Defining IP Address Values
for an NT System

In Figure 3-2, the workstation's address is 128.92.3.18, which in the example is the first available address for clients in the subnet. You'll also see that the subnet mask is set as 255.255.255.240. This setting indicates a 16-address subnet. These addresses are just examples and are not the ones you'll probably use.

If you're building an NT-based LAN without a lot of Internet connectivity, but you still want to use TCP/IP, you can pick a set of IP addresses out of thin air and use them in your internal network. For example, in my sample network I'm using a C-Class from 205.205.205.0 to 205.205.205.255. The default gateway address is 205.205.205.1, and since the NT server serves as my router, that's the address it takes. The subnet mask is then 255.255.255.0. All the NT and Windows 95 clients on my network use these values for the default gateway and subnet mask.

Other IP addresses are assigned as needed. Since none of the systems connect across a WAN to other network segments (they just dial out using RAS for Web browsing and e-mail), this arbitrary set of IP addresses works fine. In corporate environments, you don't want to make a habit of this.

TIP

If you need to select a range of IP addresses "out of thin air" for a small network, a common practice is to use the A-Class IP address range of 192.0.0.0.

If you want to investigate the Properties sheet showing these values at any time, do the following:

1. Open Control Panel.

2. Open Network.

3. In the Network Control Panel, click the Protocols tab.

4. If TCP/IP is displayed in the Protocols tab, select it and click the Properties button.

5. Close the TCP/IP Properties sheet by clicking Cancel. (Do this *especially* if you make any experimental entries in the sheet that you don't want to keep. Setup for this aspect of NT use is discussed later in this chapter.)

At any time you can also right-click Network Neighborhood and select Properties from the shortcut menu. The Network applet appears when you do this.

One more point: Recently, the IETF (Internet Engineering Task Force) and various other interested parties finally agreed on an expanded version of the IP addressing system. It's called IPv6, and it drastically expands the IP address range within the TCP/IP addressing scheme. (Each of the numeric entities in the dotted-quad notation is called an *octet*, because they're eight-bit numbers ranging from 0 to 255.) Not a big thing, right? Oh, a very big thing indeed. Once, the IETF thought they'd never run out of IP addresses in the present dotted-quad scheme. Then fifty million people got on the Internet and every business with a desk lamp and an electric outlet got on, too. Suddenly, the address space started to get cramped. So we got IPv6, which is roughly the equivalent of providing ten IP addresses to each individual grain of sand on the planet Earth. With this increase, we're unlikely to run out of address space anytime soon. The next release of Windows NT, Version 5, supports this major change in the Internet address system.

That wraps up the lovely discussion of TCP/IP theory. I've stuck to the things that have direct relevance to your use of Windows NT Server. Now it's time to demonstrate its use by installing the TCP/IP protocol on your server.

Installing TCP/IP on Windows NT Server

All the things discussed in the previous section actually start to become fairly clear once you apply them to real-world situations. Installing TCP/IP is fairly simple, but if you don't get your addressing correct the first time, you immediately can have problems. (The steps described here can also be performed when you set up the server for the first time).

1. Open Control Panel.

2. Open Network.

3. In the Network Control Panel, click the Protocols tab.

4. Click the Add button. A list of protocols appears.

5. Select TCP/IP Protocol from the list and click OK. A message appears: "If there is a DHCP server on your network, TCP/IP can be configured to dynamically provide an IP address. If you are not sure, ask your system administrator. Do you wish to use DHCP?"

6. Click No. (You'll get to DHCP later.) You are then prompted for the location of the files, which are on the Windows NT Server CD-ROM. Provide the CD-ROM drive letter and the i386 directory and click Continue.

7. When the files finish copying, the TCP/IP Properties sheet comes up, as shown in Figure 3-3

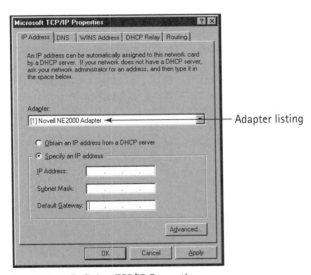

Figure 3-3: Defining TCP/IP Properties

8. Enter the IP Address for your server (it could be one assigned to you, or one of your choosing). Also, enter your subnet mask value and the default gateway value.

9. Click OK. If you're installing TCP/IP on a server that already has RAS installed, as is likely, you may be asked to configure Remote Access Service to use TCP/IP.

10. Click No. (You configure RAS later.)

11. Click Close in the Network applet. Then restart the system.

A final note: In Figure 3-3, notice that a network card is listed. This is fine, since TCP/IP is a universal networking protocol that works over Ethernet as well as phone lines. But since you're using RAS, the network card isn't used. The modem isn't listed here. What gives? The modem is set up by Windows NT to share the same IP address as the network card when it's used for Remote Access. It does this using a process called *binding*.

When binding occurs, the various networking devices, services, and protocols you use are all tied together so that everything works properly. Modems are "bound" to the network card on your Windows NT system using something called a WAN Wrapper. WAN, which as you know stands for wide-area network, is the term Microsoft uses to tell this device: "Bind this modem to your computer's network card so that this computer can dial up the server and join the network that way. Use the same IP address as well, if needed." When you use a modem to dial up the server from your client, you are really creating a type of WAN. Your network card's (and thus your system's) IP address is shared with the modem or other telecom device.

For an example of what this looks like, open the Network applet in Control Panel and click the Bindings tab. (It also appears once during Windows NT setup when you configure your network, so you've already glimpsed it before.) A list of services appears with plus signs next to them, indicating that you can go to lower levels in the list. Click the plus sign next to Remote Access Server Service, and a WINS Client (TCP/IP) listing appears with another plus sign to its left. Click there and the networking device bindings appear, as shown in Figure 3-4.

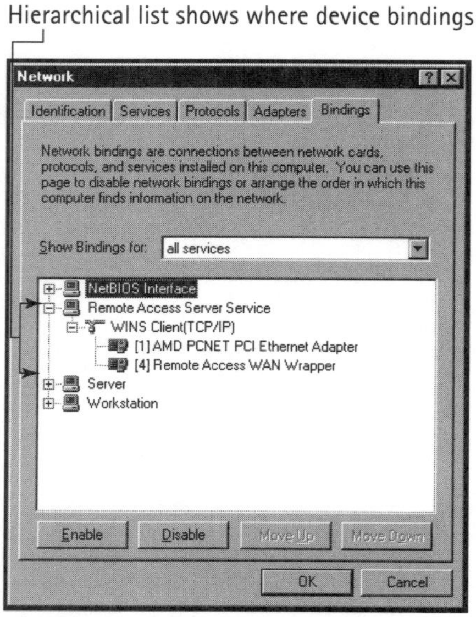

Hierarchical list shows where device bindings reside

Figure 3-4: Checking Bindings for Your Network Devices

Rarely will you need to change anything in the Bindings tab. If you have multiple network cards in Windows NT server, which creates what is called a *multihomed* server, you may want to change the order in which the operating system searches for information on each network device. Moving items higher up in the binding order for a particular service can also increase their performance. (All installed network cards in the multihomed server would appear in the Adapters list in Figure 3-4 as well.)

Now it's time to explore the vital and powerful realm of TCP/IP networking in earnest.

Expanding TCP/IP Capabilities

Although it's relatively straightforward to create a network connection that uses only NetBEUI for its protocol, there is an obvious limitation: NetBEUI is not routable and is only suitable for smaller networks. Many company LANs have network segments connected with routers. While each segment can be locally accessed using nonroutable protocols such as NetBEUI, there's no easy way to communicate through a router from one segment to another. In that case, you must use TCP/IP as your protocol from your server and your clients. (IPX, the standard protocol for Novell NetWare, is also routable and is a convenient option, but I won't be discussing its use here.)

Install TCP/IP and Related Services First on a New Server

Before digging into the details of TCP/IP-based LAN configuration, here's a key rule that I recommend following: If you plan to use TCP/IP as your primary networking protocol and need to employ WINS, DNS, and the usual suspects, do yourself a favor and start off the whole thing on a new Windows NT Server installation.

Why? Trying to install TCP/IP networking and related services on a working Windows NT server in an office, with functioning clients, is asking for trouble. The chances are that one service or another will fail to run properly without a lot of thrashing around and troubleshooting, interfere with existing services, or fail to run what should be a fairly easy TCP/IP connection.

When you install your Windows NT server, install TCP/IP *first* as your sole networking protocol. Then install WINS immediately afterwards. The process is simple; it's the usual Control Panel, Network, Services tab, Add button procedure. (I go into more detail a bit later.) After you do these things and get your TCP/IP networking up and running, continue layering in the other services, features, and protocols you need.

Unfortunately, running TCP/IP alone isn't enough for LAN access from a remote client. When you need to do this type of thing, you have to learn about some Windows NT server capabilities that haven't yet been discussed in this book, namely WINS, DNS, and DHCP. When you start dealing with multiple acronyms, things can get scary very quickly. You can buy a shelfful of Windows NT books to find out what these programs do and how to set them up properly, or you can read the next several pages and then actually *get something done.*

I briefly mentioned these three important services at the beginning of this chapter and can't avoid describing them, but I can try to do it in semi-plain English. Also bear in mind that what is discussed in the following subsection barely scratches the surface of Windows NT's TCP/IP-related networking applications. Many details are glossed over out of necessity, but nothing important will be missed.

Introducing WINS (Windows Internet Name Service)

WINS is a friendly little service that ties into some fairly arcane aspects of networked computing. WINS makes sure that your network clients' (whether remote access or on the actual network) *computer names* are properly mapped within the server. This is mainly used when the server needs to relate a computer's NetBIOS name to an IP address. And what is NetBIOS (besides another scary acronym)?

NetBIOS (Network Basic Input/Output System) is a foundation of PC-based networking. It is a low-level networking protocol, a simple set of programming instructions for creating and maintaining network connections. Then networking protocols such as NetBEUI (which is closely related to NetBIOS), IPX/SPX, or TCP/IP lie "on top" of NetBIOS and determine how the data is sent around the network, how data packets are structured, and how they communicate on the network. A NetBIOS *name* is simply the name for your computer, workgroup, or domain, such as Richs_box, Basic_workgroup, or Test_Domain. (I prefer to use underscores in my naming conventions instead of spaces.) So some aspects of NetBIOS actually sound reasonably familiar.

Where does WINS come in? It makes sure everyone who connects to the network has a fair connection. No, the server doesn't do it automatically when you start it up and dial up from a client using TCP/IP; a facility has to be running on the server that maps IP addresses to computer names when they connect on the network. It uses a database to keep records of clients and the IP addresses they use when they connect to the server. (This process is called *name resolution.* This is a grossly simplified but fairly accurate account of what WINS does). When you install WINS on Windows NT Server, a special application called WINS Manager is added to the Start menu's Programs/Administrative Tools menu. WINS Manager is shown in Figure 3-5.

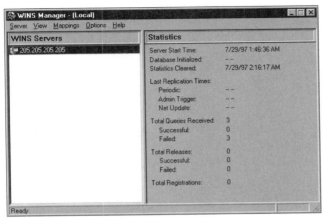

Figure 3-5: Introducing WINS Manager

In Figure 3-5, the pane on the left shows any WINS Servers present on the network (at least one on each routable segment), along with its IP address. The right pane shows the overall activity of the WINS service while the system is running. If you have a really big Windows NT network, several WINS servers will show up here. This is particularly the case if you have a Primary WINS Server and a Secondary Wins Server in the same domain. For our applications, that's a bit grandiose.

Some Windows NT Server administrators actually prefer not to use WINS. There is an alternative, called the LMHOSTS file, that you can learn about in the sidebar "About LMHOSTS Files."

About LMHOSTS Files

Some Windows NT server operators, especially in relatively small networks, may not even use WINS to perform name resolution. Instead, they can use a special file called LMHOSTS, which lives in the NT directory `C:\winnt\system32\drivers\etc`. LMHOSTS is a text-file database of NetBIOS computer names and the IP addresses that are statically assigned to each of those names. Then, when the server is directed to do so, it looks up the LMHOSTS file and performs name resolution based on the entries it finds there. It's simpler than WINS but isn't as efficient or reliable. Microsoft provides a sample LMHOSTS file in the directory we just mentioned; my examples of LMHOSTS entries are shown here:

```
205.205.205.2     RICHS_BOX       #PRE
#DOM:MAIN_SERVER
205.205.205.3     NT_STATION      #PRE
```

continued

About LMHOSTS Files *(Continued)*

205.205.205.4   BRUCE"S_BOX

where:

◆ The IP address is given first, followed by the networked computer's NetBIOS name.

◆ #PRE is an identifier that ensures LMHOST entries' compatibility with some older types of networks. This allows preloading of the computer name and address into the name cache created on the server. Windows NT-only networks will simply ignore it.

◆ #DOM is an identifier telling the server that the entry on the current line is a domain controller.

If you decide to experiment with LMHOSTS, make sure WINS isn't installed on your server. Then, in the Network Control Panel, select the Protocols tab, select TCP/IP, and click Properties. When the Properties sheet appears, select the WINS Address tab. Enable the check box titled Enable LMHOSTS Lookup. Do the same for your Windows NT clients. You may also need to import the file on your server by clicking the Import button and browsing to the folder mentioned previously. After you've added your entries, the complete LMHOSTS file must also be copied to all your Windows NT Workstations that will participate on the network.

To edit your LMHOSTS file on your server, display it in its folder, right-click LMHOSTS, and select the Open With command from the shortcut menu. Then use Notepad to open and save the file. This method prevents the file's format or naming convention from being subtly changed by the file system. Then copy the file over to the same folder on your NT clients. By default the LMHOSTS file has the file extension ".SAM" for Sample file. The extension must be removed if you want to use it for name resolution on your server.

Though this method bears explanation here, you won't be using it in this book. In networks with more than a couple of clients, it's a lot of administrative busy-work. There are easier and more efficient alternatives, such as using WINS.

WINS also offers the highly useful capability of creating and importing static mappings such as the ones used in LMHOSTS files. Remote clients that use a static address can thus dial in to the WINS server and enjoy full integration to the system. If you use static addressing, particularly with a significant collection of clients, you'll need to import your LMHOSTS mappings into WINS Manager.

WINS's primary limitation is that it handles address-to-name resolution on your private, *internal* Windows network. It's Microsoft's proprietary method for a networking function that is also common on UNIX-type network operating systems.

TIP WINS *can* be used for name resolution on larger networks, but it's not a very secure system and can easily be cracked by intruders who want to get into your network. The general method for NT 4.0 is to use WINS for internal connections and DNS for larger networks and outside connections.

If someone from outside your network needs to gain access to it — through a WAN connection, or perhaps someone dialing up an Internet Web server — something else is required to make sure those users can have proper access and to maintain general network security. That's where DNS comes in.

Introducing DNS (Domain Naming Service)

In many Windows NT networks using TCP/IP, WINS and DNS are usually teamed up for network management. DNS can be an extremely complicated business. DNS, or Domain Naming Service, is new to Windows NT 4.0. It's Windows NT's next-generation name resolution service that bears some resemblance to basic NetBIOS name resolution but goes beyond it in many important ways. It's heavily used by Windows NT Servers on the Internet to provide name resolution for all the different services that the Internet provides: e-mail, ftp, news, and so on. It can handle name resolution from any computer in or out of the network on the Internet, and it doesn't employ NetBIOS. For Internet use, DNS relies on the familiar WinSock that is so commonly used online. This is why DNS and WINS are so often combined on an Windows NT Server: they form an inside-outside combination. In Windows NT networks, NetBIOS and WINS handle the inside, while WinSock with DNS are meant to handle the outside. This isn't always true. WINS can be used for connections to computers local to the WINS server by the "outside world" and outside the LAN.

Unfortunately, as noted previously, WINS is far more vulnerable to hacking. Major security issues result if the WINS server is published on the Internet, because hackers happily eat up WINS servers to which they gain access. If you set up a WINS server for outside access to your network, it can be rapidly brought to its knees by hundreds of outside connections, some of which may be unwanted. This is where firewalls are important and almost required, to keep unwanted guests from trying to access private servers. Nothing can be done about this except to use a firewall, but they can't easily be used for Internet clients unless you use static addressing and add those IPs to the *allow access* list in the router/firewall. So DNS is a good solution.

When you install DNS on your server, a special DNS Manager program appears in the Start menu, Programs/Administrative Tools menu. It's shown in Figure 3-6.

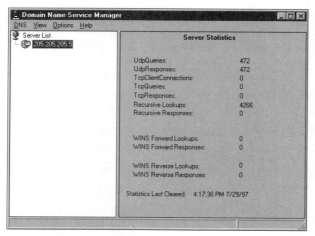

Figure 3-6: Introducing DNS Manager

In the pane on the left, the Server list displays a hierarchical list of each DNS Server on the network with its IP address. The right pane shows a list of server activities that have occurred since server startup, including WINS status queries to and from the server.

Double-clicking an IP address for a DNS Server displays the *zones* managed by the server, as seen in Figure 3-7.

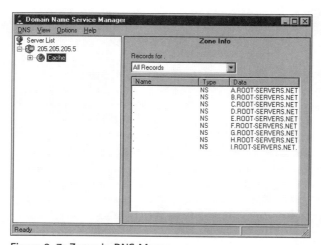

Figure 3-7: Zones in DNS Manager

On installation, DNS creates a new default zone, called *cache,* that contains the basic collection of *root servers* present on the Internet. Entries in the server list can be double-clicked down the hierarchy to open folders containing the root server listings, none of which are actually present in your network. Instead, they're reserved IP addresses (A for Address) and NetBIOS name listings (NS for Name Server) for important locations on the Internet, including InterNIC, NASA.GOV, the Army, and other agencies heavily involved in the development of the original Internet or ARPAnet. To have a quick look at the listings, click the Start button and select Find, and enter the filename **CACHE.DNS**. Then open the cache with Notepad. Within that file lie several clues about how DNS works.

The CACHE.DNS file is used by the DNS service to provide your server with the vital underpinnings for its networking TCP/IP connections to the Internet. NT Servers running as Web servers or in WANs (not just for RAS either) must have this feature enabled and undisturbed. In your server you'll also have to create a *new* zone containing your network's DNS Server name and IP address, and any other services your system provides, such as intranet or ftp. In this case, that IP address *must* be provided to you by your ISP or higher-ranking IS guy, or whatever power-that-be provides you with IPs. It's not as hard as it sounds, but you won't be getting into that in detail in this book.

If you're running a Net-isolated network and need or want to run DNS in your working network, Microsoft's sample CACHE.DNS file states that you can simply edit it and add an NS and A record for your newly installed DNS Server. A sample server entry reads as follows:

3600000 NS test_server.test_domain.

;test_server.test_domain   3600000 A 205.205.205.5

Unfortunately, every time the DNS service starts, it creates a new CACHE.DNS file that resides in the WINNT\System32\DNS folder, overwriting any previous changes. How are you supposed to make DNS recognize your server properly, as what is called the *root authoritative* server for your network?

The best solution is to create your own DNS zone, and it turns out to be quite easy to do as you'll see later. Don't delete the cache file and add something in its place. DNS Manager may not work if you do this.

When Do You Need to Run DNS?

You don't need to run DNS if your LAN is not connected to the Internet or is not part of a larger routed WAN. In general, a DNS name server is not needed on a small Windows NT Server network with a collection of clients and/or connections to legacy systems such as Novell NetWare. If your network is anything like mine (exactly two Windows NT Servers, two Windows NT Workstation clients, two Windows 95 clients, and two more Macintosh clients, plus a NetWare 3.12 server), and you want to run TCP/IP as your internal network protocol for your Windows clients, and for basic dial-up Internet access, you do not need to use DNS. You could run it anyway, and everything would be fine; however, it's a little extra work for relatively little benefit in a small, isolated network.

In a LAN with several routed segments, as is common in small- to medium-size companies, running DNS services is a good idea. And if you're planning to run an intranet on any size network, you must have it. If you plan to do this, you need to create a new primary zone (called, for example, myzone.dns), using the DNS Manager. It's a fairly simple process that's described later in this chapter.

TCP/IP Properties from the Network applet provides a special DNS tab under which you enter your basic DNS server information. Figure 3-8 shows the DNS tab.

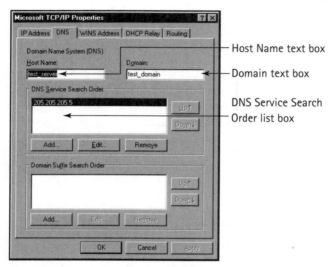

Figure 3-8: The DNS Page in TCP/IP Properties

The Host Name text box simply contains the name for the computer/server. The Domain text box can be one of two things:

◆ If your Windows NT Server is simply a Primary Domain Controller (like my servers, MAIN_SERVER and TEST_DOMAIN), you enter that PDC name there. You do this when you want to run DNS in your local domain, whether or not it's linked to the Net.

◆ If your Windows NT Server is running an Internet domain, like MYSILLYSITE.COM or something like that, with a domain name provided to you by Internet Services Inc. or your IS manager, you enter that. This is done only in Internet/intranet/extranet/ultranet (sheesh!) applications.

You must also enter the IP address for your Windows NT Server in the DNS Service Search Order list. It's simply the IP address you assigned to your server in the network; a sample address for my server is shown in Figure 3-8. Also notice the WINS Address tab in the same figure. (You'll come back to this a bit later.)

DNS is an interesting and somewhat complicated topic. The Windows NT DNS

Manager is a highly useful utility for managing and configuring your DNS services, but it's also something you should take your time with. You can't be in a complete hurry when you set up facilities like this on your server, or things are almost bound to go wrong.

Introducing DHCP (Dynamic Host Control Protocol)

DHCP, or Dynamic Host Control Protocol, is used to dynamically assign IP addresses to clients on the network, both within the LAN and for Remote Access clients. This can be a good thing, because if you have a limited collection of IP addresses to work with (a 16- or 32-address subnet) and you have to use them for a network that has twice as many clients, you must use DHCP to ensure that all your clients have fair access to the network. (Many clients could be set up with NetBEUI while some of your others use TCP/IP, which is easy to arrange, but that's a different story.)

The biggest benefit by far of using DHCP is that you don't have to perform manual TCP/IP configurations on your network clients. This is great for laptops and mobile clients, even those that move around between subnets or routed network segments, because they can automatically configure again for another IP address when they connect elsewhere. (Assuming, of course, that another DHCP server is present, or a DHCP Relay Agent service is being used from the original DHCP server across one or more routers. That service is also provided in the Services tab and has a setting tab in TCP/IP Properties. Also, routers in the company network must support DHCP or this will not work.) In practice, this results in far fewer headaches for clients.

Many RAS servers in smaller TCP/IP networks, which I discuss in Chapter 9, rely on a static set of IP addresses that can be assigned to clients as they log on to the network or dial in from the field, instead of using DHCP. But DHCP can work just as well or better. Later I discuss how to take both approaches.

When you install DHCP (using the typical Control Panel, Network, Services tab), another special application called DHCP Manager is installed into your server. It appears as shown in Figure 3-9.

Scope menu

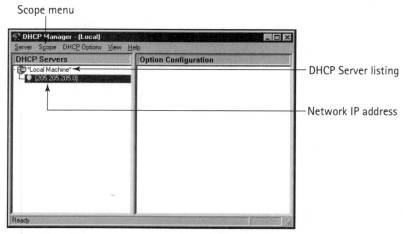

— DHCP Server listing

— Network IP address

Figure 3-9: The DHCP Manager

The key element in DHCP is a *scope*. For DHCP to work in the server, you must define a set of available IP addresses (a subnet, or whatever) for use as a DHCP scope. Multiple scopes can be created. Addresses or subnets of the subnet can be *excluded* within that scope. You can also reserve specific IP addresses for particular client systems by the clients' MAC address and some basic identification information. When a client uses an IP address from a DHCP scope for their connection, that is called an *active lease*. Figure 3-10 shows an example of a server that has handed out a couple of active-lease IP addresses to clients.

Figure 3-10: Active IP Address Leases in DHCP Manager

Don't worry too much about thse alien-sounding concepts. You'll put these ideas into practice later in this chapter and their execution is actually simple, consistent, and approachable.

About MAC Addresses

MAC addresses have nothing to do with the Macintosh computer. MAC addresses are the 12-digit hexadecimal numeric address that is hard-wired into every network card when they're manufactured. You'll run into them often enough in network operating systems like NT and NetWare to make it worthwhile to know about them. They are *not* the same as an IP address. A good way to find out the MAC address for any system participating on the network is to go to that system (or have the user do so) and type in the command NET CONFIG WKSTA in an NT Command Prompt window. (This applies only to NT Workstation or Server.) When you do so, you'll see the following screen:

```
Command Prompt                                                  _ □ ×
Microsoft(R) Windows NT(TM)
(C) Copyright 1985-1996 Microsoft Corp.

C:\>net config wksta
Computer name                          \\TEST_SERVER
User name                              Administrator

Workstation active on                  NetBT_NE20001 (00001B4E4E8C)
Software version                       Windows NT 4.0

Workstation domain                     TEST_DOMAIN
Logon domain                           TEST_DOMAIN

COM Open Timeout (sec)                  3600
COM Send Count (byte)                  16
COM Send Timeout (msec)                250
The command completed successfully.

C:\>_
```

Checking a Computer's MAC Address

The third line of text in the display shows what you're looking for. In the figure, the MAC address is enclosed in parentheses and reads 00001B4E4E8C. Every network card on your LAN has a number like this. No two cards are the same. How do we know this? Because the pantheon of network gods decreed it. (You can also use the NBTSTAT -a [Computer name here] command from any connected location to check the MAC address for any system on the network.)

For more discussion on using Windows NT's command prompt to check TCP/IP connections, please see the section in this chapter titled "Checking Your Connections Using the Command Prompt." It's a highly useful troubleshooting tool that really helps you get your hands on what's going on in your TCP/IP network.

On the client end, Windows NT Workstations become DHCP clients through a simple process. It's just a matter of selecting an option in TCP/IP Properties' IP Address tab.

DHCP has its own set of complexities beyond the basic features that I've just described. A long list of options are provided for installed DHCP scopes that affect how DHCP clients behave when they lease IP addresses. In some cases, you'll never have to mess with them (they can be examined by selecting a scope, pulling down the DHCP Options menu and selecting Scope, for a single scope, or Global for all scopes on the server). Most of the time, the option defaults in DHCP are fine for smaller networks. But when you get into multiple-server TCP/IP networking, you'll have to pay attention to some key DHCP options, which are described a bit later.

As it stands, you can't count on DHCP requests to be routable between network segments on the LAN. If your DHCP server isn't on the same network segment as a client making a DHCP request, the server may never detect the client's requests for an IP address assignment. Some routers are compatible with DHCP, as I've mentioned, but many aren't. NT Server provides a DHCP Relay Agent service that helps deal with this problem. Some DHCP Scope options also help you cut down on broadcast traffic in your LAN, which I'll describe later.

Another difficulty with DHCP is that it doesn't provide fault tolerance. If you have two DHCP servers, they don't coordinate with each other and can have Scope address conflicts as a result. If you have more than one DHCP server on your network, make sure to define Scopes with address ranges that don't conflict with each other. By doing this, you also enable a "backup" mechanism that ensures at least some clients will still receive address assignments if one of the servers goes down.

DHCP is a black art within networking. Windows NT 4.0 makes this powerful and complex feature startlingly approachable. Many network operating systems that lack a native DHCP capability force you to enter long strings of hexadecimal code just to configure a basic DHCP function. With NT, this is a thing of the past.

The main alternative to DHCP, as I've mentioned, is using a pool of static addresses and assigning them to clients from the server as they connect. I prefer to do this first, at least to test the services I already have and to make sure of a working connection. DHCP's online Help actually provides a lot of useful information about its functions and terminology, and does a good job building from introductory areas up to advanced information.

Installing WINS on Windows NT Server

At this point you begin setting up your various TCP/IP-related services. The assumption here is that you've already installed the TCP/IP networking protocol as part of your Windows NT installation. Continue here by installing and setting up WINS.

Installing Windows Internet Naming Service is a simple process. Setting it up properly on the server for basic use requires a few more steps. Once you're done, you'll be ready to start connecting your clients. Follow these steps:

1. Open the Control Panel and double-click Network.

2. Select the Services tab.

3. Click the Add button and select Windows Internet Naming Services from the list. You're prompted to give the location of the files, and when it's done, you're prompted to restart the system.

4. After installing the basic WINS service, open the Network applet again from the Control Panel.

5. Click the Protocols tab.

6. Select TCP/IP and click the Properties button. The TCP/IP Properties sheet appears.

7. Click the WINS Address tab. It appears as shown in Figure 3-11.

LMOSTS check box may be enabled by default

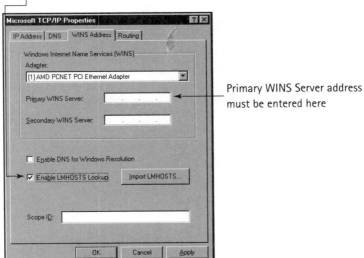

Primary WINS Server address must be entered here

Figure 3–11: Setting Up WINS Services under TCP/IP Properties

8. Enter the Primary WINS Server address. What is it? That's your server's IP address. It's that simple. For example, if your server's IP address for the network adapter is 205.205.205.5, then that's also your Primary WINS server address. (Eventually, in a larger network, you will have other WINS servers. A Secondary WINS address can be provided here if necessary.)

9. Make sure the Enable LMHOSTS Lookup check box is disabled. Using WINS, you don't need to use the LMHOSTS file. (It may be enabled by default as seen in Figure 3-11. If so, clear it.) Also, clear the Enable DNS for Windows Resolution check box if it's enabled (you won't need that yet for the client).

10. Click OK and click Close. You're prompted for another of NT's ubiquitous restarts.

That's it for WINS setup for now. Of course, you could spend time working with the WINS Manager program and its Address Mapping features, but it isn't necessary if you just want to test a successful connection.

The basic server-side WINS setup phase is done. Windows NT Workstation clients can now connect. But first they must be set up properly to do so, which is what you do next.

More on WINS Manager

WINS Manager is an important program for more advanced uses, such as enabling and executing WINS database replication from a Primary WINS Server to a Secondary WINS Server. The process is executed using the concept of Push-Pull partners. You can use an NT server, such as a Backup Domain Controller, as a Backup WINS server for your network in case things go down. Then your clients can still communicate to the server and maintain their presence on the network if the main WINS server goes down. But WINS servers don't automatically replicate, which is why the *Push-Pull* process is necessary. The WINS Manager allows you to set up this process and execute it. Appendix A of this book touches on this topic in more detail.

Configuring Client LAN Connections Using TCP/IP

When you set up Windows NT clients to connect to a WINS server, I'd like to make a couple recommendations:

◆ Start clients from scratch if possible. When I build a Windows NT client that I know is going to be connecting to a TCP/IP server using WINS and any other related services, I like to build it from scratch and set it up as I so painstakingly described earlier in this chapter. Then I install the other features and productivity applications. In many cases, this may not be possible with office computers.

◆ If you're connecting to a Windows NT domain (our default in this book), the name of your client computer should have an account on the Domain controller through Server Manager. If it doesn't, it isn't a big deal. When you've just finished setting up a new Windows NT Workstation system, the Workstation operating system will allow you to enter the domain name for the PDC in your network. Then it immediately logs on and connects using the network to register on the domain that way. (RAS connections, discussed in Chapter 9, work somewhat differently.)

Setting up the client is quite easy. Make sure your system's LAN card is properly installed and that it has the TCP/IP protocol installed as well. Bear in mind that the default is that our Windows NT Workstation client is logging on to an Windows NT domain server (or Primary Domain Controller).

Also, when you install TCP/IP on the client, make sure you have a proper IP address assigned to the computer, along with a default gateway and subnet mask value. The Default Gateway value is the same as that for the server you're connecting to; in other words, if the Default Gateway value on the server is 205.205.205.1, then that's the gateway value that should be placed in the client. Figure 3-12 shows an example for one of my clients.

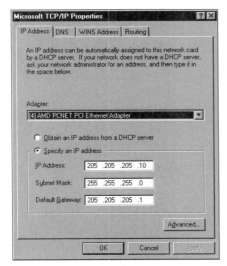

Figure 3-12: Assigning IP Values to a TCP/IP Client

With this in mind, here's how to set up a Windows NT Workstation client to connect to a WINS server:

1. On the Windows NT client, open (or have the user open) the Network applet in Control Panel.

2. Click the Protocols tab.

3. Select TCP/IP and click Properties. The TCP/IP Properties sheet appears.

4. Click the WINS Address tab. Then enter the IP address for the Windows NT Server running the WINS service. Make sure both check boxes are disabled on the page. Click OK to close TCP/IP Properties.

5. In the Network applet's Identification tab, click the Change button. The Identification Changes dialog box appears, as shown in Figure 3-13.

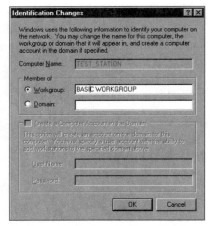

Figure 3-13: Setting Up Your Client's Identification for Network Logon

6. Click the mouse in the Domain text box and enter the name of the Windows NT domain to which your system is a client.

7. Select the Create a Computer Account in the Domain check box.

8. Enter the user name and password. On the first connection, the name of the user account must have the power to add workstation accounts to the domain server, such as the Administrator. (On the second logon, you'll use your normal assigned name and password.) The final results should resemble Figure 3-14.

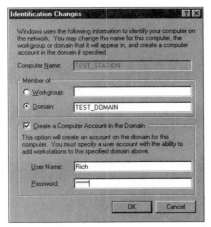

Figure 3-14: Setting Up the Initial
Logon to the Domain Server

9. Click OK to return to the Network applet. After a moment, a dialog box appears: "Welcome to Domain *Domain name.*" It's shown in Figure 3-15.

Figure 3-15: This Is What You Should See When You Set Up a TCP/IP-Based Domain Client

10. Click Close to close the Network applet, and restart your system.

    Now it's time to perform the actual network connection. This is a big moment.

11. Press Ctrl+Alt+Delete to begin the logon process.

12. Type in your name and password. You may also have to select the domain from its drop-down list. Press Enter.

13. At this point, your computer should be able to open the server in Network Neighborhood and browse through any resources shared from the server.

As noted, an administrative-level password must also be used to create the computer's account. Once that's finished and the connection has been verified, you can disconnect and then log on to the computer as a different user. When the Logon Information screen appears, enter the desired user name and password for the client computer and make sure the correct domain is also listed.

At this point, you've done the following:

♦ Configured TCP/IP on the server and placed the server IP addresses where they need to be in the various Properties sheets and dialog boxes

♦ Set up a basic WINS service on the Windows NT Server and applied the server's IP address to the needed places on the server

♦ Configured TCP/IP on the network client to connect to the WINS server, using a static IP address

♦ Connected the NT Client, registered on the domain, and browsed Network Neighborhood

Many Windows NT Server users, especially in small networks, do not need to go any further. You now have functional TCP/IP on your network. This recipe is for a small network and will not necessarily be the solution for a company with branch offices and routed connections. But if you're taking Windows NT's TCP/IP capabilities out for a spin and want to build something that works for you right away, this is a good way to go. Windows NT provides other capabilities that can ease administration and increase the versatility of your network. Two key service installations are described in the rest of this section: DNS and DHCP.

Installing and Configuring DNS on Windows NT Server

Although DNS is a bit more complicated in practice than WINS, it's still simple to install and presents little more difficulty in its setup on the server. As noted earlier, DNS isn't needed on a small, isolated NT Server-based network unless you plan to run an intranet. On an intranet, DNS is one of the required support services. That's because DNS provides name resolution capabilities for any network client that isn't part of the central LAN, and for many other services related to the Internet and internal intranets. As WINS is often used to handled name resolution for clients within the LAN, DNS handles it for clients outside the network, frequently for Winsock applications. Although your immediate applications may not require it, making provision for DNS in your network is the single most important thing you can do to allow for future growth with minimal trouble. Follow these steps:

1. Open the Control Panel and double-click Network.

2. Select the Services tab.

3. Click the Add button and select Microsoft DNS Server from the list. You're prompted to give the location of the files. When it's done, you're prompted to restart the system.

4. After installing the basic DNS service, open the Network applet again from the Control Panel.

5. Click the Protocols tab.

6. Select TCP/IP and click the Properties button. The TCP/IP Properties sheet appears.

7. Click the WINS Address tab.

8. Enable the Use DNS for Windows Resolution check box.

9. Click the DNS tab.

10. Type in the complete host name for the DNS server. It's the same as the Windows NT server's NetBIOS name, its actual computer name.

11. Enter the domain name of the Primary Domain Controller. (This could also be the domain name for your company, but that's for a different application.)

12. Click Add, type in the IP address for the server running DNS, and click Add. It appears, as shown in Figure 3-16 (your values will be different).

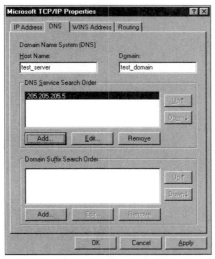

Figure 3-16: Setting Up DNS Services under TCP/IP Properties

13. Click OK, click Close to commit the changes, and restart the system.

That's the basic setup for Microsoft DNS. Nothing to it. There's a bit more to do, however, if you plan to run DNS in a network and expect to grow into a larger network or an intranet. To allow for that growth ahead of time, you must create a new DNS zone. This enables you to set your NT Server as the authoritative root domain for your network, minimizing the growing pains later. Follow these steps:

1. From the Start menu, select Programs, and then Administrative Tools, and then DNS Manager.

2. In the left pane, double-click the Server List icon. An IP address appears. It's the IP address for the DNS server.

3. Double-click the IP address. The Cache icon appears.

4. Double-click the Cache icon. Two folders appear: arpa and NET. Double-click the NET folder. The results should appear, as shown in Figure 3-17.

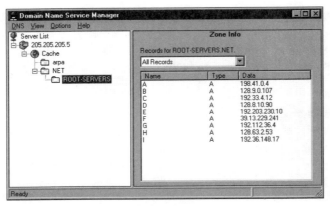

Figure 3-17: Browsing DNS Manager

This is the list of IP addresses for the cached Internet root servers in the CACHE.DNS file. It's the contents of the "cache" zone that is automatically created by Windows NT when you install DNS. Now you'll add your own primary zone for your network.

5. Select the IP address at the top of the DNS server list. This should be the address of your server.

6. *Right-click* the server IP address and select New Zone. A simple Creating New Zone wizard appears.

7. Select the Primary Zone Type option and click Next.

8. Enter the name for your new zone. A Zone File name is automatically created in the second field. Click Next.

9. Finally, click Finish. The results will resemble Figure 3-18.

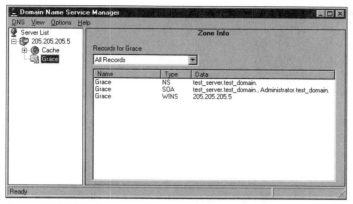

Figure 3-18: Defining Your New Primary Zone for DNS

The DNS application automatically reads in the correct IP address and the Name Server information that you entered into the TCP/IP Properties' DNS tab. In Figure 3-18, the NS record is the Name Server in its full NetBIOS name. The SOA record (Start of Authority) shows the primary source of information about the DNS domain on the network and also lists the network's e-mail address for the administrator in charge of the DNS. (In this case, it's `Administrator. test_domain`.)

When you take a look at the Cache zone (the zone automatically created by DNS when you install it), you'll also find that your own new DNS server is added to that Cache name server list after you create your new zone.

Very important: On the client side, add the Primary DNS server's IP address to the TPC/IP Properties' DNS tab. Also, in the TCP/IP Properties' WINS Address tab, enable the Enable DNS for Windows Resolution tab, to ensure full cooperation between DNS and WINS. Then DNS will provide NetBIOS name resolution for business clients connecting to your network from a WAN. Your connection will then lock in to the WINS/DNS server without a hitch.

You need do nothing else with DNS Manager for the present. DNS Server configuration for your system is essentially complete, until new and larger applications arise that are beyond the purview of this book.

The final phase in your TCP/IP integration is to configure DHCP. Remember the set of static addresses you used in RAS for client assignments? DHCP takes its place. On Windows NT, DHCP is a thing of beauty.

Installing and Configuring DHCP on Windows NT Server

Instead of using the fairly crude method of assigning static addresses to clients through RAS, or assigning a specific IP address to each and every client on your network, you can do something more versatile and graceful: employ DHCP for dynamic IP address assignment. As previously noted, this has the compelling advantage of accommodating clients without having to muck around with their TCP/IP settings.

On the NT Workstation client, just select a check box in TCP/IP Properties, and in Dial-Up Networking, and it is ready to go. (During setup you're even asked the question "Do you want to use DHCP?" Selecting Yes is all you need to do.) Server setup, including defining the necessary Scope for dynamic address sharing, is equally simple. When you're setting up your TCP/IP connections with Remote Access, using static addresses is a good way to test your setup. Once you've layered in your other services and made sure they work properly, jettisoning static addressing and using DHCP is the last step to a fully integrated small TCP/IP network.

A DHCP Scope is a collection of client computers that run the DHCP client service, running across a custom subnet mask that must also be defined within DHCP Manager when you create the scope. (You don't use the same subnet mask that is originally defined on the server when you install TCP/IP. Also, though DHCP Manager is supposed to define a suggested subnet mask for you automatically when you define your Scope, in practice you'll have to enter the correct one.) In a sense, defining a DHCP scope simulates the process of using a router to set up a subnet.

DHCP also provides a long list of options for each address scope you create. You can define a set of options that are global, which apply to all scopes created in the server. Or you can simply opt to set options for each individual scope. You'll explore that feature a bit later.

You must also name your scope.

Installing DHCP is a matter of clicking the usual Control Panel, Network, Services, and Add button. Select Microsoft DHCP Server and click OK. Then, in the TCP/IP Properties sheet's IP Address tab *on the server*, you'll notice that the Obtain an IP Address from a DHCP Server option is ghosted. You're using a hard-wired IP address for your server, which is required in any case. DHCP addresses can be handed out only to clients on the LAN and online through Remote Access.

Setting up a new DHCP Scope is fairly simple. Follow these steps:

1. After rebooting from the DHCP installation, select DHCP Manager from the Start menu, and then Programs, and then Administrative Tools.

2. Select the "Local Machine" listing in the left-hand pane.

3. From the Scope menu, select Create. The Create Scope dialog box appears, as shown in Figure 3-19.

Start, End, and
Subnet Mask addresses

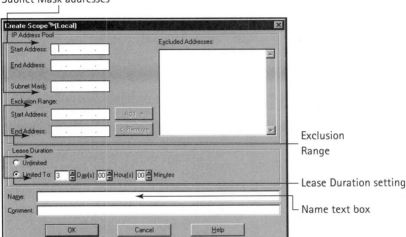

Figure 3-19: Defining Your New Scope for DHCP

4. Enter the Start Address for your new scope. It should fall within the boundaries of your server's original subnet, but you can issue any range of addresses that is desirable. Bear in mind that the scope must fit within the boundaries of the correct subnet mask value, or you'll receive a "Specific range overlaps with an already existing range or is invalid" message.

5. Enter the End Address for the new scope.

6. Type the correct subnet mask for your server's original subnet (in TCP/IP Properties) in the subnet mask field. (You're creating your own subnet in DHCP Manager; if you're setting up a scope of 16 IP addresses, the subnet mask you should enter 255.255.255.240, and so on.)

7. You can also set the Lease Duration for your scope to Unlimited or to a value in Days, Hours, and Minutes. Choose Unlimited for your present example (you can always change it later).

   Note that subsets of your scope can be excluded, using the Exclusion Range feature with its Start and End Address values. Excluded addresses must be encompassed within the scope.

8. Type in a preferred name for your scope of up to 128 characters. (If you expect to run more than one scope in your server over time, you'll want to plan your scope names accordingly.) The finished results should resemble Figure 3-20.

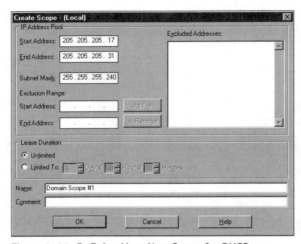

Figure 3-20: Defining Your New Scope for DHCP

9. Click OK to commit the new scope.

You'll receive a message, as shown in Figure 3-21.

Figure 3-21: Do Not Activate Your Scope Yet!

10. Click No. First, you must set your scope options.

Notice in Figure 3-23 that the scope of addresses has a range of 205.205.205.17 to 205.205.205.31. The scope address itself will occupy the IP address at the beginning of the subnet, which is 205.205.205.16, as shown in Figure 3-22.

Defining DHCP Scope Options and Enabling DHCP Address Sharing

After your scope is defined, you have a series of options that can be defined to ensure that DHCP clients are fully and properly configured across the network, no matter where they're connecting from. Scope options communicate connection information to every client that connects to the server using that scope. Several dozen different options are provided, but most are relatively unimportant. Many DHCP option values are already optimized for best performance under Windows and should not be changed. The five options you'll work with in this section are those most commonly changed in DHCP setup.

With the new, inactivated scope selected in DHCP Manager, select the DHCP Options menu and select Scope. The Scope dialog box appears, as shown in Figure 3-22.

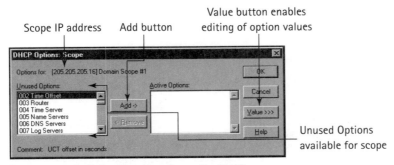

Figure 3-22: Defining Your New Scope for DHCP

In the Unused Options scroll box, each option is assigned a three-digit number from between 002 to 068. Five key options provide DHCP setup information to logged-on clients:

003   Router

        The administrator provides the IP address for the default gateway on the server.

006   DNS Servers

        The administrator lists up to three separate DNS servers on the network (required only if the network is running DNS server).

015   Domain Name

Furnishes the DNS domain name for the connected client (used only if a DNS server is present on the network)

044   WINS/NBNS Servers

Provide the IP address for the Name Resolution server (NBNS stands for NetBIOS Name Server)

046   WINS/NBT Node Type

This setting determines how the client resolves computer names. Typically, you have four node value choices: H-node (0x8), M-node (0x4), P-node (0x2), and B-node (0x1). The best value for most applications is 0x8, because it enables the client to attempt contacting the WINS server for name resolution and then using broadcasting for name resolution if the WINS server isn't available for some reason.

Here's how to set your local DHCP scope options and then activate it for use on the network:

1. Select your newly created scope in DHCP Manager.

2. From the DHCP Options menu, select Scope.

3. In the Unused Options list, select 003 Router and click Add. The option appears in the Active Options list. This is where you add the IP address for the server's default gateway.

4. Click Value. The dialog box expands to add another feature, as shown in Figure 3-23.

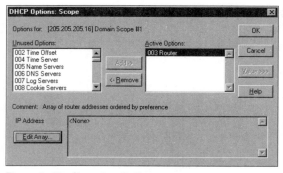

Figure 3-23: Changing Options

5. Click the Edit Array button. The IP Address Array Editor appears.

6. Enter the IP address for the server's default gateway and click Add in the Array Editor.

7. Click OK. The new address appears in the dialog box.

8. In the Unused Options list, select 006 DNS Servers and click Add.

9. Click the Edit Array button. The IP Address Array Editor reappears, this time for adding the DNS server listing.

10. Type in the IP address for the DNS server in your network and click Add to establish the value.

If you don't know the exact IP address for the DNS server, you can also type in the server's name in the Server Name field and click the Resolve button. This automatically places the server's IP address in the correct field. Then click Add to install it.

11. Click OK to set the value in the scope, and click OK to see the results in DHCP Manager. Figure 3-24 shows the results.

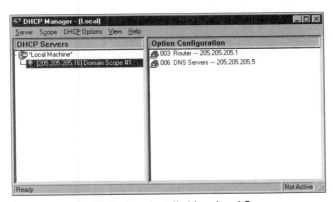

Figure 3-24: DHCP Options Installed in a Local Scope

Now, you'll add the other three options and activate the scope.

12. From the DHCP Options menu, select Scope.

13. In the Unused Options list, select 015 Domain Name and click Add, and then click Value. A new String field appears, where you enter the domain name for the Primary Domain Controller in your network. (In my example system, it's test_domain. Yours will be different.) If you're participating in a larger network with multiple domains, you may want to define this value for each scope instead of globally; the default in this section is that you're creating a single local scope for use in a relatively small network.

14. In the Unused Options list, select 044 WINS/NBNS Servers and click Add. You will be warned to set Option 46 as well.

15. Click OK to remove the warning, and click Value to set the value for the WINS server.

16. Click Edit Array to change the WINS/NBNS Server IP address, and the IP Address Array Editor reappears. Enter the address in the New IP Address field and click Add. Click OK to close the dialog box.

17. Finally, select 046 WINS/NBT Node Type and click Add, and then click Value. Figure 3-25 shows the Options window after you do this.

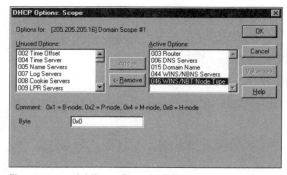

Figure 3-25: Adding a Domain Server Name to a DHCP Domain Name Listing

18. In the Byte field, enter the value 0x8 and click OK to commit all your Option changes. Figure 3-26 shows the final results, but bear in mind that your address values will be different.

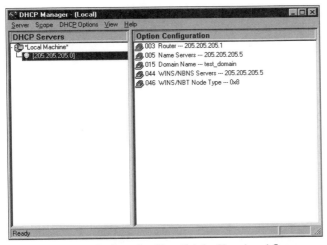

Figure 3-26: Key Options Are Now Set for Your Local Scope

19. As your final step, from the Scope menu select Activate (with the new local scope selected as shown in Figure 3-26). Close the DHCP Manager.

The five DHCP options you've defined cover all the key ones that you'll normally work with. Most of the others are customarily ignored because Windows NT DHCP clients aren't directly compatible with them. Some of the other options can be used for configuring UNIX DHCP clients, but that topic is beyond the scope of this book. The whole section you've just gone through is the most complicated process in the entire book. The Windows NT TCP/IP configuration features are actually quite approachable compared to many operating systems, but there are still a significant number of configuration methods to follow to create a successful, seamless connection, as you've seen.

Configuring a Windows NT Client for WINS/DNS/DHCP Connections

The final (and much simpler) step is to configure your Windows NT Workstation client to communicate with the WINS/DNS/DHCP server. Follow these steps:

1. On the Windows NT client, open (or have the user open) the Network applet in Control Panel.

2. Click the Protocols tab.

3. Select TCP/IP and click Properties. The TCP/IP Properties sheet appears, displaying the IP Address tab.

4. In the IP Address tab, select the option Obtain an IP Address from a DHCP server.

5. Click the DNS tab. In the Host Name field, type in the name of the client computer. Then, in the Domain field, type in the name of the Primary Domain Controller.

6. Click the Add button, enter the IP address for the DNS server (which should be the address for the Primary Domain Controller), and click Add again. If your network has another DNS server, you can also add its IP address. Figure 3-27 shows a sample result.

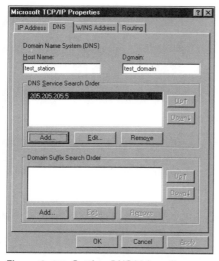

Figure 3-27: Setting DNS Values for a LAN Client (NT Workstation)

7. Click the WINS Address tab. The IP address for the NT Server that's running the WINS service should already be present.

8. Select the Enable DNS for Windows Resolution check box and click OK. You're finished with basic client configuration.

9. Click Close to close the Network applet and restart the client.

When the system comes back, log on using your normal user name and password. You'll be able to browse Network Neighborhood and any shared resources made available to you there.

That concludes the applied TCP/IP networking exercises. You now have a working knowledge of Windows NT's TCP/IP networking capabilities. Now you can work with TCP/IP features with confidence and consistency. As a vital finishing touch, please read through the last section, which provides you with a valuable networking troubleshooting tool: the Windows NT Command line.

Checking Your Connections Using the Command Prompt

Even when you understand how to apply the NT TCP/IP networking capabilities, your basic skills won't be complete without some troubleshooting techniques. The fact is, GUI-based networking tools can take you a long way but don't always provide the entire picture. Windows NT provides a powerful command prompt that bears a close resemblance to good old MS-DOS but goes far beyond the old days. In Windows NT, the command prompt is fully integrated with the operating system's complex networking capabilities. You can locate it by simply clicking the Start button, selecting Programs, and then Command Prompt.

Windows NT's command prompt offers the following commands (and quite a bit more than I can list here) for exhaustive network troubleshooting and testing:

- **PING:** For testing IP connections by sending signals between systems

- **NETSTAT:** For listing active connections on the network and displaying TCP/IP statistics

- **NBTSTAT:** For checking NetBIOS name resolution

- **NET CONFIG:** For checking basic connection information on a client or server

- **TRACERT:** For tracing TCP/IP connections through routers from end to end

- **IPCONFIG:** For checking the IP address configuration of your local system

Each command has its own permutations. Once you have a basic grasp of TCP/IP networking, none of them are difficult to understand, and they're extremely handy for checking bugs in your TCP/IP configuration.

Using the Ping Command

Ping is a simple but highly powerful command that lets you verify whether you have a successful TCP/IP connection across your network. It works invisibly no matter what kind of physical connection you have — Ethernet, phone line, or something else.

The basic syntax for Ping is

```
PING [IP address or NetBIOS name]
```

or

```
PING 205.205.205.5
PING test_server
```

The IP address shown is just an example. With the Ping command, you can sub-stitute the desired computer's IP address or name, or a Fully Qualified Domain Name (FQDN), and receive the same result. If both commands (address and name) work, you're 99 percent certain of having a good connection.

Typical results for a Ping command are shown in Figure 3-28.

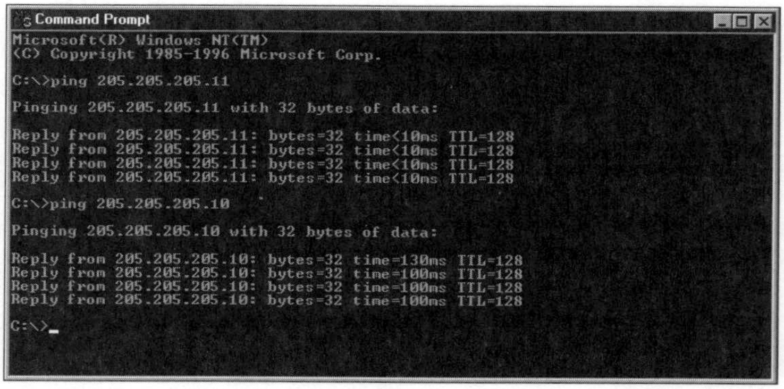

Figure 3-28: Pinging IP Addresses

What does this mean? A successful Ping requests a 32-byte packet back from the called address or computer. The process is repeated four times. When the packet is sent, the Ping command measures the response time, which is defined in mil-liseconds (ms). Figure 3-28 shows a Ping command (ping 205.205.205.10) that gets a response time measured at around 100 milliseconds, or a tenth of a second. That's a relatively slow response time, indicating that the system on the other end has a low-speed connection, most likely a phone line.

When you see a series of lines like this:

```
Reply from 205.205.205.11: bytes=32 time<10 ms TTL=128
```

it indicates either that the client you're pinging is on a high-speed connection (T1, perhaps) in the local LAN, or that you are pinging the local system.

If you are having problems with a TCP/IP network connection of any type (LAN, RAS, or whatever), the Ping command allows you to exercise a fundamental level of troubleshooting. For example, you'll often find that you can issue a Ping [IP Address] command and get a successful response formatted like the Reply line above, but when you try the same thing with the *computer name* that's associated with that IP address, such as:

```
PING test_server
```

you may receive a "Bad IP Address TEST_SERVER" error.

When this happens, it's a dead giveaway that NetBIOS name resolution is not occurring, which probably means that WINS isn't working on the server. Other possibilities are that the server or client doesn't have an updated LMHOSTS file, or that DNS name resolution isn't taking place if the other system is dialing from a completely different network over the Internet. It's very simple but indicates the most common problem in TCP/IP connectivity.

Using Netstat and Nbtstat

Netstat and nbtstat are more complex and provide more information than Ping. Without getting too exhaustive here at the end of this long chapter, both of these commands should be an important part of your troubleshooting and testing arsenal.

NBTSTAT allows you to do the following things:

◆ Display the NetBIOS name table (all the NetBIOS names the computer resolves during operation, through WINS or some other method) and the Mac address

◆ Display the number of NetBIOS names resolved by the Name Server (which basically means the number of clients successfully connected to the server, and indicates whether your clients are actually communicating with it properly)

◆ Show the NetBIOS Connection Table.

Figure 3-29 shows typical results on a small network for an NBTSTAT -A command directed to the server from a client.

```
Command Prompt                                                    _ □ ×
               statistics.

C:\>nbtstat -a test_server

        NetBIOS Remote Machine Name Table

     Name            Type          Status
──────────────────────────────────────────────
TEST_SERVER      <20>  UNIQUE     Registered
TEST_SERVER      <00>  UNIQUE     Registered
TEST_DOMAIN      <00>  GROUP      Registered
TEST_DOMAIN      <1C>  GROUP      Registered
TEST_DOMAIN      <1B>  UNIQUE     Registered
TEST_SERVER      <03>  UNIQUE     Registered
TEST_DOMAIN      <1E>  GROUP      Registered
ADMINISTRATOR    <03>  UNIQUE     Registered
TEST_DOMAIN      <1D>  UNIQUE     Registered
TEST_SERVER      <06>  UNIQUE     Registered
..__MSBROWSE__.  <01>  GROUP      Registered

MAC Address = 00-00-1B-4E-4E-8C

C:\>_
```

Figure 3-29: Checking NetBIOS Server Name Tables with NBTSTAT

Please note how you must specify both a command option (-a, -c, -s, -n, -r) and in some cases a computer name or IP address. This is another way of checking to see if you have proper name resolution or if the system even has any connection at all. For example, if you issue a sample command (commands are not case-sensitive) like the following:

```
NBTSTAT -A 205.205.205.10
```

and you receive this error:

```
Host not found
```

then the networked computer is not successfully connected and even Ping commands won't work. If you substituted the NetBIOS computer name (basically, just the computer name originally assigned to it) in the command:

```
NBTSTAT -A test_server
```

and you received the same error, try Pinging, or issuing the same command with the IP address. Sometimes a system will be connected with low-level TCP/IP, but its name isn't resolved on the server.

To check on NetBIOS name resolution for your WINS server, type in the following command:

```
NBTSTAT -r
```

In Figure 3-30, no systems are resolved by broadcasting requests, because both clients in my network correctly detected the WINS name server and had their NetBIOS names resolved to IP addresses (indicated by the line "Resolved by Name

Server = 2"). Note the lowercase "r" in the command. An uppercase "R" has a different effect in the command; it purges the remote cache name table and reloads it from disk.

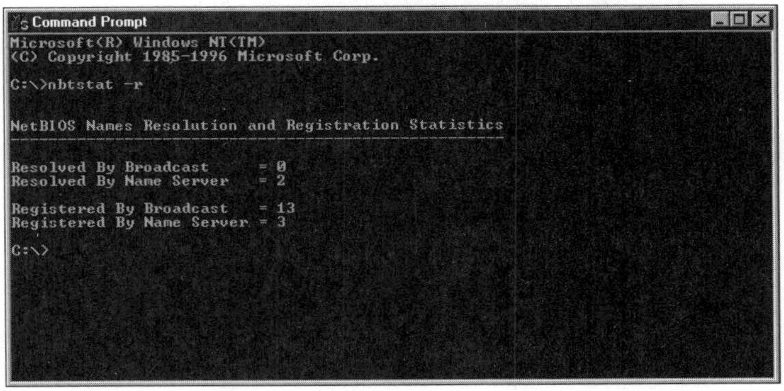

Figure 3-30: Checking NetBIOS Server Name Tables with **NBTSTAT**

Finally, to get a quick list of all the systems that are connected to the server, you can look at the NetBIOS name table using an NBTSTAT -S command.

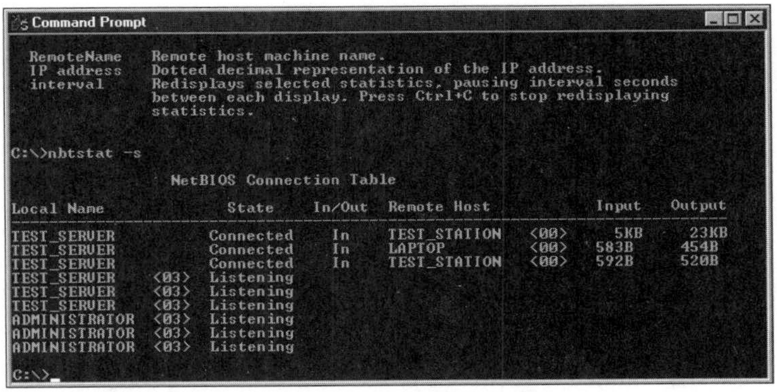

Figure 3-31: Checking the NetBIOS Connection Table

Netstat's primary job is to locate and list all the active connections on your network. Figure 3-32 shows an example for a simple netstat command.

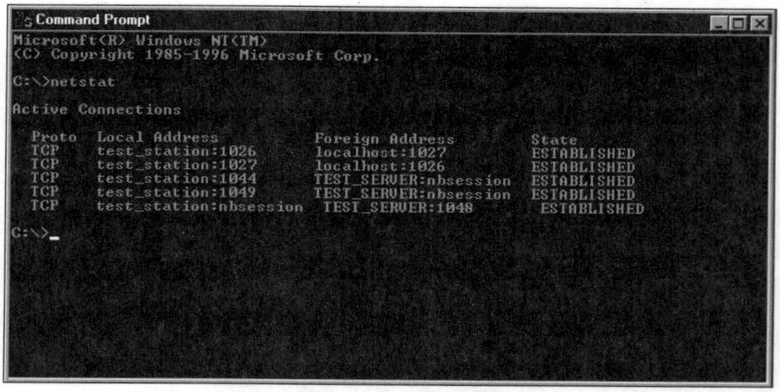

Figure 3-32: Checking Active Connections with Netstat

As you can see, netstat lists connections in terms of each system's NetBIOS computer name. Every TCP/IP connection between clients and the server is listed. By typing NETSTAT -N, you can display connections by IP address instead.

The best thing to do with Windows NT's DOS-based networking commands is to play with them. Whenever you need to have your memory refreshed about a particular command option, simply type the basic command, followed by a question mark, as in

```
NBTSTAT ?
NETSTAT ?
```

You receive a comprehensive listing of each command's wildcards and what they execute. As an example, if you type the command NETSTAT -E -S, you'll receive a huge list of the TCP/IP connection statistics in the active network.

Using the Net Command

NET is a command that gathers a huge collection of options under its innocuous syntax. You can use the Net command to add and delete network clients (NET ADD), pause and continue network services (such as WINS and DNS) with NET PAUSE and NET CONTINUE, manage shared files (NET FILE), display a list of current network sessions or disconnect a session (NET SESSION), and to perform many other functions. In fact, 22 different versions of the Net command can be used in an NT command prompt. An entire chapter could be devoted to the use of the Net command.

The quickest way to gain an overview of the options provided with the Net command is to enter NET ?. A long list of command extensions is displayed. The Net command replicates many of the same TCP/IP networking functions provided in the Windows NT GUI-based utilities. For example, if you wanted to pause the WINS service for any reason, such as testing, you issue the following:

NET PAUSE WINS

and the WINS service is stopped on the server. (Don't do this in a working network unless you want a lot of upset users!) Chapter 13 descibes the use of the Net command in greater depth.

Using the IPCONFIG Command

IPCONFIG is a highly useful reference command. As noted previously, it allows you to check the IP addressing configuration for your system. It's quite simple to use: Just type **IPCONFIG** at the command prompt to view a brief listing of the IP addresses assigned to the installed network adapters.

A better option is to type **IPCONFIG /ALL.** You receive a complete listing of all the IP address settings on your system, including Primary and Secondary WINS Servers, DNS servers, and the status of IP routing, WINS proxies, and other features in your system.

Windows 95 Client Connections Using TCP/IP

Windows 95 clients provide a set of TCP/IP properties that closely resemble those for Windows NT. When you install the TCP/IP protocol in a Win95 client, it's automatically bound to whatever network/dial-up adapters you have installed in the system. Then open up the Network applet in Control Panel, select the TCP/IP binding for the desired network adapter, and click the Properties button. A multitabbed properties sheet appears, as shown in Figure 3-33.

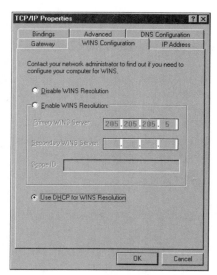

Figure 3-33: The Windows 95's TCP/IP
Properties Sheet

As an example, Figure 3-33 shows the WINS Configuration tab. You can set the
IP address for the WINS server. As you saw in Chapter 2, you can also set the
Windows 95 client to log on and obtain network client permissions from the
Windows NT Server. The Win95 client can also be set to use DHCP and look for a
DNS server, in similar ways to Windows NT Workstation.

There are some issues to watch out for when using Win95 on an NT-hosted
TCP/IP network:

◆ In the TCP/IP Properties' IP Address tab, select the Obtain an IP Address
   Automatically option if your Win95 client is going to accept IP addresses
   from the NT Server.

◆ For Win95's Client for Microsoft Networks service, its Properties sheet
   offers an option to Log on to a Windows NT Domain.

◆ Finally, if nothing else works, test your Win95 connections in the same
   fashion as you would Windows NT clients. Try working with the NT
   Server when its bare-bones WINS Server configuration is set up. Then,
   once you get successful connectivity, layer in the other NT services and
   test your Win95 connections at each step. Then you'll have a consistent
   methodology for both types of Windows clients.

A Final Word

With all that I've discussed in this chapter, that isn't even the half of it. TCP/IP networking, especially in large networks, can get extremely complicated. This book is not about building enterprise networks; it's about *getting things to work* in your office. This is probably the most important chapter in the book for that purpose, because it aims to provide a solid working knowledge of TCP/IP networking in Windows NT — a skill that is in higher demand.

For more information, see Chapter 10, which applies TCP/IP networking to Remote Access connections.

Next, in Chapter 4, you learn about connecting alternative network clients to your network.

Troubleshooting

When I log on to they Windows NT Server using TCP/IP across the LAN, I get an apparently good connection, but I can't browse through resources using Network Neighborhood, and the server isn't available!
(For Windows NT clients only.) You have a problem with name resolution, most likely on the client. If you open up a command prompt and type in the command (use your own server's IP address here)

```
PING 205.205.205.5
```

you'll get an apparently good connection. But if you then type

```
PING TEST_SERVER
```

or whatever the name of your server is, then you get an error message: "Bad IP Address TEST_SERVER." You can also type

```
NBTSTAT -A TEST_SERVER
```

and you'll get a "Host not found" error. If the server's WINS service is properly configured, which is pretty much automatic, you need to fix where the *client* looks for the WINS address resolution. It must look for it on the server, at the server's specific IP address. Follow these steps:

1. Open the client's Control Panel and double-click the Network icon.

2. Click the Protocol tab.

3. Select the TCP/IP protocol (it is installed, isn't it?) and click Properties.

4. Select the WINS Address tab. Then enter your server's address in the Primary WINS field (and the Primary DNS field, if necessary). This should fix the problem, and you'll be able to browse shared resources on the server.

(For Windows 95) When I attempt to log on to the Windows NT Server running WINS/DNS/DHCP, I get a "Domain not Found - You have been logged on using cached information" message.
There's a chance that the DHCP server has run out of addresses to hand out. Also, make sure your Use DHCP for WINS Resolution check box is enabled in the WINS Configuration tab of TCP/IP Properties for your network device. If that check box isn't enabled, not only will you not receive an IP address from the server, but the DHCP service can't give your computer the WINS server information. If you do

have an IP address for the WINS server and that check box isn't enabled, make sure your Gateway value is correct (Gateway tab in TCP/IP Properties).

I have an Windows NT Server that I inherited in my office with several dozen clients. Everyone's running static IP addresses on their computers that were handed out from the previous administrator, and they're all using LMHOSTS files. How do I do a DHCP/WINS rollout so I can get rid of this ridiculous administration problem?

Here's one way to do it:

1. Install WINS and add the proper WINS Server IP to the WINS Manager.

2. Install DHCP and create a scope that doesn't include the IP addresses of the existing computers, or create a scope that excludes whatever address ranges represent those static IP addresses. (Hope that those addresses aren't all over the map.)

3. Configure the DHCP Scope's Options with the correct node type (Option 046) and the WINS Server IP address (Option 044) so that DHCP can be used to distribute the WINS configuration as each client comes in. Check the section titled "Defining DHCP Scope Options and Enabling DHCP Address Sharing" for more on this topic.

4. Gradually enable the client computers to accept IPs from the server. Don't do them all at once. (In a Win95 client, open its network card's TCP/IP Properties sheet and enable the Obtain an IP Address Automatically option in the IP Address tab and the WINS Configuration tab's Use DHCP for WINS Resolution check box. On NT clients, open the TCP/IP Properties sheet and select the Use DHCP option.) Each client should take a couple of minutes at most to make the changes. As each client makes the change, use Ping and NETSTAT/NBTSTAT commands to check name resolution.

When I connect my DHCP-enabled clients to the Windows NT Server, I receive a "No DHCP Server was available" error!

The first thing to do is check the address range in your DHCP scope. Does it include the IP address for your DHCP Server? If so, change the scope so that it does not do so. Also verify that the IP address on the server is actually a static address. Finally, make sure enough addresses are available for the clients within the Scope.

On the server, my DNS Service will not load.

You'll have to do a full reinstall of DNS. First, remove any DNS Service you presently have installed, and reboot. Then, when Windows NT comes back, delete the entire contents of the WINNT\SYSTEM32\DNS directory, delete the DNS directory, and restart again. Then reinstall DNS from scratch.

Chapter 4

Connecting Alternative Network Clients

IN THIS CHAPTER
In this chapter, you'll dig deeper into your company's roster of network clients and learn how to connect Windows 3.1 and Macintosh computers to a Windows NT Server-based LAN. Among the jobs described here are some of the more involved client-to-server connections you'll ever perform. Even with that caveat, none of the tasks listed below present huge problems to an administrator:

◆ Connect a Windows 3.11 client to a Windows NT LAN

◆ Log on a Windows 3.11 client to a Windows NT domain

◆ Connect Macintosh System 7 clients to a Windows NT server

◆ Connect Macintosh System 8 clients to a Windows NT server

◆ Allow Macintoshes access to a Windows NT print server

IN THIS CHAPTER, you deal with networking three different operating systems to Windows NT: Windows 3.11, Macintosh System 7, and Macintosh System 8.

Windows 95 hasn't met with universal acceptance in corporations and smaller companies. Many businesses see little reason to upgrade their entire fleet of PCs just to run Windows 95. (In fact, Microsoft sold over 10 million copies of the Windows 3.*x* operating system in 1996.) Huge numbers of companies still have collections of Windows 3.*x* systems in their offices. Many have ignored Windows 95 entirely, preferring instead to do a gradual rollout of Windows NT while they continue to use their legacy computers. Those offices will expect their older 16-bit computers to participate in the network. After reading this chapter, you'll be able to meet those requirements.

If you're connecting 16-bit Windows clients to a newly installed Windows NT server, I strongly recommend using Windows 3.11. Most networked 16-bit Windows systems will probably be using this operating system, which is actually Windows 3.1 with enhanced networking capabilities. The plain vanilla version of Windows 3.1 is very painful to set up for networking and was not originally designed for it. Hence, I'll use Windows 3.11 as the standard in this chapter.

Also, bear in mind that Windows 3.1 clients can be easily upgraded to Windows 3.11 without losing any current settings. Windows 3.11 also offers the advantages of faster disk performance and an expanded collection of networking utilities, including a messaging applet (WinPopup), a simple Mail application, and even a Remote Access program!

As with Windows 3.1, there are still lots of Macs out there. They're still considered the standard in several areas of computing, primarily desktop graphics, multimedia, and publishing. Though Apple never quite gained credibility in the business market, many PC-centric organizations still use Macs in their advertising and graphics departments. Using Windows NT Server, you can insure that those Mac-based departments aren't locked out of the office LAN. Many people have dozens or even hundreds of Macs networked to a Windows NT Server. Because Mac-based applications often read and write the same file formats as their PC brethren, network participation can further ensure that the two camps in your organization "get along."

Windows 3.11 Networking: A Brief Tour

When you set up a Windows 3.11 computer, you're also offered a Network Setup sequence which bears some resemblance to Windows 95 and Windows NT clients. I won't put you through the steps to actually install Windows 3.11; the process is simple. If you need a quick refresher on Windows 3.11's networking features, follow the steps below.

Windows 3.11 does provide a Network Setup that closely resembles many features from Windows NT and 95; you can locate Setup in the Program Manager's Network group.

1. Double-click Network Setup in Windows 3.11's Network group.

   The Network Setup program window appears, as shown in Figure 4-1.

Networks button

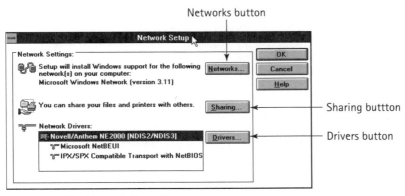

Sharing buttton

Drivers button

Figure 4-1: The Network Setup Program

2. To check the networking settings for the Windows 3.11 client, click the Networks button. The Networks dialog box appears, as shown in Figure 4-2. It provides some interesting information. Probably the most relevant to your work is that Windows 3.11 provides direct support for connecting to Windows NT servers. The basic Microsoft Windows Network is the default setup for Windows 3.11; there's no reason to change it or add to it at this point.

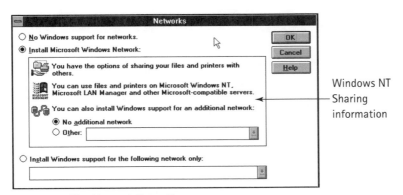

Windows NT
Sharing
information

Figure 4-2: The Network Setup Program

3. Click Cancel to close the dialog box.

4. Click the Sharing button.

   The Sharing dialog box appears, as in Figure 4-3.

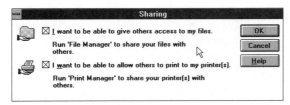

Figure 4-3: Sharing Setup for a Windows 3.11 Client

Does this dialog box appear familiar? It should. It's the same feature that's offered in Windows 95's File and Print Sharing feature in the Network control panel.

5. If the Sharing settings are as you want them, click OK or Cancel.

6. In the Network Setup program, click the Drivers button. The Network Drivers dialog box appears, similar to that shown in Figure 4-4.

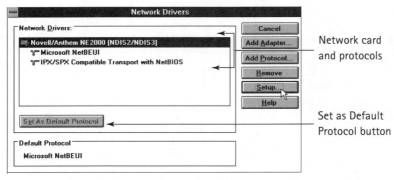

Figure 4-4: Checking Network Drivers for a Windows 3.11 System

7. In the Network Drivers dialog box, click Setup. The setup dialog box for your network adapter appears, as shown in Figure 4-5.

8. Click Cancel to close the dialog box.

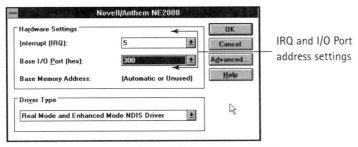

Figure 4-5: Port Addresses for an NE2000 Network Adapter

Again, if you've read the first couple of chapters, all this will be familiar. For a Microsoft Windows network such as the one you're working with in this book, make sure that NetBEUI is set as the default protocol by selecting it in the Network Drivers list and clicking the Set as Default Protocol button.

The network card type will also be shown. Windows 3.11 actually has a fairly decent ability to detect and integrate mainstream networking cards into the operating system. If you install a different card or know that the listing is incorrect, click the Add Adapter button and select the proper card from Windows 3.11's fairly extensive list.

Some words to the wise: make certain that you have the software driver disk for your network cards. They usually have a DOS-based diagnostic tool that allows you to set the interrupt and I/O Port addresses for your network adapter through software, without having to change hardware jumpers. It's also a good idea to check the settings for your network card before you finish setting up your connection.

Windows 3.11 does not automatically detect the hardware settings and addresses for your card, although it can detect its type. You may have to make corrections here. *Do not do so* unless you know the actual addresses for the network adapter! Always bear in mind that Windows 3.11 and any other flavors of 16-bit Windows do not have plug-and-play abilities of any kind, so you'll have to do a little more work.

That gives you the quick tour of Windows 3.11 networking. Once you have the basic settings defined for the client, it's fairly easy to connect it to the Windows NT Server.

Connecting a Windows 3.x Client to Windows NT Server

As you proceed through this section, you'll find that Windows 3.11's networking features closely resemble those for Windows 95. This is no accident; Windows 95 uses almost-identical features for networking as workgroups. Windows 3.11 is actually a fairly capable client OS for Windows NT networks, though primitive in its appearance compared to Windows 95 or Windows NT Workstation.

In this section, a Windows NT Server Domain called MAIN_SERVER is used for the exercises. Your server name and domain name may differ.

Because Windows 3.11 doesn't provide a Network Neighborhood or an Explorer, the best way to have direct access and connection to network resources is the File Manager. It's located in the Main group under Program Manager.

1. Open File Manager. The File Manager program appears, similar to Figure 4-6.

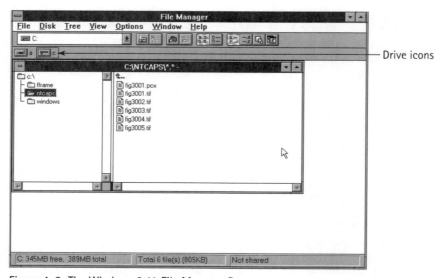

Figure 4-6: The Windows 3.11 File Manager Program

2. From the Disk menu, select Connect Network Drive. The Connect Network Drive dialog box appears. It may take a moment, because the program automatically polls the network for any available network workgroups, clients, and servers. If any resources are available, they'll appear in a similar fashion to Figure 4-7:

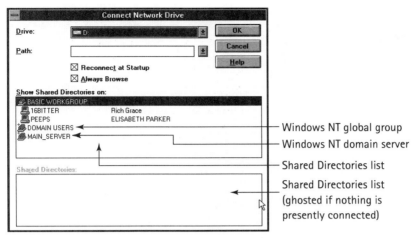

Figure 4-7: Connecting a Network Drive

The Drive list at the top automatically shows the first available drive letter, which in this case happens to be D. The Path box is blank because nothing has been selected yet. This list displays the drive letter to which your network resource will be mapped.

The key part is the *Show Shared Directories on* list box. It lists all the resources that are shared on the network, including workgroups and individual stations. More interesting yet is how Windows 3.11 can detect Windows NT Domain resources. The Windows NT Global domain group DOMAIN USERS is listed. Finally, the Windows NT domain itself, which in this case is MAIN_SERVER, appears at the bottom.

If your Windows NT server that you've logged on to is a stand-alone server without a domain, the computer's *name* will simply appear on the list.

3. Double-click the Windows NT server domain (listed as MAIN_SERVER in Figure 4-7). The client will pause for another moment while it connects to the domain server. Eventually another level is added to the Show Shared Directories list, as shown in Figure 4-8.

Domain connections are shown

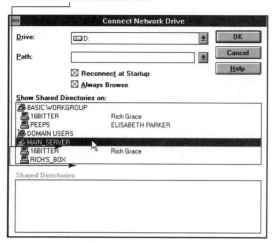

Figure 4-8: Browsing the Network

4. Select the name of the *server* in the domain (in Figure 4-8, it's RICH'S_BOX). As Figure 4-9 shows, the resources that are directly shared by the server will be listed in the previously ghosted Shared Directories list box. Also, a new path name has been added to the Path text box. Notice that the box preserves the Universal Naming Convention for the network object.

The Path name adds a new entry

Figure 4-9: Locating Shared Resources on the Server from the 16-Bit Client

5. In the Shared Directories list at the bottom (now changed to read Shared Directories on `\\RICH'S_BOX` in Figure 4-9), select a shared drive or folder.

   The UNC path name is further lengthened to show the actual share. You can now map the shared device to the system in File Manager.

6. Click OK to close the dialog box. Figure 4-10 shows an example result.

A Network Drive and CDN appear

The UNC pathname appears on the toolbar   below the toolbar

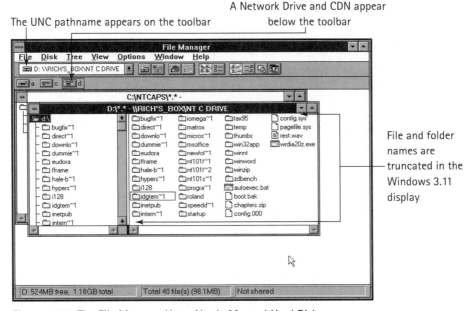

Figure 4-10: The File Manager Has a Newly Mapped Hard Disk.

File-Naming Issues

The shared device (a hard disk in this case) is automatically displayed in a window. This brings up an important point regarding the use of 16-bit Windows workstations on a Windows NT network: the long filenames problem. As illustrated in Figure 4-10, some major problems can occur because of the MS-DOS 8.3 file name format.

Any file on your Windows NT system that is read by the Windows 3.11 client is automatically truncated with a deforming "~1" "or ~2." The filenames will not be damaged on the Windows NT system by the simple act of merely reading them with the 16-bit client (or listing them with File Manager), but if the client is allowed to write those files back to the Windows NT system, the filenames will be damaged. This can have serious consequences for administrators.

The best thing to do in this situation is not to allow 16-bit clients unfettered access to any hard drive except their own. Set up the shares for your 16-bit clients' user accounts to access only a *folder* on the server that's set aside for their use. By doing so, you can save yourself a lot of headaches. User accounts for 16-bit Windows clients are set up the same way as for any other — by using the User Manager under Windows NT.

When you share a folder for a 16-bit Windows client, it's mapped into File Manager in the same way as a shared hard disk. The disk is shown as a connectivity example and as a cautionary tale of what to watch out for in Windows 3.11 connections.

Logging Windows 3.11 Clients into a Windows NT Domain

As noted before, Windows 3.11 clients are also capable of logging directly on to a Windows NT domain and becoming a member thereof. When you define your client's user accounts in User Manager for Domains, the logon for a Windows 3.11 client is functionally the same as it is for any other Windows system. The process is simple and again bears considerable resemblance to the same feature in Windows 95.

Network logon setup for a Windows 3.11 client is located in the Control Panel. Here's how to set it up:

1. Open Control Panel in the Main program group.

2. In the Control Panel, open the Network applet. The Microsoft Windows Network screen will appear as shown in Figure 4-11. This is also where you set up the client's bootup logon sequence, including user name and password. The Logon Status pane shows the current logon state, displaying the account's user name (in this case, "RICH").

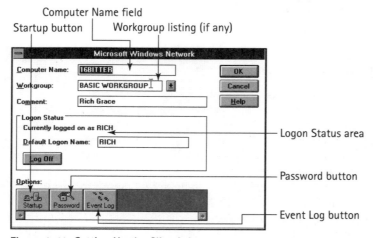

Figure 4-11: Setting Up the Client's Logon

The Computer Name shows, obviously, the name of the system on the network. This can be changed at any time by the administrator or user. (In the current figure, it's called "16BITTER.")

3. Click the Startup button as labeled in Figure 4-11. The Startup Settings dialog box appears, as shown in Figure 4-12.

Startup Options section

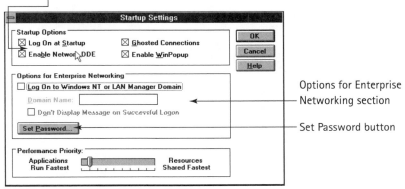

Figure 4-12: Setting Up the Client's Logon

4. To enable logon to a Windows NT domain, click in the Log On to Windows NT or LAN Manager Domain check box.

5. Enter the name of the Windows NT domain in the Domain Name text box.

6. Click OK.

Though a bit more primitive, this is the same domain logon feature that can be found in Windows 95, described in Chapter 2.

Enabling the Event Log on a 16-Bit Windows Client

Windows 3.11 provides a simple Event Log that records some network-related events between the workstation and the server. Here's how to enable and view it:

1. In the Control Panel, open the Network applet.

2. Click the Event Log button in the Microsoft Windows Network window. The Event Log Setting window appears, as shown in Figure 4-13.

Add, Remove, and Add All buttons   Enable Event Log check box

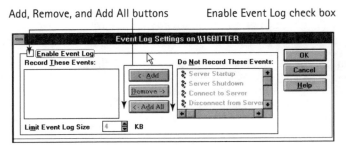

Figure 4-13: Opening the Event Log Settings Feature

3. Click in the Enable Event Log check box. The Events panes activate (Record These Events and Do Not Record These Events).

4. Click the Add All button.

5. Click OK.

6. Finally, click OK.

Windows 3.11 displays a Control Panel prompt, asking you to restart your computer.

To view the event log, open the Network group in Program Manager. Open the NetWatcher application and select View Event Log from the Connection menu. It's actually not much of an event log, providing little insight into the events on the network other than when the Windows client logs on or off. There may be times when it will be handy.

Generally, networking with Windows 3.11 on a Windows-based LAN is simple. If the hardware is functional (particularly the network card), you should have no trouble enabling Windows 3.*x* users to participate on the Windows NT LAN that you've built.

Because of file-naming issues, try to limit Windows 3.*x* client access to individual folders in the server. Make sure any users who share files with 16-bit clients are aware that they need to stick with the old DOS-based 8.3 file-naming convention to minimize confusion. (Even on the Mac, I find myself using that convention in my mixed-platform environment.) Speaking of Macintoshes, let's turn to that *other* platform.

Connecting Macintosh Clients to Windows NT Server

As it turns out, Microsoft actually did a very good job supporting Macintosh connectivity in Windows NT 4.0. No, really. (In fact, in some ways it did a better job than Apple itself.)

Macintoshes tend to do things their own way, as do their users. Only recently did Apple begin building Ethernet as a standard feature into their current Macintoshes. (You don't absolutely have to use Ethernet for your Mac clients to participate on a Windows NT-based LAN, but just try to find a network card supported by Windows NT that uses the lame LocalTalk DIN-9 connection standard.) Current PowerMacs and PowerMac clones also use the industry-standard PCI expansion bus (yes, the same PCI slots that are in your Pentium system). Some Fast Ethernet networking cards can be used in either Macs or PCs without any modification.

Many Windows NT users aren't familiar with Macintoshes or their networking capabilities. I won't be providing a complete tour of the Mac OS in this chapter; instead, you'll get a brief, functional account of the Mac's networking features and the applets it uses to manage them. When you follow the exercises in this section, you'll see both Windows NT and Macintosh screen figures. The Mac's networking functions are almost as simple as Windows NT's, though somewhat different in their appearance and nomenclature.

A Brief Survey of Macintosh Networking

Macs use a proprietary protocol stack called *AppleTalk* for their network connections. Windows NT offers a special AppleTalk protocol stack for installation with its optional Services for Macintosh. You must use Windows NT Server to enable Mac-to-Windows NT LAN connections. AppleTalk is a broadcast-based, routable protocol, combining attributes of both TCP/IP and NetBEUI, but that's where its similarities end. AppleTalk is probably the most inefficient commonly used networking protocol. Although AppleTalk's addressing scheme theoretically allows for hundreds of networked clients on any network segment, in practice it's impossible because of the protocol's constant refreshes and broadcasts. AppleTalk is a terrible protocol that should have been jettisoned by Apple long ago for TCP/IP. Then again, considering Apple's dysfunctional nature, sound technical underpinnings are clearly its least concern.

Among AppleTalk's limitations in System 7-based Macs is its single-connection nature on the client: if you're running an AppleTalk network connection over Ethernet on the Mac, and you have an AppleTalk printer connected to the Mac's serial or parallel port, you must switch your physical connection through software in order to print. Fortunately, Windows NT offers a solution to this irritating problem. You'll learn how to connect a Mac to share files and folders from a Windows NT Server, and connect to and use a Windows NT print server.

For connectivity, Macs use a special networking library called *Open Transport* (OT). Its main protocols are TCP/IP and AppleTalk. OT consists of a collection of small utilities (called Control Panels) that each manage a part of the computer's networking functions. Each utility is simple, but you may have to use several in succession to get the results you want. The Macintosh's Control Panels feature can be found in the Apple menu, at the top left of the screen, as shown in Figure 4-14.

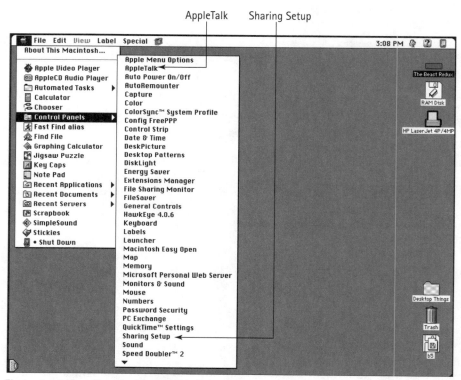

Figure 4-14: Locating the Macintosh's Control Panels

The Control Panels can also be located by opening the Mac's hard disk on the desktop and opening the System Folder; however, for convenience and speed, I'll use the Apple Menu as the interface default.

The most important Control Panel (and the one that's missed most often when connections fail) is AppleTalk, which is shown in Figure 4-15.

Drop-down list

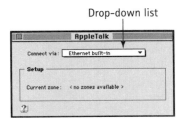

Figure 4-15: The AppleTalk Control Panel

Clicking the drop-down list reveals the complete list of possible AppleTalk net-working connections on the system. Most current Macs include the modem, printer, and built-in Ethernet ports on the list. Use the Ethernet setting for networking with Windows NT. You'll return to this utility later.

Another important Control Panel utility is the Sharing Setup, which is shown in Figure 4-16.

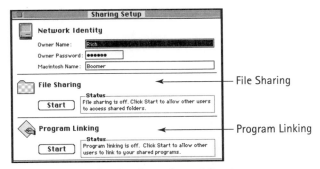

Figure 4-16: The Sharing Setup Control Panel

The File Sharing section has a Start button, which enables fellow Mac users to open shared folders and files on the host Mac. You'll need to enable this feature to use other Mac networking capabilities.

For Windows NT connectivity, the Program Linking section isn't as important since Mac programs can't run on the Windows NT desktop. If other Macs are con-nected to your network, you'll want to enable this feature as well. At the top, the Network Identity identifies the Mac and its user to the network. Make sure your fields are filled in properly here.

For monitoring network connections, Open Transport provides a File Sharing Control Panel shown in Figure 4-17.

Shared Items pane   Connected Users pane

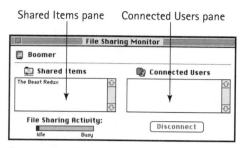

Figure 4-17: The Macintosh's File
Sharing Monitor

You can use this panel to verify network connections and disconnect users.

Finally, the Chooser utility is not a control panel, but an important application that manages every connection on your Mac — printers and AppleShare network servers being the most common. It's pictured in Figure 4-18. The Chooser is not the easiest application to work with, but you'll get acquainted with it over the course of the next few exercises.

AppleShare icon

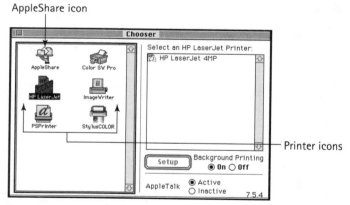

Figure 4-18: The Macintosh Chooser

AppleTalk networks are organized in terms of *zones*, which bear a passing resemblance to workgroups on the PC. An AppleTalk zone can have up to 256 networked Macintoshes and Mac-related devices, such as printers and routers, gathered within it. (In practice, this doesn't work too well.) Your Windows NT server can also manage more than one AppleTalk zone. In this case, you can name the AppleTalk zone whatever you want, since it's based on your Windows NT Server network. You'll do this a bit later. For now, the existing setup will work, and a zone doesn't even have to be defined.

Why? When the Setup status message (See Figure 4-20) refers to the default network, it means the network based on the Windows NT server. It indicates that when you restart and set up folders for sharing with connected Mac systems, the Macs will see them across this particular network, which is what you want.

AppleTalk, as noted, is a routable protocol despite its talky, broadcast-heavy characteristics. Services for Macintosh basically turns your Windows NT server into an AppleTalk router, which is what enables Macs to talk to it. It is possible to use dedicated router hardware to take the load off the server, but in most applications I've found that it isn't necessary, and the Windows NT server's performance isn't affected for most practical applications. (Each Macintosh connection occupies about 15K of memory.)

If you wind up with only a few Macs hooked up to the server (as I do in my office), the load impact is minimal. The process of setting up an AppleTalk zone will be discussed in a later section, titled "Setting up an AppleTalk Zone in Services for Macintosh."

Setting Up Services for Macintosh on Windows NT Server

The first step is to install Services for Macintosh on your Windows NT Server. It's not very complicated, but it provides a look at some other features and aspects of Macintosh connectivity that also bear explanation.

1. Open Control Panel.

2. Open Network.

3. Click the Services tab.

4. Click Add.

   The Select Network Service dialog box appears.

5. Scroll down the list of services and select Services for Macintosh, and click OK. A Windows NT Setup dialog appears, where you're prompted to enter the path.

   The Services for Macintosh files are located in the i386 directory of the Windows NT Server Installation CD-ROM. (You can also have an i386 directory located on your hard disk for convenience.)

6. Click Continue to start the service installation. The system will pause and display an ongoing message: "Installing Services for Macintosh." After a moment, the system will display the Services tab again, with the new service added to the list, as shown in Figure 4-19.

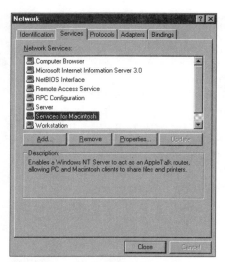

Figure 4-19: Services for Macintosh Is
Added to the List

7. Select Services for Macintosh and click Properties. The following Setup
status message appears, as shown in Figure 4-20.

Figure 4-20: A Message Informing You of the Status
of the Mac Service Installation

8. Click OK. The Microsoft AppleTalk Protocol Properties dialog box appears,
as illustrated in Figure 4-21. This is where you define the AppleTalk zone
information (in the Routing tab). At present, this isn't necessary, but keep
it in mind for later.

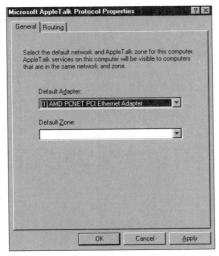

Figure 4-21: NT's AppleTalk Properties
Sheet.

9. Click OK again. (You'll come back to this in a while.)

10. Finally, click OK to close the Control Panel and commit the settings.

11. Restart the Windows NT Server.

At this point, you've finished the essential part of Services for Macintosh setup. When the server comes back, some new things will appear in your server. Among the most prominent are a new MacFile applet in the Control Panel (shown in Figure 4-22) and a new MacFile menu in Windows NT's Server Manager that you will use to set up a shared drive.

Setting Up a Secure Mac-to-NT Connection

Having performed the exercise in the previous section, you'll notice that the Services for Macintosh installation has created a new folder in the C drive of your server. It's called the Microsoft UAM Volume. Services for Macintosh adds this new folder to the first available NTFS partition on your server (in this case, drive C). The folder contains the Windows NT software for encrypting passwords from the Macintosh client. You don't have to use it, but I think it's a good idea. Why else is this new folder here?

Password Authentication: Microsoft Versus Apple

Using the Apple Standard UAMs, the Macintosh uses simple, unencrypted clear-text passwords. They can be detected by packet-sniffer programs that crackers use when they break into people's networks. (This problem is becoming more and more common; an FBI sting recently netted a very untalented cracker who used a packet-sniffer to steal more than 100,000 credit-card numbers from an Internet service provider. This guy was no genius, so the fact that he was able to do this seems to present a pretty serious security problem.) The way to eliminate this problem, at least so far as Mac-to-NT connectivity goes, is to use Microsoft Authentication. Table 4-1 lists the differences between the two methods of password authentication.

TABLE 4-1 AUTHENTICATION METHODS FOR WINDOWS NT VOLUMES ON THE MAC

Authentication Method	Purpose
Apple Standard UAMs	Enables logon to the Windows NT Server only with the Guest account. The Microsoft UAM Volume is shared and is logged on to automatically during Mac restarts. If any other shared volumes are set up on the server that require Microsoft Authentication (as described earlier), they will not be available for logon.
Microsoft Authentication	Does not permit relogon during Mac restarts, and shared resources cannot be checked off for that purpose. Guest and user accounts can be used. Volume passwords are required, if implemented on the server end. Any Windows NT Server folders that are shared can be accessed through the Chooser after the Mac is running, which is the method we use in this chapter.

Setting password authentication is simple but has important effects on how your Mac-to-NT connection behaves on your network. It will be our first step in the process of enabling our Macs to talk to Windows NT.

1. Open Windows NT Server's Control Panel (shown in Figure 4-22) and observe the MacFile applet.

New MacFile applet

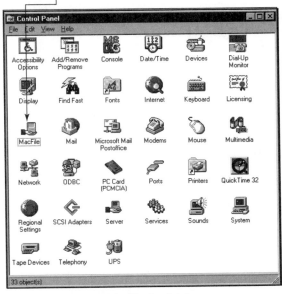

Figure 4-22: A New MacFile Applet Appears
in the Control Panel

2. Open the MacFile applet shown in Figure 4-22. The MacFile Properties
   sheet appears as shown in Figure 4-23:

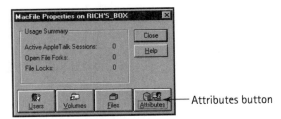

Attributes button

Figure 4-23: The MacFile
Properties Sheet

3. Click the Attributes button in the MacFile Properties sheet. The MacFile
    Attributes dialog box appears, as shown in Figure 4-24. It provides the
    basic security measures for your Macintosh client connections. The
    Change button, which I'll ignore, simply allows you to change the server
    name for your Mac clients. The actual server name doesn't change on the
    Windows NT system; the Change button allows you to enter an 'alias' that
    is sent as the server identification.

Security check boxes

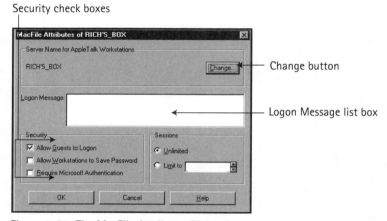

Change button

Logon Message list box

Figure 4-24: The MacFile Attributes Dialog Box

The server name, as shown in Figure 4-24, is the by-now-familiar
"RICH'S_BOX." (Yours will be different.) You'll leave it as it is for now.
You can also add a Logon Message to greet your Mac users as they log on
to the server. You'll skip these features presently; but you can change their
settings whenever you want.

Three check boxes are provided in the Security section: Allow Guests to
Logon, Allow Workstations to Save Password, and Require Microsoft
Authentication.

4. If you want your Mac workstations to be able to save their logon
    passwords, enable the Allow Workstations to Save Password check box.

    The last check box, Require Microsoft Authentication, is the one you
    really want. It enables password encryption.

5. Click the Require Microsoft Authentication check box. The effects of
    enabling this check box are significant. Guest accounts will not be able to
    automatically log on to the volume, and the Mac client will not be able to
    mount the volume to the desktop during bootup. (Table 4-1 explains this
    in more detail.)

6. Click OK.

7. Click Close in MacFile Properties.

Now you've set up your Mac clients' security features to conform to the Microsoft Windows NT standard. You can use Server Manager (a program you haven't yet seen in this book) to assign shared volumes for Mac client access.

Connecting a Macintosh System 7 Computer to a Windows NT Server

Here's where the fun stuff begins. You'll perform the following procedures to enable a Mac client connection:

◆ Define a Mac-accessible folder

◆ Set permissions for that folder

◆ Execute the actual connection

Although there are quite a few steps in the process, it's not that hard to do. One key program you'll use here is the Windows NT Server Manager, pictured in Figure 4-25. Server Manager is a program in which you'll spend a lot of time in later chapters of this book. It provides a large number of domain and user account management features, including the ability to set permissions for any shares, add connected workstations to a domain, promote a Backup Domain Controller (BDC) to a Primary Domain Controller (PDC), synchronize a BDC to a PDC, and much more. (BDCs and PDCs were discussed briefly in Chapter 1, and you'll return to them in Chapter 13.)

For now, you'll notice a MacFile menu in the Server Manager. This special menu only appears when a Windows NT Server has Services for Macintosh properly installed. This is where you set up and manage your shared devices and folders to the Mac clients.

Understanding Mac-Related Directory Permissions

Also located in Server Manager, a feature called Directory Permissions is set up to replicate Macintosh-style access privileges. There's quite a bit here, so I'll take my time explaining it.

To start with, any global or local group in your Windows NT system can be applied to a permissions setting, including the Everyone group you have seen in earlier chapters. The Everyone group itself has a set of three check boxes, all of which are enabled by default (to see them, look ahead to Figure 4-29).

All three Permissions levels (Owner, Primary Group, and Everyone) have a set of three check boxes: See Files, See Folders, and Make Changes. The first, See Files, enables the connected user to view and open files in the shared folder or volume. If there are subfolders or directories within that folder, enabling the See Folders check box allows the users in the assigned group to browse their contents and open files. Enabling the Make Changes check box for any of the Permissions groups allows the connected users to save changes to the files in the shared volume.

For the current example, you'll leave the check boxes fully enabled, except as noted.

The Owners permission setting provides a way to set ownership for the Mac-accessible volume. Unless it's absolutely necessary, *don't* change the Owner group assignment, which defaults to the Administrators group in the Windows NT Server.

The Primary group setting encompasses all the user and group accounts on your server. It also allows you to set one local or global group on your server (or a user account) to be associated with the Mac-shared directory. Though they're the same accounts as those customarily used in the Windows NT Server, they're applied only on the Macintosh side; if any of those group accounts have access to other Windows NT networked devices, they won't be able to access them from the Mac. Finally, the Everyone "group" is represented. It also offers the three check boxes.

Because of this, you may want to use the User Manager to create a special group just for the Mac user accounts on the server. Then you can assign them to a volume that they can access from the Mac.

Setting Up the Windows NT Side of the Mac-to-NT Connection

Now, after all that explanation, let's begin the real connection process between Windows NT and the Mac.

1. From the Start menu on the Windows NT Server, select Programs, then Administrative tools, and then Server Manager. The Server Manager program appears, as shown in Figure 4-25.

MacFile menu (present only when Services
for Macintosh is installed or the server)

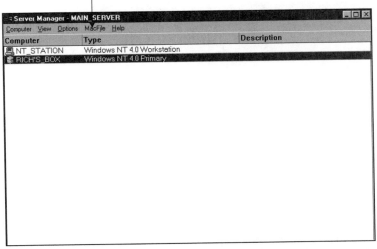

Figure 4-25: Windows NT's Server Manager Program

2. Select the system in Server Manager that contains the volumes you want to share ("RICH'S_BOX" in this example).

3. From the MacFile menu, select Volumes. A dialog box titled Macintosh-Accessible Volumes on (your server name here) appears, as shown in Figure 4-26. The previously mentioned Microsoft UAM Volume appears here, because it's automatically created by Services for Macintosh as a Mac-accessible volume. You're not limited to that single folder, however. *Any* folder or directory can be shared with the Mac client. This includes an entire Windows NT hard disk, which is treated as just another folder. The only limitation, of course, is that it must be a folder on an NTFS drive. We'll set up a hard disk to be shared as an example.

You can mount an entire Windows NT hard disk as a volume on the Mac desktop.

Microsoft UAM volume appears here

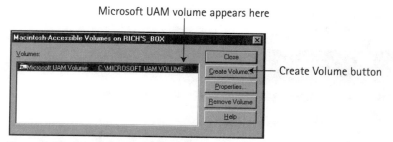

Create Volume button

Figure 4-26: Inspecting the Current Mac-Accessible
Volumes in the Server

4. In the Macintosh-Accessible Volumes dialog box, click Create Volume.

The Create Volume dialog box appears, as shown in Figure 4-27.

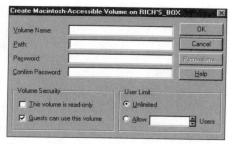

Figure 4-27: Initiating Creation of a Shared
Volume for a Mac Client

Oddly enough, Create Volume doesn't provide a way to browse for the
folder that you want to share. You must specify the path, such as C:\Mac
Shared Folders\Accounting by typing it in the Path field, and provide
a name in the Volume Name field. You don't need to use the UNC name;
the basic drive and folder path will work.

5. In the Volume Name text box, type in the name NT Shared Hard Disk.

6. In the Path text box, type in the drive letter of the NTFS-formatted hard
disk you want to share with your Mac client. (I've chosen D:\ as an
example.) Figure 4-28 shows how your entry should appear:

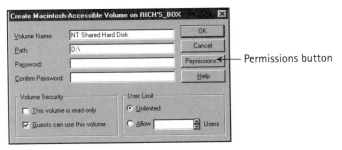

Permissions button

Figure 4-28: Creating a Shared
Volume for a Mac Client

The path you specify could be any folder you want on any NTFS-
formatted drive of your system.

7. Click the Permissions button. The Directory Permissions dialog box
appears, as shown in Figure 4-29.

Owner setting (do
not change unless
absolutely necessary)

Check boxes for each
permissions category

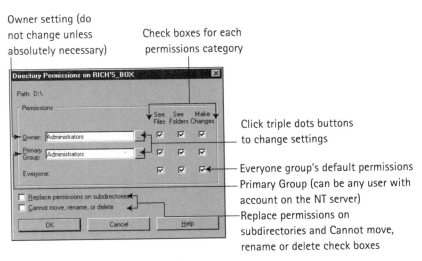

Click triple dots buttons
to change settings

Everyone group's default permissions
Primary Group (can be any user with
account on the NT server)
Replace permissions on
subdirectories and Cannot move,
rename or delete check boxes

Figure 4-29: Setting Permissions for
a Shared Volume to a Mac Client

8. Disable the Make Changes check box in the Everyone permission level.
(Other group assignments will supersede it.) You can change the Primary
group setting to a group or individual account that's more to your liking.

9. Click the triple-dot button next to the Primary group field. The Primary Group dialog box appears, as shown in Figure 4-30:

Select group from the Names list

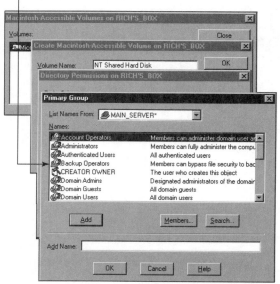

Figure 4-30: Drilling Down To Assign a Primary Group for a Mac Volume

At this point, you've drilled down through four levels of dialog boxes. This is where a Primary Group can be assigned. (A Search feature is also offered, which enables you to search over multiple servers throughout the domain for the groups or accounts you want.)

9. Select a group or individual account from the list. Unfortunately, you can use only one assigned Primary.

10. Click the Add button to add the group or user account.

11. Click OK.

The Directory Permissions dialog box reappears.

Two important check boxes are labeled back in Figure 4-29: Replace permissions on subdirectories and Cannot move, rename, or delete. Both are very useful. Enabling the *Replace Permissions* check box means that the permission levels you set at the top level of the shared volume are also applied to every subfolder or subdirectory in the volume, providing a uniformity of access to the connected Mac user.

There are advantages and disadvantages to this approach: if you're running a small LAN with just one or two Mac users and they're knowledgeable and trustworthy, you can let them have the run of the entire shared volume, and they won't run into roadblocks. The same rule applies to Mac as to PC users: sharing a whole hard disk with more than a few people is asking for trouble and big performance hits.

Conversely, if you're sharing the volume with a large collection of Mac users, disable this check box. Then, permission levels assigned to subfolders within the volume remain in effect.

Under most circumstances, you'll probably want to set up one or two folders to be shared with your Mac users, for security and simplicity.

Finally, the Cannot move, rename, or delete check box, when enabled, prevents the Mac user from moving, renaming, or deleting the shared volume or folder. I *highly* recommend doing this in a business LAN.

12. Enable both check boxes at the bottom of the Directory Permissions dialog box.

13. Click OK.

14. If desired, enter a password for the Macintosh-Accessible Volume and confirm it in the Confirm Password text box. (For Windows NT, this is called a *volume password*.) The volume password is not required for use of the resource by the client, but it does add an extra level of security.

    The password is automatically encrypted. The final result should appear, as in Figure 4-31.

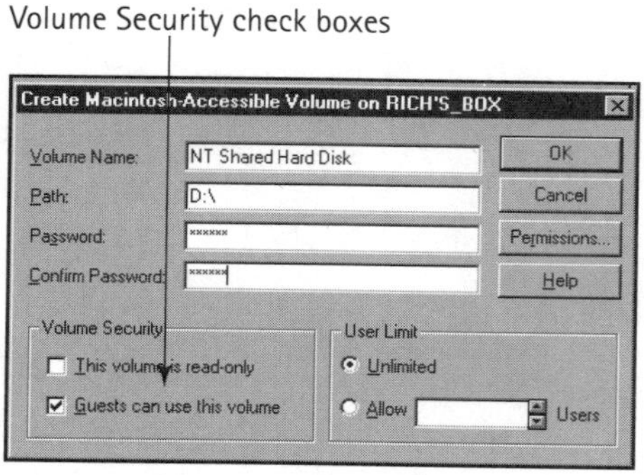

Volume Security check boxes

Figure 4-31: Finishing the Mac-Accessible
Volume

The next step is very important.

15. In the Volume Security section of the Properties dialog box, labeled in
    Figure 4-31, *disable* the two check boxes, This volume is read-only, and
    Guests can use this volume. (Otherwise, the Mac user won't be able to use
    any of the group accounts on the server, and will only be able to log on
    as a Guest.)

16. Click OK.

    The system will pause for a moment. This occurs because the Replace
    permissions check box was selected earlier in this process. The NT system
    has to go through each of the subdirectories and subfolders and change
    their Permissions settings for Macintosh users. (Any previous settings for
    PC users are unaffected. It's a beautiful thing.) If you are sharing an entire
    hard disk as a Mac-accessible volume, you'll have to wait for a minute or
    two. If it's just a folder, the pause will be much briefer. When the dialog
    box finally disappears, the Macintosh-Accessible Volumes dialog box
    reappears, showing the new shared volume, as shown in Figure 4-32.

Figure 4-32: A New Volume Is Added to the List
(In This Case, an Entire Hard Disk)

17. Finally, click Close.

Setting Up the Mac Side of the Mac-to-NT Connection

Now it's time to go over to the Macintosh client and test your new connection.

1. From the Apple menu, select Chooser. The Mac's Chooser application opens, as shown in Figure 4-33. This is where you open up your networking connection on the Mac side.

AppleShare icon

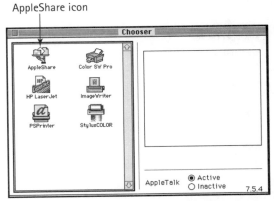

Figure 4-33: Opening the Mac Chooser Application

2. Select the AppleShare icon as labeled in Figure 4-33. The Windows NT server's name *will* appear in the Select a File Server list box, as seen in Figure 4-34 (your server's name will differ)

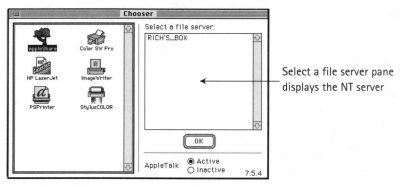

Figure 4-34: The AppleShare Connection Detects
the Windows NT Server

3. Select the server name and click OK.

   A new dialog box appears, prompting you to select a logon method.

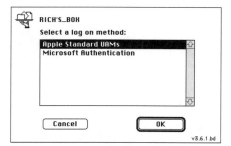

Figure 4-35: Selecting a Logon Method to
the Windows NT Server from the Mac Client

4. Select Microsoft Authentication and click OK.

   A new logon screen appears, as shown in Figure 4-36.

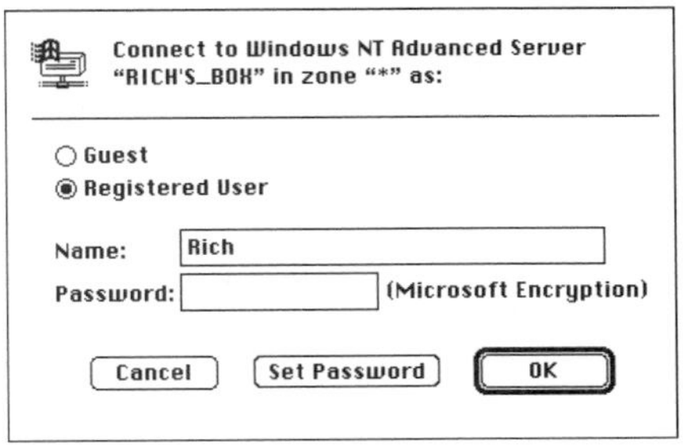

Figure 4-36: Connecting to the Windows
NT Server with an Established User
Account and Password

You have the option to log on as a guest or with an established user
account based from the Windows NT system. We'll opt for a user account.
(Notice how an AppleTalk zone is not specified in the dialog box. We'll
come back to this later.)

5. Enter your desired user account name and password. (If your account has
   the privilege, you can also change the password by clicking Set Password.)

6. Click OK.

   Another new screen comes up, similar to that in Figure 4-37, listing the
   shared volumes from the Windows NT Server.

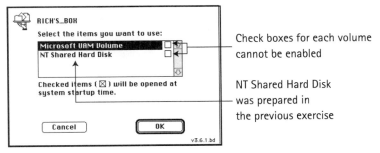

Figure 4-37: Displaying Resources
for Connection

The dialog box updates with a list of resources that can be opened over
the network. With Microsoft authentication, you can't enable either check
box (try it), because the network connection doesn't support startup
mounting of shared resources.

7. With the Microsoft UAM Volume highlighted as shown in Figure 4-37, click OK. A mounted volume icon will appear on your Mac's desktop, as shown in Figure 4-38.

Now you're making progress. A folder from the Windows NT Server, Microsoft UAM Volume, is displayed, as shown in Figure 4-38. Opening it reveals an AppleShare folder.

The Apple Share folder contained in the Microsoft UAM volume *must* be copied over to the Mac's System Folder.

8. Open the Macintosh's hard disk.

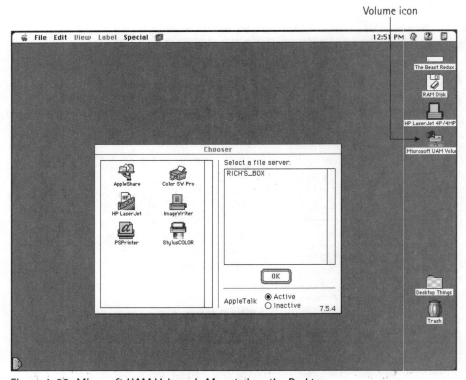

Figure 4-38: Microsoft UAM Volume Is Mounted on the Desktop

9. Open the Microsoft UAM Volume.

10. Drag the AppleShare folder from the UAM volume to the System Folder on the Mac's hard disk.

You can also copy files back and forth between the Mac client and the server using the UAM volume.

But where's the other volume, titled "NT Shared Hard Disk" or whatever you chose to name it? It doesn't show up *because it has the separate volume password* that was entered on the server.

A bit more work needs to be done to finish the connection. Back to the Chooser.

11. Select the server name again in the Chooser and click OK. A dialog box appears with a message saying you're already connected to the server as a registered user. But wait . . .

    Don't hit Cancel — there's more to do. Unfortunately, the Mac isn't very explicit in this regard, but that's why you're reading this book.

12. Click OK in the dialog box.

    The dialog box comes back with another message, listing the missing volume.

13. Click OK.

    A new dialog box appears, automatically highlighting the other volume (in the example, "NT Shared Hard Disk"). You won't be able to select the resource's check box because of the authentication method.

When you use Microsoft Authentication for the Mac-to-NT connection, you can open Mac-accessible volumes by selecting them, but you won't be able to enable their check boxes. Thus, you'll have to go through this process every time you log on.

14. Click OK.

    Now you'll be prompted to enter the password for the unmounted volume.

15. Enter the volume password (previously defined on the NT server).

16. Click OK.

The second volume shown in Figure 4-39 will appear on the desktop.

Windows network folder icons

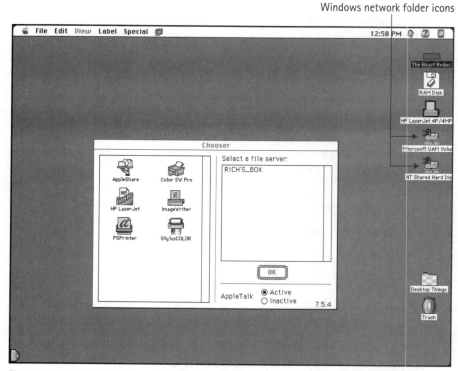

Figure 4-39: Both Mac-Accessible Volumes Are Mounted on the Macintosh Desktop

Opening the NT Shared Hard Disk volume displays the drive's contents, as shown in Figure 4-40.

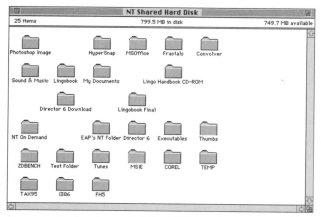

Figure 4-40: Opening an NT Hard Disk on the Macintosh Screen

Whenever you restart the Mac and you want to open the shared volume, do the following:

1. Open the Chooser.

2. Select the Windows NT file server and click OK.

3. Select Microsoft Authentication and click OK.

4. Enter the password for the server connection and click OK. The Select items list appears.

5. *Highlight the volume* you want to mount. You won't be able to enable its check box, but you *can* highlight any volume for logon by clicking its listing.

 If you want to mount all the listed volumes, hold down the Shift key on the Mac keyboard and select their names in the list.

6. Click OK.

7. Enter the volume password, if necessary.

8. Click OK.

The shared volume will be mounted on the desktop.

As noted earlier, any NTFS-based folder on the Windows NT server can be set up as a shared volume and mounted on the Mac desktop. Since a hard disk root directory is treated as just another folder, an entire Windows NT hard disk can be mounted as a Mac-readable volume in the same way as a simple directory.

This capability can be very useful for businesses where there's a lot of cross-platform creative work happening, such as desktop video and multimedia production for presentations to clients or software development.

Depending on the password authentication used, logons to shared volumes can behave very differently. If you want to make it simpler for your Mac users to log on and use shared NT folders, and security isn't a major consideration, enable the Guests can use this volume check box shown in Figure 4-31. Also have your users log on using the Apple Standard UAMs. Then the Guest account will be the Mac client's default account, and volumes can be mounted during bootup without the extra rigmarole involved using the Chooser. Because of security concerns and authentication measures, Macintosh-to-Windows NT connectivity can be a bit more complicated than you expect; once you get used to it, it's not so bad. The benefits definitely outweigh the inconveniences. Using this method, Macintosh clients can fully participate in an NT Server-based PC network. The only thing missing is a way to have Mac clients share their hard disk with the NT system. Peer-to-peer Mac-to-PC client software, such as PC MacLAN and Timbuktu, are the best solutions in that area.

Setting Up an AppleTalk Zone in Services for Macintosh

If you've been paying close attention, you may recall that you've done all this Mac-to-NT connectivity without even using an AppleTalk zone. There is no hard-and-fast rule stating that you must use AppleTalk zones to connect Mac clients to the server. In a small network, it isn't needed at all. Using AppleTalk zones is important if you have an existing AppleTalk network using its own zone and you want Windows NT to talk to it.

If you have more than one or two Macs connected to the network, or if you plan to share printers on the Mac side (or even share printers from the Windows NT side with Macs), it's not a bad idea to set up an AppleTalk zone. Windows NT also lets you maintain your existing Mac connections when you do this. Fortunately, it's not too difficult to explain or execute.

AppleTalk is a routable, broadcast-based network protocol whose addressing setup is usually much simpler than your garden-variety TCP/IP addressing scheme. A single numeric address (say, 10), which is also called a Network ID, corresponds to a single AppleTalk physical cable interconnection. As noted, you can connect up to 256 Mac-related devices per Network ID address, which also means up to 256 AppleTalk devices available per physical link. (Good luck making such a collection of devices work on an AppleTalk network, however.) An AppleTalk zone can also have *multiple* network IDs, which are defined as a *range* of addresses. As an example, you might have an AppleTalk network in the Accounting department that has a Network ID of 10. Then you might have another AppleTalk network in the graphics department, with a Network ID of 11. Both network cable lengths are joined by a router. So the address range is 10 to 11. One *or more* AppleTalk zones can be defined in that network.

In Services for Macintosh, you can assign an arbitrary network ID number if you're using Windows NT Server as your AppleTalk router. If you decided to have an AppleTalk zone with a network ID of 10, 256 AppleTalk devices can be connected to that network ID (and to the AppleTalk cable connection to the Windows NT server). If you have a range of network IDs, say from 10 to 13, you would have four separate cable lengths, each of which must be separated by a router. Then, up to 1,024 AppleTalk devices could be gathered within that AppleTalk zone (fat chance) and managed by the Windows NT server. (In most businesses, this is a very unlikely scenario. I'll stick with a single network ID for this example.)

With all that said, let's set up our AppleTalk zone:

1. Open Control Panel on the Windows NT Server.

2. Open Network.

3. Click the Services tab.

4. Select Services for Macintosh and click Properties. The AppleTalk Properties sheet will appear. It displays the default AppleTalk connection, which is an Ethernet adapter.

5. Click the Routing tab. It appears, as shown in Figure 4-41.

Enable Routing check box

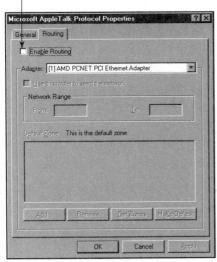

Figure 4–41: Opening Windows NT's Services for Macintosh Routing Setup

6. Click the Enable Routing check box.

7. Click the Use this router to seed the network check box, which is enabled when you click the Enable Routing check box.

   Steps 6 and 7 can be done if you don't have any other AppleTalk routers on the Mac network. If an AppleTalk router is already present on the network, NT's Services for Macintosh will automatically sense their presence (along with existing AppleTalk zones) and add them to the dialog box. (Since I don't have that large a Mac network in my office, that doesn't occur.) Zones are also automatically detected in that case.

The Network Range text boxes are where you enter the Network ID range for your AppleTalk Network ID addresses. If you have less than 256 AppleTalk devices on a single Macintosh network segment (which is very likely), a single ID will be just fine. We'll use an ID range of 10 to 10.

8. Enter the number 10 in the From field, and the number 10 in the To field.

   Using a single number in the range allows up to 256 devices in the actual zone, which you'll create next.

9. Click the Add button. The Add Zone dialog box appears, as shown in Figure 4-42.

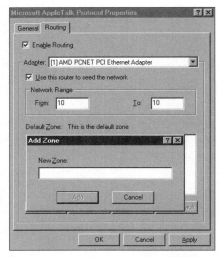

Figure 4–42: Adding a New AppleTalk Zone

10. Enter a zone name, such as **The Mac Zone.**

11. Click the Add button. You'll receive a message stating that "The AppleTalk Protocol has been configured successfully."

    This is the zone that your AppleTalk devices will be managed by with NT.

12. Click OK. An AppleTalk Protocol message comes up, stating that changes will be added when you restart AppleTalk.

13. Click OK to close the dialog. Click OK again to close the Control Panel, and restart the server.

14. Restart the Mac clients to enable them to log on in the AppleTalk zone. When you open the Chooser and begin connecting, you'll find a different message (assuming that you use Microsoft Authentication), as shown in Figure 4-43.

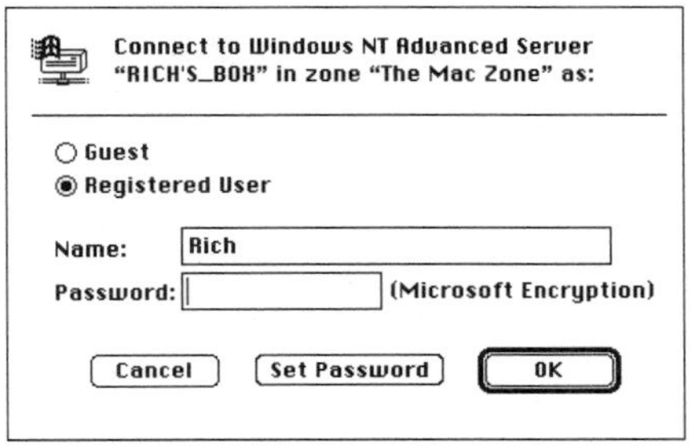

Figure 4-43: Logging in to the Windows NT-managed AppleTalk Zone

15. Enter the password and click OK. When you enter the volume pass word and finish logging on, the shared volume(s) will appear on the Mac desktop.

The process of adding Mac clients to a Windows NT Server network isn't as simple as you'd think. Nevertheless, Windows NT supports Mac networking exceptionally well. You have a good range of features, a painstaking installation procedure, and a way around the Macintosh's single-connection limitations. Why? Because Windows NT also allows Macintoshes access to its print server services. The next section shows you how to set that up.

Setting Up a Windows NT Print Server for Use with Mac Clients

To set up a Windows NT print server to use with Mac clients, follow these steps:

1. Open the Windows NT Server Control Panel.

2. Open Services.

3. Scroll down the Service list until you locate Print Server for Macintosh.

4. Select Print Server for Macintosh and click Startup. The Service dialog box appears, as shown in Figure 4-44.

Figure 4–44: Enabling Print Server for Macintosh

5. Make sure that the Automatic and System Account option buttons are enabled, along with the Allow Service to Interact with Desktop check box, as shown in Figure 4-44.

   These options ensure that the Mac can locate the printer across the network, and that any Mac user accounts can use it.

6. Click OK.

7. Open the Macintosh Chooser.

8. Select the desired printer driver icon in the Chooser. Figure 4-45 shows you what you should see.

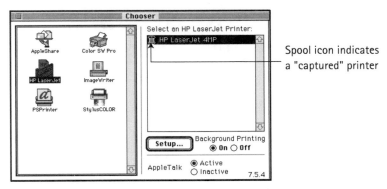

Spool icon indicates
a "captured" printer

Figure 4-45: Locating the Networked Printer in the Chooser

There's a subtle trick to this screen. Notice the tiny spool icon attached to the printer listing on the right side of the Chooser? This indicates that an AppleTalk printer on the network has been successfully "captured" by the Mac client. A print spooler is created on the Windows NT server when this occurs, and the Mac client sends the print job to the spooler, and the job prints in the background. There's not much that can be done here to change this; you trade off slower print performance from the Mac for the convenience of not having to switch AppleTalk connections to run a print job. I think it's a good trade-off. Expect a few seconds or longer wait before printer output starts. Once it begins, output will proceed at the normal speed depending on the application.

Also bear in mind that, although I'm using a PostScript printer in Figure 4-45 (HP LaserJet 4MP), you can do the same thing with good-quality nonPostScript printers that are hooked up to the server. That's because Print Services for Macintosh emulates PostScript. Thus, Mac users can send their print jobs to any nonPostScript printer on the Windows NT system and expect to get their output. Again, emulation may slow things down on the printing. Windows NT Server performance is minimally affected for normal workloads. The key thing to keep in mind is the quality of the printer's drivers. Many printer manufacturers do a less than stellar job supporting Windows NT.

All in all, compatibility issues being what they are between the PC and Mac worlds, I think Microsoft's Mac support in Windows NT Server is exceptional. You can share an entire Windows NT hard disk with Mac clients just as you can with Windows clients. Macs can see Windows NT print servers across the same network using the Chooser. Performance is more than acceptable. Mac users don't have to be left out in the cold of a PC-centric company any longer. With an Windows NT server and some Ethernet links, Macs are in like Flynn.

Networking Macintosh System 8 Clients with Windows NT

Now it's time to heap some praise on Apple. (Well, dole it out grudgingly with a spoon, perhaps.) After installing System 8 on my existing System 7 Macintosh, which uses the Windows NT networking settings so exhaustively described in the previous section, the new System 8 client worked flawlessly with the Windows NT server. All previous settings were preserved. Windows NT volumes are mounted on System 8 desktops in exactly the same way as for System 7. File compatibility is even improved.

If you upgrade an existing System 7 Mac that has a connection setup to Windows NT, the System 8 installation will read your existing settings and preserve them. Otherwise, you can follow the same procedure for network connection as described in the previous section.

Networking System 8 Macintoshes works almost identically as with System 7. Here's the basic logon process:

1. From the Apple menu, open the Chooser, as shown in Figure 4-46.

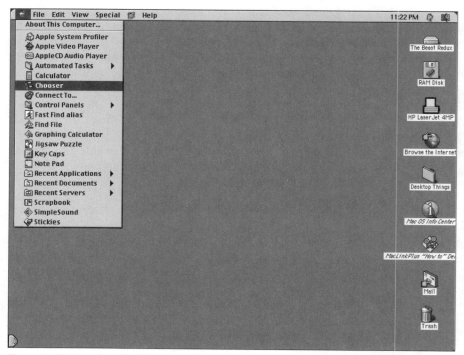

Figure 4-46: Locating the Chooser in System 8

2. Select the AppleShare icon. The resulting display, shown in Figure 4-47, should look familiar.

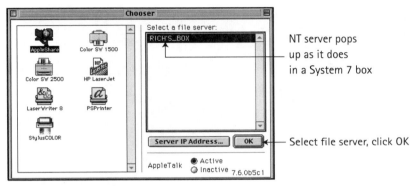

Figure 4-47: Opening the Windows NT Server in the System 8 Chooser

Though it's not used in this book, the Server IP Address button in the new Chooser opens the Macintosh Chooser up to new areas in local- and wide-area networking. Being able to issue a single IP address for a server running TCP/IP connectivity allows a System 8 Mac to have more versatility in the networking game, and bypass AppleTalk limitations. Anyway . . .

The Windows NT server also appears in the Chooser's Select a File Server pane in exactly the same way as it does in a System 7 client.

3. Select the Windows NT file server and click OK, as shown in Figure 4-47.

   The *Select a logon method* dialog box appears

4. Select Microsoft Authentication and click OK. The Connect dialog box appears.

5. Enter your user name and password.

6. Click OK. The Volumes list appears.

   Again, it's functionally identical to the process for System 7, other than some minor cosmetic differences.

7. Select a volume and click OK. (Press the Shift key and click to select more than one. Since you've selected Microsoft authentication, you won't be able to fill the check boxes.)

8. If any volume has its own volume password, enter it in its dialog box.

9. Click OK. The volumes will be mounted onto the desktop, as in Figure 4-48.

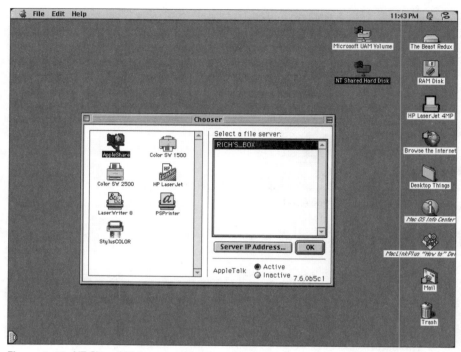

Figure 4-48: NT Shared Volumes on the System 8 Desktop

Macintosh System 8 connections (see Figure 4-49) allow you to browse through a shared volume in new ways.

In all particulars, including printing, System 8 is fully compatible with the networking practices described for Mac-to-Windows NT connectivity. If you're a new System 8 user, don't let that deter you from connecting to your office's Windows NT server. It will run just fine.

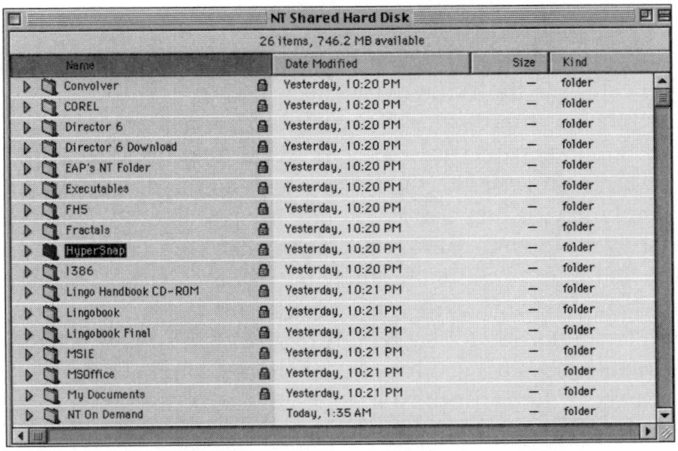

Figure 4–49: Browsing an NT Shared Volume in System 8

A Final Word

Let's face it: Macs are not a huge presence in corporate America. The AppleTalk protocol is a major reason. However, for creative-type communities, such as publishing and multimedia, they are ubiquitous. (I have received numerous stories of large Mac houses using Windows NT servers as AppleTalk routers and employing them as their workgroup servers even when they run hundreds of Macs in their organization.) You can also expect to see Macs in huge numbers of PR departments and in-house graphics organizations. So now you have the knowledge you need to see that they aren't left out of the enterprise network. Windows 3.*x* is more problematic, primarily because of compatibility. The vanilla Windows 3.1 version isn't compatible with networking, and a lot of jury-rigging has to be done to get it to work at all. If your company has a lot of 16-bit clients, buy as many copies as you can of the inexpensive 16-bit Windows 3.11 upgrade. You'll be glad you did. It's a purchase that I'd imagine even the most penny-starved IS departments would authorize with pleasure. It's cheap, and it saves a lot of unnecessary work, which will save your company money in the long run.

The next chapter discusses the topic of peer-to-peer networking.

Troubleshooting

My Windows 3.1 system can't see the Windows NT network.

This could be due to any number of problems. You may have a network card that has hardware jumpers instead of software for setting interrupts and I/O. Check your cable connections. Make sure you have the right user name and address. Beyond those issues, you may simply have a box that is too old. Many older 286 and 386 systems have chronic hardware incompatibility problems that are the bane of IS departments. I/O conflicts and interrupts are the single biggest problems with these computers, particularly when a network card and a sound card are in the system. For older PCs, documentation can also be very hard to find. If you suspect a hardware problem, strip the offending system down to its bare bones by removing every unnecessary card and then see if the network comes up.

Finally, make sure that NetBEUI is installed as the networking protocol. Also, if you're actually using a Windows 3.1 OS, it does not, in practice, support networking. Go buy the $49 Windows 3.11 upgrade. That should fix many of your problems.

My Mac client can't log on to the server at all.

The odds are that your AppleTalk connection is switched to the wrong physical connection. Open the Apple menu, and select Control Panels, then AppleTalk. The AppleTalk Control Panel provides a simple drop-down list from which you can choose the correct AppleTalk connection. If your Mac's AppleTalk is set to the Printer port and your Mac's networking connection is on Built-In Ethernet, there's your trouble right there.

If you still can't log on, check your cabling connection. It's also possible that your server may have a problem with its Macintosh services. Otherwise, few things can go wrong with a basic Mac-to-NT connection as long as the Services for Macintosh is installed and configured properly.

My Macintosh doesn't allow me to log on to a shared volume as anyone except a Guest! Also, some of the volumes I should be able to see don't appear when I log on as a Guest.

This is a minor problem on the client end. You may be using the Apple Standard UAMs for password authentication. If so, you'll be able to mount those volumes on startup that the server allows with the Guest account (mainly, the Microsoft UAM Volume). The advantage here is that you can mount those Guest-logged volumes on startup. Conversely, if the Windows NT Server makes some volumes available only under Microsoft Authentication, you won't be able to log on to any of them unless you use that Microsoft Authentication as your password scheme. Mac-accessible volumes are more secure with Microsoft Authentication and conform to Windows NT security standards. Unfortunately, you won't be able to log on to them with the Mac at startup, but must go through the Chooser every time.

I already have an AppleTalk router on my Mac-based network. Won't my Windows NT Server conflict with it if I set it up for AppleTalk routing?
Not if you check your AppleTalk Network IDs beforehand. Windows NT Server will automatically detect any AppleTalk zones you already have on the network. Do not create new zones or network IDs that use the same names and Network ID numbers that you already have, or you may clobber your existing network.

Why doesn't my Windows NT Server allow me to view the Mac hard disk?
The Windows NT operating system isn't built to work two ways. In other words, you can mount Windows NT volumes on the Mac, but not the other way around. There are third-party products that enable you to do this; among them are DataViz' MacOpener for Windows
(`http://www.dataviz.com/Products/prodinfo.html`).

When I open up Server Manager to inspect and work with my Mac volumes, I get a message saying "The network path was not found."
You have the wrong computer selected in the Server Manager. Select the Windows NT server that is running Services for Macintosh, and then select the Properties or Volumes options from the MacFile menu. You can also send a message to Mac clients from a feature on that menu.

Chapter 5

Peer-to-Peer Networking

IN THIS CHAPTER

What is *peer-to-peer networking*? Basically, it's a network of connected computers, all of which have the same status. In other words, no servers. Everyone shares and shares alike.

Peer-to-peer networking is a popular connectivity application in small businesses. Although it's limited, it's a great way for a few users (or one user with a few computers) to share resources between systems. Among the tasks you perform in this chapter are the following:

◆ Creating user accounts

◆ Connecting Windows NT Workstations

◆ Connecting a Windows 95 computer to Windows NT Workstation

MOST OF THE MATERIAL in this chapter builds on what has been discussed in Chapters 1 through 4. I won't repeat myself at great length here; I'll stick to the basics of getting your separate Windows machines to talk with one another. If peer-to-peer is the main application that you take away from this book, you won't need to read much more (unless you have intellectual curiosity).

When you're a small businessperson, you might not have the need for a server in your office. If you have just a few Win95 workstations and want to experiment with Windows NT, buying a copy of Windows NT Server may not make sense. Instead, you can buy a copy of Windows NT Workstation, which is a bit cheaper than the server, and take it for a spin. You can connect all your Windows 95 computers to it, check out its User Manager, do some basic account management, and learn more about the operating system without making a big investment in time or money. That's what this chapter is about: office connectivity with Windows NT Workstation.

Understand that there are some severe practical limitations with what you can do in Windows NT Workstation. For anything more than four or five users, account administrations can be a serious problem. Windows NT Workstation's Remote Access capabilities are effectively limited to dialing out. You can set user accounts to dial in to Windows NT Workstation, but connection support is limited, and true Remote Access services are not directly supported. Obviously, domains cannot be created in Workstation, and the security levels aren't as comprehensive as they are in a fully configured Windows NT Server. Nevertheless, you can get a lot of things done with Windows NT Workstation in a small-office environment, and this chapter aims to get you there without a lot of fuss.

Managing User Accounts with Windows NT Workstation

Do yourself a favor: If you have more than four or five client systems in your network, consider going straight to Windows NT Server. Although it's harder to set up, once you do, it's much easier to maintain than a peer-to-peer network, and also much faster.

 TIP If you have more than a few clients, I strongly recommend going straight to Windows NT Server.

Some authors actually say that you can easily have dozens of users in a peer-to-peer network without any need for a server. Whatever planet they're living on certainly doesn't have any offices. When you step through the process of networking just two puny Windows NT Workstations together in this chapter, you'll get a feel for why a server-based environment has its advantages.

What are the advantages and disadvantages of peer-to-peer networking?

Advantages:

 ◆ Cheaper

 ◆ Faster and slightly easier installation

 ◆ Fewer services to maintain or install

Disadvantages:

 ◆ More complicated user account setup and maintenance

 ◆ Sluggish performance with more than a few users on the network

Of course, Windows NT Workstation offers a User Manager. Using it, you can set up all your user accounts so that your peer users can use the resources in the local system. But Windows NT Workstation (and Windows 95) doesn't employ a centralized user database, unlike Windows NT Server. This means that on a network containing several Windows NT workstations, *every* computer in the network has to have all the same user accounts available for their shared resources. Managing multiple Windows NT workstations in a peer network can become a mess in short order.

Windows NT Workstation's User Manager is shown in Figure 5-1.

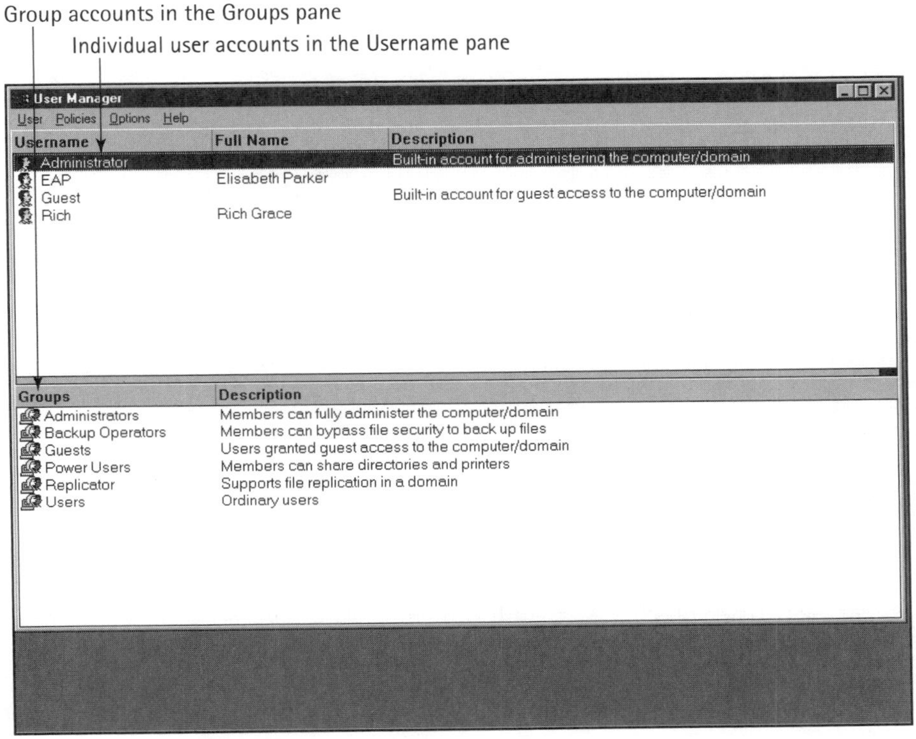

Group accounts in the Groups pane
        Individual user accounts in the Username pane

Figure 5-1: The NT Workstation User Manager

As with Windows NT Server, this is where it all begins. For any other peer-to-peer user to have access to resources on your Windows NT Workstation, they must have a user account on your system. This is where you create the accounts. For example, if you wanted your office manager Jackie to have a user account so she could read and write files from a folder on your D drive, you would have to create a special account for her on your computer. Then your computer has to be told that Jackie has the right to access the devices that you want her to. User Manager helps you do those things.

That's not all. If Jackie is also using a Windows NT Workstation, an account for her also has to be created on *her* computer so she can use her computer on the network. After all, Jackie can't simply log on to the network as the administrator. (Unless, of course, she *is* the administrator.) Once she logs on to her system using the normal Windows Networking prompt, she can use Network Neighborhood to access the resources she needs without issuing further passwords. That is, *after* everything is set up.

User Manager allows you to create individual user accounts (called *usernames*) and to gather those accounts into *groups*. Groups can be assigned to a shared device, and all users collected in that group automatically have the same access privileges for that device. They make peer-to-peer a little less complicated for Windows NT clients.

The advantage to using groups, especially in a peer-to-peer network where things can get confusing very quickly, is that you can organize all the user accounts in one convenient place on each system and have them all share the same devices in the same way. Unfortunately, you must have all your usernames organized in each computer in a peer-to-peer network, even if you're using groups. This is especially true if you're using Windows NT Workstation only for peer clients — a circumstance that's still relatively rare.

> All Windows NT peer-to-peer clients must contain all the users' accounts in a peer network that are intended to connect to those Windows NT systems.

In a mixed network of Windows 95 and Windows NT computers, the Windows NT Workstation can still allocate user accounts for the devices that it's sharing. Windows 95 computers simply designate whether a device (a hard disk or a printer, usually) is shared or not. It's easier but less flexible. Windows 95 clients don't offer a User Manager and so can't define individual accounts or groups that have access to a shared device. They just log on to the network and that's that.

I'll start off by networking Windows NT workstations and later move to Windows NT-Windows 95 connections.

Networking Windows NT Workstations

To encourage the best possible organization in your network, you need to start by properly identifying each computer. Fortunately, this is quite straightforward. Identifying a computer is a separate process from defining user accounts. When you're putting the network together, you need administrative privileges to define user accounts and set up identifications. After that, users can log on to their stations and make them their own.

In this exercise you learn how two Windows NT workstations are set up for connectivity. For the examples, one system is called Dual-P5 WS, and its workgroup is BASIC WORKGROUP. The other Windows NT system is called Windows NT_Station, and it participates in the same workgroup. (Don't worry, this becomes clear in short order.)

Remember, when you ran the Setup program for Windows NT Workstation, you were already prompted to provide a computer name and network workgroup or domain under which the computer would participate. Since you're dealing with hooking up workstations, you need to decide on a common workgroup name under which all your peers can be easily organized. Domains are not an issue here.

A workgroup is different and separate from the groups that are created in User Manager. Why?

◆ **Workgroups** are used to collect physical computers together on the network.

◆ **User groups** are used to collect user accounts so that they have uniform access rights to network resources.

For Windows NT workstations in a peer arrangement, workgroups are the highest level of organization. User groups are one step lower on the ladder.

Identifying a Windows NT Workstation on the Network

To identify a Windows NT workstation on the network, follow these steps:

1. Log on using the Administrator account.

2. Open the Windows NT Control Panel. (If you're not sure where it is, click the Start button, select Settings, and then Control Panel.) Figure 5-2 shows Windows NT Workstation's Control Panel.

Network applet

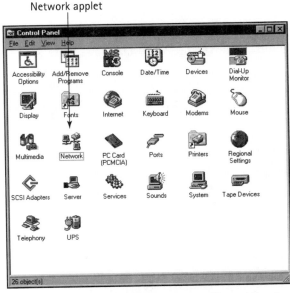

Figure 5-2: The Windows NT Workstation Control Panel

3. Open the Network applet. It is shown in Figure 5-3.

Identification tab   Change button

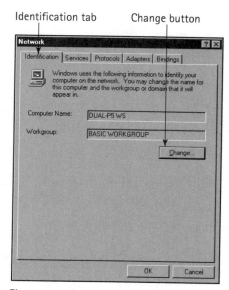

Figure 5-3: Control Panel's Network Applet

In Figure 5-3 the computer's name is Dual-P5 WS, and the workgroup is given as BASIC WORKGROUP. They are provided simply as examples.

4. Click the Change button.

The Identification Changes dialog box appears, as shown in Figure 5-4.

5. Enter the desired name and workgroup for your computer. In the example for this chapter, they're called Dual-P5 WS and BASIC WORKGROUP. You only need to remember the actual names that you're using for your own system.

6. Click OK to close the dialog box.

7. Click OK to close the Network dialog box.

Computer Name text box

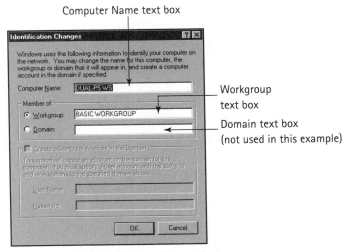

Workgroup
text box

Domain text box
(not used in this example)

Figure 5-4: NT's Identification Change Feature

In this example, the other workstation's identification looks like that shown in Figure 5-5.

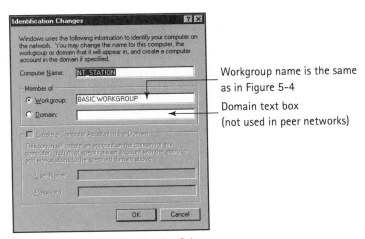

Workgroup name is the same
as in Figure 5-4

Domain text box
(not used in peer networks)

Figure 5-5: Identification for the Other
Workstation in This Example

How Should Your Peer Clients Be Organized?

In a small peer-to-peer network, all your clients should use the same workgroup for greatest efficiency and convenience. (The advantage of this will become clear a bit later.) The clients should all have different names, of course.

Another brief note: The Domain field should only be selected if your Windows NT Workstation is going to participate in a Windows NT Server-administered domain. Since you're doing peer-to-peer, this isn't an issue.

The workgroup name is the key. It's the same for both workstations in this sample network. For a small network, make sure the workgroup name is the same for all your peer-to-peer clients. The names for the computers and the workgroup don't matter; you can define them as you please. Just make sure they're all identified with the same workgroup.

Also, you need to make sure that all your network clients are using the same network protocol, which should be NetBEUI in a typical, small Microsoft network. If NetBEUI is already installed, skip the next few paragraphs and go to the next section, "Opening Network Neighborhood to Check Network Connections."

Again, using the Administrator account:

1. Open the Control Panel.

2. Open the Network applet.

3. Click the Protocols tab. Figure 5-6 shows what you should have for your peer-to-peer network.

   If the list box of the Protocols tab doesn't show NetBEUI in the list, you must add it.

4. In the Protocols tab of the Network applet, click the Add button. The Select Network Protocol dialog box appears, as shown in Figure 5-7.

Add button   NetBEUI must be on the list

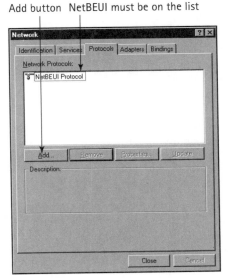

Figure 5-6: Inspecting the Installed
Network Protocols

Net BEUI Protocol appears on the list

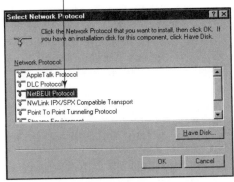

Figure 5-7: Adding the NetBEUI Protocol

5. Select NetBEUI Protocol and click OK. You may be prompted to insert the
    Windows NT CD so that the protocol can be installed.

I think it's wise to point out here that you can actually use any networking protocol for your peer-to-peer network — not necessarily NetBEUI. You can use IPX or

TCP/IP instead. The big issue here is simplicity. There's no point in being a purist when you're just hooking a few little computers together. NetBEUI is a simple, straightforward solution for doing this. With TCP/IP, you need to know a little more about IP addressing and how to apply it to each individual computer. Essentially, each individual peer machine must have its own assigned IP address that is given to the operating system. Since you're not running a server here, your TCP/IP networking capabilities are limited; nevertheless, they're still more complicated to deal with than just using the expedient NetBEUI, which requires no configuration and no special addressing schemes, and gets simple networking tasks done without fuss. I recommend sticking with NetBEUI for small peer networks. Once you get the network running, you can begin experimenting.

 NetBEUI is the simplest but not the only solution for peer networking protocols.

Opening Network Neighborhood to Check Network Connections

Once you know your protocols are in order, and your computer names and workgroup assignments are squared away, you can go ahead and restart each system and log on to them as the administrator. Then double-click Network Neighborhood on the Windows NT desktop.

With the two sample computers, Dual-P5 WS and NT_Station, and a sample workgroup, BASIC WORKGROUP, Figure 5-8 shows what you should see.

Both computers appear at the top level of Network Neighborhood.

The assumption here is that you're connecting two brand-new Windows NT Workstations, creating new user accounts and groups, and sharing devices between them. In this situation, if you're on one client and double-click the icon for the other client, the only thing you'll see is an open window with a Printers folder icon.

Even if you're the administrator, this is all you'll see. That's because the devices still need to be shared and mapped between the systems. Since I don't advise having all your users log on using the Administrator account, you'll start by creating a couple of new user accounts, and then move on to setting up device sharing for the peer-to-peer systems.

Both sample computers show up
at the top level of the neighborhood

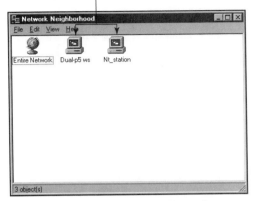

Figure 5-8: Walking the Beat in Network
Neighborhood

Creating New User Accounts on Windows NT Workstation

To create a new user account on a Windows NT workstation, follow these steps:

1. From the Start menu, click Programs, and then Administrative Tools, and then User Manager. Starting from scratch, you'll see two user accounts created by Windows NT: Administrator and Guest. See Table 5-1.

TABLE 5-1 USER ACCOUNTS CREATED BY WINDOWS NT WORKSTATION AND THEIR
         PRIVILEGES

Account	Privileges
Administrator	Full access to the system to manage the network. Power to create and remove user accounts and groups. All user rights provided. Can define access rights and shares for any devices on the system. Can also perform system administration remotely.
Guest	Can log on to the local system without a special username. Cannot create or modify accounts. Guest account is disabled by default (run User Manager to enable it).

Figure 5-9 shows the two accounts in User Manager.

Administrator and Guest accounts

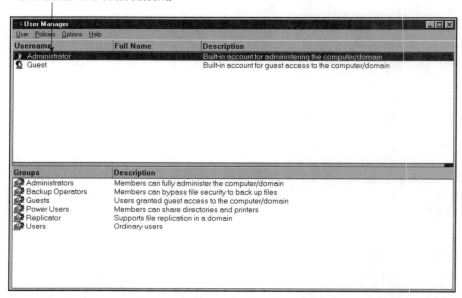

Figure 5-9: Running User Manager to Create the First New Accounts

2. From the User menu, select New User.

   The New User dialog box appears, as shown in Figure 5-10.

3. In the Username text box, enter the name by which your user account will log on.

4. If desired, enter the full name of the user and a description (not required for logon accounts).

5. In the Password text box, enter the password by which the user will log on. Windows NT automatically encrypts the password to 14 characters regardless of its length. (It won't change the password, just encrypts it.) Type the password again in the Confirm Password text box. The results will resemble those shown in Figure 5-11.

Groups button

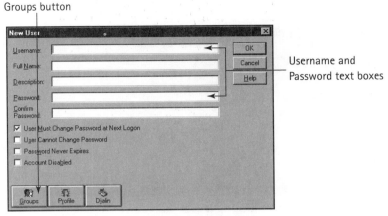

Username and
Password text boxes

Figure 5-10: Beginning Creation of a New Account

Check boxes affect how   Passwords are
passwords are used   automatically encrypted

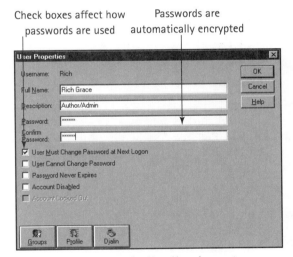

Figure 5-11: Creation of a New User Account

6. Disable the User Must Change Password at Next Logon check box, and enable only the Password Never Expires check box (if only for convenience, of course).

7. Create a second user account with the same characteristics as the previous one: a distinct user name, password, description, and the same check box configuration as described in Step 6. User Manager should have two new accounts in it, resembling those in Figure 5-12.

Policies

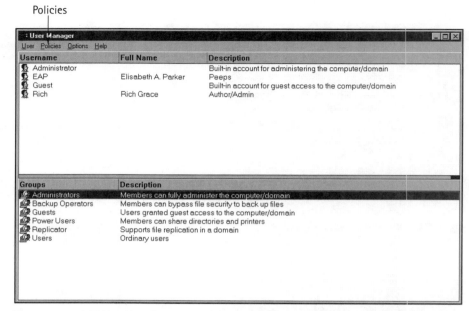

Figure 5-12: Add Two User Accounts to Your Windows NT Workstation's User Manager

8. Add the same two user accounts you just created to the second Windows NT workstation. In my sample network, one system named Dual-P5 WS is going to be the system that username Rich uses, while the system NT Station will be the one that username EAP uses for her work. Yours, of course, may differ.

Make sure you have a record of any passwords, especially if they're meant to be a more secure type of password combining letters and numbers. (For that matter, the administrator *must* remember his or her password!)

Four check boxes are provided in Figure 5-11, each of which affects how the new accounts' passwords are accepted by the system. Table 5-2 describes these check boxes.

TABLE 5-2 NEW USER CHECK BOXES

Check Box	Features
User Must Change Password at Next Logon	The next time the user logs on to the local system, the user will be prompted to change the password. This is handy for administrators who want their network users to make the decision about the password they will use (the administrator should make a record nevertheless).
	Unfortunately, selecting this Option (which is enabled by default) can also entail some headaches during network setup. In a peer-to-peer Windows NT network, user accounts must be placed on all clients sharing resources on the network, and this means that the users must change their passwords while logging on to every system in the network containing their accounts. (On NT Server, the user account only has to be created once. On a peer -to-peer network, it may need to be created many times, once on each client system.) The administrator uses a "dummy" password when he or she creates the account, and the users must change it to what they want when they log in the first time — on any system where their accounts appear. If they don't, they'll receive an error message when they try to use network resources. Since this is a royal pain, I don't recommend this option unless it's absolutely necessary. Disable this check box for any account where you think it's appropriate, and do so on all systems that will contain the account.
User Cannot Change Password	The user cannot change the password. Handy for user accounts assigned on a sporadic basis on the network, such as Guest.
Password Never Expires	Forces the password to be permanent, overriding any other settings. Overrides the User Must Change Password at Next Logon checkbox (fortunately).
Account Disabled	Useful for temporary disabling of accounts while a user is on vacation. An account can be disabled and then copied as a template for fast creation of new accounts.

Figure 5-12 shows the Groups button in the New User dialog box. Now that your user accounts are created, you can actually go ahead and start allocating your shared resources to them. But you can also increase the convenience of maintaining your peer-to-peer network. That's discussed in the next section.

Understanding User Rights

Groups are the handiest way possible for Windows NT Workstation users to organize themselves. I *highly* recommend making use of them. To do so, you need to know a few basic things about groups.

Just as with Windows NT Server, user rights can be used on Windows NT Workstation to limit peer clients' access to others' resources.

It's no accident that Windows NT Workstation provides six different default groups. As shown in Figure 5-12, the six default groups are Administrators, Backup Operators, Guests, Power Users, Replicator, and Users. (Windows NT Server has a larger collection.) Each group has its own qualities and characteristics that depend on a Windows NT feature called user rights. User rights determine how user accounts interact with the computer system and with other systems on the peer network.

To get a quick grasp of how user rights work, perform the following steps:

1. Open the User Manager.

2. From the Policies menu, select User Rights. The User Rights dialog box appears, as shown in Figure 5-13.

Rights list   Grant To list box

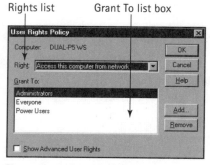

Figure 5-13: Introducing User Rights

A drop-down Rights list is displayed in the dialog box.

In Figure 5-13, an automatically selected right is at the top of the list: Access this computer from network. The Grant To list box shows the user groups that have that right assigned to them: Administrators, Everyone, and Power Users. So far, so good. All three of those are groups within the system (though Everyone is really a catch-all group and doesn't appear in the User Manager).

3. Click the down arrow in the Rights list, as shown in Figure 5-14. The list shows a selection of different privileges within the system.

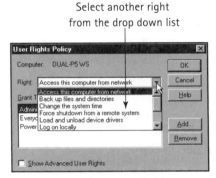

Figure 5-14: Inspecting User Rights

4. From the Rights list, select Access this Computer from network. The Grant To pane will change, as shown in Figure 5-15.

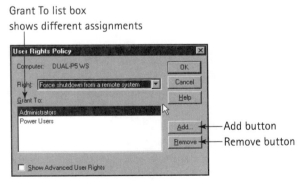

Figure 5-15: Inspecting Group Assignments for a Specific User Right

This is the key. Look at each of the rights in the list, and you'll see that only certain groups use them. The Add and Remove buttons allow you to change those assignments whenever you want.

5. Click the Add button. The Add Users and Groups dialog box appears. Here you can add groups and even individual user accounts to have that specific user right. You have to go through the same process for any individual user right. To display individual accounts here, simply click the Show Users button.

6. Double-click a group or account name to add it.

7. Click OK. The new group or account appears in the User Rights Policy dialog box for the selected user right.

You can create your own groups from scratch and assign appropriate user rights. Then add your user accounts to them. Instead of having to laboriously assign those user rights to each individual's account, you can just collect the accounts in a group and they automatically use those rights.

Since Windows NT Workstation provides six local groups (Administrators, Power Users, and so on), you might as well use those instead of creating your own. If you copy a group and create your own from it, the original group's user rights aren't copied to the new one. The six existing groups are not true templates, because their attributes (mainly user rights) are not copied to any new groups you create from them.

Windows NT provides enough basic groups so that you probably won't need to create your own in most situations.

Organizing Users into Groups

As you can see, you have to do a lot more work to create a new group and assign the user rights you want. Using the User Rights Policy dialog box shown in Figure 5-15, you'd have to check each user right and decide whether it's appropriate for the new group (and the accounts associated with it) to have those powers. (If you want to know more about group creation and assigning user rights, please see Chapter 12.)

You don't have to do that; instead, add the two new user accounts you've created to the Power Users local group for each Windows NT Workstation. Then set up the connections and shared devices while still using the Administrative account. Finally, log in using both of the new Power User accounts to see how it works.

1. In the User Manager, double-click the Power Users local group listing.

The Local Group Properties dialog box appears as shown in Figure 5-16.

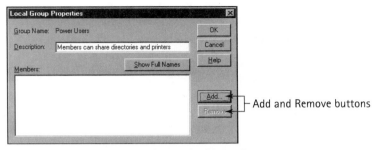

Figure 5-16: The Local Group Properties Dialog Box

2. Click Add.

   The Add Users and Groups dialog box appears. Individual accounts are listed, including the two you've just created.

3. Double-click each of your new user accounts in the Names list box.

4. Click OK. The results should resemble Figure 5-17.

Two new users are listed

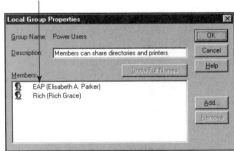

Figure 5-17: Adding Two New Accounts to the Power Users Group

5. Click OK.

6. Go to the second workstation and follow the same procedure as Steps 1 through 5.

   The Power Users group is handy in a peer network because users in that group have the right to share devices and define many things about how their system works, without impinging on most administrative tasks.

The administrator sets up the shared drives and defines the users or groups that can access them. Once the users in the Power Users group log on and start using the systems, they can use the shared devices but can't define any new shares of their own. The group does have the capability to use shared devices and directories — they just can't define them on their own. Only users with administrative privileges can do that.

7. Close User Manager.

At this point you should still be logged on to both workstations as the administrator. It's time to set up a couple shared devices between the two computers.

Setting Up Peer-to-Peer Shared Devices

This section, of course, assumes that your connected systems are capable of being networked together and have been set up using the methods described in the previous exercises. Follow these steps:

1. On either workstation, open My Computer.

2. Right-click the C drive. Its shortcut menu appears.

3. From the shortcut menu, select Sharing, as shown in Figure 5-18.

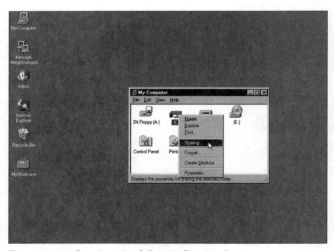

Figure 5-18: Opening the C Drive's Sharing Feature

The hard disk's Properties sheet appears.

4. Select the Shared As option button.

5. Click New share.

6. Enter a new share name. (For example, use *C Drive*.)

7. Click the Permissions button. The Access Through Share Permissions dialog box appears.

8. Click the Add button. The Add Users and Groups dialog box appears.

   Here's the key step.

9. Select the Power Users group and click Add.

   Power Users, you may recall, is where your two new accounts are grouped.

10. Under Type of Access, select Change. (You're still in Add Users and Groups here.) This sets up the Power Users group so that its users can read and write to files on the local station.

11. Click OK. The Access Through Share Permissions dialog box reappears.

12. Just for kicks, make sure the Everyone group in the share has Read access from the Type of Access list (which also shows up in Access Through Share Permissions). This prevents unwanted read/write access by rogue accounts to the shared disk.

    Don't delete the Everyone group or give it No Access status. If you do, your user accounts will not be able to use the shared device!

13. Click OK.

14. Click OK again to close the hard disk's Properties sheet.

    You should be able to go over to the other workstation, open up Network Neighborhood, and access the shared drive. Since you're the administrator, this is to be expected.

15. Follow Steps 1 through 14 above for the other Windows NT Workstation with its C drive.

    Now test your new user accounts and device shares by having your users log on to each computer (or doing so yourself with each account). You don't have to restart each system fully, however.

16. From the Start menu, select Shut Down. The Shut Down Windows dialog box appears.

17. Select Close all programs and log on as a different user? and click Yes.

18. When the system prompts you to log on, enter the name and password for one of your new user accounts. Follow the same process for the other Windows NT Workstation, using the other new account.

Because both user accounts are present on both systems, when each user logs on to the system, he or she can access the shared hard disks on the other computer by opening Network Neighborhood and double-clicking the computer icon for the other user's machine. No other passwords need to be issued.

This leads to a key issue of etiquette in peer-to-peer networks: trust. When your various users are accessing each other's systems, everyone has to be comfortable with the fact that this is going on. The larger a peer network you build, the more difficult it becomes to make sure that things aren't shared that shouldn't be. Figure 5-19 shows a diagram of the relationship between the two systems you've just networked:

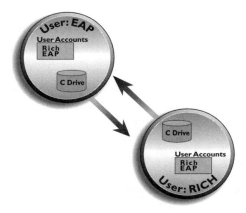

Figure 5-19: Two Windows NT Systems in a
Peer-to-Peer Relationship

If you have four systems in a similar relationship, the number of accounts each system contains would double, and the amount of work to connect the computers goes up exponentially. Not everyone in the network will necessarily need to offer the same number of resources on the network, but this is the basic trend in peer-to-peer.

Every user has a responsibility to be a good network citizen. Windows NT Workstation provides the User Manager program so that each workstation has a way to dictate which resources are going to be shared with which colleagues. Some systems may be on the network but may not share anything at all. Others might share only a printer. (I'll get to that in Chapter 6.)

Peer users need to be a bit more sophisticated about their use of the network than an average client-server user does. An administrator of a peer-to-peer Windows NT network also has a lot of work to do (perhaps more than you'd expect), particularly in building user accounts and making sure they're all in the right places. Each system also has to be managed on an ongoing basis to make sure users don't accidentally delete program files, remove directories, or lose important data files.

This section has given you the basic mechanics involved in creating a Windows NT Workstation network. It's nearly as complicated as running a server because of the multiplicity of user accounts. After a certain point, getting a server may not seem like such a bad idea. It provides a central point of management.

Networking Windows 95 Computers to Windows NT Workstation

In peer-to-peer connections, another common application is running a mixed Windows NT Workstation/Windows 95 network. In some ways, Windows 95 users have it easy. No User Manager exists on a Windows 95 system. This has several implications:

◆ If you have a Windows NT workstation with several Windows 95 systems in a small peer network, the workstation can function as a type of server because of its User Manager capabilities.

◆ Windows 95 systems can simply log on and have immediate access to shared devices from the Windows NT computer without carrying user accounts in their own system.

◆ Windows 95 machines can share devices from their computers without concern for user rights or specific accounts. All they need to control is a single password for each shared device, whether it's a folder, hard disk, or printer. Anyone who wants to access that device needs only to furnish that password.

◆ Windows 95 systems can also get a list of users and groups that are allowed access to their system from another computer: a Windows NT computer. It works with either Windows NT servers or workstations.

Windows 95 computers can participate in the same *workgroups* as Windows NT Workstation machines. In fact, that's the key to a successful connection. Here's how to connect a Windows 95 system to the peer-to-peer Windows NT network you created in the previous section:

1. In the Windows 95 system, open Control Panel.

2. Open the Network applet.

3. Click the Identification tab. It appears as shown in Figure 5-20.

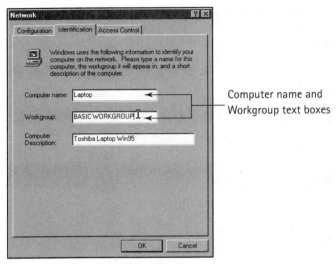

Computer name and
Workgroup text boxes

Figure 5-20: Opening Windows 95's
Identification Screen

4. Enter the name of the computer (if it isn't already defined).

5. Enter the workgroup's name that the system will join. (In Figure 5-20, it's BASIC WORKGROUP, which is automatically capitalized by Win95.)

   The workgroup name and the computer name are both important, but the workgroup name is crucial. Because the other systems are likely part of a workgroup, you must specify the same one for a Win95 client. As long as you have a functioning network connection, the rest is fairly easy.

6. Close the Network control panel. You may be prompted to restart the system. After doing so, log on to it using the new account.

   For the Win95 system to connect fully, a user account for that user must be included on any Windows NT systems that are to be its peers on the network.

7. Run User Manager in a Windows NT workstation.

8. Create a new account using whatever name and password are appropriate (as long as they correspond to the user for the Win95 client) and add it to the Power Users group (for example).

9. Close User Manager. You should now be ready to connect.

Always bear in mind that users from Windows 95 systems won't have the ability to log on to any Windows NT peer system if their user name and password do not exist on the Windows NT computer. The account must be placed on any Windows NT computer to which the Windows 95 client expects to connect.

Sharing Devices and Acquiring Accounts from a Windows NT System

Because Windows 95 doesn't have a User Manager, you can take two different approaches to sharing devices in a Windows 95 computer in a mixed network:

◆ Require a password whenever a user opens the resource in Network Neighborhood or from a mapped drive.

◆ Acquire a list of users from another computer that are permitted to use each shared device.

The only virtue of the first option is that it's simple. In a peer-to-peer network, that approach can become a nuisance, because the person sharing the device on the network has more control over the password and because everyone is forced to enter the password when trying to use the resource. Since everyone uses the same password, this can also create a basic security problem.

Instead, you can leverage your existing user accounts from the Windows NT User Manager as a database that the Windows 95 system can automatically draw from. Although you still have to follow the same steps for each shared device, the process has several advantages. First, existing user accounts and passwords are used, without generating anymore passwords that the users and administrator must keep track of. Second, once a user logs on to the network, he or she can automatically open the shared resources without having to enter a second "nuisance" password. Finally, the Windows 95 user or administrator has complete control over who can access the system — in one handy location.

Here's how to share a Windows 95 device on the network and use a Windows NT user database to do it:

1. On the Win95 client, open Control Panel.

2. Open the Network applet.

3. Click the Access Control tab. This is where you make the decision of how users can access the shared device. Two very important option buttons are provided, as shown in Figure 5-21.

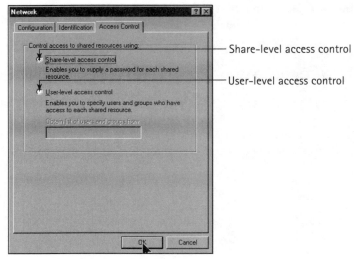

Figure 5-21: Opening the Windows 95 Access
Control Feature from the Network Applet

Table 5-3 summarizes the functions of these option buttons.

TABLE 5-3 HOW CAN USERS ACCESS YOUR WINDOWS 95 SYSTEM'S HARD DISK?

Disk Access Type	Features
Share-level access control	As mentioned, its main virtue is simplicity. You can define a password that anyone else must enter to access your device. It can prove an administrative and diplomatic nightmare, however.
User-level access control	The perfect solution for mixed Win95/NT networks of any type, client-server or peer-to-peer. The Win95 client can fetch a user account database off any connected Windows NT system, server or peer workstation, stand-alone or domain, from which users can be chosen for access rights to the shared resource.

4. Select the User-level access control option button. The Obtain list box is enabled, as shown in Figure 5-22.

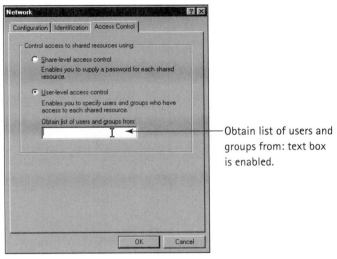

Obtain list of users and
groups from: text box
is enabled.

Figure 5-22: Enabling User-Level Access Control

5. Enter the name of the Windows NT system – to which the Win95 client is
   already connected – that contains the desired User Manager database. (In
   Figure 5-23 it's DUAL-P5 WS, but it could be any Windows NT
   Workstation system on your peer network that you're connected to.)

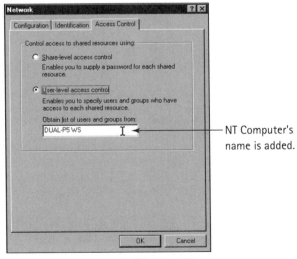

NT Computer's
name is added.

Figure 5-23: Entering the Windows NT
System for User Database Access

6. Click OK.

7. Restart your computer to let the changes take effect. (The system also prompts you.)

8. When the system is back online, open My Computer on the Win95 system.

9. Right-click a hard disk icon. The disk's shortcut menu appears.

10. Select Sharing from the shortcut menu. The drive's Properties sheet appears, displaying the Sharing tab.

11. Click the Shared As button and enter a share name, as shown in Figure 5-24.

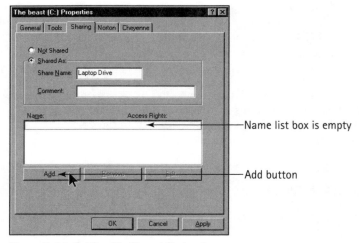

Figure 5–24: Setting Up Shared Status for a Win95 Hard Disk

The Names field is empty, but that soon changes.

12. Click the Add button. The Add Users dialog box appears, as shown in Figure 5-25, containing some interesting information.

Individual User accounts

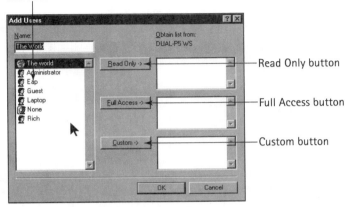

Figure 5-25: Adding User Accounts from an
NT System to an Access List for a
Windows 95 Resource

Groups from Windows NT workstations can't be displayed, but befitting a
peer-to-peer relationship, all the individual user accounts are listed in the
Add Users dialog box! (If you were hooking up to a domain server as
described in the Troubleshooting section of Chapter 2, you'd see the global
domain groups listed as well as individual accounts.)

All that remains is to decide what kind of access each user will have, and
which users will have access.

The access types are what you'd expect: Read Only (by selecting a user
and clicking the Read Only button), Full Access (ditto with the Full Access
button), and Custom.

13. Select the Administrator account and click the Full Access button.

14. Select other user accounts as desired and click the appropriate button for
    each. As you can see, this is a tremendous convenience feature for the
    network administrator. Your Windows 95 client can intelligently access
    each account and assign particular rights. Figure 5-26 shows a typical
    result.

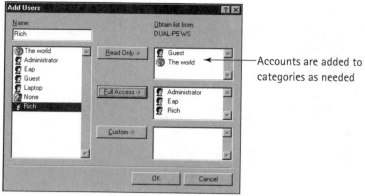

Accounts are added to categories as needed

Figure 5-26: Choosing User Accounts from the Windows NT System and the Types of Access They Have

15. Click OK. If you add a user to the Custom category, a Change Access Rights dialog box appears for that user, as shown in Figure 5-27.

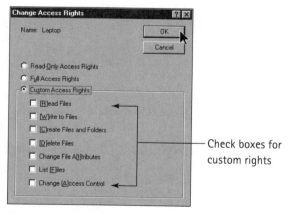

Check boxes for custom rights

Figure 5-27: You Can Change Access Rights for a Specific Account — on the Win95 Client

Again, the rights are similar to what you see in Windows NT systems. You may have a special client to whom you want to allow the ability to read and write files, but no other privileges.

If you have no users in the Custom category, this dialog box does not appear.

16. Select desired rights (if necessary) and click OK.

The Properties sheet reappears with some major changes.

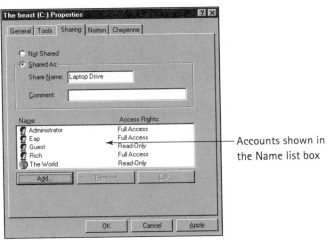

Accounts shown in
the Name list box

Figure 5-28: A Successful Share Creation,
Using an NT Account Database

17. Click OK to save the changes. The disk drive icon in My Computer
changes to a Shared type.

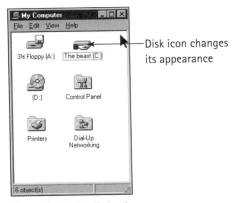

Disk icon changes
its appearance

Figure 5-29: The Drive Is
Shared in the Peer Network

Other systems will now be able to open Network Neighborhood, open the Win95 computer's icon, and immediately open the shared hard disk — if their user account under Windows NT is part of the share!

Although it takes a few more steps than doing it with a brute-force password, I recommend this method for peer-to-peer networks. This way, you're guaranteed that only those who you want to have access to the client actually have it. This is by far the best way to effectively integrate Windows 95 clients into *any* Windows NT-based network.

Even if you have a Windows NT server or three on the network, along with lots of Windows NT client workstations and Windows 95 machines, you can still employ the methods in this chapter to create small cooperative workgroups. Just make sure you keep a tight handle on the peer-to-peer configurations!

Bear in mind what I also mentioned in the previous section: In a peer-to-peer network, there are serious limits to how many users should use one workstation's shared hard disk. This goes for Windows 95 clients as well. If you have more than a few people's accounts accessing the system, you'll probably see noticeable hits in performance as other users thrash that hard drive. There are limits to the practical size of peer networks; I hope this chapter has given you a good appreciation of how they work and how to use them most effectively.

A Final Word

Now that you've gone through the basic process, you can see how going with the server-based network has some clear advantages over peer-to-peer. The latter is not a bad solution for a homogeneous Windows NT Workstation/Windows 95 computer collection, but networking options are severely limited. Considering the potential headaches, the basic NT Server software is not that much more expensive.

Macintoshes can't be peer networked unless you spend several hundred dollars for additional third-party software. TCP/IP service support is nonexistent in a peer network except for dial-out and simple, fixed addressing schemes. If you have to cut expenses down to the bone, peer-to-peer is a good way to go. If all you have are Windows 95 machines (and Windows), you actually don't even need a Windows NT workstation to connect those computers together. But since this is a Windows NT book, doing that is obviously relevant.

The next chapter discusses how to share printers over client-server and peer-to-peer Windows NT networks.

Troubleshooting

I've just received an "Unrecoverable Disk Error" when I tried to save my file back out to the network, and I lost all my work in that entire file!
You've run into one of the most painful problems in Windows networking. It's happened to me, it's happened to your office mates, it's probably even happened to Bill Gates. This error occurs when you work on a file from someone else's machine on the network, and then their system crashes or they have to reboot for some reason. Windows NT doesn't have what is called *transaction rollback*, a feature in some network operating systems that allows clients to recover gracefully from server shutdowns and maintain open files without damaging the current client session. Once the server recovers, the client can save his or her work without losing it.

Windows NT and most UNIX operating systems don't have transaction rollback. If a client has a file open from another machine and that other system shuts down, the electronic link between the file on the server and the client's session with that file is *broken*. When the other system comes back, and the user tries to save their work out, the old serving machine gets confused and that entire file can be blown away, overwritten with asterisks. It isn't pretty. There's not much you can do about it except to be careful. Perform recursive saves. This means *always* keeping a copy of your most current work on your local hard drive and saving everything there. Only when you are finished do you save your work out to the serving machine. Also, administrators on the network should always notify everyone else that they're about to restart, and would they please save out any open files they have running? These two measures should eliminate this problem.

When I try to log on to someone's shared system, I receive this message:

```
\\(System on Network) is not accessible.
The user must change his password before he logs on the first time.
```

Here's why. It's easy for the person setting up the share on their system to just enter the password they want. When they log back on to the system for the first time and are required to change the password, they simply reenter the first one. This process won't work. (Unfortunately, the system *appears* to accept it, but it really doesn't.) When you set up shares on a Windows NT Workstation, make sure that you actually change the password when you log on for the first time after setting up the share. Have the other person use a dummy password the first time and then enter the one he or she wants. That will get rid of this error.

Chapter 6

Print Serving From Windows NT

IN THIS CHAPTER
This chapter focuses on four major tasks:

◆ Setting up Print Services on a Windows NT server

◆ Making Windows NT workstations use the print server

◆ Making Windows 95 clients use the print server

◆ Peer print sharing between Windows NT workstations and Windows 95 systems

A *PRINT SERVER* is a computer that connects print devices such as laser or ink-jet printers to the network, enabling sharing of those print devices with clients on the network. Usually, those printers are hooked up to the server's parallel port and then shared on the network in the same way as other server resources.

Windows NT print serving is a fairly simple and efficient process. It also provides fairly broad operating system support, including all flavors of Windows (and Macintosh support, which was discussed in Chapter 4). In this chapter I focus on how to set up a print server on Windows NT Server, and how to make Windows NT and Windows 95 clients access the shared printer.

Setting Up Print Services on a Windows NT Server

Printer drivers are the software programs that enable the operating system to work with attached printer hardware. Windows applications use the print driver as a go-between to process and send documents for output. Of course, it isn't as simple as just sending a document to the printer.

When you set up print serving on Windows NT, you're actually setting up a sophisticated print spooler. Without getting too detailed about its inner workings, *print spooling* is a set of device drivers gathered into a multithreaded background printing system. When a Windows NT print server is created, it automatically sets

239

itself up as a background print-spooling process that arranges print jobs from clients in a linear *queue* and sends them to the print device in the order they're received.

Behind the scenes, the images you send to the printer are translated into a language the printer can understand and reproduce on paper. Windows uses a special graphics library called the *GDI* (Graphics Display Interface) to handle all the images that appear on your screen. When anything from a picture to a word-processing document is sent to your printer, that image is translated from the GDI to a format the printer can handle.

If you're using Windows clients on the network, network printer connections can be made with the protocols you're presently running, including NetBEUI, TCP/IP, or IPX. The most complicated part of the process is setting up the printer and then defining permissions for it. If you've already learned about sharing in earlier chapters, neither of those topics will present a problem. For the most part, the instructions in this chapter are not specific to any protocol.

Installing a Printer on the Windows NT Server

Installing a printer to the server is not a difficult process. Once you've done so, there are a few minor problems to watch out for. I'll point them out where it's appropriate.

This section assumes you're starting from scratch with a printer newly attached to the parallel port on your Windows NT server, and that the Windows NT server is a Primary Domain Controller, as described in Chapter 1. Basic printer installation is performed using an Add Printer Wizard. Follow these steps:

1. Open My Computer from the desktop.

2. Open Printers.

3. Double-click Add Printer. The Add Printer Wizard appears, as shown in Figure 6-1.

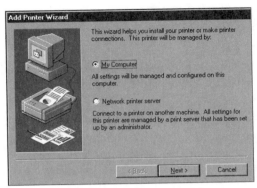

Figure 6-1: Opening the Add Printer Wizard

4. Click Next. The Wizard displays a list of available ports.

5. Select the port to which your printer is attached. Its check box must be enabled, as shown in Figure 6-2.

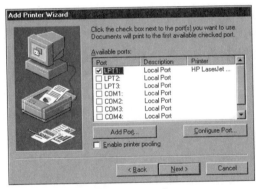

Figure 6-2: Selecting a Printer Port

6. Click Next.

Next you choose the printer type.

7. In the Manufacturers scroll box, select the manufacturer of your installed printer. The Printers scroll box changes to list the available models from the Windows NT CD-ROM.

The Printers list box shows the list of *printer drivers* that are directly supported by Windows NT. Here are a few points to keep in mind as this occurs:

◆ If you have a printer that was manufactured in the last year or so, there's a good chance that it won't show up on the list.

◆ If your printer doesn't show up, there's also a good chance that Microsoft has created a driver for it. It may be available on Microsoft's Web site (http://www.microsoft.com/) or in the latest service packs for Windows NT.

◆ Your printer may also provide a floppy disk containing the Windows NT drivers. If it doesn't, check the printer manufacturer's Web site, assuming it has one. Search engines can also be helpful in this area, because many third-party developers have their own support sites for specific products and may offer device drivers there.

8. If your printer provides a driver disk, and it doesn't show up in the Printers scroll box under your manufacturer, click the Have Disk button and follow the instructions for loading the driver software. Otherwise, go to Step 9.

9. Select the Printer model and click Next.

10. Enter the name for the printer. (I recommend accepting the default name provided by the Wizard, as shown in Figure 6-3.)

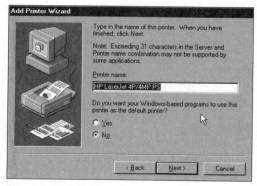

Figure 6-3: Defining a Printer Name

11. Click Next.

The Add Printer Wizard enters its sharing phase, as shown in Figure 6-4.

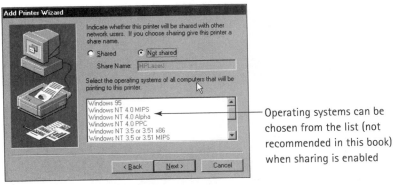

Operating systems can be chosen from the list (not recommended in this book) when sharing is enabled

Figure 6-4: Sharing a Printer During Setup

In the present exercise you'll enable printer sharing, but you can always do it later.

12. Select the Shared option.

13. Define the share name, using 12 characters or less if possible. (Windows 3.*x* network clients will not be able to detect a shared printer name with more than *eight* characters.)

14. Click Next.

The Wizard finishes its operation, and the printer is added to the Printers window. At this point you still need to set up permissions for your user accounts and perhaps tweak some settings. The next section tells you how.

Just as with a hard disk or folder on the server, network printers can be shared. Once the printer is installed on your server, setting up its sharing status is fairly simple, and the process is similar to that for other networked devices. There are major and minor gotchas to watch out for; the major one is described in the "Naming Your Printer Share for Windows 95 Clients and Other Operating Systems" sidebar.

Naming Your Printer Share for Windows 95 Clients and Other Operating Systems

Although Windows NT and Windows 95 systems support long naming conventions, there are some minor inconsistencies. The biggest one is naming a shared printer. The share name is different from the basic printer name.

Here's the key rule of thumb: Don't use more than 12 characters for the *share* name of your networked printer. Following are examples of valid printer names using this rule:

continued

Naming Your Printer Share for Windows 95 Clients and Other Operating Systems *(Continued)*

My_LaserJet

My LaserJet

John's_Laser

John's Laser

You can name a printer anything up to 12 characters if you plan to share a printer with Windows 95 clients. Spaces and underscore characters can be used, along with apostrophes and dashes. If you break the 12-character rule, Windows 95 clients will not be able to "see" the printer across the network. In such cases, you can enter the UNC-based network path to the printer when you access the shared printer from the Win95 client. For example, the name \\RICH'S_BOX\Accounting_LaserJet breaks the 12-character rule. If you do this, you may still encounter error messages at unexpected times during printing jobs. I do not recommend doing this. Stick to 12 characters for your printer share name conventions in a straight WinNT/Win95 network.

It can be difficult to install Windows 95 printer drivers from the provided list in the Sharing tab, as labeled (though ghosted) in Figure 6-4. Choosing them allows Windows NT to cache printer drivers for the other clients on the server, to be automatically downloaded by the clients when they access the printer for the first time. This saves the work of having to load drivers on each local system. In practice, this doesn't work too well for the Windows 95 selection. When you finish printer setup, you may be prompted with a request for an "*.INF" file that must be loaded from another disk. Unfortunately, loading the Windows 95 CD-ROM doesn't work in this case. (Strangely enough, it does work if you're setting up print sharing from a Windows NT workstation.) This method works fine for any other listed client type, including any flavor of Windows NT. But Windows 95 clients sharing an NT server's print services may be stuck out in the cold, needing to load printer drivers locally.

Why does this happen? In an effort to be helpful, Microsoft managed to make things more confusing. The server dialog box that requests the *.INF file is requesting the location of the printer driver files for the other requested operating systems (such as Windows 95 or other flavors of Windows NT) so that those drivers can be downloaded by the client the first time it tries to connect to the printer. Since 90 percent of your other clients are likely to be either Windows NT 4.0 (which is automatically installed) or Windows 95, you would expect to be able to insert the Win95 CD-ROM and have the server read it. Unfortunately, it doesn't work. Although it's a bit more work, you're better off installing printer drivers locally at each Win95 client so they can access the print server. Windows 3.1 clients must have the correct driver loaded locally.

Configuring Your Networked Printer

After you install your printer on the server, configuring and sharing are the next steps. For the most part, printer configuration is done automatically when you perform the installation. There are a few settings you should know about because their defaults may not be what you want. To configure your printer, follow these steps:

1. Open My Computer.

2. Open Printers.

3. Right-click the installed printer. Its shortcut menu appears.

4. From the shortcut menu, select Properties. The printer's Properties sheet appears.

5. Click the Device Settings tab. It appears as shown in Figure 6-5.

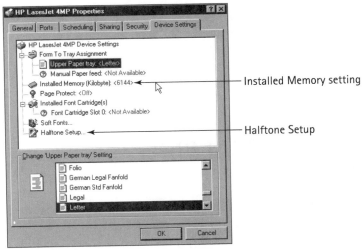

Figure 6-5: Opening a Printer's Properties Sheet

Device settings will be somewhat different depending on your printer type. Figure 6-5 shows the settings for an HP LaserJet model, which is pretty typical in an office environment.

If your printer has more memory than in its default configuration, that extra memory won't necessarily be detected by Windows NT. You'll need to enter the correct value in the Installed Memory entry. This is important because full-page graphics and complex layouts can take up a lot of memory in a laser printer, particularly with PostScript. If this applies to you, simply click the Installed Memory listing shown in

Figure 6-5. The lower half of the Device Settings tab shows a list of increasing values for memory. Select the correct one, and it appears in the listing above.

Halftone Setup is another useful setting, particularly for ink-jet and laser printers. It affects the quality of graphic printouts on a page. Select the Halftone Setup listing, and click the displayed Halftone Setup button that appears at the bottom of the sheet. A special dialog box appears, as shown in Figure 6-6.

Figure 6-6: Adjusting a Laser
Printer's Halftone Patterns

Select any feature in the dialog box and press F1 to get an explanation of its function. This is an area in which you can do a lot of experimenting. Under most office circumstances, default halftone values should be fine. If you have specialized users on your network (CAD or publishing), modifying halftone values can be a useful trick.

Now you're ready to set up user permissions.

Setting Print Sharing and Permissions

If you've already set up sharing during printer setup, you've already performed half the process. If not, and you just installed the printer locally on the server, open the printer's Properties sheet and click the Sharing tab. Click the Shared option, enter a proper share name, and click OK.

Before your clients can view the shared printer when they browse the network, their permissions have to be defined. Fortunately, it's as simple as sharing anything else under Windows NT.

Setting Access Types and Printer Permissions

Setting up shared printers is similar to sharing folders and hard disks, but there are some minor differences. Shared printers have four access types: No Access, Full Control, Print, and Manage Documents. They're quite similar to the access types used for disks and folders, and they can be located in the shared printer's Permissions list on the server:

1. Open My Computer.

2. Open Printers.

3. Right-click the installed printer. Its shortcut menu appears.

4. From the shortcut menu, select Properties.

   The printer's Properties sheet appears, displaying the familiar six tabs, as shown in Figure 6-7.

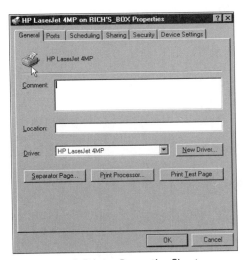

Figure 6-7: A Printer Properties Sheet

5. Click the Security tab.

6. Click the Permissions button. The Printer Permissions dialog box appears, as shown in Figure 6-8.

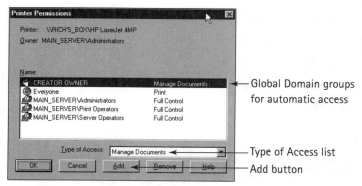

Figure 6-8: Opening a Networked Printer's
Permissions List

Table 6-1 explains each printer access type.

TABLE 6-1 WINDOWS NT ACCESS TYPES FOR SHARED DEVICES ON THE NETWORK

Access Type	Capability
No Access	Locks the user(s) or group away from the resource, rendering it invisible to that user.
Print	Provides basic access to the printer from the network. The user can send jobs to the shared printer but can't modify any settings or print queues.
Manage Documents	Enables users to browse through print queues and resume or delete jobs.
Full Control	Allows full access to the shared printer for the user account. User rights, share settings, and other administrative tasks can be managed through the network. Use this access level sparingly!

For each account or group, the type of user access is strictly up to you. You can assign them to either groups or individual accounts. I don't go into the mechanics of user account or group creation; if needed, you can brush up on that in Chapter 2.

7. Click the Add button. The Add Users and Groups dialog box appears, as shown in Figure 6-9.

Add button (ghosted until account is selected)

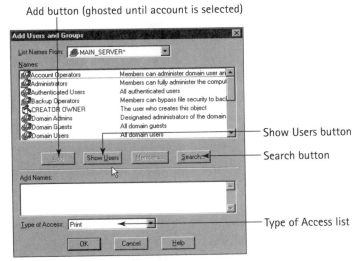

Figure 6-9: Adding Users or Groups to a
Printer's Permissions List

8. Click the Show Users button to display any individual user accounts on the server.

9. Select an account or group and click the Add button. Follow that same step to add further accounts.

10. When you're finished adding and/or searching for users, click OK.

The Printer Permissions list shows the added accounts.

11. If desired, change the type of access for added user accounts by selecting them and choosing a new setting from the Type of Access drop-down list.

12. When you're finished, click OK.

13. Finally, click OK to close the Properties sheet.

Your print server is now ready for use.

A print server is apt to have a lot of users calling upon it at different times. If you have users from other Windows NT domains that need access to your print services, then simply click the Search button as labeled in Figure 6-9. A simple Find Account dialog box appears, listing any other Windows NT domains that yours may be connected with. You can specify a group or user account, select a domain to search in, or search through all connected domains for that account/group.

This feature is not available to stand-alone Windows NT servers, although you can easily create print serving in the same way as described previously. This is another reason why I recommend creating domain servers even for a small network.

Making Windows NT Workstations Use the Print Server

Once you have your printer set up on the server, and your workstations are already properly connected and the share accounts are defined, it's child's play to set up the print service for a Windows NT workstation. The method I describe here is probably the simplest and quickest way to access and install a shared printer on a Windows NT workstation. It's called *point and print,* and it is stunningly easy. Once you set up the printer using Point and Print with an Administrator account, you can log the system back on as its typical user, and that user will be able to use the printer depending on the type of access you've granted. Follow these steps:

1. Open Network Neighborhood.

2. Open the Windows NT server listed in Network Neighborhood.

   If a printer has been connected and shared properly, it appears in the server's list of shared devices, as shown in Figure 6-10.

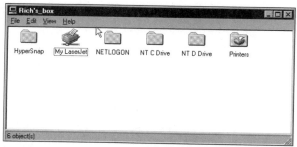

Figure 6-10: Locating a Server's Shared Printer in Network Neighborhood

3. Right-click the printer icon shown in the Neighborhood window.

4. From the shortcut menu, select Install.

The Windows NT workstation pauses briefly. After the printer connection is initialized, you're done. It's elegantly simple, because Windows NT Server automatically caches the correct Windows NT *x*86 printer drivers and sends them across the network when a Workstation client connects for the first time. (This doesn't work nearly as well with Windows 95 clients, as you've seen earlier.)

To test it out, simply open My Computer, open Printers, right-click the new printer to display its shortcut menu, select Properties, and click the Print Test Page button in the General tab.

As is typical in Windows NT, there's more than one way to perform the same task. You can also drag the network printer icon from the Network Neighborhood window onto your Printers icon in My Computer. This has the same effect as the simple steps outlined earlier.

Making Windows 95 Computers Use the Print Server

Windows 95 clients offer three ways to install a shared network printer: with the Add Printer Wizard, through Network Neighborhood, or by capturing a networked printer to the local printer port.

You can use the Add Printer Wizard either during setup of the client or afterwards, as is shown here. This is also called *establishing* a printer. Follow these steps:

1. Open My Computer.

2. Open Printers.

3. Double-click Add Printer. The Add Printer Wizard appears, prompting you to begin installing a printer.

4. Click Next.

5. Select the Network Printer option and click Next. As shown in Figure 6-11, the Wizard prompts you to enter the network path to the printer. If you're a macho UNC person, you'll be able to enter the full network path right off the top of your head. If you're like me, or the rest of us, you'll press the Browse button as labeled in Figure 6-11.

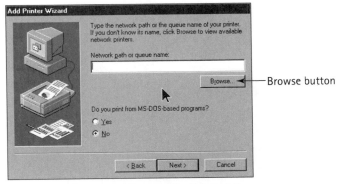

Figure 6-11: The Wizard Prompts for Entry of the Network Path to a Printer

6. Click the Browse button.

The Browse for Printer window appears, as shown in Figure 6-12.

Figure 6-12: Browsing the Network
Path To Locate Shared Printers

7. Click the plus signs (+) to navigate through the levels in the network until you locate the desired printer. An example is shown in Figure 6-13.

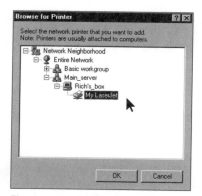

Figure 6-13: Drilling Down To
Locate the Shared Printer

8. Select the printer and click OK.

The UNC name for the printer's network path appears, as shown in Figure 6-14.

Of course, your network path will differ.

Figure 6-14: The Network Path Appears
in the Wizard

9. If you have any clients on the network that use MS-DOS-based programs to print documents, select the Yes option. If not (if you have only 32-bit Windows clients that use only Windows software programs), keep the No option.

10. Click Next. The Add Printer Wizard displays the naming screen, showing the default printer name supplied by the server, and I recommend keeping it. (This is different from the share name for the printer.) The naming screen also requests whether this will be the default printer for this client.

11. If you want to use the printer as the default for the system, click Yes.

12. Click Next again. You can elect to print a test page at this point.

13. Click Finish.

At this point you may be prompted to insert the Windows 95 CD-ROM. Some OEM Windows 95 systems (particularly laptops) come with the Windows 95 installation directory copied onto the hard disk. If that's the case, you'll see a dialog box appear and disappear while the drivers are loaded. Otherwise, put the Windows 95 CD-ROM for the client in the CD-ROM drive and click OK — the drivers are loaded. Then the test page is printed.

Browsing the Network on a Win95 Client to Install a Printer

Using Network Neighborhood, you can use the same point and print feature offered under Windows NT Workstation. Again, this is the quickest way to access and use a printer from a Windows 95 client. The printer must be shared properly from the server, and the user account must have the correct access type. You may also have to load a device driver.

In the unlikely event that you use MS-DOS applications in your Windows 95 system, the Capture Printer Port option is used to provide a way for those DOS applications to use the networked printer. Otherwise, this feature provides no specific benefit to Windows networking clients.

For the purposes of this book, printer port capturing is a non-issue. This feature applies only to MS-DOS programs running on network clients. Macintoshes actually perform a capturing action when they access a Windows NT Server's shared printer for the first time; that function is not the same as described here. Follow these steps:

1. Open Network Neighborhood.

2. Open the Windows NT Server listed in Network Neighborhood.

3. Right-click the printer icon shown in the server window.

4. From the shortcut menu, select Install. Notice that a Capture Printer Port menu option is also displayed here. (Also note that you can condense the last four steps into one quick action by simply dragging the shared printer from Network Neighborhood into the Printers window.)

   After selecting the Install option, the Add Printer Wizard appears, asking if you print from MS-DOS programs.

5. Select Yes or No depending on your client's characteristics.

6. Click Next. The Wizard displays a screen enabling you to select the printer manufacturer and model from a list.

7. Select the manufacturer and printer model and click Next. The wizard displays a default printer name. The dialog box also shows Yes and No options for setting the printer as the default printer.

8. Click Next. The Wizard asks you if you want to print a test page.

9. Click Finish.

You're prompted to enter the Windows 95 CD-ROM into the client's CD-ROM drive. When the system finishes loading the support files from the CD-ROM, you're prompted to print a test page, and the networked printer appears in the Printers window. At that point the printer is available for your applications.

Peer Print Sharing Between Windows Clients

Peer print sharing works much the same as in the previous sections. Here you will assume that the printer being shared is connected to a Windows NT workstation. Windows NT Workstation provides a User Manager program that enables creation and management of user accounts and user groups. In almost all particulars, sharing a printer between workstations behaves the same way as sharing a printer from a server.

Peer Print Sharing Between Windows NT Workstations

Installing a printer, configuring it, and setting up its share and permissions are similar processes as described in the earlier sections of this chapter. After that, the other workstation can access the printer as follows:

1. Open Network Neighborhood.

2. Open the Windows NT Workstation listed in Network Neighborhood. As part of the same workgroup, the system should show up in the first level of Network Neighborhood.

3. Open the Printers group.

4. Right-click the printer icon shown in the Printers window.

5. From the shortcut menu, select Install.

The Windows NT workstation pauses briefly while the drivers are copied. (Depending on how fast your clients are, the pause may be imperceptible.) In this case, the Windows NT workstation connected to the printer already has the correct printer drivers and automatically copies them over to the other system.

To test it out, the process is exactly the same as described earlier. Open My Computer, and then open Printers, right-click the new printer to display the shortcut menu, select Properties, and click the Print Test Page button in the General tab.

Again, you can also drag and drop the networked printer from Network Neighborhood to the Printers window.

Windows NT Workstations can share printers quite efficiently. There are some minor differences between how a Windows NT Workstation does this and how a Windows 95 system behaves.

Peer Print Sharing Between Windows NT Workstation and Windows 95

Windows 95 is quite capable as a peer-printing client. As noted earlier in this chapter, a weird anomaly occurs when you try to cache Windows 95 printer drivers in a Windows NT server. In Windows NT Workstation, if you know you're going to be sharing the printer with a Windows 95 client, here's how to set it up:

1. Install the printer.

2. Open My Computer, and then open Printers.

3. Right-click the printer. From the shortcut menu, select Sharing.

4. Select the Shared option and enter a share name or accept its default.

   Don't bother selecting any system types from the Alternate Drivers list. Even if you select Windows 95 from that list, setting up peer sharing on the Win95 end still requires copying drivers on the local system, so there's no point in bothering with it on the Windows NT Workstation side.

5. Click Next. You can also print a test page at this step.

6. Click Finish.

Assuming that everything else is in place (printer installed, sharing enabled, user accounts, and permissions), here's how to access the shared peer printer from a Windows 95 client:

1. Open Network Neighborhood on the Windows 95 client. Browse the Neighborhood until you locate the Windows NT Workstation's shared printer.

2. Open My Computer on the Windows 95 client and open its Printers window.

3. Drag the shared printer icon from the Network Neighborhood window to the Printers window.

   The Add Printer Wizard appears, asking if you print from MS-DOS programs on the Win95 client.

4. Select the Yes or No option and click Next.

5. Select the manufacturer and model of your printer.

   Watch this step carefully. The Windows 95 list of supported printers differs from those on Windows NT. Make sure the printer you're sharing has the same driver type on both ends.

6. Click Next.

7. Enter the printer name or accept the default. If this is to be the Windows 95 client's default computer, select the Yes option.

8. Click Next.

   You can elect to print a test page.

9. Click Finish.

You have to insert a Windows 95 CD-ROM into the local system's drive to finish off the installation. The printer appears in the Printers window and can then be accessed by your applications on the Windows 95 client.

A Final Word

Print serving is a fairly simple process under Windows NT, whether you're talking about client-server or peer-to-peer. If you get your basic network connections under control, setting up print serving is easy. The key is to follow the naming conventions.

In the next two chapters, you'll learn how to connect, communicate, and manage mixed Windows NT and Novell NetWare networks.

Troubleshooting

I have a fairly common printer that just came out in the last six months, but I can't find it on my Windows NT Server's printer lists.
There's a good chance that the new printer driver has been added to a service pack or separately to the Microsoft Web site. Microsoft's Web site has special pages dedicated to downloading service packs for both Windows NT 3.51 and Windows NT 4.0. Pages are also provided on which you can search for and download a specific driver without downloading an entire 10-20MB service pack. If any new drivers are created for Windows NT, this is where you'll find them:

◆ For Service Pack 3, the latest of Windows NT's downloadable service packs, go to
   `http://www.microsoft.com/ntserversupport/content/servicepa cks/default.htm`

◆ For individual Print driver updates, use the Support page on Microsoft's Web site, select Windows NT Server, and select Printer Drivers. (The name of the actual Web page is too long and too garbled to list here.)

 Microsoft constantly works on updates for Windows NT and releases them periodically. During the time that I was writing this book, the latest service pack was #3. At the risk of dating myself, there's a good chance that a newer service pack or even two have been released since. If you discover this, there's one good rule of thumb to follow: just download the latest one. For example, you don't need to download Service Pack 3, install it, and then download Service Pack 4 in order to completely update your system. Just get the newest one.

When I use the Add Printer Wizard to install a printer, I'm asked at the end of the installation to provide the location of the printer files. Even if I specify the Windows NT CD-ROM, I'm still prompted for the files.
You may have a pair of files called MISPRINT.INF and MSPRINT2.INF in your `WINNT\INF` folder on your hard disk. These are Windows 95 printer support files and will not work under Windows NT Workstation or Windows NT Server. Rename them MSPRINT.OLD and MSPRINT2.OLD and run the Wizard again. (This does not apply to shared printers and Windows 95 drivers.)

I can't print to the local printer device.
To start with, see if you can print from the command prompt:

1. Open a DOS Command Prompt in Windows NT.

2. Type the following command:

```
dir > lpt1 <return>
```

Unfortunately, this will not work with a PostScript printer. If you receive no output, a garbage printout, or get an "Unable to write to port" message, then check your cabling, remove any switch boxes, and perform a self-test on the printing device. Check to see that the WINPRINT.DLL file is located in the system (use the Find feature from the Start menu). Then remove the printers from the Printers window, delete all the files from the `WINNT\SYSTEM32\SPOOL\DRIVERS\W32x86` folder, and then reinstall your printers.

If the problem is with a PostScript printer, load the Apple LaserWriter driver. It's a basic PostScript printer driver, and using it will help determine if there's a problem with your specific driver/printer combination.

I can't print to the networked printer.
Check the basic network connections. Try copying a file over to a shared resource on the server. If you can't access the server at all, you won't be able to print. If the connections are working, check the user rights for the account, sharing names, and the networking protocols on the client system.

Another useful trick is to create a printer at the local client and redirect its output to the network print server. Follow these steps:

1. Start the Add Printer Wizard.

2. When it displays the Port section, click Add Port. The Printer Ports window appears.

3. Select the Local Port listing.

4. Click the New Port button. A Port Name window appears.

5. Enter the UNC name for the networked printer, in order of server name and printer share name. An example would be

```
\\RICH'S_BOX\MY_LASERJET.
```

Use that port for the local printer by enabling its checkbox. If this doesn't work, then check the length of the share name.

If the printer's share name is more than twelve characters, that could also be the problem. Also, make sure that the share name does not use commas, periods, or any other unusual characters other than possibly an underscore character.

Part II

Windows NT to Novell NetWare

Novell is Microsoft's primary competition in the LAN market. Although Windows NT is gaining in both market share and mindshare, a huge number of company sites use Novell for their network connectivity. You'll more than likely have to deal with Novell, even if you're building a Windows NT-based network, and that's what this section is about. Fortunately, Windows NT makes dealing with Novell relatively easy to do. So does Novell. In both Chapter 7 ("Windows NT to Novell NetWare 4.11 Connections") and Chapter 8 ("Windows NT to Novell NetWare 3.12 Connections"), you explore both Microsoft's and Novell's methods for making Windows NT talk to NetWare.

NetWare 4.11 (also called *IntranetWare*) occupies Chapter 7, in which you learn how to run Microsoft's Gateway Services for NetWare to share NetWare services through a Windows NT Server to your other users. Although the service is handy, Gateway Services for NetWare is fairly limited (perhaps by design), and Novell steps into the gap by offering several free programs from its Web site that amplify and expand upon Microsoft's built-in services. These programs are given the full treatment in Chapter 7, and if you're actively using NetWare while building a Windows NT network, I strongly encourage you to make use of them. A similar approach is taken in Chapter 8, which discusses how to link Windows NT Server and Windows NT Workstation to NetWare 3.12.

Chapter 7

Windows NT to Novell NetWare 4.11 Connections

IN THIS CHAPTER

Novell NetWare servers are almost ubiquitous in all types of companies. When you or your company decide to install and use a Windows NT server, there's a good chance you'll be expected to make it work with an existing NetWare system. In this chapter you discover how to perform the following Windows NT connectivity tasks:

- ◆ Access a Novell NetWare 4.11 server through Windows NT Server

- ◆ Access and administer a Novell NetWare 4.11 server through Windows NT Workstation

BOTH PROCESSES JUST LISTED are relatively simple to install and set up but can become complicated in practice. Windows NT Server uses a special feature called Gateway Services for NetWare, while Windows NT Workstation exploits a couple of options: the built-in Microsoft NetWare client and the specially built Novell IntranetWare Client for Windows NT.

If you want to use Windows NT in conjunction with NetWare, I recommend using a Windows NT workstation for managing all key aspects of NetWare 4.11 servers. For a basic interface and sharing NetWare server capabilities with your users, Gateway Services with Windows NT Server works just fine. If you want comprehensive NetWare management capabilities, you must use a Windows NT Workstation client connected to the NetWare server.

NetWare is a large and complicated operating system, particularly in its newest versions. A complete discussion of its features is far beyond the scope of this book, so I describe the key terms and ingredients that you'll encounter when you connect Windows NT with NetWare. However, in most cases you're expected to know what you need to get the most out of NetWare.

To help you perform NetWare administrative tasks on a Windows NT system, Novell provides some powerful utilities that go far beyond Microsoft's already capable offerings. When you install the Novell IntranetWare Client on a Windows NT workstation and set up NetWare Administrator, you have full administrative access to the NetWare server, using a GUI-based NDS management utility. The next section provides a brief introduction to NetWare, setting the context for the Windows NT services and utilities you'll use to connect Windows NT to NetWare servers. The second part of this chapter shows you where to find these free programs on the Internet, how to install them, and briefly describes their features.

A Brief Survey of NetWare 4.11

Novell basically created the PC local-area networking business with its powerful NetWare network operating system (NOS). Compared to Novell's experience, Microsoft Windows NT is a Johnny-come-lately (although an increasingly successful one). Hundreds of thousands of companies and small businesses use NetWare as the backbone of their networks. If you're running Windows NT in a company, odds are you'll have to deal with NetWare at some point. Fortunately, both Microsoft and Novell make this interaction relatively easy.

The current version of Novell NetWare is dubbed IntranetWare 4.11. (I continue to call it NetWare 4.11 for brevity's sake.) Besides the basic server package, Novell provides a collection of additional capabilities including FTP and Web servers, DHCP, DNS, and a host of other Internet capabilities that roughly mirror those found in Windows NT. Many other capabilities, such as Lightweight Directory Services Protocol (LDAP) support, are far beyond the scope of this book. Nevertheless, no one in the networking game can afford to ignore NetWare.

Despite Microsoft's steady progress in the networking market, Novell NetWare is by no means out of the game. At the end of 1996, 70 percent of corporate network users were still connected to Novell NetWare servers. In particular, NetWare 4.11 has something going for it that Windows NT 4.0 cannot match: Novell Directory Services. Novell Directory Services (NDS) is a highly elegant solution to the problem of managing complicated wide-area networks in a multinational corporate enterprise.

How does NDS work? Without going into the hard-core technical details, it's surprisingly simple and approachable. Novell's Directory Services is organized in terms of a *tree*. The NDS tree is a hierarchical organization loosely based on the ISO X.500 specification, with many modifications. The core servers in a Novell 4.11 network are called the *root*. NDS inverts the tree, placing the roots at the top of the hierarchy. The main communications links (T1 lines and so on) are termed *trunks*. *Branches* are considered to be individual networking cable lengths in the overall network. Finally, *leaves* are individual users. Since a picture is worth a thousand words, Figure 7-1 shows the basic scheme.

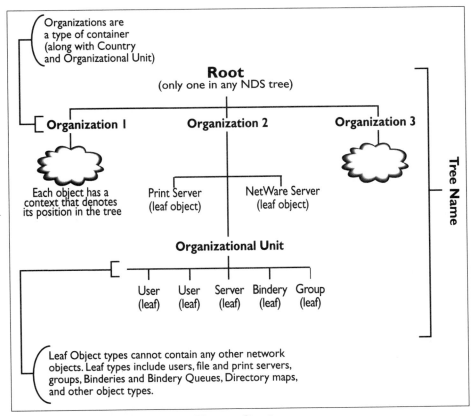

Figure 7-1: The Novell NetWare 4.11 Directory Structure

Unlike the Windows NT domain system, Novell's NDS enables you to gather all the elements of an enterprise network into one all-encompassing, elegant system. If you're dealing with international WAN systems, NDS can handle that, too, using another object classification called a *country*. Individual servers and collections of computers don't have to be isolated from one another, and a company's offices in Berne and Munich don't have to be isolated from the servers in the New York office. Using NetWare 4.11 and its NDS services, an administrator can tie those far-flung locations together on the same network. As deep and complicated as it sounds, an NDS system usually doesn't go more than five or six levels deep. Elegance doesn't necessarily mean complexity. (Nonetheless, NetWare is plenty complex if that's what you're looking for.)

Context is another key NDS term. For Novell, a context means the *position* of the computer in the NetWare tree. When you set up NetWare capabilities on a Windows NT system, the context refers to a label depicting the general identification of the server, such as *Marketing Intranet Server* or *Engineering File Server*, although the label is not the name of the actual computer.

NetWare 4.11 organizes things in terms of server *objects*. In other words, every user account, group, server process such as print serving, the servers themselves, and network segments are treated as objects organized within the NDS tree structure. The NDS object model makes it relatively easy to administer a large network and keep things manageable, no matter how large the network.

Novell also offers, or will offer, a new version of NDS specifically for Windows Windows NT Server. It's not available as a free download, unlike many of the other utilities described in this chapter. The new version is a high-end commercial networking product intended to replace the Windows NT domain service with Novell's Directory. I describe what NDS can do for your Windows NT server in a brief section at the end of this chapter.

NetWare also provides a large collection of server utilities that you can run to manage various aspects of the Novell server. Typically, those programs are run from a connected workstation that provides full access for the network administrator. (As you'll see, Windows NT Server is severely limited in its out-of-the-box NetWare administration capabilities.) For NetWare 4.11, these utilities include NETADMIN, NETUSER, and RCONSOLE. Most of NetWare's server-based programs can't be run directly on the server; you need a workstation with administrative or supervisory privileges in order to perform basic server management.

How do you connect your present Windows NT server to your company's NetWare 4.11 server? By using a bundled feature called *Gateway Services for NetWare*. If you need to share a NetWare system's resources through Windows NT server to your Windows clients, you need to install and configure Gateway Services.

Understanding Windows NT Server's Gateway Services for NetWare

Windows NT's Gateway Services for NetWare is a simple and useful solution to the problem of interfacing Windows NT Server to NetWare. It supports NetWare 3.11/3.12 and the newer and more sophisticated NetWare/IntranetWare 4.11. (NetWare 3.12 connectivity is discussed in Chapter 8.) Without Gateway Services, you would have trouble doing anything productive with Windows NT Server/NetWare connections.

Gateway Services for NetWare enables you to perform the following tasks from Windows NT Server:

◆ Log on to a NetWare 4.11 server, map its hard disk, and share its resources with Windows NT-connected users, including print server capability.

◆ Log on to a NetWare 3.12 server, map its drive, and share its resources with Windows NT-connected users (this is described in Chapter 8).

◆ Share a Novell print server with users connected to the Windows NT server.

Despite its undeniably useful features, Microsoft's Gateway Services for NetWare has some major limitations:

◆ You can't log in to Novell's Directory Services from a Windows NT server. Because of this, you can't create new user accounts, groups, and other tree objects, or modify their permissions and rights by default. To log on to a Novell 4.11 server from Windows NT Server with privileges for changing and adding accounts, you must run bindery emulation on the Novell end.

◆ Conversely, you can't run Novell's powerful NetWare Administrator utility from Windows NT Server. Nor can you run many important DOS-type NetWare utilities on the Windows NT Server as a client, including NETADMIN.

◆ Share levels are limited — you can't conveniently share folders with a large collection of individual users from the Novell server through Gateway Services.

◆ By default, several folders and subdirectories present on the Novell 4.11 server cannot be accessed from Windows NT Server — they are hidden from view. You must create an account on the NetWare server that permits the Windows NT administrator to access the entire NetWare system, but you cannot automatically use the Windows NT Server-NetWare connection to do so. You must use *another* NetWare client that has full administrator or supervisor access to the NetWare server to create an administrator account that mirrors the one used on your Windows NT server.

TIP   Although quite useful, Windows NT's Gateway Services for NetWare doesn't allow you to administer NetWare servers from a Windows NT server.

In other words, Windows NT Server's Gateway Services for NetWare is not directly compatible with NDS. For full control of a NetWare system from Windows NT, you must use Microsoft or Novell client software for Windows NT Workstation or another Windows system. (Novell actually bundles versions of their NWAdmin software for Windows 95 and Windows 3.*x* with their IntranetWare CD. As I discuss later, you can download the Windows NT version from Novell's Web site.) Microsoft also provides its NetWare Client Services on Windows NT Workstation, and Novell's software (which is a little more powerful) is free and readily accessible from Novell's World Wide Web site. Unfortunately, you can't use these programs on anything except Windows NT Workstation.

You must use the IPX/SPX networking protocol for communication between

Windows NT and NetWare. When you install Gateway Services for NetWare, the protocol is automatically installed along with the service and bound to your network interface card.

In the following section you concentrate on how to install Gateway Services for NetWare and then on how to use it for connections to a Novell NetWare 4.11 server. Then you find out how to set up Gateway Services for NetWare to allow sharing of NetWare resources through the Windows NT Server to your users.

Installing and Configuring Windows NT Server's Gateway Services for NetWare

Now that you have a basic idea of what Gateway Services for NetWare is all about, follow these steps to install it:

1. Open My Computer.

2. Open the Control Panel, and then open the Network applet.

3. Click the Services tab.

4. Click Add. The Select Network Service dialog box appears.

5. Select Gateway (and Client) Services for NetWare.

6. Click OK. You may be prompted to enter the location of the i386 directory or insert the Windows Windows NT Server CD-ROM.

7. A dialog box appears prompting you to add IPX/SPX Protocol support in your installed Remote Access Service. If this is desirable, click OK. If you don't need IPX/SPX in your Remote Access configuration (you can always add it later), click Cancel. The service finishes installing.

8. Click OK to close the Network applet. You're prompted to restart the server.

9. After the server restarts, log on to the system in your usual way. A new Select NetWare Log on dialog box appears, which provides a logon to the NetWare system. The dialog box is divided into two sections: Preferred Server (for NetWare 3.12) and Default Tree and Context (for NetWare 4.11). The 4.11 server appears in the Preferred Server list, but its logon is actually handled in the Default Tree and Context section. At the top, the Username is listed. It's the same name you just logged on with, and it's the name that NetWare automatically sees when you log on. Unfortunately, there's a good chance that you don't have an account with that Username on the NetWare server, and you'll need to create the account later on.

10. Select Default Tree and Context to enable logging on to a NetWare 4.11 server.

11. If you already know what the default tree and context are for your NetWare server, enter them in their proper fields.

12. Click OK. You're greeted by the following message: "You cannot be authenticated on [TREE(CONTEXT) *names*] due to the following reason: the specified user does not exist. Do you really want to set the preferred server or context to [TREE(CONTEXT) *names*]?"

13. Click Yes.

Receiving the *Specified user does not exist* message indicates that your normal Windows NT Server Administrator account does not have a corresponding account with the same name on the NetWare system. Not having a corresponding account is not a big problem at the moment, because you can still browse the NetWare system from the Windows NT server.

After the basic Gateway Services are installed and, most importantly, assuming you have a good network connection, you should be able to open Network Neighborhood and locate the NetWare or Compatible Network entry. After opening Network Neighborhood, you're prompted for a user name and password, which are local to the NetWare server. Under many circumstances this may be sufficient for your purposes. If you have a supervisor-caliber user name and password for the NetWare server, you can just enter them, and your Windows NT server will have access (not complete access, however, due to limitations in Microsoft's client capabilities). However, you still need to perform some configuration tasks before you can log on and share NetWare resources efficiently.

When you direct Windows NT to log on to a NetWare 4.11 server, you provide the NDS tree and the context into which the Windows NT server connects. The tree and context are not automatically detected the first time, which is what the Default Tree and Context section is for. What does this mean? The terminology reflects the nature of NetWare 4.11, in which a server is just another object in the NDS hierarchy, whether you have just a single server (as I do here) or a massive wide-area network (WAN) in which the NetWare server you're connecting to is just a small part.

Throughout the rest of this chapter, the NetWare 4.11 server for this book has a tree name of SEQUOIA, which I decided on when I originally set up the server.

The default context used in the examples for this chapter is called RGALTD. Of course, yours will be different. NetWare's actual naming nomenclature is a bit more complicated than described here, because this book is about Windows NT and not about NetWare. Fortunately, Windows NT enables you to use the basic naming elements without all the extra naming conventions sometimes required by NetWare.

In either case, you need to know those two key elements (the tree name and the context) to make a successful connection to your NetWare 4.11 server from Windows NT Server, and to configure Gateway Services for NetWare to share resources across the Windows NT network. I explain how to configure the Gateway Services for NetWare in the next section.

Configuring Gateway Services for NetWare Resource Sharing

When you open Windows NT Server's Control Panel again, you'll find a new configuration utility labeled GSNW (Gateway Services for NetWare), as shown in Figure 7-2. You use this utility to fully set up the Gateway Services on your Windows NT Server so that you can share NetWare resources with your users.

 TIP You need three pieces of information to create a successful connection: the name of the NetWare server, the name of the NDS (Novell Directory Service) tree, and the name of the server's context.

Figure 7-2: Windows NT Server's New GSNW Applet
Is Located in the Control Panel

The key pieces of information you need for proper configuration include

♦ The name of your NetWare 4.11 server

♦ The NDS tree of your NetWare server

♦ The name of your NetWare server's highest-level context

Follow these steps to configure Gateway Services for NetWare:

1. Open the GSNW applet. The Gateway Services for NetWare dialog box appears, as shown in Figure 7-3.

Default Tree and Context is used for
logging on to NetWare 4.11

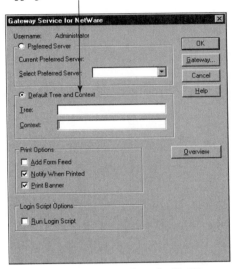

Figure 7-3: Gateway Services for NetWare
Provides Dual Logon Capabilities

The two fields in the Default Tree and Context section may already be filled, depending on how you just logged on.

2. Click the Preferred Server option and its list-down arrow to reveal the name of your NetWare 4.11 server. (Yes, your NetWare 4.11 server's name appears here, even though the Preferred Server section is used for NetWare 3.12!) Make a note of this server name because you need it later. (In my test case I've called it RICHS_411.)

3. Select the Default Tree and Context option.

4. Enter the name of your NetWare server's NDS tree in the Tree field.

5. Enter the name of your NetWare server's highest-level context in the Context field. The results should resemble Figure 7-4.

Preferred Server is disabled

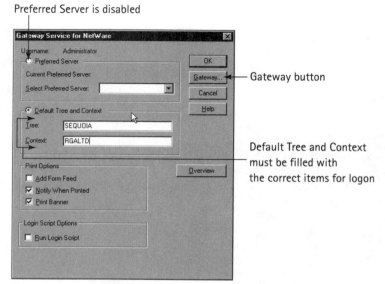

Gateway button

Default Tree and Context
must be filled with
the correct items for logon

Figure 7–4: The GSNW Default Tree and
Context Values Must Be Entered for Proper
Connection to a NetWare 4.11 Server

5. Click the Gateway button as labeled in Figure 7-4. The Configure Gateway
   dialog box appears. **Important:** In this dialog box you enable NetWare
   server resources to be shared through the Windows NT Server with your
   other Windows NT-connected users on the network. These resources
   include files, shared drives, and shared print servers.

6. Click the Enable Gateway check box. Make sure it's selected so that the
   gateway is fully enabled.

7. In the Gateway Account field, enter the Administrator account you
   customarily use for your Windows NT Server access.

8. Enter your Administrator account's password, and then reenter it in the
   Confirm Password field. The results should resemble Figure 7-5.

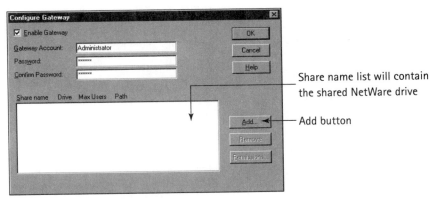

Figure 7–5: Gateway Configuration

The previous two steps do not establish your Administrator password on the NetWare server. (You still have to do that on the NetWare server, or using a Windows NT Workstation connection that enables remote administration. That process is described later in this book.) What you've done is set up your Windows NT Server Administrator account to enable NetWare gateway-sharing capabilities from your NetWare server *through your Windows NT server* to the Windows clients connected to the Windows NT server.

The next phase is to set up the NetWare drive as a share. (With normal Windows NT drives you just use My Computer and the drive's shortcut menu, but you can't do that with the NetWare gateway.) Follow these steps:

1. Click the Add button as labeled in Figure 7-5. The New Share dialog box appears, as shown in Figure 7-6.

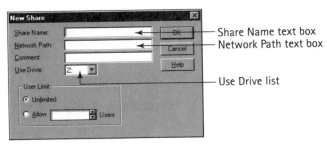

Figure 7–6: Setting Up a Shared NetWare Hard Disk

2. In the Share Name text box, enter a desired share name for the NetWare server hard disk, up to 13 characters. If you have MS-DOS/Windows 3.1 systems on your network that will be accessing the NetWare system through your Windows NT computer, make that share name a maximum of eight characters.

   Here's where you can brush up on your UNC naming conventions. Remember the NetWare server name I had you make note of in Step 2?

3. In the Network Path field, enter the UNC path to your NetWare server's hard disk (in my example, it's \\RICHS_411\SYS). Normally, a NetWare server's hard disk is automatically named SYS, but yours *may* differ, as will your server's name.

4. In the Use Drive field, scroll through the list until you locate a desired drive letter. I used the first one available, which is H. The results should resemble Figure 7-7.

Figure 7-7: Identifying a Shared NetWare Hard Disk

5. Click OK.

6. If your share name is more than eight characters, it will not be readable from MS-DOS-based workstations connected to your Windows NT server. If this is okay, then click Yes.

   Assuming that your Administrator user account is also properly set up on the NetWare server, that's all you need. The new share name appears, as shown in Figure 7-8.

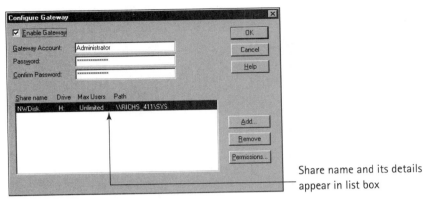

Figure 7-8: Defined Shared NetWare Hard Disk

7. Click OK.

8. Click OK to close the Gateway Services for NetWare applet.

Give Microsoft credit. Gateway Services for NetWare setup is strikingly simple and elegant if you have a few key pieces of information. The only hitch is that you need to know the UNC nomenclature for the shared NetWare drive: its server name and the shared drive's name. Also, even on Windows NT Server, Microsoft's client services don't allow you to have full administrative capabilities from the Windows NT Server to NetWare.

Using Windows NT Server and Workstation to Access a Novell NetWare 4.11 Server through Gateway Services for NetWare

After Gateway Services for NetWare is installed and configured, you can play around with things a little bit. As you saw in the previous section, Gateway Services for NetWare enables you to map a shared NetWare drive to a drive letter. After you do that, all you have to do to access the NetWare drive on the server is open My Computer. A shared drive icon appears, similar to that shown in Figure 7-9.

Shared network drive icon

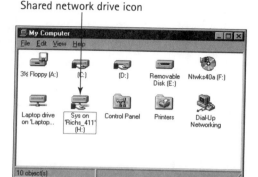

Figure 7-9: The Gateway-Shared NetWare
Hard Disk, Mapped into My Computer

As you can see in Figure 7-9, the NetWare drive icon combines the visual attributes of two different drive icon types. The tiny pipe denoting a networked drive appears, but the small hand icon also indicates that the networked drive is being shared by the Windows NT server.

A Windows NT-shared NetWare drive icon bears a slightly different appearance from the normal shared-device icon.

After the NetWare drive is successfully mapped, accessing it from Windows NT and Windows 95 workstations connected to the Windows NT server is simple. Follow these steps:

1. Open a Command Prompt or MS-DOS Prompt window.

2. From the command prompt, enter the following command:

```
net use * \\RICH'S_BOX\NTDisk <enter>
```

   ◆ RICH'S_BOX is the name of my sample Windows NT Server running the Gateway Services for NetWare (yours will differ).

   ◆ Windows NTDisk is the name of the shared NetWare hard disk as defined in Gateway Services for NetWare (again, yours will differ).

   This command is valid for both Windows NT Workstation and Windows 95 users.

3. After pressing Enter in the command prompt, open My Computer. The shared NetWare disk appears as a new drive icon.

You can also open Network Neighborhood and right-click the icon representing the NetWare server. The shortcut menu that opens is shown in Figure 7-10.

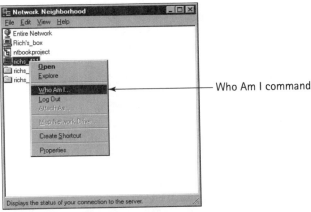

— Who Am I command

Figure 7-10: NetWare User Commands Appear on the Shortcut Menu for the NetWare Server

For example, selecting the Who Am I command from the shortcut menu reveals an example of NetWare's real nomenclature, indicated in the user name shown in Figure 7-11.

Figure 7-11: Checking the Login Status for the Shared NetWare Device

You can also log out from the NetWare server using the same method. Windows Windows NT Workstation and Windows 95 clients also have the same capabilities.

Sharing NetWare resources through Windows NT Server can be a difficult proposition in larger networks. In your Windows NT server, the best procedure for a large collection of users is to set up individual shared folders that are visible only to each individual user and to the administrator. This is unworkable when you run a

NetWare server through the Gateway Services for NetWare to your Windows clients, because granularity of your share levels is basically limited to drives and not folders. NetWare 4.11 has an excellent home directories feature that can support thousands of users and permits direct folder sharing and mapping. In fact, Novell significantly outperforms Windows NT in this important area. From Windows NT Server you can map NetWare directories to individual drive letters, but you're severely limited in the number of shares you can create this way. You have a maximum of 26 drive letters available, a few of which are already occupied by your Windows NT server's drives, so it's possible to get really stuck here.

When you share a NetWare disk through Windows NT Server, you can provide that share to as many Windows NT Server clients as necessary. Novell NetWare print servers can also be shared through Windows NT using the same Gateway-based methods described previously, and they don't suffer from this limitation.

Windows NT Server's Gateway Services for NetWare and Windows NT Workstation's Client Services provide only a few functional differences. Windows NT Server's Gateway setup is the primary difference; both systems' client capabilities are surprisingly limited. I discuss Windows NT Workstation's Client services in the following section.

For a complete discussion of how to create a new Administrator account on your NetWare server that enables you to fully use Gateway Services for NetWare, please see the section titled "Installing and Using Novell's Windows NT IntranetWare Client Service."

NetWare 4.11 Setup for the Windows NT-to-NetWare Connection

For complete use of Gateway Services for NetWare, you have to prepare the NetWare server with a new Administrator-class account and a special new group called NTGATEWAY, and make that new Administrator account a member of the NTGATEWAY group. Also, it's a good idea to provide that account with complete Supervisor rights to the entire NetWare system. You can do this using the DOS-based NETADMIN program in NetWare 4.11, running through a Command Prompt window on an MS-DOS, Windows NT Workstation, or Windows 95 client. (You can't provide Supervisor rights through Windows NT Server.) You can also use Novell's beautifully done NWADMIN software program, but there's a catch. You can't perform any of these things using Microsoft's basic NetWare Client software, described in the next section, unless you're running Bindery emulation on NetWare 4.11. Because Bindery emulation is not an automatic service of NetWare, and extensive discussions of how NetWare works are beyond the scope of this book, I don't discuss how to set up Bindery emulation or the ins and outs of the NETADMIN program. I do mention that using the NETADMIN program to create an Administrator account is quite straightforward, and any reasonably experienced networking person will find it easily approachable with a modicum of knowledge of NetWare and Windows NT networking terms, all of which are provided throughout this book.

Understanding Windows NT Workstation's NetWare Client Service

Windows NT Workstation offers a feature called Client Services for NetWare. Although Client Services for NetWare is a handy way for Windows NT workstations to have quick access to NetWare file and print servers, and it works great with both NetWare 3.*x* and 4.*x*, it has many of the same limitations as its Windows NT Server-based Gateway Services for NetWare counterpart. By itself, Client Services for NetWare doesn't provide full access to the NetWare 4.11 server. You can't fully administer the server or modify user accounts in the Novell system, although Client Services for NetWare does allow you to log on to the NDS as a normal user.

Windows NT Workstation's Client Services for NetWare is a simple way to hook up a Windows NT workstation to a Novell server.

Unlike Gateway Services for NetWare, Client Services for NetWare does not allow passing through of shared NetWare resources to other users. All you have is a local connection from your Windows NT Workstation client.

Installation and use of the NetWare client for Windows NT Workstation is simple, and you learn how to do those things in this section. For free and more powerful alternatives to Microsoft's admittedly bare-bones NetWare support offerings, you have to turn to Novell, which fortunately is easy to do. The latter part of this chapter describes how you can use Novell's free Web-based downloadable utilities to get the maximum power out of your Windows NT-to-NetWare nexus.

Installing Windows NT Workstation's NetWare Client

Follow these steps to install Windows NT Workstation's Client Services for NetWare:

1. Open the Control Panel.

2. Open the Networks applet and click the Services tab.

3. Click Add. A dialog box appears that shows a list of Workstation services you can add. Client Services for NetWare may be at the top of the list.

4. Select Client Services for NetWare and click OK. You may be prompted for the directory from which to install the files, which should be the i386 directory on your Windows NT CD-ROM (or a copied i386 directory on your hard disk).

   After the files are copied, you need to reboot the system.

5. After the server restarts, log on to the system in your normal fashion. The Select NetWare Logon dialog box appears, providing a logon to the NetWare system. It is divided into two sections: Preferred Server (for NetWare 3.12) and Default Tree and Context (for NetWare 4.11). The 4.11 server is also listed in the Preferred Server list, but its logon is actually handled in the Default Tree and Context section. The Username is listed at the top, which is the same name you logged on with; it's also the name that NetWare sees when you log on. You possibly may not have an account with that Username on the NetWare server, so you need to create that account later.

6. Select Default Tree and Context to enable logging on to the NetWare 4.11 server.

7. If you know the default tree and context for your NetWare server, enter them in their proper fields.

8. Click OK. If your user account isn't replicated on the NetWare machine, you'll see the following message: "You cannot be authenticated on [TREE(CONTEXT) *names*] due to the following reason: the specified user does not exist. Do you really want to set the preferred server or context to [TREE(CONTEXT) *names*]?"

9. Click Yes.

The system continues logging you in to both the Windows NT and NetWare servers.

When you open Control Panel on your Windows NT workstation, you find a new configuration utility labeled CSNW (Client Services for NetWare). This utility is used to record your preferred server or tree and context settings for connections to the NetWare system. Follow these steps:

1. Open the CSNW applet. The Client Services for NetWare dialog box appears.

   The two fields in the Default Tree and Context section may already be filled, depending on how you previously logged on.

2. Click the Preferred Server option and click the drop-down list to reveal the name of your NetWare 4.11 server. Make a note of this server name because you'll need it later. (In my test case, I've called it RICHS_411.)

3. Select the Default Tree and Context option.

4. Enter the name of your NetWare server's NDS tree in the Tree text box.

5. Enter the name of your NetWare server's highest-level context in the Context text box.

6. Click OK when you're finished with your entries.

The Overview button provides a decent online help resource to the key features offered by Client Services for NetWare. Otherwise, that's about it for client configuration on Windows NT Workstation. If you can compare the CSNW applet to the Gateway Services for NetWare in Windows NT Server, you'll see that they're quite similar except for Windows NT Server's Gateway feature.

Using Windows NT Workstation to Access a Novell NetWare 4.11 File/Print Server

When you've successfully installed Client Services, you can browse the NetWare file server as you would any normal shared resource — open Network Neighborhood and browse its entries in your normal way. You may be required to enter other user names and passwords depending on the resources you're trying to access. You'll also find that some key utilities, such as RCONSOLE and NETADMIN, still cannot be run from Windows NT Workstation. Something more is needed.

Installing and Using Novell's Windows NT IntranetWare Client Service

By their basic nature, Microsoft's client software on Windows NT Server and Workstation don't provide complete access to the NDS in NetWare 4.11. They're meant as features of convenience for Windows NT Server administrators and workstation users to have access, and share resources, from their *legacy* Novell counterparts, and to not-so-subtly provide a motivation to migrate sooner rather than later from NetWare to Windows NT. However, the odds are that your Novell servers aren't going away any time soon. You may even be chafing at the limits that the Windows NT NetWare client capabilities impose on you. Fortunately, help is easily at hand, but it's from Novell, not Microsoft.

For the best Windows NT Workstation-to-NetWare connection, which enables you to run any NetWare program from the server, there's one choice: Novell's IntranetWare client for Windows NT.

Why Do You Need Novell's Software for Your Windows NT-to-NetWare Connections?

There are several reasons why I recommend using non-Microsoft software programs to get the most out of your Windows NT-NetWare connections:

◆ The IntranetWare client software is free.

◆ The IntranetWare client is readily available. Although it isn't bundled with Windows NT, you can dial up Novell's World Wide Web site at the following address:
   http://www.novell.com/intranetware/ ntint/products.html/.
   The download takes about 2.9MB and is a self-extracting archive. The file is named NTENU41E.EXE. The download process is simple, but you have to register your name and other information on the Web site to be allowed to download.

◆ The IntranetWare client also bundles the NWAdmin program, which is briefly discussed later in this chapter.

◆ The IntranetWare client also provides a single logon point. From this logon point you can set up your Windows NT logon and NetWare client logon without having to enter your user name and password for each. This saves you the trouble of having to run multiple logons, which Microsoft's services force you to do.

The assumption is made here that you already know how to use a Web browser to enter a Web page address and download software.

After you download the IntranetWare client software, move or copy it *to its own folder* and double-click it to expand its contents. A new i386 folder subfolder will be created. Open it and double-click its Setup program, which is called **Setupnw**. Follow the instructions provided during setup, which are quite simple.

Because Novell's IntranetWare client cannot run concurrently with Microsoft's Client Services for NetWare on Windows NT, the setup program asks to uninstall the Client Services for NetWare if the Microsoft client is currently running. Please do so.

When you finish installing the IntranetWare client, you're asked to reboot the system. After you restart, a new logon dialog box appears, as shown in Figure 7-12. The first time you see this dialog box, you need to enter some key information — the tree, context, server name, and so on — to produce a successful logon, even if you don't yet have an Administrator account set up on the NetWare system to mirror the account on your Windows NT Server.

Login, NetWare, and
Windows NT tabs

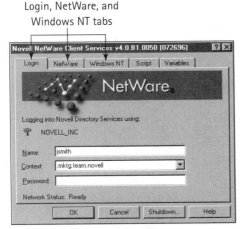

Figure 7-12: Starting Novell's IntranetWare Client

Depending on the version you have, the NetWare tab may be titled *IntranetWare*. In either case the functions are the same.

To set up your first login, follow these steps:

1. Under the Login tab (displayed by default), enter your user name in the Name text box.

2. Enter the context for your server (mine is called RGALTD, but yours will be different) in the Context text box.

3. Enter your password in the Password text box.

4. Click the IntranetWare tab.

5. Select the Tree option. (Notice the Bindery Login option. This indicates that you can use the IntranetWare client for Windows NT Workstation connections to NetWare 3.12.)

6. Enter the name of your NDS tree (in my case, SEQUOIA).

7. The Preferred Server field may not automatically show your NetWare server in its drop-down list, but it is automatically detected there. Scroll through it and select it (my server is called RICHS_411.RGALTD).

8. Click the Windows NT tab.

9. Enter your administrative account or user name in the Local Username field.

10. The name of your Windows NT workstation should automatically display in the From field. If it doesn't, enter it there.

Note the presence of a Windows NT Only check box. Leave this blank unless you plan to perform Windows NT-only logons.

11. Click OK. Assuming all your passwords and other information are correct, you'll be logged on to the workstation and its NetWare client connection.

After you achieve login to the NetWare server, you can locate its disk in Network Neighborhood. Map the NetWare disk to a drive letter on the workstation, and open a new DOS window. Use the CD command to locate yourself in the PUBLIC directory, and type NETADMIN to start Novell's main administrative program. It starts up successfully and doesn't lock you out! Novell's IntranetWare client does not require bindery emulation to provide full access to the system.

You can't run programs such as NETADMIN or the Windows-based NWAdmin (described in the next section) natively from the NetWare server. The programs are designed to run strictly across a client, so you need to configure a Windows NT workstation client to further administer a NetWare server, create accounts and groups, set up print services, and perform most other tasks.

Understanding Novell's NWADMIN Downloadable Software Program

Expanding and improving on Microsoft's NetWare client support and gateway services, Novell provides a powerful NetWare 4.11 management utility called NetWare Administrator for Windows NT. It is shown in Figure 7-13.

Novell freely distributes NetWare Administrator on its World Wide Web site at http://www.novell.com/intranetware/ntint/products.html/. After you download it and run the Setup program on Windows NT Workstation, the program provides easy access to the complete NDS tree on your Novell server. Administrator provides many similar functions to the Windows NT User Manager: You can create user accounts and groups, define account passwords and user rights, and handle all the usual server/user administrative tasks.

As shown in Figure 7-13, NetWare Administrator provides a browser window showing the hierarchy of all the objects in your Novell server's NDS. The window includes all user accounts, groups, directory contexts, and other objects in the currently logged tree.

The term *objects* is important here because every item you create on a 4.11 server is considered an object within the server's NDS. In many other cases the terminology is similar to that of Windows NT, with the concepts of groups, user accounts, user rights, and other elements translating intact. By knowing the basics of the Windows NT system, you'll also understand some of the basics of NetWare.

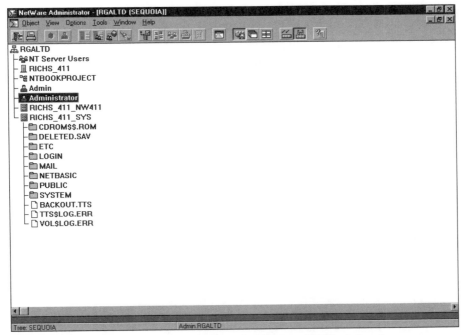

Figure 7-13: Novell's Free NWAdmin Program for Windows NT Client–Based
NetWare Administration

The top level shown in the tree is the server context, which in Figure 7-13 is titled RGALTD. You can click the context object with the right mouse button. When the shortcut menu appears, select Create. You can create an object of any kind supported by NetWare, including new user accounts and groups. Right-clicking a user account and selecting Details from its shortcut menu displays a window that enables you to change any characteristic attached to that account, including password settings, login times, group memberships, user rights, and many other elements. There are many similarities here between NetWare Administrator and the Windows NT User Manager.

Figure 7-13 also shows how the directory object RICHS_411_SYS (in other words, the hard disk) is exploded to show its various folders.

One handy application for the NetWare Administrator is to help create a more convenient logon account for the server administrator. In other words, because your Windows NT server's logon account is the same one that NetWare sees, why not make one logon do the work of two? Create a Supervisor-level account in Administrator that uses the same account name and password as the highest-level Administrator account on your Windows NT server. This way, your logon will be fast and painless. Follow these steps:

1. Obtain the correct Administrator account name and password for your Windows NT server. (Because you're the administrator, this should be no problem.)

2. Open the NetWare Administrator for Windows NT.

3. Select the object at the top of the tree. This is the server object or context. (As an example, in Figure 7-4 it's shown as RGALTD.)

4. Right-click the server object. Its shortcut menu appears. Select Create. The New Object dialog box appears, as shown in Figure 7-14.

Figure 7-14: Creating a New Object in the NDS Tree

5. Select User and click OK. The Create User dialog box appears.

6. Enter the login name for the account and then the last name, which is required by the program but is not directly used to log on. The results should resemble Figure 7-15.

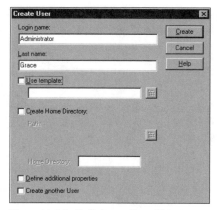

Figure 7-15: Defining a New Object in the NDS Tree

7. Click Create. (Notice how the account's password isn't defined here.) The new account is added to the NDS tree.

The next step is to add the password and access rights to the account.

8. Right-click the new Administrator account. When its shortcut menu appears, select Details. A special dialog box appears in which you define a huge number of characteristics for that new account, as shown in Figure 7-16.

Clicking the tab on the right displays a
new set of options in the dialog box

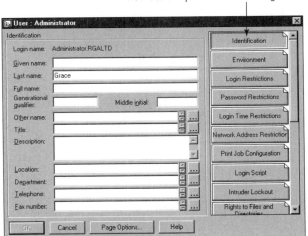

Figure 7-16: Opening the Settings for the New User Account

9. Click the Password Restrictions tab to set a new password for the account.

10. Click the Change Password button, enter the new password for the account, and Retype it to verify it.

11. Click the Rights to Files and Directories tab to set rights for the user account to the NetWare drives or directories in your server. Use the Find, Show, and Add buttons to do so. Make sure to enable the Supervisor rights check box for the selected resources.

You may want to look over some of the other settings as you go along, or even create other accounts with more restricted capabilities and rights.

For greater synchronization between Windows NT and NetWare 4.11 servers, Novell also provides a special integration utility called IGRATE.EXE that enables two-way (NDS-to-Windows NT or Windows NT-to-NDS) user account integration between the two network operating systems. Individual NDS user accounts can also be synchronized with a Windows NT account. Run the iGRATE *Update* feature first before beginning this process; the update sends Windows NT's domain information to NDS. This works only with Windows NT domain servers. The IGRATE feature can also be run inside of NWADMIN if the program is downloaded from Novell's Web site.

One final note: In the Public directory of your NetWare 4.11 you'll notice a folder titled Win95. When you open it, what do you find? Why, another copy of NetWare Administrator! This version is for Windows 95, but it can also run on Windows NT Workstation without a hitch (although *not* on Windows NT Server). If you don't want to bother downloading and installing NetWare Administrator for Windows NT, just use the version provided in the Public directory. It runs identically to the Windows NT version.

A Final Word

NetWare 4.11 (now actually called IntranetWare by Novell, who was a notable late-comer to the Internet/intranet party) remains a powerful and useful network operating system. In particular, its Directory Services and home directory capabilities are superior to the comparable features of Windows NT, particularly for larger networks. Where NetWare tends to fall down is in its modern TCP/IP support, which is essentially grafted on and is not native to the operating system. (The *IntranetWare* handle has an ever-so-slight ring of competitive desperation.) Since Novell essentially created the local-area networking market, any rational person in the field should hope that Novell rebounds from its long-standing troubles and becomes a competitive force again. Its market share is still significant, and the quality of its work is evident.

The next chapter in this book describes how to interface Windows NT to NetWare 3.12, the Clydesdale horse of network operating systems.

Troubleshooting Windows NT–NetWare 4.11 Connections

When I double-click a NetWare server utility in an open window on my Windows NT system, its window just opens and closes without running the program.
You need to map the NetWare hard disk to a drive letter. Then open a DOS window under Windows NT, change to the NetWare drive, and use the CD command to go to the Public directory. All the important NetWare utilities are located there. Type the command at the DOS prompt.

When I use Client Services for NetWare on my Windows NT Workstation to browse an NDS tree, some objects are missing from the list.
Microsoft's Client software can't handle large NDS trees. If the information requested by Windows NT's NetWare client isn't completely contained by the first reply from the NetWare server, some objects are omitted from the list. You can still connect to any existing resources; this problem just prevents some of them from being displayed in the browse list but does not disable them. The best workaround is to use Novell's Client software. Also, the Windows NT 4.0 Service Pack 3 fixes this problem.

When I try to run the NetWare NETADMIN program from my Windows NT Workstation's DOS prompt window, I get an error message saying "You are not logged in to Directory Services. You must be logged in to Directory Services before you can run NETADMIN."
In this case, the problem doesn't lie with your user name or password. This problem occurs because you're using Windows NT's native Client Services for NetWare, which doesn't provide direct access to Novell's NDS. This explains why you can run programs such as NETUSER, which enables you to change settings for your currently logged account but not NETADMIN, which is the complete administrative tool for Novell's NDS. To fix this problem, you need to download and install Novell's IntranetWare client for Windows NT (described previously).

I can't locate the information I need to identify my context or my complete Novell user name.
If you have any type of workstation connected to the server, open a DOS prompt and type **WHOAMI**. Your user ID and server ID will be displayed. Also, if your NetWare server shows up in Network Neighborhood, right-click its computer icon and select the Who Am I command. A display similar to Figure 7-11 is shown. The user name is a bit more complicated here and shows the actual NetWare nomenclature. A clue: The context is shown as the last part of the User name entry, which in Figure 7-11 is RGALTD.

Also, if you're logged on to a NetWare 4.11 server, you'll see an NDS object in the Network Neighborhood, shown as an icon with small boxes arranged in a tree pattern. Right-click this icon and select Who Am I, and you'll find the name of the NDS tree for your network.

Chapter 8

Windows NT to Novell NetWare 3.12 Connections

IN THIS CHAPTER
The following Windows NT connectivity tasks are described:

- ◆ Accessing a Novell NetWare 3.12 server through the Windows NT Server
- ◆ Sharing a Novell NetWare 3.12 print server through the Windows NT server
- ◆ Accessing and administering a Novell NetWare 3.12 server through the Windows NT Workstation

CONNECTING A WINDOWS NT server to a NetWare 3.12 server is a fairly simple matter. For more nitty-gritty administration tasks involving the NetWare system, you'll still need a Windows 95, DOS, or Windows NT Workstation computer. Any of those three types can be used to run the NetWare 3.12 applications for adding and changing user accounts and groups and normal administration.

Huge numbers of company and department servers run NetWare 3.12. It's the Clydesdale workhorse of network operating systems. Even though NetWare 3.12 is several years old, it's still incredibly common, and many companies still find it of great value. It's cheap to run, highly reliable, and provides basic, rock-solid file- and print-serving features. It's also been around a lot longer than NetWare 4.11, and many companies have stuck with version 3.12 for quite a few years now.

In many cases, you may not only be expected to set up a Windows NT server to run all the typical bells and whistles but also to maintain use of an existing NetWare print server. You can almost count on running into good ol' NetWare 3.12, whether you're a consultant, an employee at a large firm installing Windows NT Server in a department, or building your server in a smaller firm. NetWare is almost ubiquitous, and many people will expect you to be able to deal with it. That's what this chapter is about.

A Brief Survey of NetWare 3.12

NetWare 3.12 is not a fancy operating system. What it does, it does well, but much of the networking world has since passed it by. Its entire interface is based on MS-DOS character-based conventions, and it's built for two basic tasks: file serving and print serving. A huge number of utilities for management and tweaking are provided in the operating system, including:

- ◆ PCONSOLE (for managing print server configuration on NetWare, and creating new print servers; can be run in a Windows NT Server DOS window to check the status of print queues but cannot create new ones)

- ◆ RCONSOLE (for remote Administrator or Supervisor connections to NetWare; this program works correctly in a Windows NT Server DOS window)

- ◆ SYSCON (for general-purpose administration tasks; cannot create or modify accounts under Windows NT Server)

- ◆ WHOAMI (for checking the current client's logon name)

- ◆ USERDEF (for adding new users and creating/editing user account templates; cannot be run under Windows NT Server)

- ◆ VOLINFO (for checking the presence of NetWare servers and switching between servers on the network)

- ◆ DSPACE (for defining how much disk space a NetWare user account can occupy on the server; cannot be run under Windows NT Server)

- ◆ LOGIN and LOGOUT (for logging in as a new user to the server, and logging out at the end of the work day; cannot be run correctly under Windows NT Server)

Despite its graphical and functional limitations, NetWare 3.12 is still a 32-bit, fully multitasking operating system that runs multiple applications simultaneously in the course of its work. Its performance is swift, and a huge collection of third-party utilities, many in the form of NetWare's proprietary .NLM executable file format, are offered in the market. You don't need the latest multigigahertz Pentium II monstrosity to get decent performance out of it, either. (In fact, that's gross overkill.) It runs just fine on legacy 486 hardware or even 386s, and the odds are that those are the systems running it in your company.

NetWare 3.12 automatically creates a *Supervisor* account, using that name, which is used to do all the key administrative tasks on the system. When you perform Windows NT-NetWare configuration, you will need to have access to the password for that Supervisor account. Just make sure that you know what you're doing. If you are reasonably well versed in NetWare, you'll have no trouble using Windows NT Workstation as an administrative connection to a 3.12 server.

Understanding Windows NT Server's Gateway Services for NetWare

As with NetWare 4.11, you can use Microsoft's Gateway Services for NetWare to provide a Windows NT Server connection to your legacy NetWare 3.12 servers.

Logging in to Directory Services doesn't exist for NetWare 3.12. NetWare uses a Bindery scheme for server organization, and Gateway Services provides a clean and simple Bindery logon for Windows NT Server. Once you log on, Gateway Services allows you to map the NetWare server's hard disk into Windows NT's My Computer group, share Novell print servers across the network, and run numerous NetWare utilities from a DOS window.

Windows NT Server does not allow you to perform NetWare 3.12 (or 4.11) administration tasks from a local Command Prompt window, even when you're running Gateway Services. It's possible to run a command prompt, log on as the supervisor, and run NetWare's server utilities. Unfortunately, you'll quickly find that you can't create new accounts, groups, or modify the characteristics of existing accounts through Windows NT Server. Logon also doesn't work correctly. NetWare's management utilities generally allow you to press the Insert key to add new items, but this does not work under Windows NT Server connections. Similar to NetWare 4.11 connections, Windows NT's gateway provides only a functional connection to NetWare 3.12 devices and services, without any significant administrative capabilities. For more information about this topic, please see the previous chapter of this book.

Installing Windows NT Server's Gateway Services for NetWare

Gateway Services for NetWare provides a simple, functional Windows NT Server connection with resource sharing capabilities, and it is relatively easy to install and set up. Here's how to install it:

1. Open My Computer.

2. Open the Control Panel and then open the Network applet.

3. Click the Services tab.

4. Click Add. The Select Network Service dialog box appears.

5. Select Gateway (and Client) Services for NetWare.

6. Click OK. You may be prompted to enter the location of the i386 directory or to insert the Windows NT Server CD-ROM.

7. A dialog box appears, prompting you to add IPX/SPX protocol support in your installed Remote Access Service. If this is desirable, click OK. If you don't need IPX/SPX in your Remote Access configuration (you can always add it later), click Cancel. The service finishes installing.

8. Click OK to close the Network applet. You're prompted to restart the server.

9. After the server restarts, log on to the system in your usual way. A new dialog box titled Select NetWare Logon appears, providing a logon to the NetWare system. It is divided into two sections: Preferred Server (for NetWare 3.12) and Default Tree and Context (for NetWare 4.11). The Preferred Server section is what you want here. At the top the Username is listed. It's the name you logged on with and the name NetWare automatically sees during its connection to your Windows NT Server. The odds are good that the NetWare server lacks an account of that name; you can use NetWare's SYSCON or USERDEF utilities from a workstation to add a new account if necessary.

10. Select Preferred Server to enable logging on to a NetWare 3.12 server.

11. If you already know the name of your NetWare server, enter it in its proper text box.

12. Click OK. You may be greeted by another message, reading "You cannot be authenticated on [PREFERRED SERVER name here] due to the following reason: the specified user does not exist. Do you really want to set the preferred server or context to [PREFERRED SERVER name here]?"

13. Click Yes. The message merely indicates that your current logon user name doesn't exist in NetWare's bindery. This isn't a big deal, because you still can access the NetWare server and configure Gateway Services for its key sharing functions.

Creating an NTGATEWAY Group on the Novell Server

After you install Gateway Services, you need to create an NTGATEWAY group on the NetWare 3.12 server and add a user account that has the same name as your Administrator account on Windows NT Server. The assumption here is that you're using a non-Windows NT client to do this, which is directly connected to the NetWare server. A DOS, Windows 3.x, or Windows 95 system all work fine for this task. You should also have Supervisor capabilities on the NetWare 3.12 server to define all the properties you need. NetWare's SYSCON utility is fairly simple to work with, particularly if you have experience on Windows NT Server, because much of the terminology is the same and navigating Novell's menus is straightforward.

1. Open a DOS window on the client system.

2. Use the CD command to go to the PUBLIC directory on the NetWare system drive.

3. Use NetWare's LOGIN command to log in to the server as the supervisor.

4. Type in SYSCON at the DOS prompt. The System Console program appears, as shown in Figure 8-1.

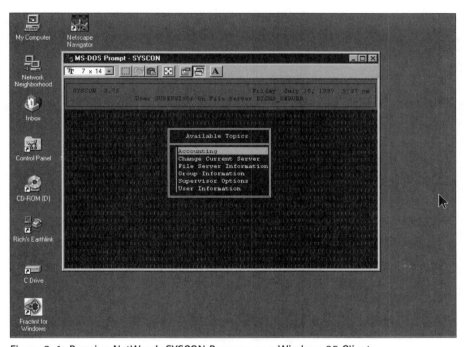

Figure 8-1: Running NetWare's SYSCON Program on a Windows 95 Client

5. Use the down-arrow key to select Group Information and press Enter. A Group Names menu appears.

6. Press the Insert key. (Note that this does *not* work on a Windows NT Server.) A New Group Name prompt appears.

7. Enter the new group name **NTGATEWAY** and press Enter. The new group is added to the menu. Press Escape.

8. Select the User Information option from the SYSCON menu and press Enter. The User Names menu appears, showing all the current user accounts on the NetWare server. Press Insert to add a new Administrator account if needed.

9. After creating the new account name, select it in the User Names menu and press Enter. Another long User Information menu appears, allowing you to change the account's password, group assignments, and Manager status, among many other features. Make sure that your new account is part of the NTGATEWAY group, and that it's added to the Managers list. The password should also be the same as that used for the Administrator account on your Windows NT system. Once you're done, press Escape a few times to back out of the program. Finally, press Escape and select Yes to quit SYSCON.

For full Gateway Services operation, you must perform this series of steps on the NetWare server. The key things to remember are the use of the Insert key and making sure the new account is part of the NTGATEWAY group.

Configuring Gateway Services for NetWare 3.12 Resource Sharing

After you have Gateway Services installed and the NTGATEWAY group is set up on NetWare with the proper account, you can set it up to allow sharing of NetWare resources through the Windows NT server to the Windows NT Windows-based clients.

1. Open My Computer and then open the Control Panel. A new icon titled GSNW appears there.

2. Double-click the GSNW icon to open it. The Gateway Services for NetWare applet opens, similar to Figure 8-3. Because you originally configured it for a Preferred Server, your Preferred Server option will be enabled, showing the NetWare 3.12 server's name in the Select box.

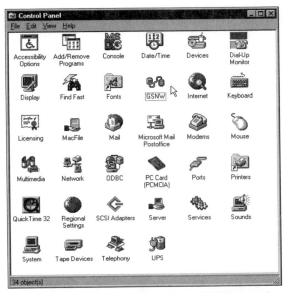

Figure 8-2: Windows NT Server's New GSNW Applet Is
Located in the Control Panel

Preferred Server section is used for
logging on to NetWare 3.12

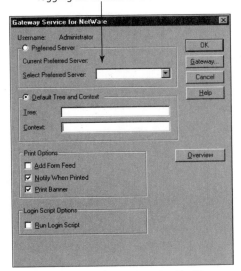

Figure 8-3: Gateway Services for NetWare
Provides Dual Logon Capabilities

3. Click the Gateway button.

4. Click the Enable Gateway check box. This check box *must* be enabled.

5. In the Gateway Account box, enter the Administrator account you customarily use for your Windows NT Server access. (*Not* your NetWare Supervisor account.)

6. Enter your Administrator account's password, and reenter it in the Confirm Password box. The Configure Gateway dialog box should appear, as shown in Figure 8-4.

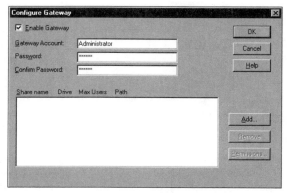

Figure 8-4: Configuring Gateway Services for NetWare
3.12 Connections

7. Click the Add button. The New Share dialog box appears, as shown in Figure 8-5.

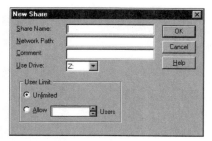

Figure 8-5: Creating a new NetWare drive share

8. Enter the desired name for your NetWare drive share in the Share Name text box. (You can't set up print server shares from this dialog box.) The name can be up to 12 characters in length. If the desired name is greater than eight characters, any Windows 3.1/MS-DOS clients on your Windows NT network will not be able to detect the share, so keep this in mind.

9. Enter the Universal Naming Convention path to the NetWare drive in the Network Path box. An example is \\RICHS_SERVER\SYS, where RICHS_SERVER is the name of the server, and SYS is the default name for the NetWare hard disk. (Typically, a bootable NetWare hard disk is named SYS.)

10. Select the first available drive letter from the Use Drive list.

11. If you need to limit the number of users who can have access to the Windows NT-shared NetWare drive, select the Allow option and type in the maximum number of users. This limits the number of connections that can share the drive through Windows NT, possibly to minimize the performance impact on the network.

12. Click OK. The Configure Gateway dialog box displays your new server disk listing, as shown in Figure 8-6.

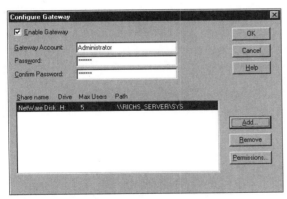

Figure 8-6: The New NetWare Drive Share

13. Finally, click OK to close the dialog box, and click OK to close Gateway Service.

What you've just done is to set up your Windows NT server Administrator account to pass NetWare 3.12 sharing capabilities *through your Windows NT server* to Windows clients connected to the Windows NT server. At this point, you're done. You can open Network Neighborhood on any connected Windows client, open the

Windows NT Server, and browse the shared NetWare drive. Now, you still need to set access permissions on the NetWare drive (and, possibly, user accounts) so that your Windows users can locate any folders they need. By default, only the Login, Mail, and Public folders are made available from the NetWare drive through Gateway Services.

For Windows 95 clients, remember that its Client for Microsoft Networks Properties must be set to log on to the correct Windows NT domain. Once this is done, the clients will be able to browse the NetWare drive without needing the IPX protocol installed in their systems.

 TIP When client access the NetWare server through NT's Gateway Services, the NT clients do not need to use the IPX protocol.

Those Windows clients will not be able to run NetWare server utilities such as RCONSOLE, SYSCON, and PCONSOLE, however (mercifully), because those Windows clients don't have a direct connection to the NetWare system. Clients to your Windows NT server are assumed to have the same access rights to the Novell server through the gateway. This makes it difficult to create individual folders for your users and to allow access to them.

Another option is to install Novell's or Microsoft's NetWare client software on all your clients that have a physical network connection of some kind to the Novell and NetWare server, and run the IPX protocol on them. When you do this, your clients can log on to both the Windows NT and Novell servers, and shared resources will show up in Network Neighborhood.

Accessing a Novell NetWare Print Server Through Windows NT Server

Unlike drive sharing, Gateway Services isn't used to share a Novell print server through Windows NT. Print server sharing is much simpler than that. To start with, open up Network Neighborhood in Windows NT Server and locate the NetWare network. When you open up the NetWare server, any print servers set up there are displayed in the Network Neighborhood window. (If you get tired of opening half a dozen windows every time you browse Network Neighborhood, pull down its View menu, select Options, and select the Browse folders by using a single window option.)

Windows NT automatically detects NetWare *print queues* that can be passed through Windows NT to other users on your network. When you open up the NetWare server in Network Neighborhood, the NetWare print queues are already available for your use. To access a NetWare print server, follow these steps:

1. Open Network Neighborhood.

2. Open Entire Network and open NetWare or Compatible Network.

3. Open the NetWare server. Any properly configured print queues created on the NetWare server automatically are displayed, as shown in Figure 8-7.

Figure 8-7: Displaying the NetWare Print
Queue in Network Neighborhood

4. Open the Printers group in My Computer.

5. Drag the NetWare printer queue icon in the Network Neighborhood to the Printers window. A "Connect to printer" message appears, reading "The Server on which the printer resides does not have a suitable printer driver installed. Click OK if you wish to install the driver on your local machine."

6. Click OK. After a moment, the Add Printer Wizard appears. Select the proper manufacturer and printer driver.

7. After the driver is installed, the new icon appears in the Printers window, as shown in Figure 8-8.

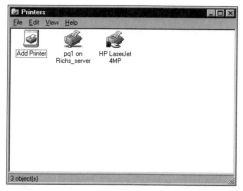

Figure 8-8: Displaying the NetWare Print
Queue in Network Neighborhood

8. Right-click the new printer icon and select Sharing. (Yes, you can do this.)

9. Select the Shared option and type in a new share name of up to 13 characters.

10. Click OK. Go to any of your connected Windows clients and open up Network Neighborhood. When you browse to the Windows NT Server's shares, you'll locate the newly shared NetWare printer! Windows 95 clients connected to your Windows NT Server may need to install a new driver, but any Windows clients (and your Windows NT Server as well) can use the NetWare print server to their hearts' content.

That wraps up Windows NT Server's most important functions for connecting to NetWare 3.12. Using the gateway, the Windows NT server becomes the front end for the NetWare network to any of its connected Windows clients, without the need to install the IPX protocol. What if you want more control? Because you can't use Windows NT Server for any kind of Novell administration tasks, you have to do some more work. The best approach is to use a Windows NT workstation, directly connected to the Novell 3.12 server, running the proper client software. Would that be Microsoft's NetWare client software? Not necessarily.

Understanding Windows NT Workstation's NetWare Client Service

Windows NT Workstation provides an important feature called Client Services for NetWare. While it's useful for Windows NT workstations that need quick access to NetWare 3.12 file and print servers, it still presents limitations. By itself, Client

Services for NetWare for Windows NT Workstation doesn't provide full access to the NetWare 3.12 server. You can't fully administer the server or modify user accounts in the Novell system, although the Client Services does allow you to log on as a normal user, mount its shared hard disk as a network drive, and use its print server.

Unlike Gateway Services, the client does not allow passing through of shared NetWare resources to other users. You have a local connection from your Windows NT Workstation client, and that's it.

Installation and use of the NetWare client for Windows NT Workstation is simple, and I show you how to do those things here. For a more powerful (and free) alternative to Microsoft's admittedly bare-bones NetWare support offerings, you'll have to turn to Novell, which fortunately is simple to do. The final part of this chapter describes how you can use Novell's free Web-based downloadable utilities to get the best use out of your Windows NT Workstation-to-NetWare connection.

Installing Windows NT Workstation's NetWare Client

Here's how to install Windows NT Workstation's Client Services for NetWare:

1. Open the Control Panel.

2. Open the Networks applet and click the Services tab.

3. Click Add. A dialog box showing a list of Workstation services you can add appears. Client Services for NetWare may be at the top of the list.

4. Select Client Services for NetWare and click OK. You may be prompted for the directory to install the files from, which should be the i386 directory on your Windows NT CD-ROM (or a copied i386 directory on your hard disk).

   After the files are copied, restart the system.

5. After the server restarts, log on to the system in your normal fashion. The Select NetWare Logon dialog box appears, providing a logon to the NetWare system. It is divided into two sections: Preferred Server (for NetWare 3.12) and Default Tree and Context (for NetWare 4.11). The 3.12 server is automatically listed in the Preferred Server list. This is what you want. At the top, the Username is listed, which is the same name you logged on with; it's also the name that NetWare sees during your initial logon. It's possible or even likely that you don't have an account with that Username on the NetWare server, and you need to create that later on.

6. Select Preferred Server to enable logging on to the NetWare 3.12 server.

7. Select the NetWare server from the drop-down list (it may already be displayed there).

8. Click OK. If your user account isn't replicated on the NetWare machine, you'll see another message.

9. Click Yes.

The system continues logging you in to both the Windows NT and NetWare servers.

Windows NT Workstation's Control Panel shows a new utility called CSNW, for Client Services for NetWare. It's useful if you need to select another NetWare server in the network (you may have more than one NetWare 3.12 server in your enterprise network, for example), and any available servers usually are automatically detected here *if* you have a direct connection.

The Overview button in the CSNW applet provides a decent online help resource to the key features offered by Client Services for NetWare. Otherwise, that's about it for client configuration on Windows NT Workstation. If you can compare the CSNW applet to the Gateway Services in Windows NT Server, you'll see that they're quite similar except for Windows NT Server's Gateway feature, which is missing here. It's extremely bare-bones and does not provide the ability to perform administrative tasks from the connected workstation. Something else is needed if you plan to use a Windows NT Workstation as a NetWare client.

Locating, Installing, and Using Novell's Windows NT IntranetWare Client

By its basic nature, Microsoft's client software on Windows NT Server and Workstation don't provide complete access to NetWare servers of any type. The software meant as features of convenience for Windows NT Server administrators and workstation users to have access, and share resources, from their "legacy" Novell counterparts, and to not-so-subtly provide a motivation to migrate sooner-rather-than-later from NetWare to Windows NT. However, the odds are that your Novell servers aren't going away any time soon. You may even be chafing at the limits that Windows NT's NetWare client capabilities impose on you. Fortunately, help is easily at hand.

For the best Windows NT Workstation-to-NetWare connection that allows you to run any NetWare program on the Windows NT Workstation client, there's only one choice: Novell's IntraNetWare client for Windows NT.

There are several reasons why I recommend using nonMicrosoft software programs to get the most out of your Windows NT-NetWare connections:

◆ The IntranetWare client software is free. It doesn't cost you a cent.

- ◆ The IntranetWare client is readily available. Although it isn't bundled with Windows NT, you can dial up Novell's Internet World Wide Web site at the following address: `http://www.novell.com/intranetware/ntint/products.html/`. The download takes about 2.9MB and is a self-extracting archive. The file is called NTENU41E.EXE.

- ◆ The IntranetWare client provides unfettered access to all NetWare 3.12 utilities from a Windows NT Workstation without the need to run any further programs.

- ◆ The IntranetWare client also provides a single logon point where you can set up your Windows NT logon and NetWare client logon without having to enter your user name and password for each.

After you download the IntranetWare client software (which I won't describe how to do here; simply follow the instructions at Novell's Web site at the address listed earlier), move or copy it to its own folder and double-click it to expand its contents. A new i386 subfolder is created. Open it and double-click its Setup program, which is called SETUPNW. Follow the instructions provided during setup.

Note that Novell's IntranetWare client cannot run concurrently with Microsoft's Client Services for Netware; it asks to uninstall it during its setup if the Microsoft client is currently running. Allow it to do so.

When you finish installing the IntranetWare client, reboot the system. A new logon dialog box appears, as shown in Figure 8-9. The first time you see it, you'll need to enter some key information — the server name, Supervisor account, and so on — to produce a successful logon and the ability to perform remote NetWare administration from the Windows NT Workstation.

Login, NetWare, and
Windows NT tabs

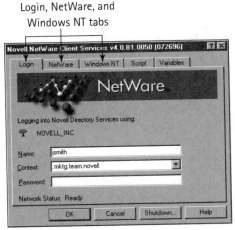

Figure 8-9: Starting Novell's IntranetWare Client

Depending on the version you have, the NetWare tab may be titled "IntranetWare." In either case, the functions are the same.

To set up your first logon, follow these steps:

1. The Login tab is automatically displayed. *Do not modify its settings.* Click the IntranetWare tab first.

2. Select the Bindery Login option and select the NetWare 3.12 system, which is automatically detected in the Server drop-down list.

3. *Now* select the Login tab.

4. Enter the supervisor's user name.

5. Enter your Supervisor account's password.

6. Click the Windows NT tab. Enter your administrative account or user name in the Local Username text box. Your Windows NT Workstation's name should be automatically displayed in the From text box. If not, enter it there.

   Note the presence of a Windows NT Only check box. Leave this blank unless you plan to perform Windows NT-only logons.

7. Click OK.

8. Enter your Windows NT password. (A check box is also provided, reading "Change your Windows NT password to match your IntranetWare password after a successful logon." You can enable this check box if desired, but I don't recommend it except for convenience. If you should enable it, you'll have a single-stop logon for both your systems. Just make sure your passwords are properly synchronized between both systems.

9. Click OK. Assuming all your passwords and other information are correct, you'll be logged on to the workstation and its NetWare client connection concurrently.

After logon to the NetWare server is achieved, you can locate its disk in Network Neighborhood. Map the NetWare disk to a drive letter on the workstation, and open a new DOS window. Use the CD command to locate yourself in the PUBLIC directory, and type NETADMIN to start Novell's main administrative program. It starts up successfully and doesn't lock you out! Novell's IntranetWare client does not require bindery emulation to provide full access to the system.

At this point, you can open NetWare drives and folders from the server. You can even double-click any of the typical NetWare utilities such as SYSCON or RCONSOLE, and they will run properly on the workstation despite the fact that they're DOS applications. You don't need to run the LOGIN program in a DOS prompt window to open NetWare utilities as the supervisor. When your client is running properly, you can run multiple NetWare utilities at once, as shown in Figure 8-10.

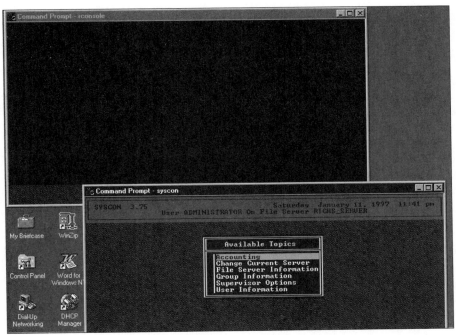

Figure 8-10: Running Novell's RCONSOLE and SYSCON Utilities on Windows NT Workstation

Full administration capabilities are offered. You can even display Novell's "server snake" in a DOS window running RCONSOLE.

A Final Word

That concludes the NetWare connectivity chapters. Generally, it's pretty simple to execute Windows NT-to-NetWare communication. It is important to understand at least the basics about NetWare so that you can provide the information that Windows NT needs to make the connection. It's a good idea to make friends with the NetWare administrator in your company (unless that's you, and then that'd be a bit weird), so you can get that information when you need it.

The next section of this book discusses some intensive online connectivity applications, including Internet connections, Remote Access, and Virtual Private Networks.

Troubleshooting Windows NT–NetWare 3.12 Connections

I have more than one NetWare server on my network, but my Windows NT system, using Client Services for NetWare, doesn't let me see them all.
NetWare 3.12 uses a mechanism called SAP (Service Advertising Process) to list any NetWare servers connected in the default or Preferred Server's local network segment. Windows NT Workstation's CSNW is capable of reading and connecting to any servers in that local segment that are listed in that preferred server's SAP table. Unfortunately, if any NetWare servers are not routed or bridged over other network segments, Windows NT won't see them. Routing/bridging is necessary for any servers in other network segments to be added to your NetWare preferred server's SAP table. Check your routing connections. Then you can type the command **DISPLAY SERVERS** in the NetWare console screen.

When I try to run Novell's NWADMIN program on my workstation, the program doesn't detect my NetWare 3.12 server!
NWADMIN is designed to work only with NetWare 4.*x*. For administration of 3.*x* servers, you need to set up Novell's IntranetWare client on the Windows NT Workstation and then run NetWare's native administrative utilities. Also, there is no feasible method to migrate NetWare 3.*x* user accounts to Windows NT as there is with NetWare 4.*x*. You have to do them one at a time by hand, using the User Manager.

When I'm setting up Gateway Services for NetWare, I receive an error message stating that I must have an NTGATEWAY group on my NetWare 3.*x* system, and that my gateway user account must be part of the group.
You need to use SYSCON on the NetWare system to create a new Windows NTGATEWAY group and add the Administrator account to it. Please see the section titled "Creating an Windows NTGATEWAY Group on the Novell Server" for details.

Windows NT Workstation takes a long time to display NetWare folders and files in Network Neighborhood when I'm running CSNW.
Normally, Windows NT Workstation takes about 20 seconds to display NetWare disk contents. To fix this, make sure you're running at least Service Pack 3 for Windows NT 4.0, which you can get from Microsoft's Web site.

Part III

Internet and Online Connectivity Tasks

Part 3 focuses on online connectivity applications. Windows NT provides a broad array of features in this area. One essential tool for any network manager is ensuring that your users can use a standard modem-phone line connection to connect to the network. You can do this in two different ways: using Windows NT's Remote Access Service (RAS) from an NT Workstation or Windows 95 system to an NT Server, or creating a Virtual Private Network. Chapter 9, "Setting Up Remote Access on Windows NT Server," concentrates on more conventional Remote Access connections in which the client computer dials the server directly and initiates a network connection. In this way the client behaves just like a normal networked system, except at *much* slower speeds. You also become acquainted with Microsoft's must-have free upgrade, called Routing and RAS.

Chapter 10, "Internet Connections and RAS Upgrades," builds on basic remote access by offering two key Internet access applications: setup for standard Web browsing and e-mail, and creating a Virtual Private Network through your ISP to your server. Virtual Private Network is a new technology, and Windows NT 4.0 is one of the first network operating systems to support it. NT does so by means of Point-To-Point Protocol (PPTP), which enables the use of standard Internet connections as an *invisible* medium to create network connections without the normal long-distance fees entailed by Remote Access. You can do this using a normal ISP connection, although dedicated connections are a good idea on the server end. Finally, Chapter 11, "Setting Up Microsoft Exchange for Electronic Mail," describes how to configure and use Windows NT's free Microsoft Exchange group e-mail software.

Chapter 9

Setting Up Remote Access on Windows NT Server

IN THIS CHAPTER
This chapter covers the following topics:

- ◆ Configuring and using Remote Access Server (RAS) with the NetBEUI protocol
- ◆ Configuring and using Remote Access Server (RAS) with the TCP/IP protocol

THE PERMUTATIONS OF using remote access on your Windows NT-based network are potentially huge, spanning almost every important service Windows NT Server has to offer. First, you'll learn how to create simple Remote Access Server connections using Windows NT's RAS services and NetBEUI protocol. Then you'll segue into the use of TCP/IP to do the same thing.

Even if you only use Windows 95 and Windows NT Workstation clients on your network with your Windows NT Server (which is the assumption), remote access with TCP/IP is loaded with pitfalls and potential problems. Nevertheless, compared to other widely used network operating systems that use TCP/IP, Windows NT does a good job making this key networking tool approachable.

Before digging into the details of Remote Access configuration, you should spend a short period of time exploring two key topics regarding RAS: its basic mechanisms and security issues. Both areas can get quite complicated. My goal in this beginning section is to reduce complex topics to understandable terms without minimizing their importance. That's the approach I take throughout this important chapter.

Understanding RAS and Its Mechanisms

As was discussed briefly in Chapter 1, Remote Access Service (RAS) is a feature provided by Windows NT for clients who need to access the network when they're away from the office. RAS can also be used by Windows NT servers and workstations to access the Internet for browsing and e-mail. For business applications, you might have a company executive out for a trade show who needs to access the network to get company e-mail or to download the new PowerPoint presentation cranked out by the graphics department back home.

Windows NT's basic Remote Access Service is a fairly simple and efficient tool for this purpose. Using Windows clients, you can dial in to the LAN or domain administered by the server running RAS, and browse the network just like you would on your LAN. You can use any conventional networking protocol for remote access, including the usual TCP/IP, NetBEUI, and IPX protocols supported by Windows NT. Other key Windows NT features are intended to expand the RAS and TCP/IP reach in your network by providing dynamic IP addressing (DHCP), seamless name resolution for clients on the server (WINS), and Internet/intranet domain name management (DNS). All these features and more can be mixed in different combinations to produce TCP/IP network connections in differing ways. I discuss them later in this chapter. In some cases those features can also be used with other networking protocols such as NetBEUI.

RAS's simplicity is an asset for many people out in the field, because once you're successfully connected, you have nothing else to worry about. Network Neighborhood opens up its shared resources just as it normally does, and any mapped hard disks and printers appear in My Computer. You can set clients to browse only on the server, or on the entire network. The biggest difference is speed. For practical purposes, remote access isn't usable for anything except file serving. Application serving is a nonissue, especially when you're dealing with 33.6 Kbps modems from your boss's laptop. As an emergency gateway for getting to important data files or transferring them long-distance to someone else's system, though, it can't be beat. It's also becoming one of the most important applications in general networking.

Another application for RAS is client dial-up to the Internet. This is a simpler application discussed in Chapter 10.

Remote access provides a rare instance where 56 Kbps modems can genuinely help the business user. For example, your boss can have a 56 Kbps modem with his or her laptop and be able to dial up the server, which can have another 56 Kbps modem connected on its end. By setting up this way, you get the benefits of using higher-speed modem technology without having to worry about ISP termination or compatibility issues. If you must use analog modems for remote access, hook up a 56 Kbps modem to your server and distribute the *same model* modem to your remote access clients. The price premium for 56 Kbps modems is a mere $20-$30 over other modems; for client-server remote access applications, they're a decent investment.

Understanding Security and Firewalls

In this chapter, I don't have the space to tell you about the vast security issues confronting anyone who builds any kind of outside link to their network. On the most basic level, beyond building secure user accounts in Windows NT with "uncrackable" passwords and careful maintenance of user rights, there is one fact: You need a firewall. In the present day this shouldn't be big news. Although break-in risks from hacking tend to be overhyped, the problem is real.

Firewalls have a simple purpose: keeping outsiders away from your company's private internal networks. When your network has access to the Internet, uses the Internet for communication across a WAN, or uses a remote access gateway, you really need a firewall. If your company has a Web site administered within your company, and especially if you plan to have some kind of order-taking mechanism on your Web site or private network, a firewall is an absolute must. If done right, firewalls don't even have to be an inconvenience to your remote users.

Among the biggest problems involved in using firewalls is that most people who buy them simply don't set them up properly—because they either don't know how or are too busy to attend to the crucial details. Do not fall into this trap! Firewalls don't have to inconvenience your remote users, but neglecting them can sure cause a huge inconvenience for *you* if some prankster or criminal gets loose inside your network. Firewalls are also expensive. Nevertheless, you can't afford not to consider them.

Two basic mechanisms are used by firewall packages. The first is called *packet filtering*. It dynamically checks incoming data packets to see whether they're coming from a trusted location somewhere else in the Internet "cloud," and whether the packet can be allowed access to the services it's asking for. They're a convenient routing mechanism and rely heavily on the security rules defined by the administrator. Packet filtering is a basic form of security that can deal with inherently insecure forms of access such as Telnet and FTP. The biggest drawback is that packet filtering still allows for direct communications between your network and the Internet cloud, and is an inadequate measure in many cases. It tends to be cheaper and readily available in freeware and shareware packages, and in commercial programs. That makes it easier for crackers to reverse-engineer them and devise easy workarounds.

The second type of firewall mechanism is called a *proxy server*. It's a more effective measure in some ways than packet filtering because it isolates your network from the Internet by using a so-called *bastion host* as a physical barrier between the inside (you and your network) and the outside. A *bastion host* is usually another computer using two network connections, one to the outside and one to your network. At the same time, user transparency is preserved, and the proxy server doesn't interfere unduly with your boss trying to get that PowerPoint presentation downloaded to his or her laptop. Microsoft offers a proxy server package as an extra to Windows NT that provides some highly useful firewall features, beginning with Proxy Server version 2.0.

Firewalls can be expensive and complicated, requiring several man-months to set up, which is probably the biggest reason why they tend to be neglected in time-pressed IS departments. You'll have to decide how to balance your department's needs. If you have frequent or constant employment of the Internet or remote-access dialup to the server, a firewall is still a necessity. You may want to consider taking the increasingly popular third-party route for addressing complex security requirements. Nevertheless, outsourcing critical management functions of this type can introduce new sets of problems that you'll have to carefully consider. But that's why you're getting a paycheck . . .

Other Security Considerations

As a network administrator within your organization, probably the biggest conflict you'll face is the issue of security versus ease of use. No other networking mechanism highlights this problem more than your dial-up remote-access facilities. You're guaranteed an ongoing problem with your users' passwords and account names as your network grows. Why? To start with, your users are going to resist using assigned passwords with "uncrackable" alphanumeric combinations. They're hard to remember.

Changing account passwords on a fairly regular basis, which many administrators have to do, makes things even more difficult. It's an administrative headache. Because dial-up remote access is becoming such an important part of business connectivity, you'll find yourself juggling the trade-off between ease of use and security almost constantly. Remote access also provides a huge window of vulnerability. If you use it along with corporate Web sites that handle any sort of transaction (a topic that's far beyond the scope of this book), it isn't a question of *if* you get attacked, but *when*.

What can you do to minimize or cope with the problems presented here? There are a number of things:

♦ Define a coherent security program and make sure the business managers in your company are on the same page as your IS department in this critical area.

♦ Use a separate authentication server (or even a third-party solution).

♦ Make sure all your user accounts are gathered in groups for consistent resource privileges.

♦ Constantly monitor traffic for break-ins.

♦ Back up your event log files daily.

♦ If and when a break-in occurs, cut off the connection as quickly as possible, and check your event logs and service text files for clues.

There's an awful lot more that can be said, but these are the basics.

One of the coolest things about the Internet is how it allows you to research topics like this in a strikingly efficient fashion. Go to some of the major IS magazine Web sites, such as *InfoWorld Electric* (`http://www.infoworld.com`), *ZDNet* (`http://www.zdnet.com`), and *ComputerWorld* magazine (`http://www.computerworld.com/`). Most major IS magazine sites contain searchable article databases on any relevant topic, including firewalls and their mechanisms, comparative reviews, security issues, and recommendations.

Do You Need TCP/IP?

Flatly stated: No, not in many situations.

Once you get past the basic functions, so many issues are involved with remote access that a book could be written about RAS alone. TCP/IP configuration for remote access by your clients may be the most unpleasant and difficult task you'll ever undertake in Windows NT; it's one reason why I advocate using NetBEUI for small Windows NT networks. There are numerous ways to configure TCP/IP for remote client access, including the following:

◆ Defining a static set of IP addresses to assign to clients as they dial in. This is good for many applications, and if your server will never dial out to the Internet to use it as a Virtual Private Network (VPN), it's also an excellent way to test out your setup. You may use the basic TCP/IP configuration dialog box to do this.

◆ Using Dynamic Host Configuration Protocol (DHCP) to dynamically assign IP addresses to remote clients as they dial in (best for situations where you have a limited number of IP addresses to work with). Address scopes must be defined using the DHCP Manager. It's a very good substitute for using static addresses and is much better for larger networks.

◆ Defining a specific IP address for each Windows NT client using the LMHOSTS file.

◆ Setting up Windows Internet Naming Service (WINS) on your Windows NT Server. This is required if your local-area network spans router connections and you expect to have access to a workstation across a router boundary. It's also a much better name resolution method than using the LMHOSTS file. Typically, WINS is set up in conjunction with DHCP on larger Windows NT networks.

TIP WINS is also highly useful for managing NetBEUI client connections over routers. Considering that NetBEUI is inherently a nonroutable protocol, this can be a beautiful thing.

◆ Combining WINS and Domain Naming Service (DNS) to provide NetBIOS/Internet domain name resolution, which maps computer names on the network to specific IP addresses and ensures a firm communication link. This is the method I describe in this chapter. You can also combine them with DHCP to eliminate using static address pools from the server.

TCP/IP connections provide so many options under Windows NT that it is easy to get lost in the details. As discussed in Chapter 1, how you set up TCP/IP depends heavily on your application. If you plan to route between different LANs, you need to use TCP/IP for your basic networking protocol, and by extension, for remote access. If you have a fairly small network without a lot of outside connectivity, and you're using Windows-type clients exclusively, you don't need TCP/IP and can get along with the nonroutable NetBEUI protocol.

Many writers and technicians urge people to use TCP/IP exclusively, no matter what kind of network they're dealing with. I do not always agree with this approach. Admittedly, TCP/IP is ideal for large networks and is the networking standard for the Internet. For simpler connectivity applications like the ones described in this book, TCP/IP is unnecessary, and it adds another level of complexity to the process. (It is also slower in small networks.) If you just want to get a basic, reliable remote access connection to the server for a small business, home office, or an unrouted LAN in an office department, you *can* use NetBEUI or IPX exclusively. Using either is the simplest way to get a quick connection to the local-area network over a phone line. You can also use NetBEUI or IPX in conjunction with TCP/IP, along with DNS, DHCP, and WINS, to make sure all your bases are covered. (Not so fast!)

You begin with the basics, and add layers in later sections.

Setting Up and Configuring Remote Access Services for NetBEUI Connections

There's a good chance you've already installed Remote Access Service on your server when you set up the operating system. You can check by opening the Control Panel, opening Network, and clicking the Services tab. If the Remote Access Server isn't there, simply click the Add button, select the server from the list, and insert the CD when the system asks for it (unless you have an i386 directory on your hard disk).

An Add RAS Device dialog appears, listing any installed modems in the system. You can also install a new modem by clicking the Install Modem button. Afterwards, the familiar Remote Access Setup dialog box appears, as shown in Figure 9-1, showing the modem(s) installed on the system.

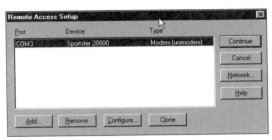

Figure 9-1: The Remote Access Setup Dialog Box
Is Deceptively Simple

1. Select a modem and click the Configure button. The Configure Port Usage dialog box appears, as shown in Figure 9-2.

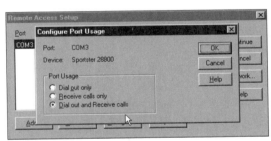

Figure 9-2: Configuring for Dial-Up or Receiving Calls

2. Make sure the Dial out and Receive calls option is selected, and click OK to close the dialog box.

3. Click the Network button. The Network Configuration dialog box appears, displaying the protocols that can be used for dialing out and receiving calls.

4. Enable the NetBEUI and TCP/IP check boxes in the Dial out Protocols and Server Settings sections, as seen in Figure 9-3.

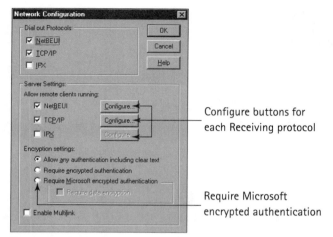

Configure buttons for
each Receiving protocol

Require Microsoft
encrypted authentication

Figure 9-3: Deciding on the Network
Protocols To Be Used on the Server

The type of RAS connection used by the server depends on what the client requests. If a client dialing in to the server uses NetBEUI, the server will use that protocol for the network connection, even though it also supports TCP/IP.

Notice the Configure buttons shown next to each protocol.

5. Click the NetBEUI Configure button. The RAS Server NetBEUI Configuration dialog appears, as shown in Figure 9-4.

Figure 9-4: Simple NetBEUI Configuration Options

6. Select Entire network (you can always change the setting later). You'll see the same options for any of the three networking protocols: This computer only or Entire network. Selecting This computer only ensures that the dial-up client can only access the server that answers the call. If Entire network is selected, the dial-up user can explore the network just as they normally would.

7. Click OK.

8. In the Network Configuration dialog box, select the Require Microsoft Encrypted Authentication option. This enables the best level of security for a client-server remote access connection.

9. Click OK.

10. Click Continue, and then click Close to close the Network control panel. You're prompted to reboot.

I use both NetBEUI and TCP/IP for dial out and receive, because if a remote client wants the server to call them back, the server should be able to use the same protocol used when the client initiates contact and requests a callback. In other words, if a client calls in using the supported NetBEUI protocol, and the server attempts to call back using TCP/IP, you may run into problems. Both ends need to be on the same page.

You'll come back to this dialog box when you set up RAS to use TCP/IP, later in this chapter.

After you restart the system, your Remote Access settings are enabled on the server. This is only the beginning.

Setting Up User Accounts for Remote Access

A RAS user account is exactly the same as a normal user account created in the User Manager. All the same rights apply, and the logon mechanism is transparently the same. A few minor details must be checked to make sure the user can dial into the server. The most important is allowing the client user account to dial in. Another is the callback features for the client. Office users with laptops may be dialing in to the server from hundreds or thousands of miles away during business trips. When this occurs, server callback offers convenience to the remote user. Three different settings are possible for Remote Access callback, as listed in Table 9-1.

TABLE 9-1 RAS CALLBACK TYPES

Setting	Function
No Call Back	No call backs requested, and the user logs in over the RAS connection "on their dime."
Set by Caller	Used frequently when remote users move from place to place and need long-distance callbacks. When the user connects to RAS, a dialog box pops up requesting a callback number. The user will probably want to speak to the front desk of their hotel to make sure of the direct dial-in number to their room before issuing this number.

continued

TABLE 9-1 RAS CALLBACK TYPES *(Continued)*

Setting	Function
Preset To	Most useful when the remote user is consistently in one place. Then the server automatically dials back at the prescribed number.

The callback options depend heavily on what the user wants and what their individual situation is. You may have to change these settings from time to time as users' circumstances change. Here's how set up an account for dial-in privileges:

1. In the User Manager or User Manager for Domains, select the user account and then select Properties from the User menu.

2. Click the Dialin button. The Dialin Information dialog box appears.

3. Enable the Grant dialin permission to user check box.

   The Callback options are displayed: No Call Back, Set by Caller, and Preset To.

4. If the user expects to enter phone numbers from different locations, select Set By Caller. If the user expects to be in one location for the entire trip or always uses Remote Access from one location, select Preset To and enter the number.

5. Click OK to commit the settings.

In all other particulars, user accounts for remote access behave the same way as they would on the local network, with the same user rights and abilities to browse the network.

Because you're using your normal user accounts, this isn't as dire as it sounds. For example, if you have a remote user whose access on the network is customarily for a single shared folder on the server, that's what they'll see when they dial in. Everything looks the same, just slower.

For business purposes, I actually prefer the This computer only setting in the protocol setup, because it minimizes the possibility that someone with a purloined account can wander throughout the entire network and pillage other users' hard drives. Using the This computer only setting, the dial-in client can still access any folders on the server that they ordinarily would in the course of their work. If their files are on a local network client, selecting Entire network allows the remote user to browse through the network until they locate their own computer (or someone else's if necessary).

Now you're finished with the basic setup for Windows NT Remote Access on the server end. Of course, there's a lot more that you may eventually need to do. You haven't looked at any kind of TCP/IP setup. Nor have you looked at setting up Windows NT Server's other facilities, such as WINS and DHCP. All in good time . . .

Setting Up a Windows NT Workstation Client for Remote Access with NetBEUI

Now you'll see how to set a Windows NT Workstation client to dial in to your server. All in all, it's rather simple, especially with NetBEUI. (Your boss will thank you.)

At this point, I assume that you already have Remote Access Service installed in your Windows NT Workstation client. If not, the procedure is the same as for installing Remote Access on a Windows NT server, as described earlier. Follow these steps:

1. Open the Control Panel.

2. Open the Network applet and click the Services tab.

3. Select Remote Access Service and click Properties. The Remote Access Setup dialog box appears. If the service is set up properly, the client's modem should appear here.

4. Click the Network button. The workstation's Network Configuration dialog box appears, as shown in Figure 9-5.

Figure 9-5: Deciding the Network Protocols To Be Used on the Windows NT Workstation

If the workstation is set up to dial out and receive calls, this dialog box will appear the same as in Figure 9-3.

5. Select NetBEUI. (Its check box should then be enabled.) Disable any other protocols for the moment. You use NetBEUI to create a basic connection.

6. Click OK. Click OK again to close the Properties sheet, and click Close to close the applet. You're prompted to restart.

The Identification tab provides two fields: the Computer Name and the Workgroup/Domain field. Depending on whether your computer's account is part of a workgroup from a Windows NT stand-alone server, or a participating member of a domain, this field will change its contents. The assumption in this book is that your server is a Primary Domain Controller and not a stand-alone.

The best way to ensure that Windows NT Workstation or Server clients are a member of your domain is to use the Server Manager on Windows NT Server. (Windows NT Servers can also be RAS clients. Unfortunately, Server Manager doesn't offer the capability to add Windows 95 clients as domain members.) For more information on that topic, please see Chapter 2.

Configuring Dial-Up Networking (DUN) for Remote Access Using NetBEUI

Another important process is making sure that your Windows NT client's Dial-Up Networking application uses the correct protocol (in this case, NetBEUI). Follow these steps:

1. Open My Computer.

2. Double-click the Dial-Up Networking icon. This is the DUN application you'll be using for RAS connection.

3. Click New to create a new connection listing. The New Phonebook Entry Wizard appears. (If you're running DUN for the first time, this is the first thing to appear.)

4. Type in the name for the new connection and click Next.

5. Three check boxes appear, as shown in Figure 9-6.

6. Select the check boxes that apply to you and click Next. (The top check box should be selected *only* if you're calling an ISP; see Chapter 10). I keep all three check boxes cleared in most applications.

7. Enter the phone number for your dial-up connection. Click the Alternates button if more than one dial-up number is provided from the RAS server. This enables the client to try other numbers if the first one is busy.

8. Click Next and then click Finish.

   Now you need to set up DUN's properties to use the proper protocols.

9. Open the DUN application.

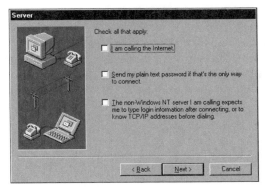

Figure 9-6: Configuring DUN

10. Click the More button and select Edit Entry and Modem Properties. The Edit Phonebook Entry dialog box appears.

11. Click the Server tab. It appears as shown in Figure 9-7.

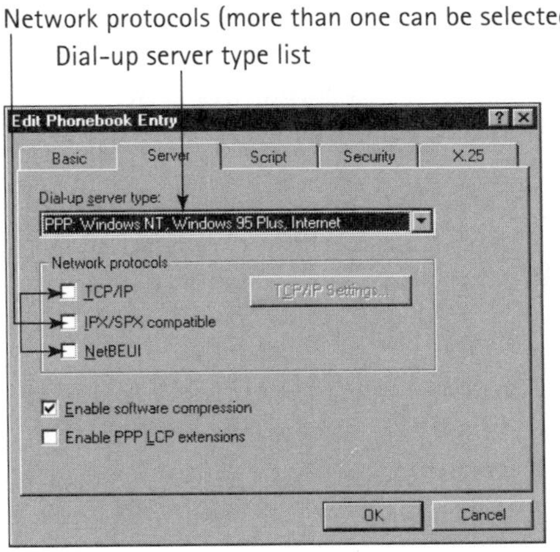

Network protocols (more than one can be selected)

Dial-up server type list

Figure 9-7: Configuring DUN, continued:
Set Up DUN Properties

12. In the Dial-up server type list, make sure the listing "PPP: Windows NT, Windows 95 Plus, Internet" is displayed, as shown in Figure 9-7.

13. Select NetBEUI. Leave the other protocols blank. (If the protocol isn't installed in your client, you're prompted to do so by the program.)

14. Click the Enable software compression check box to enable it. (This provides somewhat better network connection speed.) The Enable PPP LCP Extensions check box can also be enabled if you're using this phone listing to dial up *only* a Windows NT server. In some other systems, the Enable PPP LCP check box may actually prevent you from connecting properly, but for straight remote access to the server it can be enabled or not as you choose.

15. Click OK. DUN is now set up for a proper NetBEUI-based RAS connection to the server.

Client Dialing and Logging On with a Windows NT Workstation Using NetBEUI

At this point, your Windows NT workstation client should have a fully configured modem and phone line, and have a new DUN (Dial-Up Networking) phone listing set up for dialing into the server. The server should also be set up to receive remote access calls from clients. It must also be able to accept NetBEUI connections over RAS. All this is done in the preceding sections. There is much to do, but it's all pretty basic.

Here's how to dial in with a Windows NT workstation RAS client:

1. On the dial-up client, open My Computer and open your Dial-Up Networking applet.

2. Click Dial.

3. You may be prompted to enter a user name and password. If so, enter them and press Enter. The domain to which you're logging on will also be listed.

   The computer will dial the number and begin to connect.

4. If the user account is set up with Callback capabilities (in User Manager, Dialup), the server will prompt for a callback number, as shown in Figure 9-8. If no callback is desired, click Cancel or press the Escape key.

5. If needed, enter the phone number and click OK. The client and server will briefly disconnect, and the server will immediately call back.

6. In either case, your logon continues and your connection is authenticated by the server. (Check the Troubleshooting section at the end of this chapter for a list of things that can go wrong here and how to fix them.)

You are connected to the server over a phone line. Now you should be able to open up Network Neighborhood. If your Windows NT workstation client is a member of an Windows NT domain, its name and that of the server will appear in Network Neighborhood. Other domain clients may also appear (as many as the user account has permissions for).

You can also try a search using a computer name if you don't want to fiddle around with opening a bunch of windows. Right-click Network Neighborhood and select Find Computer. Then type in the name of the computer on the remote network. If your server permits browsing through the entire network, and you have the appropriate permissions, the computer appears in the window.

Setting Up a Windows 95 Remote Access Client Using NetBEUI

Considering that the huge majority of laptops in corporate use run Windows 95, and since Windows NT is rather difficult to set up on a laptop (due to problematic device support and Windows NT's much heavier use of resources), you have to deal with Windows 95 clients in this context. Fortunately, that's fairly easy to do.

One thing to keep in mind is that Windows 95 systems can't be counted as domain members under Windows NT. Instead, they appear in Network Neighborhood as part of a workgroup that transparently appears in the network. Typically, in the Neighborhood you have to open Entire Network and then Microsoft Windows Network, and then the workgroup name should appear. (The Windows NT domain may also reappear here as well.) Of course, Windows 95 clients can actually log on to a Windows NT domain; they just can't be members.

Windows 95 clients have a special Dial-Up Networking group, which is located in My Computer. Unlike Windows NT, each individual phone listing runs its own copy of Dial-Up Networking. To set up a new RAS dial-up account for a Windows 95 client, do the following:

1. Open My Computer.

2. Open Dial-Up Networking.

3. Open the Make New Connection applet. It's shown in Figure 9-8.

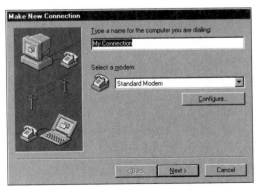

Figure 9-8: Creating a New Dial-Up Connection for a Win95 RAS Client

4. Enter a name for the new dial-up connection, and make sure the correct modem for the client is selected and configured correctly. (For example, name it "Windows NT Server Connection.")

5. Click Next.

6. Enter the phone number, area code first, for the server's dial-up number.

7. Click Next, and then click Finish. A new dial-up connection icon appears in the Dial-Up Networking group.

The next phase is to ensure that the new connection uses the proper networking protocols. Follow these steps:

1. Right-click the dial-up connection icon you've just created. Its shortcut menu appears.

2. From the shortcut menu, select Properties. The dial-up connection's Properties sheet appears, as shown in Figure 9-9.

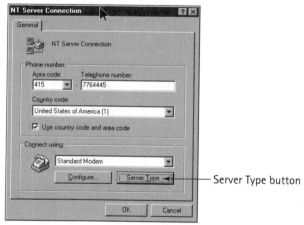

Figure 9-9: Opening Properties for the New Windows 95 Dial-Up Connection

3. Click the Server Type button. The Server Types dialog box appears, as shown in Figure 9-10.

4. In the type of Dial-up Server list, select "PPP:Windows 95, Windows NT 3.5, Internet," as shown in Figure 9-10.

Type list (best value is shown here)

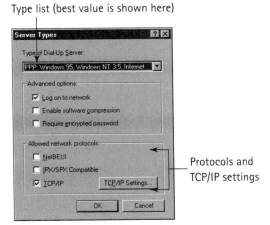

Protocols and
TCP/IP settings

Figure 9-10: Checking the Server
Type for Dial-Up Under Windows 95

5. Enable the NetBEUI check box. Leave the other protocols disabled for now.

6. Click OK, and click OK again to close the Properties sheet.

You're using NetBEUI to start with so that you can get a functional connection. Make sure the NetBEUI protocol is installed on the Win95 client. When you do so, it's automatically bound to the "Dial-Up Adapter", which is, of course, your modem.

Dialing and Logging On with a Windows 95 Client Using NetBEUI

For convenience, you can drag and drop a shortcut to the Dial-Up Connection on the Windows NT desktop. The convention here is opening it up from My Computer:

1. Open My Computer, and open up the Dial-Up Networking group.

2. Open the Dial-Up Networking applet for your server dial-up connection.

3. Click the Connect button. You may be prompted to enter the password for your account. If so, simply type it in and press Enter.

   The Windows 95 system then dials out.

4. If the user account is set for callback, the server responds with a prompt for the phone number on the client end. Click Cancel if you don't need a callback.

5. The server continues logging on the client to the network.

Windows 95 connectivity for Remote Access is actually simpler to perform than for Windows NT Workstation. Networking protocols are automatically bound to connection devices, including network cards and modems. Just make sure that the Win95 client's Server Type has the correct specified protocol. When you use TCP/IP with Windows 95 clients, you'll need to define a few more settings, but it's still fairly straightforward.

Installing and Configuring Remote Access for TCP/IP Connections

Although it's relatively straightforward to create a remote access connection that uses only NetBEUI for its protocol, there is an obvious limitation: NetBEUI is not easily routable and is only suitable for smaller networks. Many company LANs have network segments connected with routers. While each segment can be locally accessed using nonroutable protocols like NetBEUI, there's no easy way to communicate through a router from one segment to another. In that case, you must use TCP/IP as your main protocol from your server and your clients. For RAS, if you have a desktop machine that you need to access on another network segment, TCP/IP is required.

I've already discussed WINS, DNS, and DHCP in Chapter 3, and there is no reason to repeat the same information. Windows NT's TCP/IP networking capabilities function the same way across a phone line as they do in a LAN. (The big difference is the obvious one: speed.) If you haven't yet read that chapter, I strongly urge you to do so before trying to use TCP/IP networking with RAS.

Now the big moment has come: to set up RAS to use TCP/IP on your server, and fold in the services you need to run it on the network. When you're finished, you'll have a basic working knowledge of the key aspects of Windows NT's TCP/IP networking techniques. They apply to LAN usage as well as remote access applications, which are basically just a slower networking connection.

I've already described how to use NetBEUI for a remote access connection under Windows NT. In practice, a TCP/IP RAS connection works the same way. It functions invisibly to the user. It's the process of lining up your ducks in a neat row for TCP/IP use that can be difficult.

Before you start, the assumptions are:

◆ You already have RAS installed on your server and on a Windows NT client, and user accounts, passwords, and share permissions are squared away.

◆ The TCP/IP protocol is installed onto your server and your Windows NT client but is minimally configured.

◆ The RAS/WINS server is a Primary Domain Controller.

You'll perform five major tasks in the following exercises:

◆ Setting up Remote Access Service to use TCP/IP as its dial-in protocol, and using a set of static IP addresses for handing out to clients.

◆ Setting up a Windows NT dial-up client to connect to the server.

◆ Connecting a Windows NT workstation to the RAS/WINS server over a dial-up line and browsing the network. (At this point, this may be all you'll need to do for your connectivity applications; if so, you can stop here.)

◆ Installing DNS and configuring it for your TCP/IP network, and reconnecting with your Windows NT client to verify successful communication.

◆ Installing DHCP, eliminating RAS's static address list, creating a new DHCP scope in its place, and connecting a Windows NT client to the RAS/WINS/DNS/DHCP server.

The last step is quite a mouthful, but it's not as bad as it sounds. Layering and testing each service in sequence is the key.

Chapter 3 provides an overview of each of the three key Windows NT connectivity services for TCP/IP networking; the key alternatives to using WINS, DHCP, and DNS were also mentioned. You'll take them into account as you go through the exercises for RAS connectivity.

Configuring Remote Access for TCP/IP with Static IP Addresses on Windows NT Server

Everything discussed in this section relates to Windows NT Server. RAS client setup is discussed a bit later. Follow these steps:

1. Open the Control Panel and double-click the Network icon.

2. Click the Services tab.

3. Select Remote Access Service and click Properties. The Remote Access Setup dialog box appears, displaying a list of the currently configured modems, ISDN devices, and other dial-up devices on the server.

4. Select the desired dial-up device if necessary, and click the Network button. The Network Configuration dialog box appears, as shown in Figure 9-11.

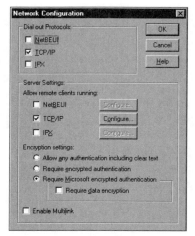

Figure 9-11: Enabling TCP/IP for RAS

5. Select TCP/IP for both Dial-out Protocols and Server Settings, as shown in the figure. The Configure button for TCP/IP is enabled.

6. Click the Configure button for the TCP/IP protocol. Now the RAS Server TCP/IP Configuration dialog box appears. You've drilled down to the point where critical RAS setup is defined, as shown in Figure 9-12.

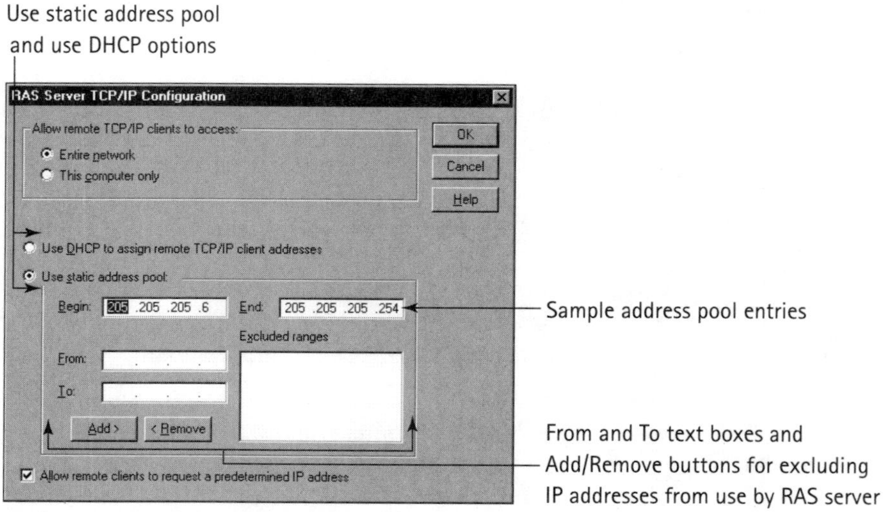

Use static address pool
and use DHCP options

Sample address pool entries

From and To text boxes and
Add/Remove buttons for excluding
IP addresses from use by RAS server

Figure 9-12: Defining RAS Server's Address Scheme

7. Enable the Use static address pool option.

8. Enter the beginning and ending IP addresses for the selection that you want to allocate to your users. In practice you'll probably use much fewer addresses than are pictured in Figure 9-12, perhaps half a dozen or so. You can also exclude address ranges within the pool by adding the beginning and end address range values for them and clicking the Add button. Also, make sure the IP address for your server isn't included in the pool.

Be sure not to include the RAS server's IP address among the addresses you allocate to RAS!

9. Make sure the allow clients to request a predetermined IP address check box is enabled.

10. Click OK.

11. Click Continue to close Remote Access Setup, and click Close to close the Network applet.

At this point, can you connect clients to the RAS Server using TCP/IP?

No, you can't. Some sort of name resolution is *required* for successful connections. For your applications, you can use WINS for that because it's easiest (trust me) and most efficient. For a more complete discussion of this feature, please see the section in Chapter 3 titled "Installing WINS on Windows NT Server." Presently, you'll see how to enable a RAS client to properly use the name resolution features of a WINS-enabled RAS server.

Configuring Client Dial-Up Networking (DUN) for Remote Access Using TCP/IP

When you set up a Windows NT client to connect to a RAS/WINS server for the first time, I'd like to make a couple of recommendations:

◆ Disconnect any networking cards in the client computer, particularily if it's a laptop. When I build a Windows NT client that I know is going to be dialing in to a server using RAS and TCP/IP, I like to build it from scratch and set it up as I've described so painstakingly earlier in this book. Then I install my other features and productivity apps. If that isn't possible, the odds are that it will work, but layering ensures a more efficient configuration process.

◆ If you're connecting to a Windows NT domain (the default in this book), the name of your client computer should have (or will have when you're finished) an account on the Domain controller through Server Manager. If it doesn't, such as when you've just finished setting up a new Windows NT Workstation system and the OS doesn't allow you to enter the domain name for the PDC in your network, which it won't, you can connect using RAS and register on the domain that way. There's a trick to it, particularly since the Windows NT Server is running WINS.

Setting up the client is fairly easy, but there are many steps involved in doing it correctly. Follow these steps:

1. On the Windows NT client that will be doing dial-up remote access, open (or have the user open) the Network applet in the Control Panel.

2. Click the Protocols tab.

3. Select TCP/IP and click Properties. (This is on the *client*, remember.) The TCP/IP Properties sheet appears.

4. Click the WINS Address tab. Then enter the IP address for the Windows NT Server running the WINS service. Make sure both check boxes on this page are disabled.

5. Close the Properties sheet and the Network control panel. You're prompted to restart.

6. After the computer comes back, open the client's DUN application or create a new one using the correct phone number.

7. Click the More button and select Edit Entry and Modem Properties. The multitabbed Edit Phonebook Entry dialog box appears.

8. Click the Server tab. DUN's Server tab for connection setup, appears as shown in Figure 9-13.

9. Select the TCP/IP check box and click the TCP/IP Settings button. All other protocols should be disabled. (If you have more than one running at once, they will not interfere with each other and will work together if needed. I advocate disabling the other protocols just to keep things simple.)

10. Select the Server Assigned IP Address option.

11. Select the option Specify Name Server Addresses. Four IP address fields, all of which should be empty by default, become enabled and ready for data entry.

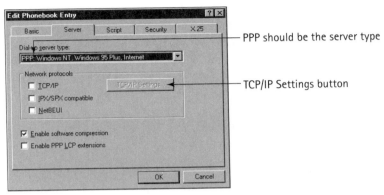

PPP should be the server type

TCP/IP Settings button

Figure 9-13: DUN Setup for Server Connections

12. Enter the IP address for your WINS server (which is the IP address for the server itself — the WINS service resides on the same address in the network) in the field titled Primary WINS. For the RAS/WINS server type, this is all you need to do. Because the WINS service is part of our connection system for TCP/IP, this value must be provided by the user. A sample setting is provided in Figure 9-14.

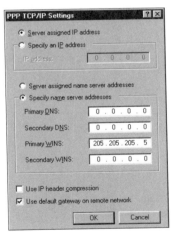

Figure 9-14: Setting Up the DUN
Application with the WINS Server
IP Address

13. Click OK, and click OK again to close the Edit Phonebook Entry dialog box.

Notice what you just did? The same WINS server IP address present on the WINS Address page in TCP/IP Properties must also be placed in the Dial-Up Networking application! This is the trick. It ensures that NetBIOS name resolution works properly with the Remote Access connection. By doing this, the client is able to see the server after you dial in, even if the identification tab in the Network applet doesn't allow you to enter the domain name.

Connecting a Windows NT DUN Client to the RAS/WINS Server

Now it's time to perform the actual RAS connection. This is a big moment. Follow these steps:

1. Log on to your Windows NT Workstation client.

2. Open Dial-Up Networking.

3. Click Dial and enter your password. The client computer dials out. After a few moments you're connected. You should see the following message, as shown in Figure 9-15.

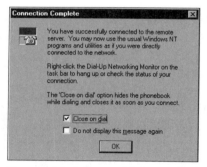

Figure 9-15: A Successful Connection Is Indicated

A small indicator light appears on the taskbar, which flashes blue when data is exchanged. Use this to track your connection.

4. Open the Control Panel and double-click the Network icon. The Network applet appears, automatically displaying the Identification tab, which is what you want here.

5. Click the Change button. The Identification Changes dialog box appears, as shown in Figure 9-16.

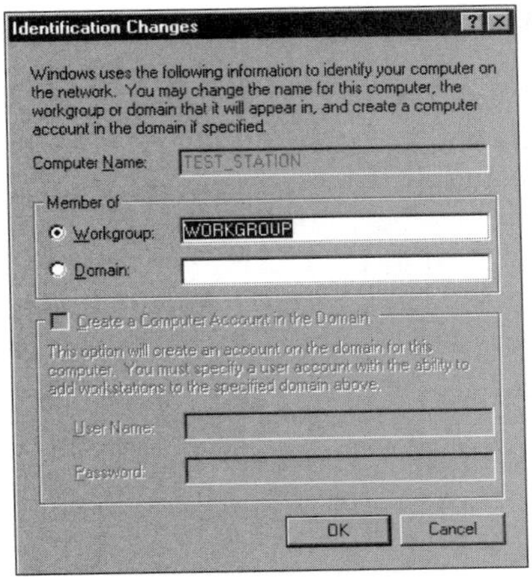

Figure 9-16: Changing Identification To
Register With the Domain Server
Through RAS

By default, a new Windows NT workstation account is forced to be a
member of a workgroup if it isn't directly connected to a domain server. If
you use Remote Access to create the client membership to a domain, this
is where you perform it — *after* you connect with RAS.

6. Select the Domain option and type the Windows NT domain name (for the
   Primary Domain Controller).

7. Select the Create a Computer Account in the Domain check box.

8. In the User Name text box, enter the name of the administrative or other
   user account that has the power to add workstation accounts to the
   domain server.

9. Enter the password for the account.

10. Click OK. After a moment, a dialog box appears, reading "Welcome to
    Domain \\[*Domain name*]."

11. At this point your computer should be able to open the server in Network
    Neighborhood and browse through any shared resources.

Notice how the NetBIOS-type domain name was used. An administrative-level
password must also be used to create the client computer's account. Once that's
finished and the connection has been verified, you can have the client user log on
to the computer with their normal user name and password. When the Logon
Information screen appears, enter the desired user name and password for the client
computer, make sure the correct domain is also listed, and select the Logon using
Dial-Up Networking check box. Or you can simply log on the client without dialing

up the server through RAS. In that case, you'd be logging on to the local workgroup and then dialing up the server when the need arises.

Basic RAS connections, especially those using TCP/IP, could use some streamlining in Windows NT. If one simple thing is left out of these lengthy procedures, connections won't behave the way they should. If you do run into difficulties, the troubleshooting section at the end of this chapter will help you track down many problems preventing you from getting a successful connection using the methods described here.

At this point, you've done the following:

◆ Configured RAS to use TCP/IP on the server (with WINS as the name resolution feature on the server, and static IP addresses being handed out from there)

◆ Configured Dial-Up Networking and RAS on the client to dial up the server

◆ Connected the Windows NT Client, registered on the domain, and browsed Network Neighborhood

Many Windows NT Server users, especially in smaller networks, will not need to go any further. You now have functional TCP/IP RAS connections on your network. Nevertheless, Windows NT provides other capabilities that can ease administration and increase the versatility of your network. You will concentrate on two key services in the rest of this section: DNS and DHCP, and how to integrate them into your RAS installation. For a deeper discussion of how those two services work, please see Chapter 3.

Configuring DNS and DHCP for Remote Access Client Use

If the Windows NT server you're dialing in to uses it, you need to add the primary DNS server's IP address to the TCP/IP Properties' DNS tab on the *client* side. Because your client is running Remote Access over a modem as its network connection, add that DNS server's IP address to the client's Dial-Up Networking application, in its Server tab's TCP/IP configuration. It's a process similar to adding the Windows NT RAS server's WINS address. Your dial-up connection then locks in to the WINS/DNS server without a hitch. Here's how to set it up on the client:

1. Open your client's Dial-Up Networking program. Make sure its correct Phonebook listing is displayed.

2. Click the More button and select Edit Entry and Modem Properties.

3. Click the Server tab.

4. Click the TCP/IP Settings button.

5. Enter the DNS server's IP address in the Primary DNS field. (The server's Primary WINS address should already be in its field.)

6. Click OK, click OK again, and click Close to close DUN.

7. Open the Control Panel and double-click Network. When the Network applet appears, select the Protocols tab.

8. Select TCP/IP and click Properties. The TCP/IP Properties sheet appears.

9. Click the DNS tab.

10. In the Host Name text box, add the name of the Windows NT Server you're dialing in to.

11. In the Domain text box, add the name of the Windows NT domain to which your RAS client is connecting (and will be, or is a member of).

12. In the DNS Server Search Order text box, click the Add button. The TCP/IP DNS Server dialog box appears, with a single entry box.

13. Type in the IP address of the DNS server, and click OK. Figure 9-17 shows a typical result.

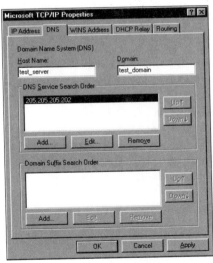

Figure 9-17: Enabling Client DNS Server Acknowledgment

14. Close out of the Network applet and restart the system.

Watch those IPs carefully!

When your users are setting up the dial-in clients, you may want to keep a beady eye on the process. Better yet, circulate concise, exact instructions. A wrong IP address in the wrong place can cause serious problems and completely blindside you. One of the best examples occurs if an inexperienced user mistakingly puts your DNS server's IP address into their client computer's IP address for dialing in using a static address. If this happens, the client can literally kill the DNS for the whole system, and bring much of your network to a screeching halt — not just the remote-access connection, but quite likely the LAN, too. At least make sure everyone who wants to use RAS dialup has solid instructions on how to set up their computer.

Now, instead of using the fairly crude method of assigning static addresses to clients through RAS, or assigning a specific IP address to each and every client on your network, you can do something more versatile and graceful: employ DHCP for dynamic IP address assignment. As I've noted, this has the compelling advantage of accommodating clients without having to muck around with static TCP/IP settings for each system. Although DHCP is truly a black art of networking, Windows NT 4.0 uses it in such a way to make your life much easier. Of course, using RAS to assign from a collection of static addresses is reasonably graceful and efficient, but many companies will opt for DHCP because of convenience and improved integration.

On the client, just select a check box in TCP/IP Properties and in Dial-Up Networking, and it is ready to go. Server setup, including defining the necessary scope for dynamic address sharing, is equally simple. When you're setting up your TCP/IP connections with Remote Access, using static addresses is a good way to test your setup. After you've layered in your other services and made sure they work properly, jettisoning static addressing and using DHCP is the last step to a fully integrated small TCP/IP network. Chapter 3 goes into considerably greater detail about DHCP setup and its various options.

Setting up RAS on the server to use DHCP is simple. Follow these steps:

1. Open the Control Panel, open Network, and click the Services tab.

2. Select Remote Access Service and click Properties. The Remote Access Setup dialog box appears.

3. Click Network.

4. Click the Configure button for TCP/IP.

5. Select the Use DHCP to assign remote TCP/IP client addresses option, as shown in Figure 9-18.

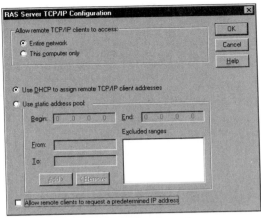

Figure 9-18: Enabling DHCP in RAS Server

6. Clear the Allow Remote Clients to request a Predetermined IP Address check box. With DHCP you don't need it. This only applies if you're using DHCP. If you're using a predetermined group of IP addresses on the server and handing them out, leave this check box enabled. (If you need a bit of brushing up on this, have another look at Chapter 3.)

7. Click OK. Then click OK, click Continue, and then click Close to close Network. Once again, you're prompted to reboot.

Here's what you do on the client side:

1. On the Windows NT client that will perform dial-up remote access, open (or have the user open) the Network applet in Control Panel.

2. Click the Protocols tab.

3. Select TCP/IP and click Properties. The TCP/IP Properties sheet appears.

4. Click the IP Address tab. If you're running a network card in your RAS client, select the Obtain an IP Address from a DHCP Server option.

5. Close the Properties sheet and the Network control panel. You're prompted to restart.

6. After restarting, open the client's DUN application or create a new one using the correct phone number.

7. Click the More button and select Edit Entry and Modem Properties. The multitabbed Edit Phonebook Entry dialog box appears.

8. Click the Server tab. DUN's Server tab for connection setup appears.

9. Click the TCP/IP button. All other protocols should be disabled.

10. Select the Server Assigned IP Address option, or make sure it's enabled. This is the key. (In fact, if you've been using static addresses assigned from the server, this option remains unchanged!) If your client is dialing in to a server that supports the full panoply of TCP/IP services (RAS/WINS/DNS/DHCP), Figure 9-19 shows typical settings for a Windows NT Workstation dial-up client.

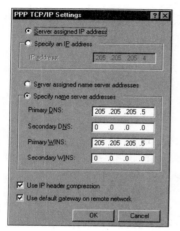

Figure 9-19: Client Settings for Connection to a RAS/WINS/DNS/DHCP Server

11. Click OK, and then click OK again to close the Edit Phonebook Entry dialog.

You are now ready to connect your Windows NT client. Please note that your Primary DNS and Primary WINS server addresses may be different. If clients are connecting to a large network, many managers like to run WINS or DNS separately on another member server within the domain. If that's the case, simply enter that member server's IP address. (This also applies to LANs, by the way.)

Simply dial up and log on. When you do so, using the same methods discussed earlier, an IP address is provided by the DHCP server to the client as an active lease. It happens invisibly to the client. There is no particularly big thing involved in DHCP setup, as you now can see. *Explaining* it is more difficult than doing it. (That's done in Chapter 3.) That concludes the applied RAS networking exercises. You now have a working knowledge of how to use Windows NT's basic Remote Access networking capabilities. Now you can work with TCP/IP features with confidence and consistency on both LANs and remote connections. As you can see, it's pretty simple to work with once you have your networking protocols together and understand the IP addressing scheme if you're using TCP/IP.

The last section in Chaper 3, "Checking Your Connections Using the Command Prompt," offers a brief discussion of Windows NT's command-line utilities for checking the status and operation of your networking connections. Those commands apply in much the same way for RAS network connections as they do across the LAN. If you need a refresher, please refer to that section.

Windows 95 Client Connections Using TCP/IP

Settings for Windows 95 clients using TCP/IP are extremely similar to those described here. Windows 95 has good TCP/IP networking features and uses similar addressing entry features to those for Windows NT. Just bear in mind that Win95 clients can't belong to a Windows NT domain, so their initial behavior on connection will be a bit different.

In particular, Windows 95 clients provide a set of TCP/IP properties that closely resemble those for Windows NT. When you install the TCP/IP protocol in a Win95 client, it's automatically bound to whatever network/dial-up adapters you have installed in the system. Then open up the Network applet in Control Panel, select the TCP/IP binding for the desired network adapter, and click the Properties button. In the WINS Configuration tab, you can set the IP address for the WINS server. As you've seen in Chapter 2, you can also set the Windows 95 client to log on and obtain network client permissions from the Windows NT domain. The Win95 client can also be set to use DHCP and look for a DNS server, in similar ways to Windows NT Workstation.

There are some issues to watch out for when using Win95 on a Windows NT-hosted TCP/IP network:

◆ In the TCP/IP Properties' IP Address tab, select the Obtain an IP Address Automatically option if your Win95 client is going to accept IP addresses from the Windows NT server.

◆ TCP/IP Properties also provides a WINS Configuration tab. It offers a field to enter the WINS server address. Don't select the Use DHCP for WINS Resolution check box unless the server is running a fully configured DHCP scope that provides a WINS server address as part of its option configuration. With Windows 95-Windows NT Server RAS connections, it's best to keep things as simple as possible.

◆ Also, disconnect any PCMCIA or internal network cards in your Windows 95 system when you're testing your RAS TCP/IP connections on a Win95 system. Windows 95 can get confused during a RAS connection and default its network connections to the Ethernet LAN even though the connection "appears" to be working across the modem. Although Windows 95 is a pretty solid networking client, it is not as bulletproof in its TCP/IP as Windows NT Workstation.

A Final Word

The next two chapters build further on your Remote Access knowledge. Chapter 10 discusses another key RAS application: Virtual Private Networks using Point-to-Point Tunneling. At the beginning of that chapter you'll find out how to perform the basic function of connecting to the Internet. Then you'll learn how to use Point-to-Point Tunneling to create a Virtual Private Network across the Internet. Finally, you'll learn the basics about one of Windows NT's hottest new upgrades, Routing and RAS, which is offered free to any Windows NT Server administrator.

Chapter 11 describes the installation and configuration of Windows Messaging, Windows NT's bundled version of the Microsoft Exchange e-mail messaging application. Although Windows NT's bundled e-mail isn't the fanciest or cleanest you'll ever see, it is provided free and is worth looking into. The end of Chapter 11 describes Microsoft's new Exchange 5.0, a BackOffice application that is most decidedly not free, but it also offers much more powerful capabilities.

Troubleshooting

When I log on to the RAS server using TCP/IP, I get an apparent good connection, but I can't browse through resources using Network Neighborhood, and the server isn't available.
(For Windows NT clients only) You have a problem with name resolution, most likely on the client. If you open up a command prompt and type in the command (use your own server's IP address here)

```
PING 205.205.205.5
```

you'll get an apparent good connection. But if you then type

```
PING TEST_SERVER
```

or whatever the name of your server is, then you get an error message, "Bad IP Address TEST_SERVER." You can also type

```
NBTSTAT -A TEST_SERVER
```

and you'll get a "Host not found" error. If the server's WINS service is properly configured, which is pretty much automatic, you need to fix where the *client* looks for the WINS address resolution. It must look for it on the server, at the server's specific IP address. Follow these steps:

1. Open the client's DUN application, click More, and select Edit Entry and Modem Properties.

2. Click the Server tab.

3. Click the TCP/IP button.

4. Select the Specify Name Server Addresses option, as pictured back in Figure 9-26. Then enter your server's address in the Primary WINS field (and the Primary DNS field, if necessary). This should fix the problem, and you'll be able to browse shared resources on the server.

When I try to dial up the server, I receive an error 733 on my client: The PPP control protocol on this network is not available on the server.
(For Windows NT and Windows 95 clients) The problem is that the client isn't getting an assigned IP address from the server. This could be due to several problems:

◆ The server is running DHCP services, but a scope hasn't been properly defined for it.

◆ The server has run out of static addresses to assign, because other clients have taken them all.

◆ The DHCP server is properly set up, but its scope of available addresses is fully occupied.

◆ Your dial-up adapter is not properly set up.

If the problem is the first one listed here, have the server manager use DHCP Manager to set up a new scope or expand the existing one. The server must also be able to assign DHCP addresses through RAS. Make sure the server's Use DHCP to Assign Remote TCP/IP Client Address option is selected, and that the Allow Remote Clients to Request a Predetermined IP Address check box is *disabled*. This should fix the problem. If not, check your hardware setup on the client and make sure the IP addresses are correct in TCP/IP Properties.

When I try to run the Windows NT Server with RAS and DHCP, I get an error message number 20091 in the Event Viewer.
Make sure your DHCP server is properly configured with a scope of addresses. Also make sure that your RAS Server TCP/IP Configuration (found in Control Panel/Network/Services tab/Remote Access Service/Properties button/Network/-TCP/IP button) is set to use DHCP instead of static addresses.

Chapter 10

Internet Connections and RAS Upgrades

IN THIS CHAPTER
The following Windows NT topics are discussed in Chapter 10:

◆ Using Dial-Up Networking to establish a client connection to the Internet (applies equally to Windows NT Server and Workstation)

◆ Using Point-to-Point Tunneling Protocol to create a Virtual Private Network (VPN) connection across the Internet

◆ Understanding, installing, and using Microsoft's new Routing and RAS upgrade to Windows NT Server

CONNECTING TO THE INTERNET from Windows NT is about as simple as doing so through the more common Windows 95. You have a few more details to attend to and a couple of simple tricks to watch out for, which will be pointed out when appropriate in this chapter. Internet connection is a simple but key connectivity application without which no general-purpose networking book would be complete.

When you connect to the Internet, you use Windows NT's DUN (Dial-Up Networking) application, which can be found in the My Computer group. As you learned in Chapter 9, DUN is used to create a Remote Access networking connection to your server across phone lines or some other telecom connection. But DUN can be used for other things, such as:

◆ Connection to the Internet for Web and news browsing, e-mail, and other typical Net applications

◆ Secure connections to your network RAS server using PPTP

Point-to-Point Tunneling Protocol (PPTP) is a particularly interesting connectivity application, and one that has a lot of relevance to you if you've already read Chapter 9. Imagine a way that you could take advantage of your typical Internet service provider (ISP) connection to create the same type of RAS networking connection that was described in Chapter 9, but without the bothersome long-distance toll call costs. This is great if your boss's laptop has a modem, and he's been e-mailing you about getting those phone costs down.

345

You'll learn about the fairly straightforward concept of a Virtual Private Network (VPN), which I've mentioned in passing at other places in the book. The VPN enables you to use a dial-up ISP connection as the underpinning to connect to your Windows NT server. You can even browse the Internet and perform any of the other typical Internet functions at the same time, across the same connection.

Logically enough, I begin this chapter with the steps you need to build a basic Internet connection in your Windows NT system.

Everything in the Internet connectivity section of this chapter applies equally to Windows NT Server and Windows NT Workstation. I treat both generically except where otherwise noted.

Setting Up Windows NT Internet Dial-Up Connections

When you set up your system for Internet access, you have to install Remote Access Service on your computer and set it to use the TCP/IP protocol. (There's a good chance that you have both of those items already installed on your computer, but I won't assume that here.) You also need the following things:

- Dial-up name server IP addresses from the ISP

- A reasonably up-to-date browser program (frame-capable preferably)

- An e-mail program

- A news reader (if desired)

Windows NT 4.0 provides a copy of Internet Explorer 2.0 with every copy of Windows NT, but it's most decidedly not an up-to-date browser. (In fact, it's pretty much useless.) If you'd just as soon not rush out and buy more software, you can download newer versions of Netscape Navigator or Microsoft Internet Explorer from the Internet. Both programs also offer special news readers with which you can explore and contribute to special mailing lists, which are vast caches of e-mail devoted to discussions of specialized topics. Mail lists abound across the Internet and are a useful source of research and even technical support should the need arise. Figure 10-1 shows an example of a news reader, bundled with Microsoft Internet Explorer, that can be used to browse and read e-mail collections on specialized subjects in new groups.

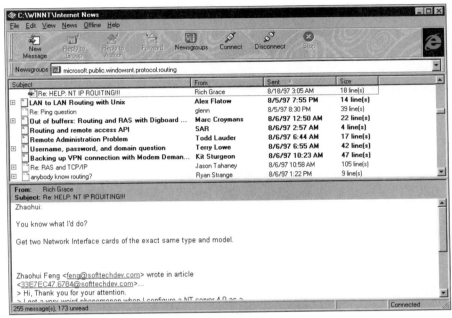

Figure 10-1: Microsoft Internet Explorer's Newsreader

The same goes for e-mail programs. Windows NT also provides a built-in e-mail program called Microsoft Exchange (it's started by double-clicking the Inbox icon on your Windows NT desktop). I describe how to set up and use Exchange in Chapter 11. Nevertheless, freeware and shareware e-mail programs are offered for downloading on the Internet, many of which are much easier to set up and use than Exchange. (Qualcomm's Eudora Light is an example.) Internet Explorer also provides a useful e-mail program, called Internet Mail.

The biggest requirement is to have the DNS name server IP addresses from your ISP. This information is almost always provided by your ISP when you sign up for Internet service connections. Normally, a primary name server address and a secondary address are both provided. For Windows NT Internet connections, you place those addresses in your Dial-Up Networking program's TCP/IP setup section, which I describe a bit later. Although you need those DNS server addresses, you do not need to have DNS installed and running on your system to connect to the Internet.

You don't have to worry about defining an IP address for your own computer when you connect to an ISP, because those addresses are assigned dynamically by the service provider when you connect to their server.

Installing and Configuring Remote Access for Internet Dial-Up

On the Internet, TCP/IP is the standard protocol. However, it's much simpler to set up your Internet connection to use TCP/IP than for conventional network connectivity. Follow these steps:

1. Open the Control Panel and double-click the Network icon.

2. Click the Services tab.

3. Select Remote Access Service and click Properties. The Remote Access Setup dialog box appears, displaying a list of the currently configured modems, ISDN devices, and other dial-up devices on the server.

4. Select the desired dial-up device and click the Network button. The Network Configuration dialog box appears, as shown in Figure 10-2.

Enable the TCP/IP dial-out protocol

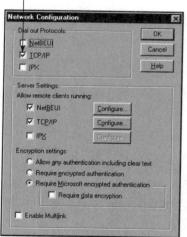

Figure 10-2: Configuring Remote Access for Your Internet Access

5. Select TCP/IP for Dial out Protocols, as shown in the figure. No other settings are required. TCP/IP is the only valid protocol you can use for Internet dial-up.

6. Click OK.

7. Click Continue. You're returned to the Network applet.

8. Click Close. You're prompted to restart the system.

That is pretty much the whole thing for your networking setup. Most of your setup work is done in your Dial-Up Networking program.

Configuring DUN for Internet Dial-up

Perhaps the most difficult part of Internet connectivity preparation is setting up the actual dial-up connection. As you'll soon see, it isn't that big a deal. There are a few minor tricks to watch for; for those of you who've read through other parts of this book, it's duck soup. Follow these steps:

1. Open My Computer.

2. Open the Dial-Up Networking application.

3. Click the New button. The New Phonebook Entry Wizard appears.

4. Enter the desired name for your dial-up entry and click Next.

5. Select the I am Calling the Internet check box and click Next.

6. Enter the phone number of the ISP that you'll be dialing. You may also provide alternative phone numbers if the first one is busy; DUN automatically uses any alternate numbers when necessary.

7. Click Next, and then click Finish.

That's the simplest part of the setup. Now you need to configure your DUN Internet connection with the correct name server IP addresses.

1. Open My Computer.

2. Open the Dial-Up Networking application.

3. Click the More button and select Edit Entry and Modem Properties. The Edit Phonebook Entry dialog box appears.

4. Click the Server tab, as shown in Figure 10-3.

5. In the Dial-up server type list, make sure the listing "PPP: Windows NT, Windows 95 Plus, Internet" listing is displayed, as shown in Figure 10-3.

Dial-up
server type

PPP should be
the server type

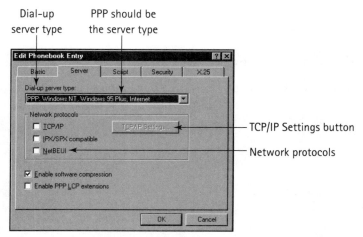

TCP/IP Settings button

Network protocols

Figure 10-3: Configuring DUN for Internet Access

6. Enable the TCP/IP check box. Leave the other protocols blank. (If the protocol isn't installed in your system, you're prompted by the program to install it.)

7. Click the Enable software compression check box to enable it. (This provides somewhat better network connection speed.)

Here's the key trick in this whole procedure.

When editing your phonebook entry for Internet connection, disable the Enable PPP LCP Extensions.

8. *Disable* the Enable PPP LCP extensions check box. As shown in Figure 10-3, that check box is cleared, which is what you want. In most Internet connections, the Enable PPP LCP check box may actually prevent you from connecting properly. What occurs is that you can dial up properly, and your account name and password are authenticated by the server on the other end, but you will be unable to browse the Web, send e-mail, or use any Internet-related services.

9. Click the TCP/IP Settings button. The PPP TCP/IP Settings dialog box appears, as shown in Figure 10-4.

Primary and Secondary
Enable this option   DNS IP addresses

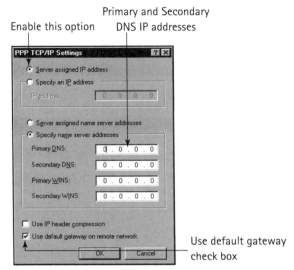

Figure 10-4: Configuring DUN for
Internet Access, PPP TCP/IP Settings

Use default gateway
check box

10. Select the Server assigned IP address option at the top of the dialog box. This enables your system to accept a dynamically assigned IP address from your Internet service provider. For a successful connection, you must have this option enabled.

11. Select the Specify name server addresses option. As shown in Figure 10-4, four IP address fields, all of which should be empty by default, become enabled and ready for data entry.

12. Enter the ISP-provided Primary DNS IP address. (Also often called the "Server assigned name server address.")

13. Enter the Secondary DNS address provided by your ISP. (WINS addresses are not provided except in rare cases.)

14. Enable the Use IP header compression check box.

15. Enable the Use default gateway on remote network check box. Figure 10-5 shows the result after doing all these steps.

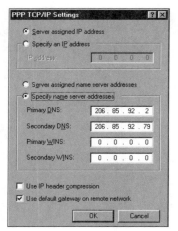

Figure 10-5: Setting Up the DUN Application with the DNS Server IP Addresses

Your DNS name server addresses will be different from those shown in the figure.

16. Click OK to commit the new settings, and click OK again to close the Edit Phonebook Entry dialog box.

You've just finished the key part of preparing your system for Internet access. Notice that none of the process you've gone through has anything to do with TCP/IP preparations in the Network Control Panel. What you've done is completely separate from setting up TCP/IP connections for network use, which can be much more complicated.

When using your Windows NT-based Internet connection in a remote location, such as a hotel or in an office, you may need to add more characters to your dialing string. Hotels, office buildings, and even some apartment complexes use digital PBX (Phone Bank Exchange) systems to manage their internal phone networks. When you dial a telephone number, a one or two seconds' delay occurs while the PBX tries to resolve the call. Otherwise, you will probably not be able to connect. In order for your connection to work via a PBX, you need to dial a "9" to access an outside line. You may also need to enter one or two commas between the "9" and the dial-up number to connect to your server successfully. A comma tells the dialer to pause for one second. A one- or two-second pause gives the PBX time to connect your computer to an outside line. The best way to fix this problem is to insert a "9," predial entry in your dial-up connection. You should do this only if you're dialing to an outside phone line to reach your ISP.

Of course, you don't need the "9," if you're just dialing out from home or an office where a PBX isn't present.

The "9," entry imposes a brief delay on the DUN program to allow the PBX to furnish the outside connection for the modem. Here's how to set this up:

1. Click the Location button in the DUN application. The Location Settings dialog box appears, as shown in Figure 10-6.

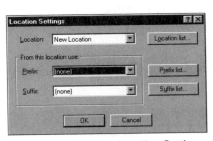

Figure 10-6: Defining Location Settings in the DUN Application

2. Click the Location list button.

3. Type the desired name of the location in the Location text box and click Add. Make sure your new entry is selected, and click OK.

4. Select the Prefix drop-down list. A short list of dial-up prefix settings appears.

5. Select the "9," entry.

6. Click OK. The DUN phonebook now appears, similar to Figure 10-7.

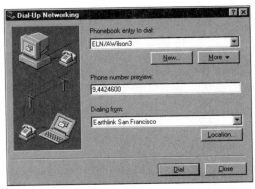

Figure 10-7: Setting Up the DUN for Dial-Out Through a PBX

Your Internet setup, other than your browser and e-mail programs, is now complete. Note that DUN provides a scrollable list of connections. Whenever you create a new connection, as you've done here, it's added to the Phonebook entry list. Its Location settings may need to be modified.

Connecting to the Internet

After your settings are complete, all you need to do is click Dial in the Dial-Up Networking application. The connection dials up and goes through the process of logon and authentication for your account.

You may need to modify some of your other settings as you go through the process of Internet connection. To do this, click the More button and select User Preferences. Four tabs are offered: Dialing, Callback, Appearance, and Phonebook, as shown in Figure 10-8.

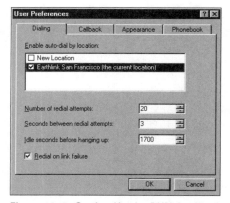

Figure 10–8: Setting Up the DUN Application with the DNS Server IP Addresses

The Dialing tab provides for multiple redial attempts, delays between redial attempts, and setting of the time period before the DUN program automatically hangs up its connection. If you run into a lot of busy signals, frequent redials with minimal time delays are the order of the day. When you're connected, start your browser program, e-mail, or other program to do your electronic business.

Introducing PPTP and VPNs

After you have your Internet connection squared away, you have another compelling use for it. You can use your Internet connection not only for those cool browsing and e-mail programs but also as another connection to your network! You do this using a special networking feature called PPTP, or Point-to-Point Tunneling Protocol.

The basic point behind PPTP is that it allows you to use existing local-call Internet access connections as actual networking connections to your server and your LAN. This is called a VPN (Virtual Private Network). Essentially, you overlay a long-distance LAN connection over a dial-up Internet connection. An electronic "tunnel" is built across the Internet from your computer to the server that conveys your normal network transactions back and forth.

Although it's not as simple as some other Windows NT networking applications, PPTP is relatively easy and definitely inexpensive to implement. It also offers protocol independence, relative ease of use on the client side, good security, and ready monitoring and management on the server/administrator side of things. In general, PPTP is a good, no-hassle way to solve the expense problems associated with using Remote Access.

Virtual Private Network Advantages

VPNs do have some advantages, not the least of which is eliminating the long-distance toll call charges so common to remote access connections and the catholic protocol support already mentioned. Your VPN connection is built on the Internet-standard PPP (Point-to-Point Protocol), of which PPTP is an additional layer that enables the virtual network connection. Although a VPN/PPTP connection behaves like a normal network connection while it's used, it's a nonpersistent connection, used only as long as the user requires. This is what makes it a "virtual" private network, since it's based on resources provided by a completely outside entity and does not rely on a permanent connection.

Another benefit is security. When you establish a VPN link through PPTP, you use full Microsoft-enabled encryption schemes for every communications packet and data packet sent between your machine and the server. Using encryption, no one can eavesdrop on your connection, even though it's using the Internet as its underpinning. If you use the latest service packs to update your Windows NT server and workstations, RAS uses 128-bit encryption in domestic networking. You can also opt to set the server to accept only PPTP-encrypted data packets across its Virtual Private Network, to further limit unwanted intruders.

PPTP Security Holes

If you decide that PPTP is a useful tool for your organization, *make sure* to update your Windows NT Server installation with the latest Service Pack from Microsoft's Web site after you install the PPTP protocol.

Why? According to documentation available on www.microsoft.com, a gaping security hole exists in the original version of PPTP that allows a user to take control of the Administrative account on the server and thus do whatever they want to do within the network. When you install the Service Pack after installing PPTP, the Service Pack automatically updates the protocol and fixes this security gap.

continued

> **PPTP Security Holes** *(Continued)*
>
> It's particularly important to pay attention to this issue if your server has a dedicated connection to the Internet. As discussed in Chapter 9, security issues and Remote Access go hand in hand.

 Any networking protocol can be used on a VPN.

You can use any networking protocol you want on a VPN, just as you would in a normal LAN connection. Although your Internet service connection uses TCP/IP exclusively, your VPN connection can use NetBEUI, IPX, or TCP/IP again as the LAN/WAN-type networking protocol, and all your data packets sent across your tunneled Internet connection use that entirely separate protocol. (The process for doing this is called *encapsulation.*) PPTP, running over your RAS service, makes it possible. Client-side connections are simple; the server-side configuration requires some work and some careful planning.

One thing PPTP does *not* require is reassigning or changing your internal IP addressing scheme in your private network. All your existing TCP/IP networking services (DNS/WINS/DHCP) will run invisibly.

If your boss is using Remote Access to dial in to the server, you can add PPTP to his client, set up RAS to use it, and have him use the exact same DUN application to establish the VPN connection to the server. All he needs is a local dial-in number to the Internet.

You need to perform a significant number of steps to ensure a successful PPTP connection:

◆ Install the Point-to-Point Protocol on the server and any clients that plan to use it.

◆ Configure RAS on the server and the clients to use new VPN ports created during PPTP installation.

◆ Enable PPTP Filtering and IP Forwarding on the server (PPTP Filtering does not need to be enabled on the client; the server imposes that requirement on the connection).

◆ Obtain an assigned IP address from your Internet service provider, or a recognized Internet-registered DNS name, so that your remote clients can locate your private server on the Internet.

◆ Configure DUN on the client with separate entries for the Internet PPP connection and for the PPTP server connection, and execute the connection.

Virtual Private Network Limitations

There are limits to VPNs. First of all, the Internet is a huge public networking resource. If all companies suddenly decided to use VPNs as their long-distance WAN or Remote Access networking connection, there wouldn't be any bandwidth left over for anyone else to use, and Internet traffic would be even slower and more crowded than it is now.

Also, VPN connections are only as fast as your modem. You should resort to them only if you have to. Similar to normal dial-up Remote Access, VPNs are only good for transferring files for people out in the field — especially on analog modem connections. In some cases a VPN connection can be as much as two-thirds slower than a normal RAS connection.

VPNs are also a little more complex to set up and use, although not so much that they can't be done without a little patience on the client side and cooperation from the server side. Also, Point-to-Point Tunneling Protocol is bundled only with Windows NT clients and servers; most Windows 95 clients can't automatically use it, which leaves the vast majority of laptop users out of the action for the present. (Fortunately, some Internet partisans might add.) Microsoft has promised an update to Windows 95 that provides PPTP support, and by the time you read this, it should be available. (It's called Dial-Up Networking 1.2.) Windows 98 should have it built in.

Perhaps the biggest obstacle to PPTP support is your ISP. Most consumer-level ISPs do not support server-side VPN connections and do not plan to do so. Many ISP routers lack PPTP support, because Microsoft is so far the only major OS vendor to directly support PPTP. Client-side VPN connections are straightforward and can be executed across any ISP Internet connection. It's the server-side connection that's tricky. Even many "professional" ISPs do not support PPTP. This can be a key selling point when you search for an ISP to meet your company's needs, particularly if you want to take advantage of this technology to cut down on remote-access toll call costs.

Microsoft also provide PPTP client support for Windows 95, Windows 3.x and even Macintosh client computers. That support is enabled through Microsoft's Routing and RAS upgrade. This chapter focuses only on Windows NT Workstation, but the methods are similar for other client types.

Why is this the case? PPTP is a new technology. Microsoft first introduced it with Windows NT 4.0 and led its design and implementation. Although it's based on open networking standards, many ISPs don't use Windows NT 4.0 for their Internet server platform, and support in other UNIX-based operating systems is scanty. Finding an ISP in your local area that can directly support VPN/PPTP connections is a real challenge. In many cases, ISPs may never support VPN/PPTP because of the additional maintenance and investment it can require and the additional traffic it imposes on the network. Then, you'll have to "piggyback" a VPN on an ISP connection using the methods described in this section. Otherwise, if you do find ISPs that support PPTP, you'll probably have to pay a premium charge for it. VPNs are becoming a hot topic in the commercial networking world, and there are signs indicating that all this will change eventually. In most cases at the present, you're going to need an Internet-registered DNS name for your server or an accompanying IP address.

In this chapter I do *not* make that assumption. There is a way to use tunneling if you have only conventional ISP connections at your remote client and server ends. After you go through it and see how it works, you'll understand why a dedicated PPTP server connection to the ISP may be a good idea in the long run, and why it is a pain in the short run. But you *can* create a tunnel through a normal consumer-type ISP network (Earthlink, Netcom, and so on) if you really need to do that. That's the method described here.

Installing Point-to-Point Tunneling Protocol and Configuring RAS on the Server

The basic process of protocol installation is quite simple. This first procedure is for the server end of things:

1. Open Control Panel and open the Network applet.

2. Select the Protocols tab.

3. Click Add. The Select Network Protocol list appears, as shown in Figure 10-9.

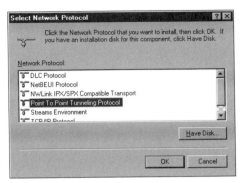

Figure 10-9: Installing Point-to-Point Tunneling Protocol

4. Select Point-to-Point Tunneling Protocol, as shown in Figure 10-9, and click OK. You are prompted for the location of the files from the Windows NT CD-ROM or i386 directory.

5. After the files are copied, you'll see the PPTP Configuration dialog box, as shown in Figure 10-10.

Figure 10-10: Telling Your Server How Many
Virtual Private Networks You Plan to Use

6. The number of Virtual Private Networks you plan to use roughly corresponds with how many telecom devices (modems, IDSN adapters, and so on) your server is running. If your server is running multiple connections, select the desired number. You can have as many as 256 VPN connections set up on your Windows NT server. If you have just a modem, keep the default value of 1 and click OK.

7. The system prompts you that "Remote Access Setup is about to be invoked. Please configure the PPTP ports in RAS setup to enable you to use RAS over PPTP." Click OK again. The familiar Remote Access Setup dialog box appears. Now comes a key step.

8. Click the Add button. As shown in Figure 10-11, the list of new RAS-capable devices appears, showing the new VPN ports. You can now see how tightly PPTP/VPN is coupled to your computer's basic RAS services.

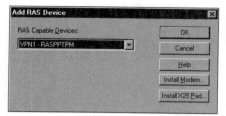

Figure 10-11: RAS Detects the New VPN Port

9. Select the first (or only) VPN port from the list and click OK. Each VPN port you create during PPTP installation is numbered VPN1, VPN2, and so on. Its device type is listed as RASPPTPM. Figure 10-12 shows the appearance of a new VPN port in the RAS setup.

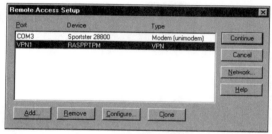

Figure 10-12: Installing a New Virtual Private Network Port into RAS

10. If you plan to use more than one VPN port on your server, click OK and repeat Steps 8 and 9 for each VPN port in the Add RAS Device list.

11. After your VPN ports are accounted for in Remote Access Setup, select the first one and click Configure. Make sure each VPN port is capable of dialing out and receiving.

12. For your VPN port(s), click the Network button. The Network Configuration dialog box appears, as shown in Figure 10-13.

13. Select the desired protocols on the server that you know your dial-up/remote clients will need. Don't worry; the settings you define for your VPN ports will not affect the settings for your other networking connections.

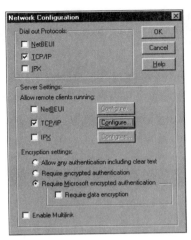

Figure 10-13: Selecting Protocols for a Virtual Private Network Port

14. Click Configure for each protocol, to define the settings for each one. (For more information regarding TCP/IP networking configurations, please see Chapters 3 and 9.) All this should look fairly familiar. As with a normal RAS connection, a VPN port can use any networking protocol available under Windows NT. All of Windows NT Server's services, including WINS, DNS, and DHCP, function properly over a VPN/PPTP connection if the client is using TCP/IP as the main networking protocol. (That's quite a mouthful, isn't it?) All the servers work transparently and nothing needs to be changed. The TCP/IP data packets are sent normally through the tunnel. If your client is going to use NetBEUI or IPX, tunneling will still work fine, just as a remote access connection does. But make sure both ends support the right protocol.

    The next step is to ensure security on your VPN connections.

15. For each VPN port connection, make sure both the Require Microsoft Encrypted Authentication option, and its corresponding Require Data Encryption check box are selected. RAS and PPP then automatically use Windows NT's security features to authenticate all remote clients using the VPN connection.

16. When you're finished with the configuration for your VPN ports, close out of RAS setup. You're then prompted to restart your system.

Enabling PPTP Filtering and IP Forwarding

For even deeper security, you can enable PPTP Filtering on your Windows NT server. This is another desirable security feature because it prevents any information *except* PPTP data from coming across your VPN connection. All other data

packets across the Net are ignored by the server. The only drawback is that it prevents connections from being tested by command-line utilities such as PING and
TRACERT, thus making troubleshooting more difficult. A good process to follow is
to make sure your connections work first before enabling PPTP Filtering. But if
you're running your PPTP services while the same system is connected to the enterprise or company network, filtering is an almost mandatory security measure (so is
plugging possible security holes by always using the latest Service Pack).

Also, for proper PPTP functioning, you must enable IP Forwarding, which is a
matter of enabling another check box and restarting. IP Forwarding is needed
because if you have only the Remote Access/PPTP connection over a modem or
ISDN device, and a network adapter in the server to which the LAN is connected,
you are running a *multihomed* server. (If your server has more than one NIC
installed, that's another multihomed configuration.) IP forwarding enables your
remote client to have access to the network and not just to the server. If the remote
client is running a routable protocol such as IPX or TCP/IP, they can browse
through the network via the tunnel to get to their desktop machine (assuming they
have one back at the office). So IP Forwarding is a good thing. To enable PPTP
Filtering and IP Forwarding, follow these steps:

1. Open the Control Panel and double-click Networks.

2. Click the Protocols tab and select TCP/IP Protocol, and click the Properties
   button. The TCP/IP Properties sheet appears, showing its IP Address tab.

3. Click the Advanced button. The Advanced IP Addressing dialog box
   appears, as shown in Figure 10-14.

LAN Network adaptor

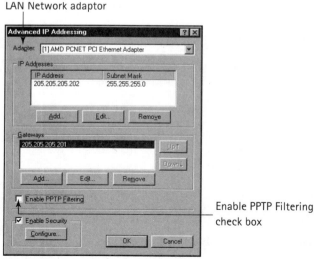

Enable PPTP Filtering
check box

Figure 10-14: Selecting Protocols for
Virtual Private Network Port

4. Select the Enable PPTP Filtering check box. Note that the network adapters installed in your computer are the only devices listed here. As noted in Chapter 9, RAS dial-up networking connections are bound to the system's network adapter. The same applies here.

TIP   As a security measure, PPTP Filtering should be enabled on the server (it doesn't need to be enabled on the client).

5. Click OK to return to the TCP/IP Properties dialog box.

6. Click the Routing tab.

7. Click the Enable IP Forwarding check box tab.

8. Click OK and then click Close. You're prompted to restart.

That's it for the basic setup of your server. Unless you have an assigned IP for the server and an Internet-registered DNS name, you can't perform PPTP connecting, right? What if you don't have those things?

There *is* a workaround. If your Windows NT server and your clients have only a typical ISP Internet connection to work with, you can still use tunneling. It works very nicely, and the next section tells you how. However, for PPTP networking, your internal IP addressing structure in the server or the client *does not need to be changed*. All your existing LAN-based network settings will work over a tunnel.

Installing PPTP and Configuring RAS on a Windows NT Client

Although PPTP client setup is similar to that on the server, many PPTP users may not have access to the server, so a full procedure is given here. Follow these steps:

1. Open Control Panel, and open the Network applet.

2. Select the Protocols tab.

3. Click Add. The Select Network Protocol list appears.

4. Select Point to Point Tunneling Protocol and click OK. You are also prompted for the location of the files from the Windows NT CD-ROM or i386 directory.

5. After the files are copied, the PPTP Configuration dialog box appears, as shown in Figure 10-15.

Figure 10-15: Setting Up a Client-Side
Virtual Private Network Connection

6. Unlike the server, it's practical to have just one VPN port installed in the client computer. You can have as many as 256 VPN connections set up on a Windows NT Server, but a client uses just a modem or an ISDN device. Therefore, keep the default value of 1 and click OK on the client.

7. Next the computer prompts you that "Remote Access Setup is about to be invoked. Please configure the PPTP ports in RAS setup to enable you to use RAS over PPTP." Click OK again. The familiar Remote Access Setup dialog box appears.

   The next step is important.

8. Click the Add button in Remote Access Setup. As shown in Figure 10-16, the list of new RAS-capable devices appears, showing the new VPN port. You can now see how tightly PPTP/VPN is coupled to your computer's basic RAS services.

Figure 10-16: RAS Detects the New VPN Port

9. On the client, select the VPN port from the list and click OK. The VPN port created during PPTP installation should automatically be numbered VPN1. Its device type is listed as RASPPTPM.

10. Select the VPN port in Remote Access Setup, and click Configure. If your client is set up in RAS only to dial out, you'll see the Network Configuration dialog box, as shown in Figure 10-17.

Figure 10-17: Selecting Your
VPN Dial-Out Protocol

11. Select whichever dial-out networking protocol you plan to use when connected to the server. (You'll take a generic approach here. For more information on using NetBEUI or TCP/IP for client networking connections, please see Chapters 2 or 3, respectively.) Note that the settings you define for your VPN port will not affect the settings for your other networking connections, such as a standard Remote Access modem connection.

12. Click OK to close the Configuration dialog box.

13. Click Continue in Remote Access Setup.

    As on the server, you must ensure security on your VPN connections from the client end.

14. Click Close in the Network applet. Restart the system.

For the client, there's no need to enable the Enable PPTP Filtering check box in the TCP/IP Properties' Advanced sheet. In fact, enabling this feature may disable your client from using standard TCP/IP connections. Filtering should be enabled on the server only.

Configuring DUN on the Client for the New VPN Connection

Now you'll need to set up another DUN configuration on the client for your Virtual Private Network connection. The assumption here is that you already have a functional Internet connection from the client, as described in the first section of this chapter. Follow these steps:

1. Open My Computer and double-click Dial-Up Networking.

2. Click the New button to create a new phonebook entry.

3. Click the Server tab.

4. Select the appropriate protocol(s) for your networking connection. If you use TCP/IP, click the TCP/IP settings button and make sure its settings match what you would normally use on the network (name server address, WINS server address, whether it accepts a server-assigned IP address, and so on). All your TCP/IP client settings will work invisibly across the tunnel.

5. For the Dial-Up Server Type, select PPP.

6. Click OK.

7. In the Entry name field, type the name for the new PPTP connection.

8. Select the client's VPN port from the Dial using list, as shown in Figure 10-18.

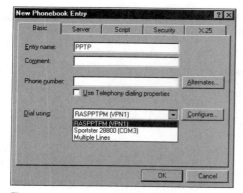

Figure 10-18: Selecting the VPN Port
in the DUN Application

Here's the big issue: if your Windows NT server doesn't have a dedicated connection to the Internet, with an assigned IP or DNS name, how can you connect your humble client? You can still do tunneling even if this doesn't apply to you. It's even relatively easy. The first thing to keep in mind is that both the server and the PPTP client must be connected to their ISP using their typical DUN connection.

When a computer connects to the Internet for the usual prosaic browsing and e-mail, it automatically gets an IP address assigned from the ISP. This IP changes every time the system connects, dynamically allocated by the service provider. This also goes for your Windows NT server, if it's just using the normal DUN connection.

But how do you obtain the IP address for the Windows NT Server so the client can use its VPN port to tunnel in? It's shockingly simple. Here's what the administrator must do.

9. Open a command line on the Windows NT server presently connected to the Internet.

10. Enter the following command: IPCONFIG / ALL.

11. Press Enter. After a second, the command line returns a listing of all the IP addresses assigned to the various WAN wrappers and network adapters in your server, as shown in Figure 10-19.

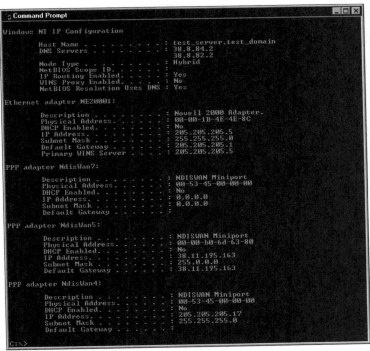

Figure 10-19: Checking for Your Windows NT Server's Dynamically Assigned IP Address (from the Internet service provider)

The one you're looking for is a PPP Adapter labeled, in my test system, NDISWAN5. (Yours may be differently numbered; it's one of the WAN Wrappers listed in the TCP/IP Properties' Bindings tab on the server.) In Figure 10-19 it shows an address of 38.11.195.163. This is the address dynamically assigned by the ISP to the Windows NT Server when it connects using its modem, ISDN, or other telecom device using your typical nonpersistent Internet connection. (Of course, your address will be different.)

This is the IP address that your PPTP client uses in Dial-Up Networking to execute tunneling through the ISP's routers to the server.

This is the key that unlocks the door.

The client *must* somehow get this address from the other end, the server end, before the connection can be made. Voice mail, e-mail, or an alphanumeric pager are good, efficient ways to do it. Your boss will thank you.

12. Back on the *client* end, in the Phone Number field of the Dial-Up Networking dialog box for your PPTP entry, type in that IP address for the server, *not* the phone number for your Internet connection. An example is shown in Figure 10-20.

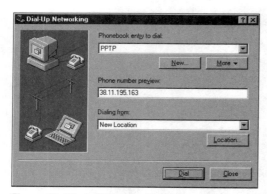

Figure 10-20: A DUN–Based VPN Port, Set Up with an IP Address

13. Click OK to close the phonebook entry.

14. If the server is already connected to the ISP, use DUN on the client side to dial up the ISP on that end.

15. After the client connects to the Internet, select the PPTP listing in DUN's Phonebook list and click Dial. After a few seconds you will see the Connection Complete dialog box, as shown in Figure 10-21.

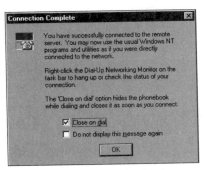

Figure 10-21: VPN Connection Is
Successfully Completed

You are now connected to the server using a tunnel through your ISP's network. The client can now browse the server and network exactly the same way as the client customarily would from the LAN or a conventional remote access connection. The big difference? No long-distance charges. (It may also be slower.)

Whenever the DUN clients need to tunnel to the server, they'll need to get another IP address from the server end, because unless the server uses the same connection more or less constantly, they'll receive new addresses from the ISP every time they connect. This is one reason why many Windows NT server administrators often prefer to get a registered domain name and IP address, so that tunneling clients can rely on the same consistent address when they dial in. The whole thing is basically black magic anyway, so getting it to work at all is an interesting project.

By the way, you can also run the same IPCONFIG /ALL command on the client end to see what address it receives from the ISP when it logs on. Doing so, the client and server can Ping back and forth to check the connection, if PPTP Filtering isn't enabled.

One final tip: I also recommend having some kind of visible indicator light to check for data flow, especially if the client has an internal modem. Here's how to set this up on either the client or the server:

1. Open up the DUN program.

2. Click More and select Monitor Status.

3. Click the Preferences tab, as shown in Figure 10-22.

4. Select the As a window on the desktop option, and click the Lights button.

5. Select All Devices and click OK. (You may have to be a little more choosy about this on the server, but for the client this is fine.)

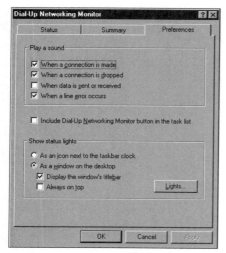

Figure 10-22: Setting Status Light
Indicators in the DUN Application

That's the basic process of running a PPTP connection. As you can see, it can be a bit complex. Once you get used to it, it's not that difficult, and your company can save a few bucks here and there using it. If you're a startup or small business dependent on venture capital or outside financing, and thus in a place where every dollar counts, this kind of thing can be a lifesaver. Ultimately, you'll want to shop around for an ISP that directly supports PPTP so that your server-side PPTP connection can be consistent, reliable, and convenient. For most applications, though, the method just described will work.

Perhaps the most fascinating thing about this whole section is that it demonstrates that you can run your ISP Internet connection and do Web browsing and e-mail simultaneously with a remote LAN connection. I've been running my entire WINS/DNS/DHCP TCP/IP LAN configuration through the ISP-based tunnel without modification of any kind. You can, too, using the methods I describe in this book. Or you can use the much simpler NetBEUI.

By the way, you can do this tunneling stuff over a LAN or a high-speed WAN. The methods are identical except that you don't have to dial up an ISP.

Upgrading to Routing and RAS (Steelhead)

Microsoft's basic RAS and IP routing capabilities are fairly simple. (Sometimes their *execution* can be a bit complicated, especially in the previous section.) For the most part, the TCP/IP and other networking functions described in this book can be performed without so much as a single extra download after you've purchased and installed Windows NT Server (and in some cases, Windows NT Workstation). Microsoft's new Routing and RAS upgrade, which can be downloaded for free from Microsoft's Web site, is something you really should have. It updates Windows NT's entire remote access structure, adding depth and a central point of administration for your entire TCP/IP or IP-based network. It also provides simulation of a small departmental-level Cisco-type router in software. This particular feature has become popular among experienced Windows NT network users in a short period of time. In the examples, I use a TCP/IP-based network to show Routing and RAS's features.

About RRAS and Service Packs

To work properly, the RRAS upgrade requires the Service Pack 3 update, which can be found on Microsoft's Web site at

`http://www.microsoft.com/ntserversupport/`.

A large collection of software for Windows NT Server and Workstation can be found in this section of Microsoft's Web server, and it's worth a lengthy browse by itself.

The Service Pack 3 filename is NT4SP3_I.EXE, and it's a self-extracting archive. It's also over 17MB in size, so it takes a while to download. Install Service Pack 3 (SP3) first, before doing anything else. (There's a good chance that Microsoft will have released even newer Service Packs by the time you read this. If so, download the latest one instead, because it will already incorporate everything in the previous packs along with a new batch of fixes.) This is the first thing you should install on your server when you get ready to install RRAS.

The Routing and RAS upgrade file is named MPRI386.EXE, and it's almost 6MB.

New Features of Routing and RAS

For basic remote access applications, your users won't see too much of a difference. Dial-up connections work pretty much the same, and most of the options are identical, if subtly updated. PPTP connectivity is updated, as are the basic RAS services. One big change is that Routing and RAS enables you to run your Windows NT Server as a TCP/IP or IPX router within your network, without the need for dedicated routing hardware. In practice, this is a wiser decision for smaller enterprise networks and small businesses than for larger organizations, particularly if they have a significant Internet presence. Nevertheless, for many small- and medium-size businesses, Routing and RAS (which I call RRAS for brevity's sake) gives them an opportunity to add new money-saving functionality to their

Windows NT server. RRAS users tend to compare RRAS's routing features to a "baby Cisco" department-size router, which is about right for its capabilities.

A new Routing and RAS Admin program is added to the Administrative Tools group, substituted for the Remote Access Admin program that originally comes with Windows NT. This program gives you a central point of administration for the following:

◆ All local and remote routers in your network

◆ All Remote Access ports configured in the server, including modems and VPN ports for Point-to-Point Tunneling

◆ Communicating routing information and updates to routers across a WAN, and connecting to other routers – known as a Demand-Dial Interface

◆ The IP routing performed by your Windows NT server, based on the network adapters

Figure 10-23 shows an example of a Routing and RAS Admin screen.

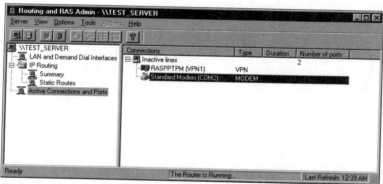

Figure 10-23: Routing and RAS Admin Offers Much Wider Functionality Than the Original RAS Admin Program

The original RAS Admin is a more-specialized program whose sole purpose is monitoring and managing dial-up Remote Access connections. Routing and RAS Admin changes much of that, subsuming the basic dial-up connections into a larger organization gathered into the local domain server under which RRAS is running.

If you double-click the Active Connections and Ports listing, as shown in Figure 10-23, you can view the status of any VPN and RAS modem ports configured in the server. This points out another advantage of the (free) RRAS upgrade – the ability to monitor and close out any VPN connections in the same application as your Remote Access connections.

You can check any IP routing or LAN connections for the network adapters in your server, *or the routers in your network*, and close them or start them up again with the click of a mouse button.

For administrators who have it available or are not satisfied with Windows NT's user authentication services, RRAS also introduces a new service called RADIUS client. RADIUS, which stands for Remote Authentication Dial-in User Service, is a versatile authentication standard on UNIX platforms and is common in UNIX-administered WANs. RADIUS allows Windows NT Server to become a RADIUS server client, turning over all RAS clients and dial-up router connections to the RADIUS server for authentication. I don't get into this topic in any depth; complex authentication and routing applications are beyond the scope of this book. (And possibly beyond the scope of most readers who want to work with Windows NT Server.)

RRAS allows you to communicate with other routers in your company's WAN using a Demand-Dial Interface. The Routing and RAS Admin program even provides a wizard for creating a new Demand-Dial connection, by pulling down the Actions menu and selecting the Add Interface option.

All you need to set up the connection is the correct IP address for the remote router. One benefit of Demand-Dial Routing is that when you use VPNs with Point-to-Point Tunneling Protocol as described in the last section, the server end doesn't need to have a persistent, "nailed-up" Internet connection for a Virtual Private Network to be executed.

All in all, the RRAS upgrade is something that every Windows NT Server user really should have. Even if you don't use its greatly expanded routing management features, the fact that all of your routable connections of any kind are gathered together in one place can greatly simplify network administration, even in small networks.

Routing Essentials

Although an exhaustive discussion of routing is beyond the scope of this book, any reader wanting to know more about Windows NT networking can benefit from at least understanding the basic terminology. Routing is the core of the Internet and a vital networking technology, and it is seldom explained in understandable terms. The beauty of TCP/IP is that when you send an e-mail to someone across the country, that message could travel through a dozen different routers to get to its destination, yet the application that created and sent the message in the first place remains blithely unaware of the tortuous path that message has to take. The client doesn't need to know the network topology to do its business. The same is true in a LAN or a WAN.

For such a system to work, every device on the network, whether it's the Internet, a small LAN, or a company-wide WAN, must have exactly one IP address. (IP addressing

continued

Routing Essentials *(Continued)*

is discussed in Chapter 3, so I won't recap it here.) Remember how subnet masks were also discussed in Chapter 3? They play a special role in routing. They determine to the host machine whether an IP address of a networked device is available locally or if it's a foreign device located across a router. This is one of the core mechanisms behind routing — what is a local network object versus what is a foreign networked object.

As you now know, each system with an IP address is also assigned a subnet mask. To determine if a destination address is in the local segment or elsewhere in the network (across a router), the server or other machine uses some basic binary math (using the XOR expression) for a comparison against its own IP address; that result is also compared against the subnet mask using the AND expression. If the result is zero, that destination address is located in the local network. If the result is not zero, that destination address is located across one or a dozen routers. The process is actually quite interesting and not as difficult as many technical writers seem to think it is.

Another common feature you'll run into is a routing table, a small database located on routers containing information on IP paths to different networks.

Windows NT enters the discussion here. Routing and RAS updates Windows NT Server's routing capabilities to the point where it's actually usable as a simple department-level router — a baby Cisco, as others have described it.

For an excellent discussion of the techniques and methods of routing, please visit the InfoWorld Web site at `http://www.infoworld.com`. Click Search and type in the title IP Routing Protocols. If you need to know more about routing, you'll be glad you read this article. It's also in the September 8, 1997 print issue of InfoWorld. It's written by InfoWorld editor Brooks Talley, and it's great stuff.

Installing Routing and RAS

When you decide to install Routing and RAS, the decision should not be taken lightly. You have to remove your existing Remote Access Services to perform the upgrade. When you do this and install Routing and RAS in its place, you have to rebuild your RAS client entries and configurations from scratch. Make notes of all your client configurations before you take this step. Also, make sure you've installed Service Pack 3 before you do anything else, or RRAS setup will not work at all. If any of the following components are installed in your server at present, they must be deleted before installing RRAS:

◆ DHCP Relay Agent

◆ Remote Access Services

- ◆ RIP for Internet Protocol

- ◆ RIP for NWLink IPX/SPX

- ◆ SAP Agent

All these components are updated by RRAS. You can keep your PPTP/VPN installation, if any. To remove these components, open the Control Panel and double-click Network. Select the Services tab, select in turn each of the services installed in your system, and click Remove.

After you download the self-extracting executable, you'll immediately see that its setup process isn't the normal Windows NT-type application setup. You basically have one chance at a time to install RRAS properly; if you have to pause the installation for any reason, you can't pick up where you left off, and you must start again from scratch. This isn't a big problem, but it's something of which you should be aware.

1. To begin RRAS installation, double-click the MPRI386 icon.

2. You're asked to agree to the licensing terms for the product. Click Yes. The installation then asks you where you want to install the Routing and Remote Access Service program files, as shown in Figure 10-24.

Figure 10-24: Placing RRAS's Installation Files in a Convenient Directory

3. I advise accepting the default. The program is merely asking where the installation files should be placed, not in which directory the new Routing and RAS installation should be done (unfortunately, that's not entirely clear). Routing and RAS updates your key files in the WINWindows NT directory *from this location*.

   Also, bear in mind that a set of Word for Windows-format documentation files are provided in a DOC folder within this directory.

4. Click OK. The installer copies the files to the directory and then asks if you want to continue the installation.

5. Click Yes. (Click No if you realize that you still have a service you need to delete.) Routing and Remote Access Setup begins here. You're prompted to select the RRAS components you want to install, as shown in Figure 10-25.

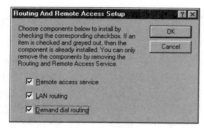

Figure 10-25: Selecting RRAS Components

6. Select all three options and click OK. (It's not mandatory to have all three, but they won't hurt, either.) The Setup program begins copying the RRAS files into your Windows NT directory. Eventually, a familiar-looking Remote Access Setup dialog box appears, as shown in Figure 10-26.

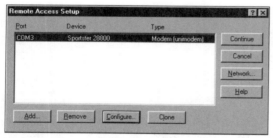

Figure 10-26: Continuing Remote Access Setup

7. Click Configure for each displayed Remote Access device. (If you have PPTP installed, your VPN ports will also show up here.) The Configure Port Usage dialog box appears, as shown in Figure 10-27.

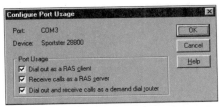

Figure 10-27: Port Usage for Routing and
Remote Access Setup

8. Because this is on the server, make sure that the top two check boxes (Dial out and Receive calls) are both enabled. If you plan to perform routing with the server in a company WAN, select the third check box as well.

9. Click OK and then click the Network button for each RAS device. The Network Configuration dialog box appears, as shown in Figure 10-28.

10. Select the encryption scheme for the RAS device, and select the Dial out and Server Setting protocols. Click Configure for each protocol, to define their networking settings. Figure 10-29 shows the slightly revised RAS Server TCP/IP Configuration dialog box.

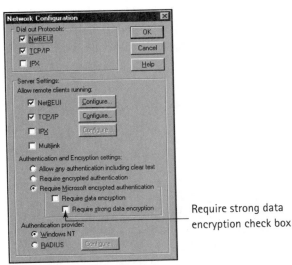

Require strong data
encryption check box

Figure 10-28: Configuring Network
Devices in RRAS

11. Select the DHCP or static address pool options as desired and configure them accordingly.

Encryption Schemes in Routing and RAS

Network Configuration is pretty much the same as described and used in Chapter 9 and earlier herein; the biggest difference is its Authentication and Encryption settings.

If you opt to use Microsoft Encrypted Authentication, a new feature is offered: Require strong data encryption. What does this mean? If this feature is enabled in your installation, enabling this check box means that your Microsoft-encrypted network data uses the 128-bit data encryption key we discussed earlier in this section.

The Require data encryption check box simply uses the old 40-bit encryption scheme that is the old RAS default.

Allow remote clients options

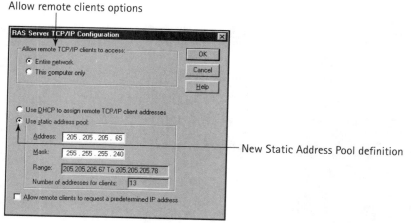

New Static Address Pool definition

Figure 10-29: TCP/IP Configuration in RRAS

Static Address Pools in RRAS

Defining a static address pool for IP address assignments to RAS has subtly changed. You may recall the discussions of the basic underpinnings of TCP/IP addressing: what subnet masks are, and how a specific address in any subnet is allocated to the router and the broadcast address, with the first address as the subnet or network address. Well, the new RAS Server TCP/IP Configuration more closely reflects those principles.

In the Address box, enter the first address for the subnet or address pool you want to share with TCP/IP RAS users. Then enter the subnet mask in the Mask box (as discussed, a subnet mask of 255.255.255.0 indicates a full C-Class of 255 address in the pool; a mask of 255.255.255.240 indicates a 16-IP address subnet, and so forth). When you enter the subnet mask, RRAS automatically calculates the number of addresses that are available for users from the subnet. In Figure 10-30, a 16-IP subnet has been defined. When the IP address for the subnet, the router address, and the broadcast IP are subtracted, 13 addresses remain available. (If you defined a 4-IP subnet, only one address would remain.)

As before, DHCP can also be used. Define a DHCP scope to replace the address pool, as described in Chapter 3.

12. For the RAS port you're dealing with, select whether connected users will be able to access the entire network or just the server in the Allow section, as labeled in Figure 10-29.

13. Click OK, and click OK again to commit the changes for the RAS port. Continue the same Steps 9 through 13 for each RAS port in Remote Access Setup.

14. When you're finished, click Continue in Remote Access Setup. After a moment, you'll receive a message stating that RRAS has been successfully installed, as shown in Figure 10-30.

Figure 10-30: Concluding RRAS Setup

15. Click OK. Finally, a Steelhead Installer message appears, shown in Figure 10-31.

Figure 10-31: The Old Steelhead
Code Name for RRAS

16. Click Restart to restart the computer and enable the new RRAS services.

Routing requires entire books to explain. A lengthy discussion of routing is far beyond the scope of this book. The bookstore shelves are groaning with meaty tomes that attempt to explain enterprise-level routing and networking topics, most with mixed success at best. For immediate help, the best places to go for Windows NT-specific information on routing are RRAS's own bundled document files mentioned earlier, and some of Microsoft's own information on its Web site and in the Windows NT Server Resource Kit. RRAS's routing features are rapidly gaining popularity as a kind of "baby Cisco" in software. Routers, of course, are expected to be available constantly, which you still can't expect of a Windows NT Server. Nevertheless, for department-level routing tasks, RRAS is certainly worth experimenting with. For full use, you'll need a multihomed server with at least two network interface cards installed. As noted way back in Chapter 1, do yourself a favor and use the same make and model cards in each slot.

A Final Word

That concludes the online connectivity section. In this chapter and in Chapter 9, you've gained working knowledge of several key dial-up networking applications under Windows NT. In Chapters 11 and 12 you'll find out about Windows Messaging, which provides both LAN/WAN-based and Internet Mail-based mail capabilities. Chapter 11 describes how to configure the Windows Messaging features offered free with every copy of Windows NT. Chapter 12 takes you to the next level in this area, describing the installation and basic applications for Microsoft's Exchange 5.0, which is a much more powerful (and expensive) messaging and groupware upgrade for Windows NT Messaging.

Troubleshooting

When I dial up my Internet connection and try to dial in to my server using the VPN port, I get a "no answer" message.
If you know that you've received the correct IP address, the PPTP server on the other end may have accidentally dropped its connection or the ISP may have cut it off. Also, if you were provided with a NetBIOS name for the server, you may not be getting proper name resolution. If you're connecting to tunnel through a typical consumer ISP, using NetBIOS names will seldom work. Always make sure you have the right IP address for the other end. There's not much you can do until the server comes back online.

I've had a lot of problems with my online connectivity since I installed Routing and RAS. What can I do to restore my old RAS without wrecking my server?
Follow these steps:

1. In Control Panel, double-click Network. When the Network applet appears, select the Services tab.

2. Select Routing and Remote Access Service and click the Remove button.

3. Click Close and then click Yes to restart the server.

4. After restarting, open a command line and use the EXPAND command to copy and expand the original OEMNSVRA.INF file into your server's WINWindows NT\SYSTEM32 folder. An example of this command might be the following:

```
EXPAND E:\I386\OEMNSVRA.IN_  C:\WINNT\SYSTEM32\OEMNSVRA.INF
```

where E:\ is the drive letter for the CD-ROM, and C:\WINWindows NT\SYSTEM32\OEMNSVRA.INF is the destination folder and filename (which EXPAND requires).

5. Reinstall the original Remote Access Service from the CD-ROM, using the Network applet in Control Panel. *Do not restart the system when the process is done!*

6. Reapply the latest service pack before restarting. If you do not do this, the system may fail to restart properly.

   In fact, some of your RRAS problems may have resulted from not using the latest service pack. If that isn't the case, check hardware compatibility. The simpler things are usually the things that go wrong first.

Do I need RRAS to set up multiple default routes in case my original Default Gateway fails?

No, RRAS doesn't hurt, but you don't need it. All you need to do is open Network, select Protocols, TCP/IP, Properties, and then select Advanced. You can then add other default gateways as needed. This is handy because you can have multiple network interface cards in the same system, each of which requires its own default gateway address. This is, of course, a multihomed server.

When I dial up my Internet server, set up my tunneling, and connect to the server, I can't browse the network in Network Neighborhood!

In all likelihood you're not getting name resolution from the server. Check to make sure that you have the right WINS and DNS (if needed) server addresses in your TCP/IP Properties' DNS and WINS Address tabs, and in your RAS's TCP/IP configuration. If the other end, the server, isn't using these capabilities, it's probably using static addressing and an LMHOSTS file instead. Make sure that the LMHOSTS file you have on your workstation has the correct entries from the server's copy. There may also be name resolution problems on the server. (This is a little beyond the normal client's ability to handle and is a definite chore for the administrator.)

My Internet connection seems to dial in correctly, and I get a successful logon, but my browser software, or News, or e-mail programs don't work and I get no data.

In many cases, this is a matter of disabling a single check box. Open Dial-Up Networking. Click More and select Edit Entry and Modem Properties. Click the Server tab. If the Enable PPP LCP Extensions check box is enabled, clear it. This should fix the problem.

Chapter 11

Setting Up Microsoft Exchange for Electronic Mail

IN THIS CHAPTER
This chapter covers the following topics:

◆ Setting up Exchange 4.0 on Windows NT Server and Workstation

◆ Setting up clients' internal office e-mail accounts

◆ Adding and editing entries in e-mail address books

◆ Sending and receiving e-mail from clients through Windows NT Server

◆ Exploring Exchange 5.0, Microsoft's next-generation messaging package

ELECTRONIC MAIL IS probably the most widely used communications tool in business. At your desk you're expected to maintain contact with your coworkers, and with outside business contacts, using the e-mail features provided to you on your computer. Windows NT Server and Workstation provide a free set of features for creating, managing, and sending and receiving electronic mail. It's called Microsoft Exchange. The topic of this chapter is how to set up and use Microsoft Exchange on your Windows NT servers and clients.

Using Exchange's features, you can send e-mail to any other user on the network, and to computer users anywhere in the world. Actually, e-mail is a lot less sensitive and time-intensive than browsing the Web and is also a good way to maintain your outside working contacts without taking too many resources from the network. Windows 95 also uses a version of Microsoft Exchange, so you can also integrate Win95 clients' e-mail on your network.

Exchange 4.0 is already superannuated by a new version of Exchange, called Exchange 5.0. Unlike 4.0, version 5.0 is an expensive add-on that is part of the Microsoft BackOffice suite of groupware and enterprise applications. Exchange 5.0, which offers a greatly expanded messaging system and new groupware collaboration features, is discussed in the final section of this chapter.

Why discuss Exchange 4.0 at all? Because it's free and comes with the operating system. Many of your Windows NT Workstation clients may be running it or will need it to send intraoffice e-mail. It provides a reasonably useful way to get your intraoffice messaging up and running until your IS manager or CIO comes up with the budget to buy the new BackOffice applications. Exchange 4.0's setup, however, leaves a lot to be desired. In this chapter, the half dozen or so of you who actually want to *use* it will get the straight story. If you plan to execute a more professional-level messaging system, consider Exchange 5.0 or some of the other powerful solutions available from Lotus and Netscape, among others.

Understanding Exchange 4.0

Exchange 4.0 is a peer-to-peer-based messaging system provided with both Windows NT Server 4.0 and Windows NT Workstation 4.0. Perhaps the most important aspect about Exchange is the fact that all messaging services are set up under the umbrella of a *user profile*. When you set up a profile, you determine what services are going to run under it, and, by extension, on that particular client. The most important services that typically run under a user profile are

- Internet Mail (for e-mail to clients and contacts across the world and outside the company)
- Microsoft Mail (internal, LAN-based e-mail)
- Personal Address Book
- Personal Folders

During the Exchange setup process, you'll become familiar with all of these elements. Of the four services, the two most important are Internet Mail and Microsoft Mail. The other two, Personal Address Book and Personal Folders, are support services and are described as you go along in this chapter.

Installing Exchange 4.0

The basic Exchange software is organized under the basic category of Windows Messaging when you set up Windows NT for the first time. Control Panel's Add/Remove Programs applet also provides a way to install Windows Messaging if you bypassed it the first time around. If you open the Control Panel and see the Mail and Microsoft Mail Postoffice icons displayed, you don't need to do anything else.

If you don't see the Mail and Microsoft Mail Postoffice icons, you'll need to install the software before proceeding with the rest of this chapter. This applies to both Windows NT Server and Workstation. Follow these steps to install the software:

1. Open Control Panel and double-click Add/Remove Programs.

2. Click the Windows NT Setup tab.

3. Scroll down the Components list to Windows Messaging. If its check box is already filled, its features have already been installed and you can just cancel out of the program. An empty check box indicates that you need to install the Windows Messaging features (although that fact is not exactly made clear by the program).

4. Select the Windows Messaging check box and click OK.

5. When the system prompts you for a file location, provide it with the drive letter of your CD-ROM drive and the CD-ROM's i386 directory (as in E:\i386). Your Windows NT system's CD-ROM disk should be in the drive, of course.

6. Click OK or press Enter and the software copies to your hard disk. Close out of the Control Panel when you're done.

After the software is installed, you use the Control Panel icons to perform part of the Windows Messaging setup, along with the Inbox icon on your Windows NT desktops. (For Internet mail you'll also use the Dial-Up Networking program.) The Inbox icon resides on your Windows NT system's desktop, whether it's a server or a humble workstation. (It's also provided on the Windows 95 desktop.) Inbox is the client software you use to create and manage your e-mail.

On Windows NT clients you can begin Exchange 4.0 setup by double-clicking the Inbox icon on your desktop. All the following steps assume you haven't started trying to set up your e-mail on those clients. But don't rush ahead. There's a lot you need to know. Unfortunately, Exchange 4.0's setup is complicated enough that trying to set it up by starting off with the Inbox icon may result in annoying messaging problems on the local system.

Exchange setup can be a bit complicated. Because of its decentralized, workgroup-oriented nature, it can be difficult to define a solid, manageable setup for the basic Exchange services. In many cases you will be responsible for assigning e-mail addresses and e-mail user names to clients within your company; you must also furnish and maintain a long list of information for each and every messaging client. That list includes the following:

◆ The Exchange Postoffice path

◆ The user name to be added to the Postoffice address list

◆ The name for your Internet Mail server, *or* an IP address (IP addresses are discussed in Chapter 3), if necessary (many systems may not use Internet e-mail on the network, sticking only with Microsoft mail)

◆ An e-mail password

◆ An e-mail address

◆ A mailbox account name

◆ A path to the user's Personal Folder file

◆ A properly set up Dial-Up Account (unless clients have to do this on their own)

The list is formidable. *Make sure* you and your client users have everything on this list before configuring Exchange for the first time on the users' computers, or tracking all this stuff down will be an unholy pain, and part or all of Exchange will not work on their systems. Even with all this information given to start with, setting up Exchange correctly is not a simple task. Imagine how difficult it was before Windows NT 4.0 came along. (Most people didn't even bother before, preferring to use third-party e-mail programs.) Now many companies will use Exchange 4.0, because it's free with the operating system and they don't have to buy another program to do e-mail. A lot of users will have to deal with it.

Exchange's Mail mechanisms are split into two areas:

◆ Microsoft Mail (for internal company e-mail)

◆ Internet Mail (for communicating to others using e-mail across the Internet)

When you start up Exchange's so-called Wizard by double-clicking the Inbox, you're presented with two options: Microsoft Mail and Internet Mail. If you select both of them, Microsoft Mail is set up first.

Setting Up Microsoft Mail

If you plan to use internal messaging, Microsoft Mail is a serviceable tool. Otherwise, if you're just planning to use Internet e-mail, and you have full DNS-based name management on your network, you don't have to install Microsoft Mail at all and can stick with Exchange's Internet Mail feature. The assumption here is that you'll want to use all the tools at your disposal. (After all, many Windows NT servers are simply small workgroup servers.) In any case, Exchange's internal Microsoft e-mail setup is much more complex than it needs to be, and no clear methodology is provided. Once it's up and running, it provides a fairly simple and convenient mechanism for internal e-mail.

As I've noted, Internet e-mail connectivity uses Windows NT's Dial-Up Connectivity application to connect. Exchange's Inbox allows you to use DUN to connect to your ISP for e-mail, providing the basic e-mail client for your Internet connection. As you'll see later, the Inbox client software is barely adequate for that purpose.

Before you run the Inbox's Wizard application for e-mail setup on any system, you *should* do the following things:

◆ Create a Postoffice on the Windows NT server or peer client that you designate as the central place to administer e-mail.

◆ Create your e-mail user accounts in an Address List.

◆ Create a set of Personal Folder files mirroring the collection of e-mail users in your network.

Then you can run the Inbox application on each system. I strongly recommend following these methods before setting up your e-mail clients, or maintenance of even a small e-mail system can prove chaotic and unmanageable.

Creating a Postoffice for Microsoft Mail on Windows NT Server

The first important step is to create a Postoffice. If you have a glance at the Control Panel, you'll find a Microsoft Mail Postoffice icon. For Exchange 4.0, Postoffices are the basic item around which your intra-office e-mail is organized. Follow these steps:

1. Open the Control Panel and double-click the Microsoft Mail Postoffice icon.

2. Select the Create a new Workgroup Postoffice option, and click Next. The next screen reads, "There should only be one workgroup Postoffice in your workgroup. Please specify where this new workgroup Postoffice should be located. The Postoffice should be put in a location that can be read by other users in your workgroup." Clearly, this is not an application ideally suited for complex domain-based Windows NT networks. In this case, I'll assume that your Postoffice is going to be located on your Windows NT domain server.

   For placement of a Postoffice, I prefer creating a new folder just off the root, called "Company Mail" or "Postoffice" or something of that nature. Then when the setup is done, you'll need to set up the folder as Shared among the users in your workgroup.

3. Enter the folder/directory path where you want the Postoffice to be placed, and click Next. Figure 11-1 shows an example.

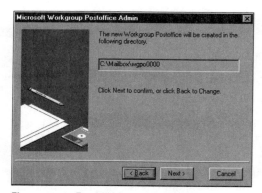

Figure 11-1: Establishing a New Postoffice

Don't enter a name for the actual mailbox; Exchange automatically names it for you. This is one of many reasons I recommend spending the extra money and upgrading to Exchange 5.0 (or another system). If you want to use native Windows NT messaging, Exchange 4.0 provides no flexibility and little real help. There's only one right way to do things here, and Exchange 4.0 is one of the few components of Windows NT that doesn't measure up in terms of online help, Windows NT conventions, or logical setup methods.

4. Click Next. You're prompted to enter the information for your Administrator account, including the account name, the name of the new *mailbox* for the account, the account's password, and several other items. Figure 11-2 shows a set of example entries.

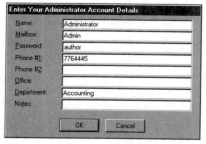

Figure 11-2: Providing Postoffice
Administrator Information

The mailbox name for each account is very important, although the setup program gives you no help and no clue about why. Mailboxes are subordinate to the Postoffice and are gathered within the Postoffice for administration. They contain the actual e-mail. When you create an Administrator account for Exchange messaging, make *sure* you know its mailbox name, because you'll need to use it when you open the program again to add user accounts as the administrator and to create Personal Folders. In Figure 11-2 I've called the administrator's mailbox "Admin."

Another annoyance is that password entries are not encrypted when you enter them. Anyone walking by your cubicle can glance over and see your password. If you can, provide a password for your mailbox that is distinctly different from the password you use for network access. And make sure no one else gets their hands on it.

5. Click OK. The server admonishes you to share the folder in which you've created the Postoffice, as shown in Figure 11-3.

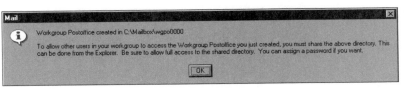

Figure 11-3: Make sure to follow this instruction.

6. Click OK to finish.

Simply right-click the new Postoffice folder you've created, and select Sharing from the shortcut menu to assign sharing and rights. (At this point you probably know about that, so just move on here. Sharing methods are discussed in detail in Chapter 2.) The Postoffice folder must be shared so that Mail clients can access it.

The next phase is to create the user accounts that your Microsoft Mail network clients will use.

Adding User Accounts to a Postoffice (Administrators Only)

The next phase is to add the user accounts for Exchange Mail to the server. The methods are similar to those just described above, except that you must use the existing Administrator account under Exchange to do this. You must also know the name of the administrator's mailbox, or Exchange will not allow you into the application. Follow these steps:

1. Open the Control Panel and double-click the Microsoft Mail Postoffice icon.

2. Select the Administer an Existing Workgroup Postoffice option, and click Next. You may need to enter the path for the workgroup Postoffice, but the path to the one you've created should be displayed by default. (Well, that's why you're the administrator.)

3. Click Next. Enter the name of your administrator mailbox and the password.

4. Click Next again. The Postoffice Manager appears, as shown in Figure 11-4. This is where you add your users' Postoffice mailbox accounts.

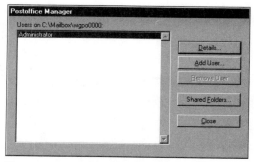

Figure 11–4: Opening the Postoffice Manager

5. Click the Add User button. The Add User dialog box appears. It's the same dialog box shown in Figure 11-2, except that its title is changed, as shown in Figure 11-5.

6. Enter the new user records for their name, their personal mailbox, password, and other information (an example is shown in Figure 11-5).

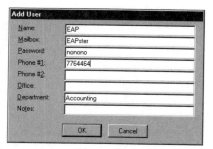

Figure 11–5: Entering New User and Mailbox Information

7. Click OK, and the new account and mailbox added to the system.

8. Continue adding user accounts as desired. When you're finished, a list of users is created, as shown in Figure 11-6.

9. Click Close to save your accounts and close the application.

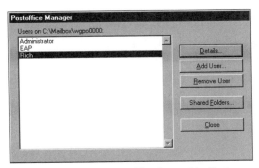

Figure 11-6: A New User List Created in Exchange on the Server

The list of users shown in Figure 11-6 (yours, of course, will be different) is set up as the Postoffice Address List. All e-mail clients that use your system can draw upon this list for communicating with other clients. A second item called a Personal Address Book can also be created; this is done on each client and can be used to collect e-mail addresses of people outside the company.

Without properly setting up the Postoffice and defining your user accounts beforehand, attempting to set up Windows Messaging on clients is a wasted exercise. There's another key step that you'll have to perform, particularly if you want to centralize the office e-mail in one place: create the Personal Folder Files for each of the e-mail clients.

A Personal Folder File is used to cache information that you want to send to other users, such as data files. Exchange treats these files as a user profile. It is encrypted and actually termed in a contradictory way; although it's a file, it's actually treated as a folder because it contains the messages and data that clients send and receive. When the information (such as attached files) is accepted, that information is removed from the Personal Folder File (whose extension is .PST) to prevent it from getting too large. I recommend making sure that all personal folders be centralized on the server; it also doesn't hurt to have the Personal Address Books for each client gathered in one location, although that aspect isn't as sensitive.

Each client on your network that will use e-mail services must have a personal folder file, or their e-mail clients will not work properly. Here's how to create them:

1. Open the Inbox on the Windows desktop. The Windows Messaging application appears.

2. From the Tools menu, select Services. The Services dialog box appears, as shown in Figure 11-7.

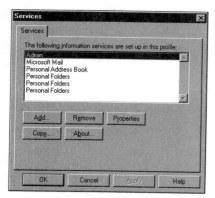

Figure 11-7: Adding Services to the E-Mail Client

3. Click Add. The Add Service to Profile dialog box appears.

4. Click the Personal Folders listing and click OK. The Create/Open Personal Folders File dialog box appears, as shown in Figure 11-8. It closely resembles the familiar File/Open dialog box you see in so many Windows applications. In the File name text box, you'll see a listing: .pst.

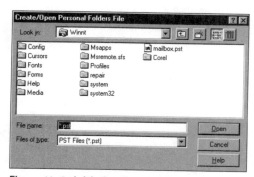

Figure 11-8: Initiating Personal Folder Creation

5. Browse through the folder list on the server until you locate the folder where you want the personal folder files to go. (I place mine in the C:\WINNT\Profiles folder of the server.) Open the folder and display its contents in the dialog box (merely selecting it won't get the job done).

6. In the File name text box, type the name of the Personal Folder File, keeping the .PST extension. It's wise to keep the filename consistent with the account user names for simplicity.

7. After entering the filename, click Open. The Create Microsoft Personal Folders dialog box pops up, as shown in Figure 11-9.

Figure 11-9: Creating Personal Folders, Using User Account Information

8. In the Name text box, enter a name for the Personal Folder that corresponds to the user of the folder.

9. Enter the account password for the Personal Folder and verify it. If needed, enable the Save this password check box. Also, choose an encryption method if desired.

10. Click OK. The new Personal Folders listing is added to the Services list. Figure 11-10 shows how a set of Personal Folders, along with some other services, looks when you're done.

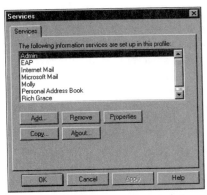

Figure 11-10: Personal Folder Creation for a Workgroup

Note: if you happen to skip naming the folders properly, they're automatically named Personal Folders. If you have several or more of these things, it can get very confusing, so here's what to do in that case:

1. Select the desired Personal Folders listing and click the Properties button. A dialog box appears, listing the folder's basic characteristics.

2. Enter a new name for the Personal Folder in the Name box. The name does not have to match the user name or name of the file. Also note that you can compress the file in this dialog box if needed.

3. Click OK to commit the changes.

When you set up Exchange clients, have the clients refer to the server's collection of Personal Folder files for the one that applies to them. Then each Exchange client will always refer back to each file as its profile and reference point for their e-mail software, and all clients can be managed at a single location.

Don't go through the *next* section on your clients without performing the previous steps on the server, or the peer client that you've designated to handle these things. You'll save yourself a lot of grief, and you'll have to perform those steps only once.

Setting Up Windows Messaging and Active Profiles

Now that you've created your Postoffice and your user accounts, you can continue on to setting up the full messaging system on your clients. When you set up Exchange for the first time, you're prompted by a Windows Messaging Setup Wizard when particular pieces of information need to be entered.

Two key items must be accounted for during client e-mail setup: the Personal Folder file, the creation of which was described in the previous section, and the Personal Address Book.

By pulling all these things together, you create an *active profile* on the client. On the server and on any clients, I recommend placing exactly *one* active profile on each system until you finish getting the office e-mail system up and running. The server (or peer client that you designate to handle the e-mail Postoffice and mailboxes) does not contain the whole galloping bunch of active profiles for a functional intraoffice e-mail system, even though the Personal Folder files for each client can be based on a single system. This is where the peer-to-peer nature of Exchange 4.0 for Windows NT really starts to become evident.

Here's where to begin:

1. Double-click the Inbox icon on your desktop. A splash screen pops up, and the Windows Messaging Setup Wizard appears, as shown in Figure 11-11. Windows Messaging is the out-of-the-box limited edition of Exchange that comes with Windows NT 4.0.

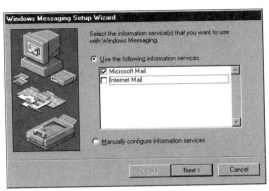

Figure 11-11: Starting the Exchange Setup Wizard

2. Select the Mail options as required by your setup.

3. Click the Next button. The Wizard begins by setting up your Microsoft Mail e-mail account for participation in the network. Here you enter the Postoffice path. On the client you need to issue the path over the network to the Postoffice resident on the server. (If you're doing client peer-to-peer stuff, the principle is basically the same. All that needs to be done is to decide whose system will handle e-mail administration.)

4. If you have previously created a Postoffice (which I strongly recommend) on the server, enter the path and the Postoffice name. Hint: Your e-mail clients can map the shared hard disk or shared Mail directory to a drive letter. This makes defining the Postoffice path a lot easier and doesn't require a UNC path. An example of a networked (and drive-mapped) path to a server's Postoffice is shown in Figure 11-12.

    Do *not* create another Postoffice on the client.

    This step can potentially annoy users and cause administrative headaches: having to enter the Postoffice path on the network users' own initiative. The Postoffice is the basic component of Microsoft Mail, and it is used to provide the central location for all the electronic mail processed through the network. What does all this mean for you? Well, it means that you, as the network administrator, will either have to distribute a memo painstakingly describing the entire process of setting up each e-mail client, or go around to each system following the steps described here.

Figure 11-12: Setting a Networked Postoffice Path
from the Exchange Client

5. Click Next again.

6. Select your client's user name from the list of available user accounts
   in the Postoffice, which is automatically displayed if the Postoffice is
   properly located by the client from across the network. It will be the same
   list as originally shown in Figure 11-6. If your name isn't displayed on the
   list, you need to add it or ask your network administrator to place it there.
   (This is one key reason why preliminary creation of the Postoffice is so
   important to correct Microsoft Mail configuration.)

7. Click Next. The user name and actual mailbox name are shown, as is an
   empty field requiring password entry. The next step is to enter the
   assigned e-mail password, which is originally defined with the list of user
   accounts on the server. (If you're a humble client, most companies will
   assign one to you, if you're really nice to them.)

8. Enter your password, as shown in Figure 11-13. Here, the password is
   actually encrypted by the application.

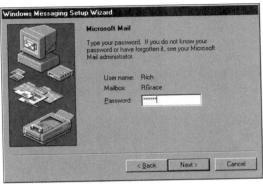

Figure 11-13: Password Entry on the Local Client

9. Click Next again.

10. Enter the path for your user account's Personal Address Book, which can be placed on the local system or the server as desired, and click Next.

11. Enter the path for the user account's Personal Folder file, which may also be placed on the server as described above. Figure 11-14 shows a sample networked path to a Personal Folder file. (Although I strongly recommend placing all those folders in one location on the server, technically each client can also create its own. For administrative purposes, I don't recommend this.)

Figure 11-14: Issuing a Network Path to a Client's
Personal Folder

12. Enter the assigned password for the Personal Folder and click OK. You're now finished with Microsoft Mail setup for your network client. Click Finish, and the Inbox application appears for the first time, fully configured.

The 12 steps you've just followed can be repeated for any electronic mail client that will participate on your network. Whether it's the Admin on the server or dozens/hundreds of clients, each and every Exchange client is set up in exactly the same way. Windows NT's basic messaging services are essentially peer-to-peer, even those bundled with Windows NT Server. With lots of people on the network, this fact makes it even more important for you to make sure that messaging administration is kept centralized and manageable.

If you're only setting up internal e-mail in your network, you've completed the steps to set it up on any client and to set up the underpinnings (Postoffice, and so on) to manage internal e-mail. If you're also setting up Internet e-mail, Exchange's Wizard continues on to that installation phase.

Setting Up Internet E-Mail in Microsoft Exchange's Wizard

Internet e-mail can be set up with the Wizard during initial setup, or after you've finished setting up and begun using the basic Microsoft Mail system. I'll describe both methods, starting with the basic Wizard setup.

In medium-to-large office environments, it's unlikely that you'll have a modem directly hooked up to a client computer. Many offices actually *network* a few modems that a larger group of users share between them. Then the central server handles the direct Internet connections and ensures that any Internet mail sent to you gets to its proper destination. For our example, I'll assume that you're using a modem and that you already have a dial-up account set up on your computer.

For a proper Internet connection using Windows NT, Microsoft Exchange runs the Dial-Up Networking (DUN) program from My Computer. When you run Dial-Up Networking for the first time through this process of setting up your Internet e-mail, you're greeted by another Wizard that steps you through the brief process of setting up a dial-up account. Chapter 9 describes how to set up an Internet dial-up connection in Windows NT in greater detail than I can do justice to here. Follow these steps:

1. Select either the Modem or Network options.

2. Click Next.

3. Select your dial-up account (called the Connection in the dialog box) for Internet Mail.

4. Click Next again.

   The next phase is to provide the Wizard with the name for your Internet Mail server. In many cases, you may have to provide an IP address rather than a DNS server name. This can be an outside Internet company such as

Earthlink, Netcom, or any other Internet service provider (ISP), or one based inside your company.

5. Enter the name for your Internet e-mail server.

6. Click Next.

7. Select the mode for how you want your computer to transfer e-mail messages: Off-line or Automatic. The Off-line option allows you to send and receive your e-mail when you want and to be selective about the e-mail that you receive. The Automatic option simply establishes your Internet e-mail connection and transfers all your e-mail whenever you start up the Exchange program. It saves some work but gives you somewhat less control.

8. Click Next. Now you have to give the Wizard your e-mail address.

9. Enter the e-mail address and click Next again.

10. Now you have to give a mailbox account name and a password. The password will probably be the same one you use for your e-mail, and your mailbox account name must also be given to you by the administrator.

11. Click Next again. The Wizard then requests a path to your Personal Address Book. The Personal Address Book will eventually contain all the e-mail addresses for your coworkers and contacts. It doesn't contain them automatically — you must enter them as you use your e-mail. The Wizard also displays a default path to a Personal Address Book, which is just another file in your system. Most of the time the default should be fine.

12. When the Personal Address Book screen appears, its default path should be acceptable. Make a note of where your Personal Address Book is. As time goes on, you may want to make a backup copy onto a floppy disk or such. If it ever gets lost, such as when the computer goes down or Windows NT ever needs to be reinstalled or upgraded, you'll still have all those e-mail addresses safely stored where you can use them again without laboriously retyping them.

13. Click Next. The Personal Folders screen appears. Enter the path to the Personal Folders file. (Hint: if the network client shares the disk or the folder containing the Personal Folder from the server, it's a lot easier to locate.) As discussed earlier, the Personal Folders file should not be created directly on the client if he or she is part of a network that's larger than a few users. For central administration reasons, it's better to consolidate personal folders in one place so they can be backed up, tracked, and managed more efficiently.

14. Click Next. You have finished! You've finally managed to install the Windows Messaging services for Internet Mail, Microsoft Mail, Personal Address Book, and Personal Folders.

15. Finally, click Finish to conclude the setup. After a moment, Windows Messaging will display the Inbox for your e-mail accounts.

Setting Up Internet Mail on an Existing Exchange Client

If you've opted to set up the Microsoft Mail internal e-mail client first and decide to set up Internet Mail later, there's no need to run the Wizard again. (In fact, you can't.) In this case, Internet Mail must be set up from the Inbox application. It's not too difficult and actually gives you a bit more control than using the Wizard. Here's how:

1. Open the Inbox application on the client's Windows desktop.

2. From the Tools menu, select Services. The Services dialog box appears, as shown in Figure 11-15. If Internet Mail is not among the services listed, it must be set up on this client.

Figure 11-15: Checking for Installed Services

3. Click OK. The Add Service to Profile list appears, as shown in Figure 11-16. This is where you begin the process of adding another mail service to the Exchange user profile.

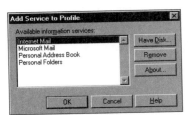

Figure 11-16: Selecting the New Service

4. Select Internet Mail and click OK. Exchange's Internet Mail dialog box appears, displaying two tabs, General and Connection, as shown in Figure 11-17.

Full name and E-mail address text boxes

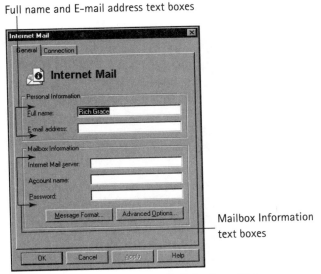

Mailbox Information text boxes

Figure 11-17: Starting Internet Mail Configuration

5. Enter the client's full name and intended e-mail address.

6. Enter the domain name of the mail server in the Internet Mail server text box. (It could be something like "Earthlink.net," "Microsoft.com," or whatever your company's server defines.)

7. Enter the user's account name in the Account name text box, and enter the password. (The password will be encrypted.) The final result should resemble Figure 11-18.

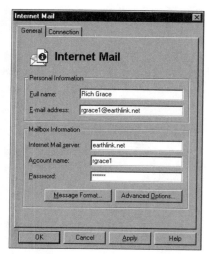

Figure 11-18: Configuring Internet Mail

8. Click the Connection tab. Here you provide Exchange with the information it needs to perform a successful connection. Two key options are provided: Connect Using the Network, which requires a fully configured Mail server (which the basic Exchange 4.0 system decidedly is not), and Connect Using the Modem, which requires that a modem be installed. In this book the default for Exchange 4.0 setup is that you're using a modem on the local client.

You provide dial-up connections using Windows NT's DUN application, which is accessed by using the Add Entry and Edit Entry buttons. Figure 11-19 shows the Connection tab.

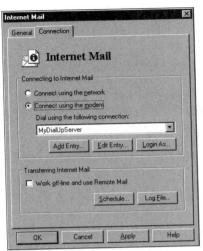

Figure 11-19: Configuring Internet Mail

The Dial list automatically displays any DUN connections you presently have on the client. This includes any Remote Access dial-up connections that may have been previously defined, and any Internet connections you may have set up, as described in Chapter 9. If that's the case, and you plan to use that connection for Internet Mail access, there is nothing else you need to do. If you need to create a new connection, simply click Add Entry.

9. Select the option Connect using the modem.

10. To create a new DUN modem connection, click the Add Entry button. The New Phonebook Entry Wizard appears. Follow its instructions as described in Chapter 9. To change the entry's characteristics, click the Edit Entry button, which displays the DUN application's multitabbed Edit Phonebook Entry dialog box.

11. Click OK to complete Internet Mail setup.

Using Internal E-Mail with Microsoft Exchange

After you have things up and running, office e-mail is a real convenience for your users. Composing and sending a message is simpler than setting up the actual messaging service; basic information is provided here that highlights the key things you and your clients need to know. Everything discussed here applies to both Microsoft Mail and Internet Mail, because the Messaging application is used for both mail types.

Open the Inbox application by double-clicking its icon on the Windows desktop. Figure 11-20 shows an example of what you'll see.

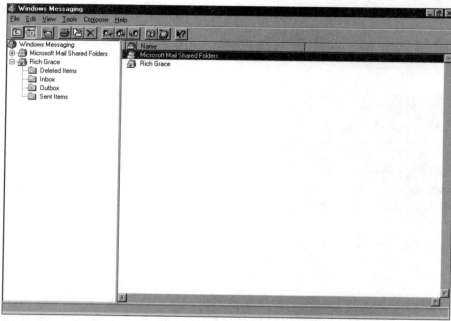

Figure 11–20: Opening Exchange's E-Mail Application

The Windows Messaging View menu provides a Folders view option, which is enabled in Figure 11-20. Until the user becomes accustomed to using the program, it's a good idea to enable it, because the client can easily browse through the folders that are organized under their account. In Figure 11-20, the user, "Rich Grace", has four e-mail folders: Deleted Items, Inbox, Outbox, and Sent Items. Every user in Exchange will have a set of these four folders arranged under their account:

◆ **Inbox** contains any messages sent to the user from around the network or the Internet.

◆ **Outbox** contains messages that the user has composed and clicked the Send button for.

◆ **Deleted Items** compiles a list of all the messages that the user has deleted from their Inbox and Outbox.

◆ **Sent Items** provides a record of all the e-mails you've sent to other clients.

Selecting any of the folders displays the folder's contents.

To create a new e-mail message, select New Message from the Compose menu. The New Message window appears, as shown in Figure 11-21.

Send tool   Insert File tool

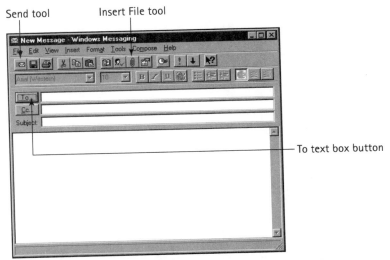

To text box button

Figure 11-21: Composing a New Message

Notice the paper clip button on the toolbar? It's called the Insert File tool, and it allows you to attach files to your message and send them along with the message. This goes for internal e-mail as well as the Internet. Click the Send button to set up the message for delivery (sending e-mail is described a bit later).

The most important thing to point out here is the To field. You can enter the e-mail address from memory if you want, but it's a lot easier to just click the To button as labeled in Figure 11-21. When you do so, the Address Book appears, as shown in Figure 11-22.

You select colleagues' and contacts' addresses for your messages in the Address Book. It's divided into two parts: the Postoffice Address Book, whose sample entries from my system are shown in Figure 11-22, and the Personal Address Book. The Postoffice Address List is (ideally, at least) provided by the server with its central-ized database of user names and addresses. Individual clients can't modify the Postoffice list. You can display the Personal Address Book by selecting it from the Show Names list, as labeled in Figure 11-22.

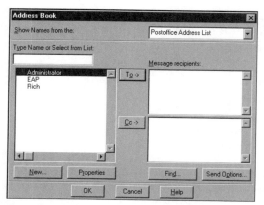

Figure 11-22: Selecting E-Mail Addresses

You can add new e-mail addresses to the Personal Address Book. Figure 11-23 shows an example of a new Personal Address Book (PAB) with a couple of new Internet Mail entries added to it.

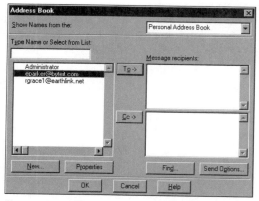

Figure 11-23: Personal Address Books Can Contain the Client's Private List of E-Mail Addresses

Select an address and click the To button as labeled in Figure 11-22, or double-click an address listing, to add it as a message recipient. You can select as many addresses as you want to receive a message. Microsoft Mail and Internet Mail address types are both collected here.

How do you add new addresses? In the Address Book window, click the New button. Then select the entry type, click OK, and add your entries.

Sending e-mail messages is a two-step process, which is one of the annoying quirks about Exchange's mail client. Why can't you just click Send to fire off a message?

1. When you finish composing the message and want to send it, click the Send tool in the New Message window as labeled in Figure 11-21.

2. Close the Message window.

3. From the Tools menu, select Deliver Now Using, and then select All Services (or Internet Mail/Microsoft Mail), depending on your application. If you're sending Internet mail, the client will dial up the Internet. Otherwise, the internal e-mail will just be sent.

Many details have been skipped to bring you the overall picture of how to work with the basic e-mail package. The basic Inbox is not a particularly well-designed application; compared to many of Windows NT's other capabilities, the bundled Windows Messaging doesn't really compete in terms of up-to-date design, ease of use, or general execution. Nevertheless, since it's free and doesn't require any upgrades to use, it's worth your while to experiment with it. Instead of boring you with the details of describing the functions of every button on the Messaging toolbar, just keep an eye on the tool tips that appear under each button. Also remember (and inform your users) that sending e-mail with Exchange 4.0 is a two-step process: click the Send button, and then select the Deliver Now feature under the Tools menu.

The next section expands on the basic concepts discussed here and takes you on a brief tour through Microsoft Exchange Version 5.0. It is decidedly not a free product (it is a commercially available part of Microsoft BackOffice and costs several thousand dollars to get in on the ground floor). Nevertheless, it's worth a quick look to help you determine whether it's the right choice for your office in the future. Exchange 5.0 is a full-bodied messaging system that also includes drastically enhanced Internet mail service support, which I'll briefly explain and explore below.

Understanding Exchange 5.0

The mere task of installing Exchange 5.0 on your server is beyond the scope of this book. Exchange occupies over 160MB of space on your server for a full installation, and Microsoft recommends running Exchange on a dedicated server within your domain or enterprise network. The setup process takes a while as well; although the Setup Wizard is quite well designed, you also have other tasks to perform, such as the Exchange Migration Wizard, which allows mail system migration from MS Mail, Novell GroupWise, Lotus CC:Mail, and Netscape Collabra. All the necessary utilities are placed on the Start menu after the basic installation. If you're migrating from MS Mail, your existing mailboxes and Postoffices can be converted over to the new system. You can still use the same Exchange client software that you spent so much time painfully configuring in the previous section of this chapter.

Exchange 5.0 effects some interesting changes on your server once it's installed. You'll find that some of your server utilities have expanded functions, but it takes a little digging to find out what those extensions are. Perhaps the biggest changes are in the User Manager for Domains. When you open the program after installing Exchange 5.0, you'll notice a new Exchange menu, as shown in Figure 11-24.

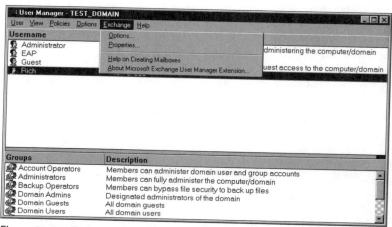

Figure 11-24: Exchange 5.0 Adds Significant Functions to the User Manager

Selecting Options from the new Exchange menu provides a simple but thought-provoking dialog box, as shown in Figure 11-25.

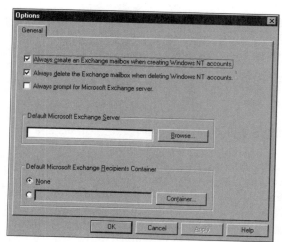

Figure 11-25: You Have the Option To Automatically Create New Mailboxes with New Accounts, and To Delete Them Accordingly

When you simply finish creating a new user account in User Manager and click Add in the New User dialog box, you'll receive a new multitabbed dialog box that provides a huge number of new communications options for the account, as shown in Figure 11-26.

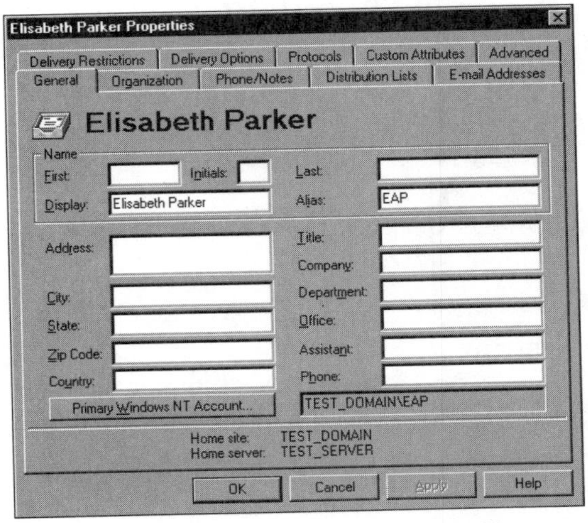

Figure 11-26: The Exchange–Enhanced User Manager
Provides a Huge Set of Communications Options
for User Accounts

Adding this type of functionality to User Manager seems logical, because accounts really should be tied in to the enterprise network, and particularly e-mail and communications options, with as little fuss as possible. In this area Exchange 5.0 really does deliver. As an example of Exchange's greater support for industry-standard Mail systems, have a look at the E-mail Addresses tab, which contains a full panoply of automatically created e-mail addresses for all the mail systems supported by the program, an example of which is shown in Figure 11-27.

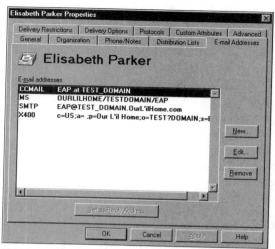

Figure 11-27: Exchange 5.0 Generates an Automatic
Set of E-Mail Addresses for Microsoft Mail,
Lotus CC:Mail, SMTP (Internet) E-Mail,
and x.400 for Each User Account

This is quite a fascinating capability, since this means that you have much less work to do to create and support electronic mail addresses for several key mail formats in the business world. It's particularly handy for large companies with WANs, because the confusing issue of defining mail addresses for so many different standards, all of which are widely used in the business world, is finally solved with this relatively simple application. Elsewhere, the Protocols tab (shown in Figure 11-28) also indicates just how radically Exchange has been improved from version 4.0 to version 5.0.

Mail and communications protocol support has taken a huge leap in Exchange 5.0. Windows NT user accounts can now be fully enabled for the World Wide Web-based HTTP protocol, Lightweight Directory Access Protocol (LDAP) for networking directory access across the Internet, POP3 Internet e-mail with a full selection of encoding options, and Internet/Intranet News integration with NWindows NTP. So what does this do for you? An Exchange client, using the vanilla user account, can connect to Microsoft Exchange using any of these protocols. Clients from other systems can, too.

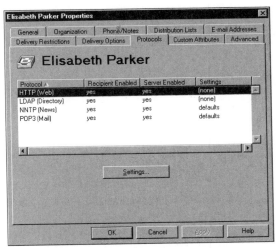

Figure 11-28: Protocol Support in Exchange 5.0

Explaining Exchange 5.0 Protocols

HTTP stands for Hypertext Transfer Protocol. It's the foundation of the World Wide Web, and it's used to transfer hypertext documents and information between a graphical browser and the Web service (or "Web page") to which the browser is connected. It's been in use since 1990, and its basic concept is straightforward. Anytime you click a link in a Web page, you're using HTTP to jump to a new location on the Internet.

NNTP stands for Network News Transfer Protocol. Without discussing the technical underpinnings of NNTP, it's an Internet standard that enables clients to read, create, and post news articles (such as letters on a topic thread) into newsgroups. The Usenet is based on the NNTP protocol. It's highly efficient and allows for rapid transport of information throughout the entire Usenet to any related newsgroups in a matter of hours or even minutes. NNTP is typically used over TCP/IP connections.

POP3 is the standard Internet e-mail protocol.

LDAP is one of the up-and-coming industry standards, whose name pops up persistently in publications like *InfoWorld* and *Network World*. Lightweight Directory Access Protocol is a relatively new communications standard that allows clients to access Directory tree information across the Internet (examples of Directories include Novell's NDS and Microsoft's upcoming Active Directory).

continued

Explaining Exchange 5.0 Protocols *(Continued)*

What is a directory service? It's similar to a database, but in this context generally applies to a method for structuring an enterprise network. Most of the time, a directory is merely read for information by its clients and servers that are connected to it, and when a directory change is made, the entire database is updated. Whereas Windows NT uses a potentially complicated domain-based system for typing together huge networks with multiple domain servers, a directory system can be used to simplify the process of integrating all the different levels of clients and servers in a network. Novell's NDS is the classic example of such a system (and a highly effective one).

LDAP is a global directory model that is supposed to be cross-platform, allowing disparate operating systems to let each other's users communicate. The basic information unit of an LDAP directory is called an *entry*. Entries contain multiple pieces of information, called *attributes*, which, taken together, comprise the entry. Attributes include such things as e-mail addresses and the entry's position in the directory tree.

LDAP uses a hierarchical tree structure, which should sound familiar to you if you've played around with NetWare 4.11 and have gone through the Windows NT-to-NetWare 4.11 chapter earlier in this book. The structure can include geographic and organizational (and even political) boundaries, which again sounds very similar to NetWare. LDAP client computers connect to an LDAP-based server and query for locations of entries, mainly for other users elsewhere in the system. And that, my friends, is as deep as I'm going to go into *this* topic.

Now that you have a vague idea of the alphabet soup of all these protocols, you can see where Exchange represents a serious advance over the Exchange messaging features that are bundled with Windows NT. Exchange 5.0 brings Windows NT into the messaging big leagues. Of course, it's not the only solution (or necessarily the best one) available. But if you plan to use your Windows NT Server in a larger network, Exchange 5.0 is definitely an option. Although it's very well-documented on the CD-ROM, I strongly recommend taking your time with any prospective rollouts of Exchange 5.0. It's an expensive investment, and other solutions are available that may be a better match for your needs. Despite its many admittedly nice features, if you're running a relatively small network, Exchange 5.0 is overkill.

A Final Word

Managing user accounts and e-mail can be a huge topic, especially if you plan to use a more powerful messaging package than that bundled with Windows NT. This chapter simply presents the basics of what you need to know to handle Exchange messaging, without going into extensive detail about how to create and edit e-mail (this is a connectivity book, after all) and other basic tasks. If you need to know more, bookstore shelves are groaning with fine, meaty tomes on the subject.

Troubleshooting

My e-mail isn't getting sent to the client destination.

Did you check to see whether the message has actually been sent? If your message(s) are still in the Outbox, select the Deliver Now Using feature from the Inbox's Tools menu. When the Outbox is empty, check the Sent Items directory in your e-mail client. Your sent messages should appear there. This indicates a successful connection.

If your message still hasn't arrived, wait a few minutes. Exchange takes a few minutes to send a message across even the smallest network.

My Windows Messaging e-mail program keeps trying to dial the Internet every 15 minutes. It's driving me nuts!

Here's how to fix this annoying problem:

1. From the Tools menu, select Options.

2. Select the Services tab.

3. Select Internet Mail and click Properties. The Internet Mail properties sheet appears.

4. Click the Connection tab.

   For a quick fix, click the Work Off-line and Use Remote Mail check box. Otherwise, click the Schedule button and set a new value in minutes in the Check for New Messages field. The Work Off-line check box is handy because the Inbox is prevented from automatically dialing up on the modem if that check box is enabled. When you're ready to send, just use the Deliver Now feature as you would normally and Exchange will dial up and send and receive messages normally.

Part IV

User Management and System Maintenance

Part IV provides many key network management tools and techniques to bring your Windows NT network to its fullest flower. Chapters 12 and 13 cover a huge number of topics. Chapter 12, "General System Management," describes interdomain communications using trust relationships, and how trusts are the key method for building enterprise networks in NT. You also learn how the trust relationship mechanism presents serious limitations when you try to build larger enterprise-type networks using NT.

Chapter 12 features much more, however. When you build a network of any size, you may need to enforce consistency between client computers, especially if many of your users are relative novices. Companies often require fairly tight methods for governing the network. Because maintenance and control is a key issue in network management, this book wouldn't be complete without a serious discussion of NT's tools in this area. System policies, home directories, and user profiles are the key tools that can be used to reach that goal of building a network. If you combine a consistent system policy with a well-designed set of home directories and user profiles, you'll be well on your way to a secure LAN.

Chapter 13, "Typical Tasks You Need To Do," introduces you to the process of writing logon scripts, which basically reproduces most GUI-based networking functions on the Windows NT command line. If you've ever edited batch files in MS-DOS or Windows (AUTOEXEC.BAT and CONFIG.SYS, for example), you'll be familiar with NT logon scripts, which operate in a similar fashion and use a Windows NT-based command set. Further topics include how to build an NT boot floppy (and why you need one), exploring the highly useful Performance Monitor program, and basic backup tips and strategies.

Chapter 12

General System Management

IN THIS CHAPTER
In Chapter 12, the following topics are discussed:

◆ How to establish communications between Windows NT domains

◆ How to create various types of system policies and why they're a useful tool

◆ How to create home directories in Windows NT

◆ How to create roaming user profiles

JUST WHEN YOU thought you had gotten through all the really complicated stuff, you expected a break, didn't you? If you really want to organize your Windows NT network, many tools are provided to you. Three of the most important tools are the System Policy Editor, home directories, and user profiles. You receive a good functional introduction to these tools in this chapter. They're not the easiest things in Windows NT to wrap your mind around, and they could take much more coverage than they get here. In this chapter I'm striving for conciseness and conveying direct understanding of some pretty complicated topics in Windows NT network management. Home directories in particular are a bit tricky and can affect several key areas of your network's functionality. They're also a bit of work to set up properly, no matter what you do.

The big payoff is better and safer network organization. When you have a large collection of users, you have to start thinking in different ways than you would for a small server-based network with, say, half a dozen users. In a situation like that, you can't afford to have any users that have access to an entire hard disk on the server. It's just too uneconomical and risky. Network organization is the compelling application for home directories – a way to have many different users participating on the network, without the performance penalties or the dangers of unfettered access by dozens of people to broad swaths of your system.

System policies, home directories, and user profiles are also Windows NT's key elements for addressing a controversial topic – simpler network administration. Many network administrators tend to tear their hair out over the issue of maintaining control of their desktop computers across the network. Although Windows NT's

417

capabilities in this area are not perfect, if you use the tools provided to you in this chapter properly, you'll make a lot more progress towards that goal than you expect. Appendix A discusses the associated topic of *thin, lean,* and *fat* clients, which are also of compelling interest to the overworked administrator.

When you work for organizations of more than a dozen or so people, you may also have to think about enforcing some consistency and predictability in your network environment. When companies roll out an operating system for clients and/or servers, many create specific policies governing how users are supposed to work with client computers. User accounts may be disallowed from having Network Neighborhood on their desktop, for example. Or users may have access only to certain prescribed applications. Although configuring an office application suite for use on a network is beyond the scope of this book, Windows NT offers capabilities to manage just such a situation with its System Policy Editor.

Leading off in this chapter, you learn about trust relationships, which are a strikingly simple mechanism for getting Windows NT domain servers to communicate and cooperate with each other. They are Windows NT's key mechanism for building larger, Enterprise-type networks. Within this simple trust mechanism, however, lies a very complicated tale.

Understanding Trust Relationships

If you have two separate domain servers that have some kind of physical network connection, even if they're on the same network segment, they do not automatically acknowledge each other. (Big surprise.) All other things being equal, such as the correct networking protocols being present on both servers, different domains still don't know the other exists. It's not like connecting another client to a Windows NT Server-based network. To effect a connection between two or more domain servers, you must create what is (somewhat endearingly) called a *trust relationship.*

Creating a trust relationship turns out to be strikingly easy. You need to know two minor pieces of information: which server is going to be *trusted,* and which server will be *trusting* the other. What do these two terms mean?

- A *trusted server* simply means that one server is given full administrative-level access rights to connect directly to another primary domain server. The connecting server is called a trusted domain.

- A *trusting domain* is the primary domain server that allows the administrative-level connection.

Say you have two domain servers, in different departments. If one domain is trusted by the other one, then you basically have a *one-way* trust relationship. This relationship has the following attributes:

◆ One domain server (the *trusted* one) can open and access resources from the other domain server (the *trusting* one), but the reverse is not true.

◆ User accounts from the *trusted* domain can join local groups on the other, *trusting* domain. The reverse is not true.

◆ The *trusted* domain can open network resources from the *trusting* domain and add user accounts and global groups from its own domain to that shared resource.

In Figure 12-1, domain TECHWRITING trusts the other domain named GRAPH-ICS, but not the other way around. In other words, just because TECHWRITING trusts GRAPHICS, that doesn't automatically mean that GRAPHICS trusts TECH-WRITING. Figure 12-1 sketches out the basic scheme.

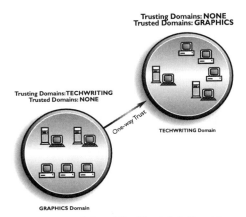

Figure 12-1: A One-Way Trust Relationship

In this situation, the administrator from the GRAPHICS domain can access resources from the TECHWRITING domain. Because of the one-way trust relationship, users from the GRAPHICS domain can even log on at workstations in the TECHWRITING domain. GRAPHICS domain user accounts can also be added to local (not global) groups in the TECHWRITING domain. Not only that, but the workstation *users* from the GRAPHICS domain can also access resources from the TECHWRITING domain. (I discuss how to do that later.)

The reverse is not true, however. Users and administrators from the TECHWRIT-ING domain cannot access information and resources from the GRAPHICS domain. They can't log on to workstations in the GRAPHICS domain or integrate their user accounts. Everything's a one-way street. You may also notice something else in Figure 12-1: The trusting domain is defined on the *trusted* domain server! Conversely, the trusted domain is set to be trusted on the *trusting* server. (I return to this point in a moment.)

You may think this is kind of unfair. After all, why should one domain get all the goodies and not share with the other? Leaving aside the ethical issues, many situations can arise in which such a trust relationship is appropriate. For example, an INFORMATION SYSTEMS domain might need to have trust relationships with several other domains so that data backups can be performed from each domain. However, the other domains would almost unquestionably not need a reciprocal capability.

All this sounds more complicated than it actually is to perform in your network. (But when you have many different domains in a company, many of which may need trust relationships, then things can get squirrelly in short order, as you'll soon see.)

But because a true relationship is built on mutual trust (no, this is not a manual about how to patch up a marriage), a highly useful inter-domain connection can be defined around both servers being both trusting and trusted. For two domains that have evenly matched security levels or a compelling reason to cooperate, you can easily create a *two-way* trust relationship. In such a case:

◆ Each of the two domain servers can open and access resources from the other domain server.

◆ User accounts from each domain can join local groups on the other, *trusting* domain.

Figure 12-2 depicts the essential characteristics of a two-way trust relationship.

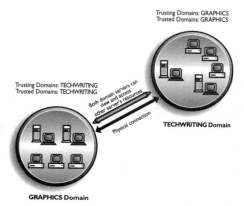

Figure 12-2: A Two-Way Trust Relationship

In a two-way setup, both domain servers can open and access each other's shared resources. Clients from both domains can log on to the other domain's workstations and see their *home* domain servers just as they normally would. User accounts from either domain can add their names to local groups on the other domain server.

Finally, another important point to keep in mind is that the trusted and trusting domains are both defined on the opposite server. Here's how it shakes out:

Host Domain: GRAPHICS

- ◆ Trusting Domain: TECHWRITING
- ◆ Trusted Domain: TECHWRITING

Host Domain: TECHWRITING

- ◆ Trusting Domain: GRAPHICS
- ◆ Trusted Domain: GRAPHICS

In the one-way trust relationship described earlier, here's how the relationship is defined:

Host Domain: GRAPHICS

- ◆ Trusting Domain: TECHWRITING
- ◆ Trusted Domain: NONE

Host Domain: TECHWRITING

- ◆ Trusting Domain: NONE
- ◆ Trusted Domain: GRAPHICS

With these two short lists, you have all the information you need to create either a one-way or two-way type of relationship; of course, you can substitute the names of your own servers for the examples above to create your own scheme. What is described here is just the beginning. The next section shows the basic mechanism for creating a trust relationship between two primary domain servers. Afterwards, I introduce you to the implications behind all this trust relationship stuff: how it's used to organize larger Windows NT networks, and the distinct shortcomings that Windows NT's domain-based model presents in an enterprise-wide network context.

Building a One-Way Trust Relationship

When you perform the process of building a trust relationship, you do so using the by-now familiar User Manager for Domains. One final point: For all the entries you perform in the next couple of exercises, you enter the names of the domains to be trusted or trusting — *not* the actual domain servers themselves. Here's how to set up a one-way trust relationship:

TIP   When you build a trust relationship, you use the domain names, not the
        server names.

1. Open the User Manager for Domains on the server that will be *trusted*.

2. From the Policies menu, select Trust Relationships. The Trust Relationships
   dialog box appears, as shown in Figure 12-3.

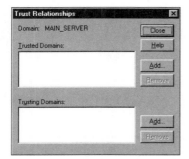

Figure 12-3: Opening UMD's Trust
Relationships Feature

In my sample network I have two domains: TEST_DOMAIN and
MAIN_SERVER. Those names appear in the next figures; you have to
substitute your own systems in the following steps. (If the server is not a
PDC or BDC, you cannot select the Trust relationships menu option; it is
grayed out.)

3. Click the Add button next to the Trusting Domains box. (Remember, this is
   done on the server that will be *trusted* in the connection between servers.)
   The Add Trusting Domain dialog box appears with a couple of simple text
   boxes, as shown in Figure 12-4.

Figure 12-4: Adding a Trusting Server
to the Server That Will Be Trusted in
the Relationship

Note you can add a password here and also confirm it. In most cases this should be unnecessary. The password only applies during the initial connection between the two servers, and since you may be the administrator for both servers (or even if you're not), a trust connection between two domain servers is so private and isolated from the rest of your network's connectivity that passwords may be beside the point. The decision is up to you and any other administrators you may be working with.

4. In the Trusting Domain text box, enter the name of the *other* domain — the one you plan to have as the trusting server to the current one. Also enter a password if need be (my default is to ignore it), and click OK.

5. Leave the Trusted Domains box, on top, empty. This ensures that the other server will not be able to connect.

6. Click Close. The domain is quickly added to the list. Finally, close the Trust Relationships dialog box. You're finished on that end for the one-way connection.

7. Now open the User Manager for Domains on the server that will be doing the *trusting*.

8. From the Policies menu, select Trust Relationships. The eponymous Trust Relationships dialog box appears, as shown previously in Figure 12-3.

9. Click the Add button adjacent to the Trusted Domains box. The Add Trusted Domain dialog box appears with a couple of simple text boxes, as shown in Figure 12-5.

Figure 12-5: Adding a Trusted Server
to the Trusting Domain Server

10. In the Domain text box, enter the name (and password, in the unlikely event that it's required) of the trusted domain — the one that you plan to allow access to from the current server. Click OK. If all goes well and your network is set up properly, you'll receive a message announcing a successful connection to the other server.

11. Leave the Trusting Domains box empty and click Close, and then close User Manager.

Setting up a one-way trust relationship is basically pretty simple. You just have to make sure both servers support the same protocols and, if they're running TCP/IP, that their name resolution services both work properly (preferably, they should mirror each other). Because TCP/IP is likely to be the standard protocol used in your network, you'll get quite a workout if something goes wrong. (Chapter 3 discusses TCP/IP networking and its various facilities in greater detail.)

Building a Two-Way Trust Relationship

Creating a two-way trust relationship is similar to creating a one-way trust relationship. In fact, you use the exact same entries on each server for both the trusting and the trusted domain. Follow these steps:

1. Open the User Manager for Domains on the server that will be "trusted."

2. From the Policies menu, select Trust Relationships. The Trust Relationships dialog box appears.

3. Click the Add button next to the Trusting Domains box. (Remember, this is done on the server that will be *trusted* in the connection between servers.) The Add Trusting Domain dialog appears.

4. In the Domain text box, enter the name of the *other* domain – the one that you plan to have as the trusting server to the current one. Also enter a password if needed (my default is to ignore it) and click OK.

5. Click the Add button next to the Trusted Domains box. The Add Trusted Domain dialog box appears.

6. In the Domain text box, enter the name (and password, if desired) of the same Windows NT domain – the one you just entered as the Trusting server. Click OK. You'll receive the message announcing a successful connection to the other server.

7. Click Close. The domain is quickly added to the list. Finally, close the Trust Relationships dialog box. You're finished on that end for its connection.

8. Now open the User Manager for Domains on the other server.

9. From the Policies menu, select Trust Relationships.

10. Follow Steps 3-7 for the second domain server, always keeping in mind that you must name the other domain, the one you just worked on, as the Trusted and Trusting entries.

The only slightly odd thing about setting up a connection like this is that you must specify the opposite server for both the trusting and trusted systems. You'd expect to define the trusting domain on its actual server, but that turns out not to be the case.

No matter how your domain servers are connected, they must have an explicitly defined trust relationship. Say you had three different domains: GRAPHICS, TECHWRITING, and ISDEPARTMENT. The ISDEPARTMENT domain is a *trusted* server for TECHWRITING, which means that ISDEPARTMENT can access the TECHWRITING domain server and its resources. The TECHWRITING domain is a *trusted* domain for the GRAPHICS domain, which means that TECHWRITING can access GRAPHICS. Does this mean, as a result, that the ISDEPARTMENT domain server can communicate with the GRAPHICS domain server? No! Trust relationship connections are not passed on through servers. Every domain server-domain server connection must be explicitly defined. Figure 12-6 illustrates exactly what I mean here.

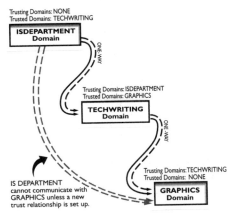

Figure 12-6: Domain Relationships Are Not Passed Through

Anytime you expect a domain server to have communications with another, a trust relationship must be established.

Accessing Shared Resources Across Domains

When your domain users want to access shared resources across domains, the process is fairly simple.

- ◆ Any share that includes the Everyone group can be accessed across domains. When trust relationships are established, the Everyone group on any domain server includes all users from *any* trusted domains.

- ◆ Use the normal Share-level permissions to search for individual groups and user accounts on the other trusted domains. Then add them to the resource's share permissions in the normal way.

Here's how to assign cross-domain user accounts to trusting domain resources:

1. On the *trusting* domain (one allowing the other server to access it), right-click a shared resource such as a hard disk, folder, or printer, and select Sharing from the shortcut menu. The Properties sheet for the resource appears, displaying the Sharing tab.

2. Select the correct share name from the Share Name list, and click Permissions. The Access Through Share Permissions dialog box appears, showing the existing list of users and groups that can access the resource.

3. Click Add. The Add Users and Groups dialog box appears.

4. Select the List Names From list in Add Users and Groups. A list of currently trusting domains appears, as shown in Figure 12-7.

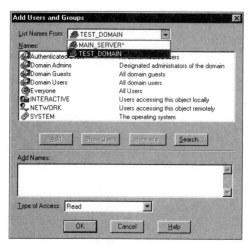

Figure 12-7: Locating Other Domains in Add
Users and Groups

5. Note in Figure 12-7 that two Windows NT domains are listed: TEST_DOMAIN and MAIN_SERVER. (These are not the actual servers; they are Windows NT domains.) The asterisk next to the MAIN_SERVER entry indicates the host domain for this operation. Your names, of course, will be different, not to mention that you can have more than two domains in the list, depending on how many trust relationships you have.

6. Select the desired domain in the List Names From list.

The selected domain's Global domain groups appear automatically.

7. To reveal the other domain's user accounts, simply click Show Users.

8. Select as many user account names or global groups as desired and click the Add button. Check the Type of Access list for proper access levels for the accounts.

9. Click OK, and then click OK again to finish up the Permissions setup.

10. Finally, click OK to close the Properties sheet and commit the Shares.

This is a rather elegant solution to interdomain resource sharing.

If you never need to do anything else with it, establishing a trust relationship is a nifty and relatively simple method to get two or three Windows NT domains to communicate with each other. When you've completed the connections for a two-way relationship, it does seem simple. But there's a serious issue involved with Windows NT's domain-based system. Once a network grows beyond a certain point using a domain-based system, it begins to resemble a briar patch.

Explaining the Various Domain Models

Consider for a moment how a trust relationship system would work with, say, 20 or 30 different domains. Imagine if several domains or more had two-way relationships with each other. To understand just how complicated trust relationships can be, you also have to know something about how larger Windows NT networks can be organized. Four key models are available for Windows NT network organization:

- Single-domain
- Single-master domain
- Multiple-master domain
- Fully trusted multiple-master domain

Each of these models is described in the sections below. As you read each one, you'll get a quick appreciation of the escalating levels of complexity that result from employing the simple trust Relationships tool in larger networks.

Single Domain

A single-domain system can contain more than one server and many clients. Everything is gathered into the one domain. Any administrative account can manage any server or client on the network. Local groups can function throughout the network, and no trust relationships need to be defined. It's a good model for small businesses and organizations that don't require separate departmental areas such as different floors or buildings. The downside is that performance suffers as more and more resources and clients are loaded onto the network. The best way to limit performance problems is to split off as many service functions onto other servers within the domain as you can — a separate WINS server, for example. But this model is decidedly the slow-growth method.

Single-Master Domain

A single-master domain system proves to be a very capable network arrangement. Building on the trust relationship methods you've already explored, single-master domain is probably the most economical and logical way to organize a multi-domain network for a small-to-medium-size company.

In a situation similar to that shown in Figure 12-8, trust relationships are strictly one-way. (They don't always have to be this way; secondary domains can conceivably have trust relationships as well, but it's a good foundation.) The master domain provides the highest level of server machine power, and no clients are directly connected to the master domain, except perhaps one for remote management. The master domain is the main hub for the network. Backup domain controllers are a necessity here, because the account databases for the entire network are maintained on the Primary and Backup Domain Controllers (BDC) in the master domain. All network clients and users are connected to the secondary domains, as are many key resources such as printers.

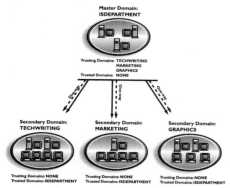

Figure 12–8: Illustrating a Single-Master Domain Architecture

It gets more complicated, but not much. All global groups and user accounts originate from the master domain. Department-level servers can offer their own local groups. If a company has several decently delineated departments and expects to grow in the future, this model is the best one to start with. This model's greatest vulnerability is that it provides a single point of failure. If the master domain server goes down, the network is crippled, even though basic services can be maintained through the BDC. Also, whenever a client needs account authorization, it must go through the master domain server, which can slow things down.

Multiple-Master Domain

A multiple-master domain network provides many of the same advantages as a single-master domain, with two compelling strengths and two compelling weaknesses. Strengths include:

◆ Maintenance of central administration.

◆ Multiple-master domains provide a better fail-safe defense against a catastrophic point of failure.

The weaknesses are:

◆ Local and global groups must be defined, modified, and maintained in more than one location on the network.

◆ More complicated trust relationships between domains.

◆ All accounts cannot be present (or replicated) across all master domains. They must be distributed more or less equally among the masters.

Through its weaknesses, the domain-based/trust system begins to break down, although it's still manageable.

When you look at Figure 12-9, the first thing you think is that most companies have more departments than that. And so it is. The only domains that have a two-way trust relationship are the two (or more) master domains. All other trust connections are one-way, from the master domains (the trusted ones) to the secondary domains (the trusting ones). All secondary domains possess the same one-way trusting relationships with each master domain. Again, no clients are directly connected to the master domains except for a remote management workstation.

You can also perform basic load balancing. User accounts can be distributed across the master domains in whatever scheme seems most logical: by alphabetic order or by groups roughly corresponding to each department. No user account appears more than once, however. Alphabetic schemes seem to have more favor with many experts in this area because accounts don't have to be messed with as much when users move around between departments. Global group management is made more time-consuming, however.

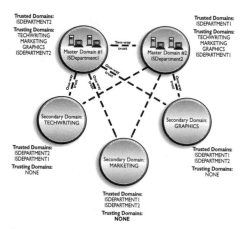

Figure 12-9: Illustrating a Multiple-Master Domain Architecture

Now, can you imagine what this would look like if you had seven or eight different departmental domains connected as secondaries to your master domains? The only thing that limits the complexity at all is that most of the trust relationships are one-way affairs. (Does this sound vaguely Freudian?) That makes things a bit easier.

This is nothing, though. Although multiple-master is a good scheme and provides good room for growth, you can go beyond this.

Fully-Trusted Multiple-Master

A fully-trusted multiple-master network assumes that every single domain in the enterprise, secondaries and masters, possesses a two-way trust relationship with every other domain regardless of type. This can get quite bloody, as Figure 12-10 indicates.

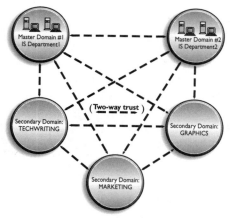

Figure 12-10: Illustrating a Fully-Trusted Multiple-Master Domain Scheme

Every department's domain really requires a separate administrator at this level. You need to have faith in the other administrators on the network.

What are the advantages to such a system? None are especially compelling. Whatever advantages exist in this scheme are also present in the standard, one-way multiple-master model. Those advantages are more than countered here by the distinctly web-like latticework of two-way trust relationships that ensue from the logical extreme of building a network in this fashion. And this is a small example; as noted, most companies carry far more departments than are illustrated here. After a point, the number of domains in the network makes such an enterprise interconnection almost too complicated.

Consider how many domains you have in your network. Say you have 10, including the master domains (this is by no means unlikely). It's quite simple to calculate how many trust relationships you need in this case. The basic formula is

$$n * (n - 1) = \text{\# of trust relationships}$$

Here, n = 10, so the result is

$$10 * (10 - 1) = 90!$$

Each individual domain requires a total of *nine* trust connections. (In Figure 12-10, five domains require a total of 20 trust connections, with four for each domain.)

Building networks of this type is far beyond the scope of this book. You can also see why other operating systems using directory services, such as NetWare, tend to be better suited for larger enterprise networks. It's also a reason why Microsoft plans to roll out Active Directory services with Windows NT 5.0. Domain-based networks are fairly easy to maintain and construct, *up to a point*. After a certain level of complexity, the domain system starts to become nearly unmanageable. For a larger network, a Fully-Trusted scheme is impractical.

One thing I can suggest doing to document a complex web of trust relationships is to use truth tables. For example, say you were to create a truth table showing the trusting domains for a multiple-master domain network consisting of five domains (MIS1, MKTG, TECH, GRPH, and MIS2, perhaps). The setup is strictly two master domains and three secondaries, with no two-way trust relationships except that between the master domains. Table 12-1, which corresponds to Figure 12-9, shows how such a truth table might appear.

You can see how the basic mechanism is preserved. Obviously, IS1 cannot trust itself (another Freudian slip), as is also the case with IS2 and any of the secondaries. Each column/row intersection represents a case where a trusting or trusted relationship does or does not exist according to the basic scheme. For example, in the MKTG row there are no trusting domains. In the MKTG column, two trusted domains are present: IS1 and IS2. This corresponds to the network depicted in Figure 12-9.

TABLE 12-1 A TRUTH TABLE FOR A SMALL MULTIPLE-MASTER DOMAIN NETWORK

Multiple-Master Domain Trusted Domains

		IS1	MKTG	TECH	GRPH	IS2
Trusting Domains	IS1	0	1	1	1	1
	MKTG	0	0	0	0	0
	TECH	0	0	0	0	0
	GRPH	0	0	0	0	0
	IS2	1	1	1	1	0

Table 12-1 shows a relatively simple setup. As your network gets more complicated, your diagrams and truth tables will be equally complex. After a certain point, diagrams are almost impossible, and lists/tables of trusting and trusted servers are the only feasible way to document complicated trust connections.

You've probably had just about enough of the concept of managing an enterprise-wide Windows NT network. This section has given you most of the basic tools to at least *design* one. As you can see, designing a network can take some significant planning. Implementing it is quite another matter. Now I'll turn to a more user-oriented method for creating a consistent network: system policies.

Using the System Policy Editor

If you're curious about ways to ensure that your client users have a consistent user interface, you can do two things. You can just let everyone use the basic Windows NT interface, with no restrictions at all and the freedom to do whatever they want, or you can impose some control and use the management features built into Windows NT — the System Policy Editor and user profiles. With these key features you can ensure that users "who know enough to be dangerous" can't cause any trouble in the larger network.

What Is the Registry?

Up to this point in the book, the Registry has barely been mentioned. That's by design, because the Registry is a highly sensitive and complex underpinning of the Windows 95 and Windows NT operating systems. Where Windows 3.1 used WIN.INI and SYSTEM.INI files (plus a huge collection of application-specific INI files) to manage and configure how Windows runs, Windows 95/Windows NT gathers most key aspects of system configuration into a crucial database called the Registry.

Many Windows NT books describe registry editing procedures and methods. In fact, entire books exist on the topic. The key utility for browsing, inspecting, and editing the registry is a program called REGEDIT.EXE, which is located in the C:\WINNT directory. Figure 12-11 shows the Registry Editor screen.

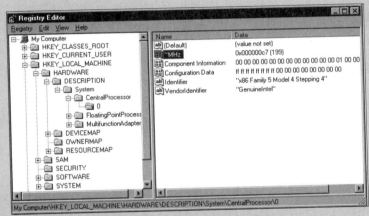

Figure 12-11: Viewing the Registry with Registry Editor

REGEDIT isn't present on the Start menu or the Administrative Tools group, although you can place it there. Editing individual values isn't usually too difficult, but some values are quite obscure, and it always seems that the most obscure and hard-to-read values are the most critical to the system. If you're a serious registry hacker, you'll have to find another source of more complete information, because this is mainly an introductory book. Intensive registry editing is far beyond the scope of this chapter. Also note that Windows NT offers a REGEDT32.EXE program, which is also widely used and offers the same powerful features as REGEDIT.

Instead of battling with the complications of directly editing Registry settings with the REGEDIT program, the network manager can employ a more graceful solution, at least for specific applications: the System Policy Editor. The Editor provides an efficient, easy method for editing key client settings for any Windows NT client on the network. The Editor's primary use is for determining the look and feel of your client computers' desktops *en masse*. Key configuration settings can also be made. This has several benefits for the administrator:

◆ **Consistent management.** Create policy templates so that every client can use them without tweaking and changing profiles for each client.

◆ **One-point integration and security.** Create a domain-wide system policy that's activated and used by all clients when they log on to the network. You can also enforce use of screen savers and associated password security on all the desktops of the connected network, thereby severely limiting the potential for prying eyes in someone's cubicle.

◆ **Good client support.** Use System Policy Editor for Windows NT *and* Windows 95 clients. Windows 95 systems must support user profiles, which is not automatically done in that operating system.

◆ **Interface consistency.** Define uniform front-end interfaces for all Windows NT clients on the network. Templates can be applied for consistent Registry entry settings on Windows 95 and Windows NT clients.

◆ **Simpler use restriction.** Regulate certain desktop features, including the Display Control Panel, network browsing through the Explorer, permitted applications, restrictions on registry editing, and many others.

◆ **Simple client Registry modification.** Modify the contents of a client computer's Registry without recourse to risky and complicated editor programs.

You already know that the User Manager provides the key features for creating and setting access permissions for the clients on your network. You've also glanced at User Profiles in Chapter 2 of this book. While it's not a complete substitute for user profiles, the System Policy Editor provides a tool for uniform management of all those accounts and groups in your network. Policies can only be edited on Windows NT Server.

Policies can also be added and modified for user accounts, specific groups, and domain groups. I strongly recommend making your changes as global and uniform as possible for simplification of user-management tasks. The larger a network is, the more important that many facets of it be as manageable and predictable as possible. Specific user accounts, such as your boss, can still have special treatment.

The System Policy Editor also provides limited but useful features for editing and changing the contents of each client computer's System Registry. But navigating the Editor isn't at all like using the REGEDIT program. Hierarchical lists of check boxes are provided for easy modification of User property settings, as shown in Figure 12-12.

Selecting a check box displays the setting

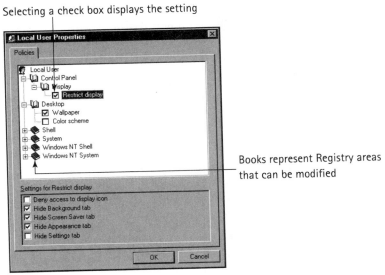

Books represent Registry areas
that can be modified

Figure 12-12: Changing Policy Properties

Book icons contain areas of the client's Registry. You can double-click a book or click its plus sign to move down the hierarchy, eventually uncovering individual settings.

The System Policy Editor works on two key categories of Registry entries, titled HKEY_CURRENT_USER and HKEY_LOCAL_MACHINE. Even in this area, the Editor hides some of the complexities from you. When you open a user's account, you'll see two icons — the computer and the user's actual account, as shown in Figure 12-13.

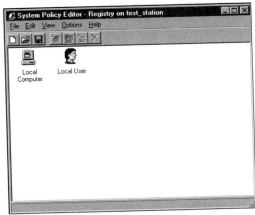

Figure 12-13: Exploring System Policy Elements

Double-clicking either icon displays its policies list. Individual check boxes represent Registry listings for the client computer. Policy categories for client computers are shown in Table 12-2.

TABLE 12-2 LOCAL/DEFAULT COMPUTER POLICY SETTINGS

Categories	Function
Network	Enables or disables remote updating of client System Policies.
System	Provides a few basic tools for network performance monitoring using SNMP (Simple Network Management Protocol.) SNMP is supported by Windows NT and must be installed through the Network applet in Control Panel. (More on SNMP below.)
Windows NT Network	Enables or disables the creation of hidden default drive shares.
Windows NT Printers	Provides a few settings for print server interaction, including error beeping on the client.
Windows NT Remote Access	More settings for clients and networked machines for interaction with their Remote Access Service.
Windows NT Shell	Enables the use of shared Programs and Startup folders, Start menu, and desktop icon arrangements.
Windows NT System	Provides client Logon and File System settings, including special logon banners (messages, greetings, or warnings that appear immediately after the user presses Ctrl+Alt-Del), execution of logon scripts before Windows NT boot-up resumes, and long/short file name settings.
Windows NT User Profiles	A few user profile settings for detection and timeout of slow network connections, and removal of cached roaming profiles (to save disk space).

Local User settings concentrate on individual user accounts. Although the categories are fewer, several go into considerable detail regarding user interface settings for the user account. Those categories are shown in Table 12-3.

TABLE 12-3 LOCAL/DEFAULT USER POLICY SETTINGS

Categories	Function
Control Panel	Settings for the Display applet in Control Panel, including whether to even display it, and which tabs to display in the applet.
Desktop	Determines the client settings for overall appearance, including background wallpaper and color scheme.
Shell	Numerous adjustments for networked clients and how they interact with the user interface. Elements in the Start Menu, Network Neighborhood, My Computer, and others can be changed to appear or disappear in the user's profile, regardless of what system they log on to. This is one area where you'll probably spend a lot of time experimenting and defining uniform interface settings for your users.
System	Provides a feature for disabling Registry editing on the clients using the policy, and a list defining which application programs can be run by the user account.
Windows NT Shell	Allows you to define a custom user interface for the user account, such as a third-party solution or the use of Windows NT Explorer as the main interface. Custom folders, Start menus, and other elements can be loaded by the user account during logon. The Restrictions sub-category allows the removal of various features from the Start menu, such as Common program groups (Administrative Tools is an example). Other networking features can be disabled, such as Map Network Drive and Disconnect Network Drive.
Windows NT System	Enables inclusion of AUTOEXEC.BAT batch file commands in the user's environment (a relatively rare thing in Windows NT) along with minor tweaks to run batch files before continuing with the boot-up sequence, disabling the use of Task Manager, and showing welcome tips at logon.

General-use system policies employ the same settings as for individual Registry editing functions.

As you can see, the Policy Editor doesn't go too deeply into crucial Registry settings. Some of the settings are trivial, particularly on the local computer side. Some, especially on the local user, can be used to craft uniform interfaces across the network, and to aid in creating roaming user profiles; these are the functional areas on which you'll concentrate.

Although it's easy to make changes to Registry settings in this context, you must still exercise caution. Changing one Registry setting can render a system unusable or cripple important areas of client functionality. When you make new policies for a user account, domain group, or entire domain, back up your existing policy files and Registries first (they're defined with the suffix .POL). You can also take advantage of Windows NT's support for long filenames by employing dating and naming conventions that clearly indicate the position and role of a policy file in your network's history.

Another problem with the System Policy Editor is its primitive interface. Little or no online help is provided. Many features either provide no clue about how to locate particular items for lists or require hand-edited entries. The System Policy Editor, in short, does not match Windows NT's normal user interface specifications and thus presents some annoyances to the administrator.

Connecting to a Network Client's Registry

One extremely handy and convenient Policy Editor feature is its capability to easily connect to a client's System Registry. If your network clients are all connected, all you have to do is select the File menu and choose Connect. The Connect dialog box appears, as shown in Figure 12-14, bearing a text box for entering the client name.

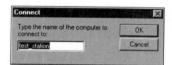

Figure 12-14: Connecting to a Network Client Through the Policy Editor

Click OK and the name of the current user on that client system appears (see Figure 12-15).

Figure 12-15: Viewing the User Account Logged On to the Client

Click OK again. Then the Local Computer and Local User icons appear (refer to Figure 12-13), and the title bar for the Policy Editor changes to display the name of the connected client (*Registry on test_station,* for example). After you connect through the Policy Editor, you've chosen to administer the policy for both the client computer and the user account. When you do so, you'll need to make sure that the user's account is the right one for the task at hand. If not, don't make changes to that account's settings while you're in the Editor, or chase any users off the system. (Hey! You don't belong here!)

When the two icons appear, you are connected to the client's Registry. Double-clicking either icon brings up its Properties window, with the Registry listings described in Tables 12-2 and 12-3. The changes you make to the local user only apply to that user account's profile *on that particular machine*; if the user was to move over to another system and log on, assuming they had proper permissions to do so, the new user profile settings will not migrate with them unless their profile is set to be roaming. (roaming user profiles are discussed later in this book.)

For now, if you want to make changes to the local server's policy, simply choose Open Registry from the File menu. The same icons (Local Computer and Local User) will appear. Unfortunately, the Policy editor doesn't preserve the naming conventions, so it's fairly easy to lose track of whose settings you're monkeying with. The title bar provides the name of the policy, so naming conventions can also be quite helpful here.

Changing Policy Settings

After you've connected to the client or opened the registry directly on the server, you can change any available settings for that system. In this example you set up a sample account to change various aspects of their desktop when they log on, including their Display applet in Control Panel, Start menu settings, a password-protected screen saver, and the items that appear in Network Neighborhood. Then you'll find out how to apply settings of the same type to a global Policy. Follow these steps:

1. Double-click the Local User icon for the connected system in the Policy Editor. The Local User Properties sheet appears, showing a list of *book* icons containing their various Registry settings.

2. Double-click the Control Panel book. The Display book appears. Its Restrict Display tri-state check box is grayed out by default, as shown in Figure 12-16.

3. Click in the Restrict Display check box to enable it. The five Settings check boxes are activated.

4. Select all the Settings check boxes except Deny access to display icon and Background. The Deny access check box blocks the appearance of the Display icon in the client's Control Panel. If all four of the other check boxes are enabled, the Display icon appears but does not open up. (This is just an example.)

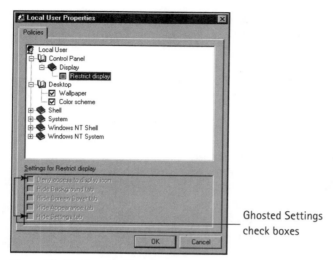

Figure 12-16: Opening User Account
Registry Settings

Ghosted Settings
check boxes

5. Click OK.

6. From the File menu, click Save.

7. On the client's system, open the Control Panel and open Display. (You won't have to restart the system in this case.) Figure 12-17 shows the results of the new settings on the Display properties sheet.

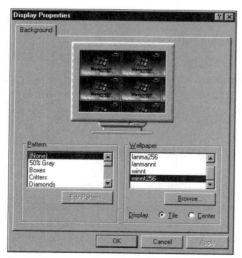

Figure 12-17: The Display Applet's Contents
Are Radically Changed

In Figure 12-17, a single tab is displayed instead of the normal four or five. (Some video card drivers add their own tabs to this applet.) Some Registry settings don't require a restart or a new logon to test their effects on the client. Most do require it. Here's an example of how to alter the user interface for a client's User account:

1. Connect to the client computer in System Policy Editor.

2. Open the Local User Properties sheet by double-clicking the Local User icon.

3. Double-click the Shell book. The Restrictions book appears. Double-click that, and a long list of check boxes appears, as shown in Figure 12-18.

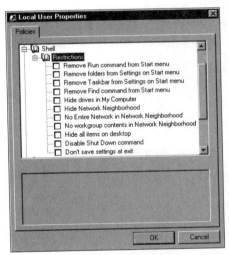

Figure 12-18: Opening Shell Settings in the User's Registry

4. Enable the following check boxes:

   ◆ Remove Run command from Start menu

   ◆ Remove Find command from Start menu

   ◆ Hide all items on desktop

   ◆ Don't save settings at exit

5. As you can imagine, the possibilities for practical jokes are almost limitless (Hide all items on desktop?). Some settings are somewhat dangerous, such as the Disable Shut Down command. After all, Windows NT has been known to crash on occasion, shocking as that may be to some readers. Other check boxes allow the administrator to limit the number of items that show up in Network Neighborhood, such as the No Entire Network or No Workgroup Contents check boxes. In any case, click OK.

6. From the File menu in System Policy Editor, choose Save. Then restart the client. Figure 12-19 shows a different Windows NT Workstation computer screen.

Figure 12-19: A Heavily Modified Client Screen, Done with Registry Edits from the System Editor

As you can see, a drastically shortened Start menu is provided to the user. Every icon previously displayed on the desktop has also been removed. I don't suggest you do this for all your clients, but it is an example of what you can do to simplify and alter how your collection of users interact with their systems.

Some aspects of the System Policy Editor are not particularly easy to work with, and they give the impression of an application that was basically slapped together at the last moment. For a good example of this, open the Local User's Properties sheet and double-click the System book. Then double-click the Restrictions book. Select the Run Only Allowed Windows Applications check box. Figure 12-20 shows what you should see.

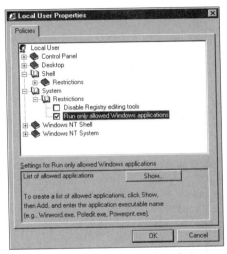

Figure 12-20: Inspecting the Run Only
Allowed Windows Applications Setting

Merely enabling this check box and saving the Registry changes prevents the client user from running *any* programs on their system, other than those you specify. This includes any Administrative Tools, Windows NT Explorer, and any other application in the system. Click the Show button on Figure 12-20. A list of allowed applications appears. Now click the Add button. A minimalistic Add Item dialog box appears, as shown in Figure 12-21.

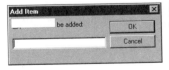

Figure 12-21: Attempting to Add an Application to the
Allowed List

In fact, not only do you have no way to browse for the desired applications, as is normal for Windows NT (you must type in the entire path from memory), but there's even a display bug in the actual feature, in the top left. (Many of the Policy Editor's features simply provide a Path text box without any browsing or search capability.) Use Windows NT Explorer to locate the program, type its path in the dialog box, and click OK. Figure 12-22 shows an example.

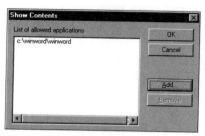

Figure 12-22: A Sample App List

Unfortunately, it's not self-evident whether you're supposed to specify the local path on the server to the application, or the path according to the mapped Network drive on the client, or *the local path on the client*. In either case, the entry is not likely to work. The client may also receive spurious error messages during startup.

Windows NT is a very capable application server; the System Policy Editor's capabilities in that particular area are almost laughably bad. You have several different ways to approach application serving through Windows NT; using the Policy Editor is possibly not the best method. It is a way to go if you want to lock users away from using those classic time-wasting programs such as Minesweeper, FreeCell, or Solitaire. If that's the case, your boss will thank you and maybe even send you to Tahiti. (Fat chance.) In general, user interface configurations work much better through the Policy Editor.

Adding Users and Domain Groups to a New Policy

When you're in the process of crafting a new system policy, you can add any user account, group, or even a specific Windows NT Workstation computer to it. This allows you to select parts of the network, such as an individual department or part of a department, to run under a particular policy while other areas of the network can make use of entirely different settings. Policies can be more flexible. Here's how to apply it:

1. In the System Policy Editor, from the File menu select New Policy. A new Policy, with Default Computer and Default User objects, is created in the Editor.

2. To add new users, from the Edit menu select New User. The Add User dialog box appears. Here you can browse for user accounts on the server.

3. Click the Browse button. The Add Users dialog box appears, as shown in Figure 12-23.

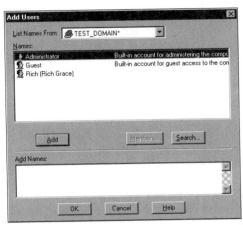

Figure 12-23: Adding User Accounts to a New Policy

4. If you want to select more than one account, hold the Shift key down as you click each account name.

5. Click Add and the accounts are added to the Add Names list box. Finally, click OK in the dialog box. New accounts are added to the policy.

6. To add Domain groups to the policy, select Add Group from the Edit menu. (Domain groups are the only type you can include. You can also click the Add Group button in the Policy Editor's toolbar.) Type in the name of the group and press Enter, or click Browse to view the list of groups on the server.

Here's where another quirk of the Policy Editor surfaces. If you click Browse, you'll see that only the global Domain groups are listed, as in Figure 12-24.

Domain Admins, Domain Guest, and Domain Users are the only groups available. The quirk is that if you just type the name of any group in the Add Group window and click OK, the program will accept it uncritically. Unfortunately, other groups besides the three Global domain groups won't work correctly. You won't even get an error message – the changes will simply fail to happen. In this area, the Policy Editor fails to provide user feedback for which most of the operating system's other features are much more effective. You can only use Global domain groups – so plan your policy installations accordingly.

Global (domain) groups are displayed

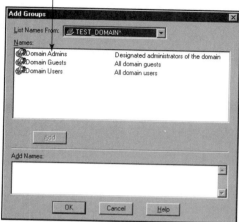

Figure 12-24: Attempting to Add an
Application to the Allowed List

7. Select the Domain groups you want included in the new policy, click Add, and click OK.

Figure 12-25 shows the results for a typical policy.

Figure 12-25: Users and Groups in a Policy

Your policy list could be much larger than this. Even better, all your user accounts could be gathered within your groups, minimizing the amount of work you'd have to do to set up their desktop configurations.

To add a networked computer to the mix:

1. From the Edit menu, select Add Computer. The Add Computer dialog box appears.

2. Click the Browse button. One of System Policy Editor's nice features appears: the Browse for Computer dialog box. It's a hierarchical list of the contents of your Network Neighborhood, and an example is shown in Figure 12-26.

Figure 12-26: Browsing the Network Neighborhood for Client Computer Additions to the Policy

3. The Policy Editor is a bit deceptive here. You can locate your Windows 95 clients in the Browse for Computer list. Since Windows 95 machines can't be direct members of a Windows NT domain (which seems pretty stupid when you think about it), they can't easily participate in system policies or user profiles. Nonetheless, you can select and add Windows 95 computers to the policy from here. Any new settings will simply not work, so don't bother. You can only use Windows NT computers in the policy system.

    Windows NT clients and servers who are members of the domain show up at the top level of the hierarchy.

4. Browse through the network until you locate the desired Windows 95 (or Windows NT) computer, and then select it, as shown in Figure 12-27 (the list may be much longer than is shown here).

5. Click OK.

Continue the same process until all your user accounts, computers, and/or groups are added to the desired policy. Then select each object and edit its settings accordingly. The only problem with this approach is that it's hard to know what you're going to do with it: where it's supposed to go when you're finished, how each system's Registry settings are affected, and so on. There's a better way to go, one which not only enforces consistency for your network clients but is much simpler to perform. That is to create a global policy.

Figure 12-27: Selecting a Computer
in the Policy Editor

Creating a Global Domain Policy

You'll find the easiest way to create a consistent system policy is to make it global. Unfortunately, the Policy Editor doesn't make how to do this explicit. There is a particular method for doing so, however.

In some of your client logons, you may have noticed that a folder called NETL-OGON keeps showing up when you open the domain server. The NETLOGON folder is used as a global "catch-all" for configuration information that you want all your clients to use when they log on to the network. Often, this folder remains empty. Creating a default policy that can be used throughout the domain (with the exception of Windows 95 clients) requires that you set up your policy and save it out to this NETLOGON folder. Fortunately, that's not hard to do, but there are a couple of tricks to it. Follow these steps:

1. Open the System Policy Editor.

2. From the File menu, select New Policy. A new policy appears, with the familiar Default Computer and Default User objects. Those are the only ones you'll need.

3. Open the Default Computer object and edit its settings according to your requirements. (For example, add a Logon banner under Windows NT System, Logon.)

4. Open the Default User settings and define your settings in each desired category.

5. From the File menu, select Save As. In the normal file views for the Save or Save As dialog boxes, you won't see the NETLOGON folder.

Also, the policy file must be named "Windows NTCONFIG." This name is required for clients to properly use it during their logons. (This doesn't apply to Windows 95 clients.)

6. To save your new global policy, enter the UNC (Universal Naming Convention) path to the server's NETLOGON folder. An example is:

\\test_server\NETLOGON\Windows NTCONFIG

where Windows NTCONFIG is the required name for the file. (The .POL suffix is automatically but invisibly added to it by the program.) The only significant change in your own entry will be the name for your actual server. Figure 12-28 shows an example.

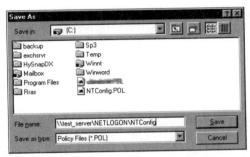

Figure 12-28: Selecting a Computer in the Policy Editor

7. With the path properly entered, click Save.

If you run into the problem of not being able to save the Windows NTCONFIG.POL file in the NETLOGON folder, your sharing capabilities for that folder haven't been set up on the server for the Administrator account. You'll receive an error message. Fortunately, this is easy to fix.

8. Open the Server Manager (in the Administrative Tools menu from the Start menu).

9. In the Server Manager, select the Primary Domain Controller listing.

10. From the Computer menu, select Shared Directories. The Shared Directores dialog box appears, as shown in Figure 12-29.

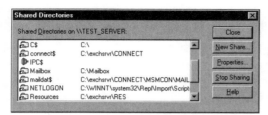

Figure 12-29: Opening the NETLOGON Folder
in Server Manager

The NETLOGON folder should appear in the dialog box, because even if it's hidden in your server, which is normal, it's the logon server share for all your network clients and thus is an element in Server Manager.

11. Scroll through the Shared Directories list and select the NETLOGON folder.

12. Click the Properties button. The Share Properties dialog box appears, as shown in Figure 12-30.

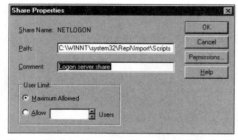

Figure 12-30: Changing Share Properties in Server Manager

13. Click the Permissions button. The Access Through Share Permissions dialog box appears, which should look rather familiar at this point.

14. Add the Administrator account to the share list, and give that account Full Control (from the Type of Access list) over the share for the NETLOGON folder.

15. Click OK, click OK again to close Share Properties, and click Close to close the Shared Directories dialog box.

16. Finally, close the Server Manager. You should now be able to save your new default policy in the NETLOGON folder. You'll have to enter the UNC path name in the Save As dialog box, as shown in Figure 12-31.

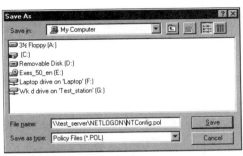

Figure 12-31: Issuing the Proper UNC Path in
the Policy Editor's Save As Dialog Box

Make sure the file is called Windows NTCONFIG.POL.

This is by far the best way to create a global policy setup. Any logon banners (from the Default Computer Registry settings) will appear when the clients log back on to the network, and user account Registry settings are also executed. Global policies override any individual client settings that may have been defined in the local Registry.

Each part of a system policy has some intriguing settings. One of the best things to do is to simply experiment with them and see what they can do, bearing in mind that you do have to be somewhat careful as noted earlier. As you'll see in the later section describing user profiles, a system policy can be combined with profiles to provide consistent, reliable Windows NT desktops for your users — even if more than one person uses the same workstation during the course of a long workday or over multiple work shifts.

The security features of the System Policy Editor are an important facet of your work, especially if you plan to administer a reasonably large network. Security is critical, and in many cases it may be a good idea to remove features like the Control Panel or even Network Neighborhood from your users' desktops. Allowing client users unfettered access to the Control Panel, with its sensitive Network applet, is most decidedly not a wise move. There's a good chance that you'll have to use the System Policy feature of Windows NT in more depth than we've been able to convey here. But now you have a good introduction to it.

A Note on Creating New Policy Templates

When you create a new policy containing all your user accounts in their appropriate groups, you would expect the policy of those accounts to be fluid, moving with the user to whichever client they happen to be using. That is not the case. A user's individual policy or user profile characteristics (which is what it is) are saved on the Registry for their primary client computer, and that's it. Policy information does not "roam" around with them. The nearest approximation of this technique is to use the global policies as described above.

System Policy Editor is one Windows NT feature that could use some serious revamping. There are interface flaws throughout; the program makes you work much too hard to issue a simple Permitted Application list, which *should* be, but isn't, a key capability of what is otherwise a very useful application server system. Many other policy settings behave in similarly cryptic ways. It'd also be nice to be able to use local groups in policies. More than anything else, it would be nice to be able to define true roaming user profiles within the central System Policy Editor utility (or in a better substitute application), because that's the logical place for it. In any case, I discuss how to create a roaming profile later in this chapter.

The next topic at hand is the process of creating home directories on the server for your collection of users, and mapping those home directories to a client's drive letter so they can access and use it easily. This is another Windows NT management feature that should enable you to use those system policies with greater discretion. Though use of home directories in Windows NT is another feature that could also use some refinement, it also can be a powerful feature for network client management.

Understanding Home Directories

Essentially, a *home directory* is a special folder on the server that's assigned to a specific client, and *only* to that client. There are some subtle tricks to creating and enabling home directories for a large collection of users. Home directories aren't mandatory for use on Windows NT Server, but they're definitely a good thing to have.

I've already touched upon the subject of home directories in Chapter 2. The first thing you need to know about home directories is that you're well-advised to create them in the first place, but that they'll require some work to get it right. If you define a complete set of home directories for your users and have them always save their company-related work data to those directories, you'll be able to ensure consistent, effective data backup policies. (The Backup facility for Windows NT is, in a word, pathetic. I discuss backup solutions in Chapter 13.)

When you create user profiles, you'll notice that the home directory feature is also present in the same dialog box when you inspect or create the settings for a user profile, shown in Figure 12-32.

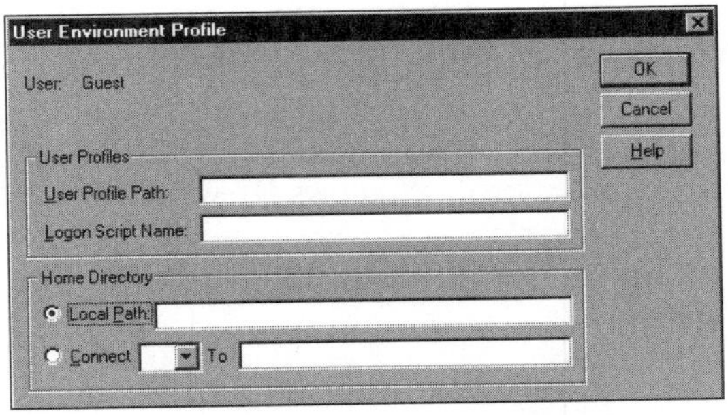

Figure 12-32: Opening a User Account's Profile Features

There's a certain amount (actually, a lot) of confusion that can be involved in creating and using home directories. It's our aim in this section to dispel that confusion, or at least to help you navigate that confusion to get the job done.

Here are the key characteristics of home directories:

- ◆ They are meant to be accessed solely by the eponymous user (and perhaps by the administrator). You can create as many home directories as you want, using Windows NT's User Manager for Domains. You can also create multiple user accounts at a time that can take advantage of home directories, by using a special Windows NT wildcard in the User Profile dialog box. Unfortunately, this feature doesn't work as well as advertised. A workaround is provided in this section.

- ◆ Users' home directories must be nested inside another directory, which is always named USERS and created just off the root of the server. (You could name it whatever you want, but keep to the standard name if you can.) The USERS directory is specifically defined with a Share-level permission, with Everyone as the only *user or group*, having Full Control access rights.

- ◆ Home directories are just another folder in the system, but they also use a different sharing scheme, called a *directory permission*. This is a key to making home directories work. To work properly for your users, you must define both a share-level permission and a directory permission for their home directories.

- ◆ When the home directory is created properly, it appears as a high-level share in Network Neighborhood within the server.

- ◆ Home directories can be mapped to a drive letter on the network client, and when this is done, files can be saved directly to that home directory. Some (but not all) Windows applications will also automatically use the home directory as their base, as I'll demonstrate.

◆ When you map a home directory to a drive letter, the mapping can prove very confusing. I'll explain why later.

It could take many pages to explain those six points. A couple of key concepts need to be explained before getting started: Windows NT wildcards and directory permissions.

Understanding NT Wildcards

Windows NT allows the use of special *logon scripts* for configuring special things about your computer when you log on. It's similar to the concept of batch files in MS-DOS, and in fact logon scripts are batch files, just with a slightly more sophisticated syntax. Windows NT provides a lengthy set of wildcards that can be used to define statements in logon scripts. Some of them are listed in Table 12-4.

TABLE 12-4 LOGON SCRIPT WILDCARDS FOR WINDOWS NT

Wildcard Variable	Function
%HOMEDRIVE%	User's local drive letter that's associated with the account's home directory
%HOMEPATH%	Full UNC path of the user's home directory
%HOMESHARE%	Share name for the account's home directory
%OS%	The account's operating system
%PROCESSOR_ARCHITECTURE%	Processor type on the Windows NT workstation
%PROCESSOR_LEVEL%	Processor level on the Windows NT workstation
%USERDOMAIN%	Domain in which the account originates
%USERNAME%	Account's user name (you'll be using this one here)

The eight variables described here can be combined with Windows NT command-line commands to do various things.

As the administrator, you can write *logon scripts* and assign them to your users. In some ways, this can be a powerful tool. Take a look at Table 12-4. The wildcard variables and their meanings aren't hard to fathom. The %HOMEDRIVE%, %HOME-PATH%, and %HOMESHARE% variables all have a direct relationship with the home directories you're working with in this section of the chapter.

For creating home directories in User Manager for Domains, you won't need to resort to logon scripts, and you won't be going into them in detail here. (Logon scripts are discussed further in Chapter 13.)

However, you will be using the %USERNAME% variable in a very special way in User Manager for Domains, to help you create multiple home directories for a collection of users on your network. User Manager's Profiles feature also enables you to execute some of these scripting variables within the GUI, without the time-consuming writing of batch files.

Now you must turn to another highly relevant topic in the discussion of creating home directories: file and directory permissions.

Understanding File and Directory Permissions

Directory permissions are different from the share-level permissions you encountered in Chapter 2. I'm discussing them here instead of in Chapter 2, because there is an immediate application for directory permissions in this chapter.

Directory permissions can only be used on Windows NTFS volumes, and they provide an extra level of security for folders on your system. File and directory permissions have a number of distinctive characteristics:

◆ File and directory permissions are located by right-clicking the folder or file, selecting Properties, clicking the Security tab, and clicking the Permissions button.

◆ When you create a folder, its directory permissions are also automatically created.

◆ Both file permissions and directory permissions create a longer list of accounts that automatically have access.

◆ Both file permissions and directory permissions also provide a longer list of access types.

◆ The biggest difference between share-level permissions and directory permissions is that in directory permissions, you can determine whether or not any files saved to that folder inherit the same permissions as that folder. In other words, if "Helen" creates a word processing file and saves it in her home directory, the file acquires the same permissions as its home directory. If only Helen and the administrator have access rights to the home directory, then they are the only ones who have access to open and edit that file as well. This is a major security enhancement.

The last point is the most important.

Locate a folder anywhere in your system. Right-click it and select Properties, and click the Security tab. Then click the Permissions button. The Directory Permissions dialog box appears, similar to Figure 12-33.

Replace Permissions check boxes

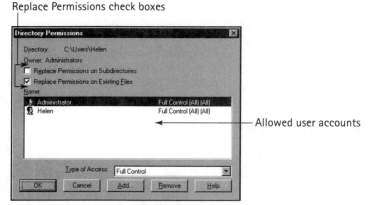

Allowed user accounts

Figure 12-33: Viewing the Directory
Permissions for a Folder

The main thing to note here is the two check boxes, Replace Permissions on Subdirectories and Replace Permissions on Existing Files. As Figure 12-33 shows, the check boxes are in their default state. Table 12-5 describes the conditions under which these check boxes operate.

TABLE 12-5 DIRECTORY PERMISSIONS CHECK BOX SETTINGS

Check box	Setting
Replace Permissions on Subdirectories	If disabled, (the default) permissions set in this directory apply only to it and any files it contains. If any subdirectories are present, they use their own sets of permissions.
	If enabled, all contents of the folder (or directory, if you will), including any subfolders, will have the same permissions as the "mother" directory.
Replace Permissions on Existing Files	If disabled, all permissions on any files within the directory use only their own permissions settings.
	If enabled (the default), all files created and then saved to that home directory will gain exactly the same permissions as the home directory.

The Directory Permissions feature ensures that the user of the home directory has significant control over it. If the administrator enables both check boxes, the user who creates any files for folders will have an exclusive privilege for them (unless the administrator sees to it that he or she has a Full Control access type for the home directory as well, which I recommend).

Speaking of access types, file and directory permissions offer a significantly larger collection of settings than the share-level permissions you've previously worked with. If you open a Directory Permissions dialog box, click the Type of Access list, as Figure 12-34 shows.

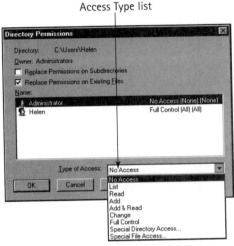

Figure 12-34: Access Types in the Directory Permissions Dialog Box

Table 12-6 describes each access type.

TABLE 12-6 DIRECTORY PERMISSIONS ACCESS TYPES

Type	Meaning
No Access	Exactly what it means. The account is locked out. Prevents access even if the account is a member of a group that has access to the directory or file.
List (RX)(Not Specified)	Enables browsing and listing of filenames and subdirectory names if any, and changing location to the subdirectories. Editing or reading the files is not allowed.

continued

TABLE 12-6 DIRECTORY PERMISSIONS ACCESS TYPES *(Continued)*

Type	Meaning
Read (RX)(RX)	Enables browsing and listing of filenames and subdirectory names if any, and changing location to the subdirectories. Files can be read and applications run.
Add (WX)(Not Specified)	Allows the account to add new files and subdirectories to the directory, but no access to files.
Add & Read (RWX)(RX)	Enables browsing and listing of filenames and subdirectory names if any, and changing location to the subdirectories. Files can be read and applications run. Finally, the account can add new files and subdirectories to the directory.
Change (RWXD)(RWXD)	Enables browsing and listing of filenames and subdirectory names if any, and changing location to the subdirectories. Files can be read and applications run. Finally, the account can add new files and subdirectories to the directory, and delete them. Files can be modified and saved over.
Full Control (All)(All)	Enables browsing and listing of filenames and subdirectory names if any, and changing location to the subdirectories. Files can be read and applications run. Finally, the account can add new files and subdirectories to the directory, and delete them. Files can be modified and saved over. Account can change permissions on the directory and its contents, and take ownership thereof.
Special Directory Access	You may be wondering what those funny letters are for each of the access types. Read (R) allows viewing of filenames and subdirectories. Write (W) permits adding files and subdirectories to the current directory. Execute (X) permits navigating between subdirectories in the directory. Delete (D) allows deletion of the directory. Change Permissions (P) grants privileges for changing the directory's permissions. Finally, Take Ownership (O) permits the taking of ownership of the directory by the user account. (All) obviously means that all of the capabilities involved are included in the access type. The letters are combined in various ways to define the capabilities of each access type.

It's a long and fairly complicated list, but once you look things over, it's quickly understandable.

I recommend that for every home directory you create on your server, you have only two directory permissions, similar to those pictured in Figure 12-32: the administrator and the person to whom the home directory belongs. Both should have Full Control privileges, or the user can have Change privileges. That allows them all the necessary abilities to change and save data without giving them the chance to mess around with Share or Permission settings. Then anything created by your users and placed in their private home directories remains theirs, but you have a monitoring capability and can access data when you need to. (Backup is also made considerably easier!)

You can also set up any home directory to allow exclusive access to its assigned user, and not to the administrator. That is the default, in fact. If something happens and the administrator needs to get into that home directory, all he or she has to do is right-click the folder and select Properties from the shortcut menu. Click the Security tab and then click the Take Ownership button. This enables the administrator to set up any home directory so that he or she can gain access in an emergency. I discuss the issue of ownership later in this chapter.

Directory permissions offer both enhanced security and increased granularity in your share levels. They're brought up here because you have an immediate context and application for them with home directories. In this topic, you may have noticed that the issue of ownership comes up. Ownership is also a mechanism for data management under Windows NT, and we glance at it next.

Understanding Ownership

Ownership is something I won't go into in great detail; I'll explain it in the context of how it's affected by the use of file and directory permissions. For example, say you create a home directory called "Helen," for a user of the same name, and you give her Full Control in Directory Permissions. Then she creates spreadsheet and word processor files to her heart's content. If Helen were to right-click one of her files and select Properties, click the Security tab, and then click the Ownership button, she would see the dialog box shown in Figure 12-35.

Figure 12-35: Checking Ownership
for a Data File

Logically enough, Helen is the owner of the file, as she should be. But if the file is saved into a home directory, its file permission will be exclusively hers. Since the file has its own set of permissions bequeathed from the user's home directory, no one else can monkey around with it. The administrator can take ownership in an emergency, however.

As shown in Figure 12-35, the Ownership dialog box also provides a Take Ownership button for taking over the ownership of a file when necessary. The administrator can do this when necessary.

Now, finally, it's time to get to the nitty-gritty of creating your home directories.

Defining Home Directories for One or More Users

Again, I'll skip the process of creating user accounts (you should already know how to do *that*) and cut straight to the heart of the matter. The assumption here is that you'll want to create more than one home directory; it's fairly easy to extrapolate the same process to performing it for a single user, which you'll also have to do from time to time. There are also some tricks you'll have to perform to make home directories work properly under Windows NT. Follow these steps:

1. To start with, create a new folder called USERS just off the root drive of your server if there isn't one there already. This is the place where all your home directories will live. It's also the place where Windows NT automatically looks for home directories unless you happen to define another folder. As I've mentioned before, I recommend sticking with the standard USERS folder.

2. Right-click the new folder and select Sharing, and set the folder's sharing to be Everyone and Full Control. That is sufficient for home directory use.

3. Open the User Manager for Domains. Your list of user accounts appears.

4. Hold down the Ctrl key and select the user accounts for whom you want to create home directories.

TIP To select more than one account in User Manager, hold down the Ctrl key. If you just want to select a whole list of users, hold the Shift key and drag the mouse.

5. Either press Enter or select Properties from the User menu. The User Properties dialog box appears, displaying the list of user accounts you've selected, as shown in Figure 12-36.

6. Click the Profile button. The User Environment Profile dialog box appears, showing the scrollable list of the selected user accounts.

7. Ignore the User Profiles section for now. You'll create user profiles in the next section of this chapter. (It's too confusing to even attempt to do both of these things at once unless you really know what's going on.)

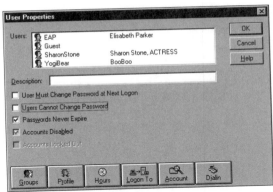

Figure 12–36: Open Properties for Multiple Users

8. Click the Connect option, and select drive Z or another high drive letter that you know does not correspond to any user's locally installed hard disk or disk share. This is the feature in User Enviroment Profiles that corresponds to the %HOMEDRIVE% variable described in the previous section. That Connect drive letter is the letter that the *client user* sees and is not related to any disk drive mappings on the server.

    Here's the "wildcard" trick I mentioned earlier.

9. In the To field, enter the UNC (Universal Naming Convention) path to your projected home directories. The UNC path with the %USERNAME% wildcard should be:

    \\TEST_SERVER\%USERNAME%

    in which you must simply substitute the name for your Windows NT server. (Mine is TEST_SERVER.) If you're just doing a single user (named HELEN), the path should read simply:

    \\TEST_SERVER\HELEN

    No, it's not \\TEST_SERVER\USERS\%USERNAME%. The reason will become clear shortly.

10. Click OK. You'll receive an error message, as follows in Figure 12-37, for each user account.

Figure 12-37: User Manager Cannot Automatically Create the Folder
for the Home Directory

11. Click OK again to return to the User Manager. When you close the dialog boxes, User Manager saves the planned home directory path with each user account. You've already saved yourself some work, but not as much as you were hoping for, I'd wager.

12. Open your new USERS folder. You'll have to create all the individual folders for your users there. You will also have to set all their directory permissions separately, one at a time. It's a pain, but it's the only way this will work.

    Now you've created all the folders for home directories, and perhaps labored mightily doing so. (If you're just adding one or two new users, it's not so bad. But if you have dozens or hundreds, it becomes a real chore. This can be quite tedious; however, once the bulk of your users are taken care of, it only has to be done once.)

13. Right-click any user folder you've created and choose Properties from the shortcut menu. The Properties sheet appears.

14. Click the Security tab and then click the Permissions button. The Directory Permissions dialog box appears, similar to that shown back in Figure 12-33.

    The next step is very important if you're the administrator.

15. Delete all default accounts by clicking the Remove button until none are left.

16. Click Add in the Directory Permissions dialog box, add the user account that is to belong to the folder, and apply Full Control or Change access. Then add the Administrator account with Full Control access.

17. Click OK. Follow the same process for each user's designated folder.

18. Finally, for each user folder, click the Sharing tab, set them to be Shared, and click the Permissions button. Delete the Everyone account and add the user's account as the only Permissions entry, using Full Control access.

Now, whenever users create new files and save them to their home directory, the directory permissions for that folder will also be applied to their data files. Thus, their information will be safe from prying eyes. (Always bear in mind that I'm using the terms *folder* and *directory* more or less interchangeably.) Again, this is a good reason to apply the Administrator account to each home directory, so there's some kind of back-door mechanism to access the information whenever needed. (An employee might get sick and someone may need access to that file, for example. Changing ownership may also be a factor here at times.)

The path business back in Step 8 with the wildcard is tricky. Namely, why isn't the UNC path written as \\TEST_SERVER\USERS\%USERNAME% in the To field? There's a specific reason. If you do this, all your users will get a new local drive letter, but it will be mapped to the server's USERS folder, which is *not* the way it's supposed to work.

Why?

A home directory gets automatically promoted over the network through the User Manager to a higher priority than just a normal share-level shared folder, which you would have to browse several levels deep in Network Neighborhood to locate. So this whole process gets very sneaky and very tricky, because if you follow the logical course of issuing the full UNC path of \\TEST_SERVER\USERS\-%USERNAME% in the User Manager's User Profiles dialog box, every single user will automatically have a new home directory with the correct directory permissions provided for it. Unfortunately, they will not have their special home directory mapped to drive Z. The USERS folder will be mapped to drive Z. Then your users may have to open up and browse through hundreds of folders before they find their own. Not a very graceful solution. Frustratingly enough, Windows NT is not really designed to efficiently do this type of thing.

Creating the home directories by hand and assigning their proper permissions is the only way to make this work effectively. It's brutal, but again, you'll probably only have to do it once, and if you do a gradual rollout, it shouldn't be so horrible. Also, chances are you may not have to do it for all your users. Unfortunately, in a bigger organization, home directories are an important manageability application.

Now it's time to view your handiwork.

Have a user with a proper account log on to the server (or do so yourself). When the system comes up, open up Network Neighborhood. Also open up My Computer. Have a look at both to see the new goodies that are placed therein, as shown in Figure 12-38.

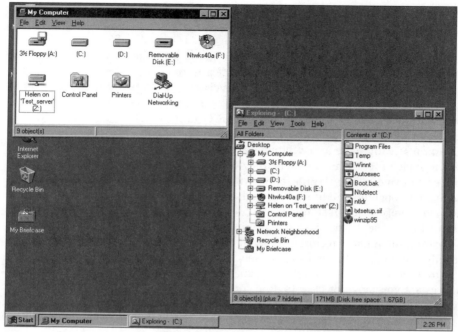

Figure 12-38: The User's Home Directory Shows Up as a Mapped Drive in Both My Computer and Windows NT Explorer

This is the payoff for all the initial confusion. The mapped folder works exactly as it should. Another payoff is that you can open some Windows NT facilities and they'll automatically adopt the home directory as their default. One example is shown in Figure 12-39, which shows a Windows NT Workstation's DOS prompt window that automatically maps to the drive letter Z, because it's the user's home directory:

Not all Windows programs will do this, particularly any office productivity programs that allow you to set its automatic paths for Open and Save. Fortunately, you can usually use that feature in your programs to set the path to the home directory.

The only problem with this whole scenario is that every single shared home directory will show up in Network Neighborhood. If you double-click the domain server in the Neighborhood, you'll see every single blinkin' home directory listed at the same level as any other shared devices such as hard disk or networked printer folders. (Fortunately, if you've done the share-level and directory permissions correctly, the only person who will be able to open the folder will be its owner.)

There's not much you can do about this. In a larger domain network, this is where your new knowledge of System Policy Editor comes in handy, because, realistically, if your users can easily locate their home directory in My Computer or Windows NT Explorer, they have little need for Network Neighborhood. Once the

Figure 12-39: The User's Home Directory Shows Up As the Default in the
Windows NT Workstation's DOS Prompt

users have their printer shares and any other disk shares from other clients or the-
server mapped to other drives or fully installed in their system, you can use the
System Policy to remove Network Neighborhood entirely from the clients' desktops, thus removing this source of potential confusion.

All in all, creating home directories for a large roster of user accounts is not as
convenient as it should be. Novell NetWare, for example, does a much better job in
this area. Now, though, you have a workable solution for this vital management
task. Combine this with a well-planned system policy and user profiles, and you're
on your way to a good solid network installation.

About Local Home Directories

Home directories can also be defined to reside on the user's local hard disk. That's the
meaning of the Local Path entry in the User Environment Profile in Figure 12-32.
That path is not local to the server — it's local to the client. If you specify
C:\USERS\PAM for the account, a new home directory will be created for the user
account on Pam's machine, assuming her system is properly connected to the network
when she logs on.

Also, please note that you must use a drive-letter-based pathname for the client's
local drive — not a UNC path. When you set up this capability, you must also create
the directory on the user's computer by hand. Then it shows up as the default path in
the DOS Prompt window and in other applications. Otherwise, local home directories
function much like server-resident ones, with the caveat that the administrator really
should make sure they have Full Control access to the same folder as the user.
Otherwise, the user can be allowed to have total control over their home directory.

Running the NET USE Command to Map a Directory to a Drive Letter

If you're in a smaller network, there's another more decentralized way to create directories on each client, and it doesn't require jumping through hoops with the User Manager. The downside is that employing this other method makes it harder to keep track of what's going on.

Windows NT offers another way in which any client computer can map a home directory (or almost any directory they want) to a drive letter. It's called the NET USE command, and it's used in a Windows NT command prompt window.

NET USE is a command you haven't seen before. It's a command for enabling the use of network resources from a Windows NT DOS prompt. The only requirement for a successful connection using this command is that the resource in demand must already have a share-level permission for the user issuing the command.

The basic syntax for NET USE is:

```
NET USE [Drive Letter] [UNC Path] [/HOME, /DELETE or /PERSISTENT
  (Yes or No)]
```

In Figure 12-40, NET USE is used to issue a command to map a directory from the UNC entity TEST_SERVER\HYSNAPDX to the drive letter M.

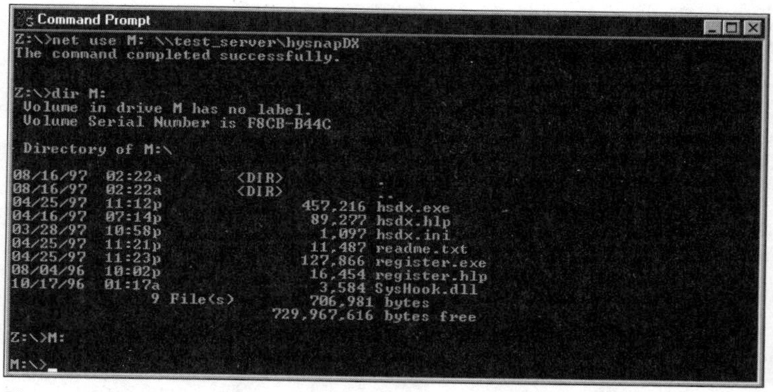

Figure 12–40: Running a NET USE Command

If it works, you'll receive a "The command completed successfully" message. It will immediately show up in Network Neighborhood and in My Computer, and in the server's top level in Network Neighborhood. You can run DIR commands, change drives over to it, and do anything else you want.

As another example, a command of immediate interest to your little home directory project might be:

```
NET USE Z: \\TEST_SERVER\RICH
```

This command maps a previously existing home directory called "Rich" to the drive letter Z on the client. Note that the USERS directory doesn't show up in the path.

If you entered the same command with the extra argument:

```
NET USE Z: \\TEST_SERVER\RICH /PERSISTENT: YES
```

then the connection becomes "persistent," and will be renewed every time the user account logs on to the network. This works for any NET USE command.

NET USE can go considerably deeper than this, but for our current application it's best to observe that it's really suitable for smaller networks where you can trust your users, or for use in logon scripts (which are discussed in Chapter 13, as are other NET USE commands). Any shared folder in the server or another person's system can be mapped this way with NET USE. All they have to know is the name of the computer, which is the head entry in the UNC path, and then the pathway of directories leading to the one they want.

Understanding User Profiles

User profiles are one of the ubiquitous elements of Windows NT. Whenever a person is added to the user list and logs on to a Windows NT network, a new profile is created and maintained for them. Windows NT computers can have multiple user profiles — as many as there are users that log on to the system. User profiles are also closely associated with home directories, being that they're created in the same dialog box in User Manager. You can also place user profiles in home directories. Profiles actually work in conjunction with system policies to form a complete environment for each user account.

There are significant differences between a user profile and system policy. A policy is defined exclusively at the server end, whereas a profile is inherently a user-defined object. When users log on to a system and set up their Windows desktop with some custom icons, such as a shortcut to their word processor or to a shared hard disk or folder, those changes don't go into the policy — they are embedded in the user profile. The network resources the user enjoys are also recorded in the user profile. If changes to the user's interface are effected in the system policy (such as removing items from the Start menu), those changes are also recorded in the profile.

Normally, whether you're working with Windows NT Server or Workstation, user profiles live in a particular place on the system: in the WINWindows NT\PROFILES folder. Each user profile is itself a folder or directory, named after its user account, containing a significant collection of content, as shown in Figure 12-41.

Figure 12-41: Inspecting a User Profile

Several folders are created for each profile, each of which contains separate data about the account's configuration after logon. (A number of hidden folders are also created.) Without getting into it in great detail, almost every element of how an account interacts with the computer is affected by its profile, including the contents of its taskbar and desktop, settings in the Windows NT Explorer, the Control Panel and the Accessories menu, network printer connections, and Windows NT programs with user-definable settings. Any or all of these will be present in the profile, depending on how the user works on the computer.

You've already seen many of the same settings in the previous section, so all of this should be familiar. Now that you've seen how to control things on your network through use of system Policies, you can also take the next step to provide your users with some more flexibility (that is, if your boss will let you), by using user profiles. User profiles usually reside in the PROFILES folder, but they don't always have to be located there, as you'll soon see.

There are three key types of user profiles:

◆ **Local Personal.** The normal user profile created by a person whenever they log on to a Windows NT computer. It stays only in the local client where they originally logged. If they have to go over to another system and log on there, any settings and changes they made for their preference will not appear on the second system. Instead, a new profile is created for them on other system.

◆ **Roaming.** A much more powerful profile type that can actually move around between machines. The place of creation can be complicated. A roaming profile can be defined at any computer that runs a copy of User Manager – any Windows NT Workstation or Server can create roaming profiles. The default in this chapter is that the accounts and profiles are being modified on a Windows NT Primary Domain Controller, but most of the process for creating a roaming profile is pretty generic. The User Manager also offers the capability to define home directories on the server, where network clients can automatically save their data during the course of the working day for easy backup after office hours.

◆ **Mandatory.** A type of roaming profile that offers much greater control to the administrator. The network administrator can define any or all of the settings for the user account (interface settings, and so on), save them in the profile, and set the profile to be roaming so that the user still has a consistent appearance and functionality regardless of where they are logged in. Mandatory profiles resemble system policies but bear the functional differences described earlier.

I'll basically ignore local profiles since they're pretty self-evident. The use of roaming profiles is of great interest, and (mercifully) considerably easier to deal with than home directories, which are created in the same User Profiles dialog box in User Manager for Domains. The next subsection gives you a recipe for efficiently combining roaming user profiles with your users' home directories.

Defining a Roaming User Profile

Roaming user profiles are one of the Holy Grails of networked computing. It actually goes beyond the simplistic concept of determining what kind of wallpaper and color scheme a particular user gets to see when they log on to their system. As you've already seen, you can make major changes to the Start menu and the desktop on any Windows NT client. When you have a user account that moves around to different systems, it becomes more difficult to enforce consistency unless you use a global policy, which lacks flexibility.

That's what roaming user profiles are meant to address. Ideally, a roaming user profile moves around from computer to computer within the network, and can be run by the user account no matter what client computer they're logging on to. The feature works well for Windows NT machines on the network (I mean both Workstation and Server here), but Windows 95 clients cannot make use of this feature.

On Windows NT the job is fairly simple to do. You'll need to use the User Manager for Domains to create a user profile that's capable of roaming to another system. Assuming you've already created the user accounts, here's how:

1. Open the User Manager for Domains.

2. Double-click the desired user account. Its User Properties dialog box appears.

3. Click the Profiles button. The User Environment Profile dialog box appears, as shown in Figure 12-42.

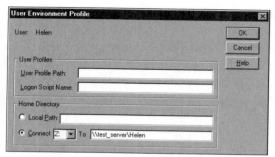

Figure 12–42: Initiating a Roaming User Profile

The User Profile Path is the key value. In the previous section I showed you how to create a home directory for your users. I had you ignore the User Profiles section of this dialog box. Now, here's where you make use of it. Notice the Home Directory path in Figure 12-42? You can also use that value for the User Profile Path. But there's another little trick you must use to make this work right – add the USERS directory to the User Profile Path.

Enter the full \\SERVER_NAME\USERS\USERNAME path if you want to place a user profile in a user's home directory, in which SERVER_NAME is the name of the domain server, and USERNAME is just the name for your user's profile. This subtly differs from the path you enter to create the home directory, as described in the previous section.

4. Enter the User Profile Path as a UNC path, similar to that shown in Figure 12-43.

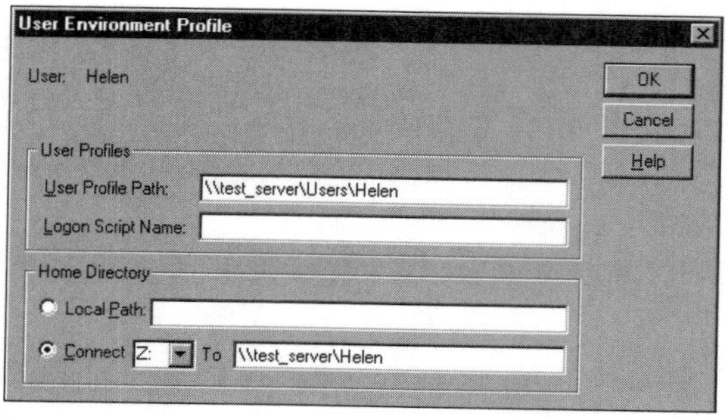

Figure 12–43: Entering the Path for the Profile

The Profile will be placed in that folder, and automatically used for that account whenever the user logs on. Notice the subtle but significant difference between the User Profile Path and the Home Directory path. Namely, the USERS directory is added to the User Profile Path.

If you don't want to clutter up a user's home directory with their profile, that's not a problem. Simply use the directory path (look closely here):

C:\WINWindows NT\PROFILES\USERNAME

in which USERNAME is just the name for your user's profile. A new folder will be created in the WINNT\PROFILES folder if you specify it. But what's different here?

Whoa! That isn't a UNC path! That's a standard directory path showing the drive letter, because if you specify a user profile to be created in the WINNT\PROFILES folder, you're *not* specifying the profile to be created in a *home directory*, which requires the UNC path. You're specifying a Windows NT directory (PROFILES) that is more or less a normal one, and not used for any special configurations. In this special case, that requires a normal drive-based path with no server name at all. Unfortunately, it's easy to take for granted that you can use UNC's for everything in the User Environment Profile dialog box. Not so! Absolutely twisted, isn't it?

Remember this: Windows NT automatically creates the PROFILES folder inside the WINWindows NT folder when you install the operating system. If you don't place the user profile in an account's home directory, it *must* be placed in the PROFILES folder.

5. Click OK. It's as simple as that. The profile is created. It's only five steps. Now wasn't that easy?

   To check the results, open the user's folder (if you've allowed administrative access to it). If you created the profile in the C:\WINWindows NT\PROFILES folder of the server, then the new profile will automatically be present there.

6. To check the correct functioning of the profile, simply have the user log on to their system and open the Control Panel.

7. Double-click the System icon. The System Properties sheet appears. Click the User Profiles tab. Figure 12-44 shows the results.

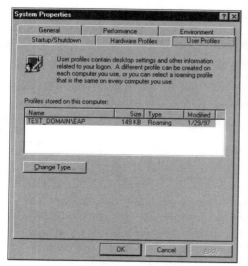

Figure 12-44: The User Profile Is,
Indeed, Roaming

Wherever the user logs in, their preferred system settings will always migrate with them on the network (assuming all else is in order: routing, the protocol type, and so on) to any other Windows NT workstation. Moreover, no one else's screen settings will be messed with. Any user changes are automatically saved to their profile and go with them to other client machines. The profile is easily defined to roam across the big wide ranges of your network. Once you have roaming profiles combined with a consistent system policy, you have an almost ironclad consistency governing your network and how it interfaces with its various users.

Using Cached Profiles

When you use roaming profiles, you may run into situations where there's a lot of network traffic. Or you may be using a Remote Access connection. If either is the case, you can enable the use of Cached user profiles for the user. Simply click the Change Type button shown in Figure 12-44. (Windows NT Workstation clients also have this button.) Figure 12-45 shows the Change Type dialog box, which is the same on Windows NT Server and Workstation:

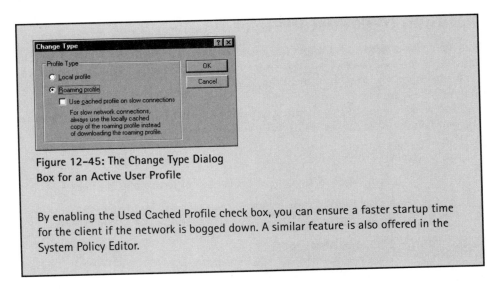

Figure 12–45: The Change Type Dialog Box for an Active User Profile

By enabling the Used Cached Profile check box, you can ensure a faster startup time for the client if the network is bogged down. A similar feature is also offered in the System Policy Editor.

Here's a full accounting of the frustrating subtleties lying in wait for you in this innocuous little User Environment Profile dialog box:

◆ To create a home directory in the USERS folder of the server, you must specify a UNC path that excludes the USERS folder and only specifies the server name and the username (e. g. \\TEST_SERVER\DINGLESNORT).

◆ To create a home directory on the user's local hard disk, specify the user's hard disk (usually C) and the directory you or they prefer. UNC paths won't work here.

◆ To create a user profile that lives in the user's home directory, you must enter the entire UNC path, *including* the USERS folder (e. g. \\TEST_SERVER\USERS\DINGLESNORT).

◆ To create a user profile that exists in the server's WINWindows NT\PROFILES folder, you must specify a normal drive-base directory path (e.g. C:\WINWindows NT\PROFILES\DINGLESNORT).

The brightest minds in the computer industry labored long and hard to bring you, the user, the wondrous complexities contained here. This section gives you a complete roadmap to those complexities, and what they're intended to provide, so that you can get the job done without a long series of 18-hour days.

Defining a Mandatory User Profile

But what about creating a mandatory roaming profile? In other words, a profile capable of moving around with the user but also contains the standard user interface settings demanded by your company? All you need is a user profile that matches those standards and is visually configured the way you want it. Assuming you know whose profile you want and where it's already located, here's how to create a mandatory roaming user profile for another user:

1. Open the Control Panel.

2. Double-click the System icon. The System Properties applet appears.

3. Click the User Profiles tab. It appears, as shown in Figure 12-46.

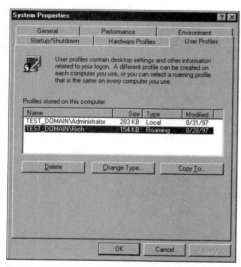

Figure 12-46: Preparing To Copy a User Profile for Setting as Mandatory

4. You have several ways you can go. For the moment, select a roaming profile that's currently active and displayed in the User Profiles tab, and click the Copy To button. The Copy To dialog box appears, as shown in Figure 12-47.

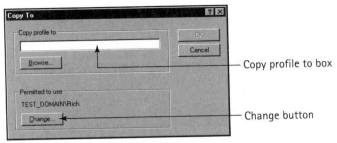

Copy profile to box

Change button

Figure 12-47: Preparing to Copy a User
Profile, Continued

Here you copy the desired profile from its present location and name to a
new user name in the WINWindows NT\PROFILES folder.

5. Enter the drive-based path in the Copy Profile To box (no, it's not UNC
   this time) as:

   C:\WINWindows NT\PROFILES\NEWUSERNAME

   where NEWUSERNAME is the name for your user's new profile. Make sure
   the correct user's name is specified. It can be a user that doesn't have a
   current roaming profile, or an existing user that you want to change to a
   Mandatory profile.

TIP

What's really annoying about this particular feature is that if you press F1 in
the Copy profile to box, to check its online Help, you'll be instructed to use a
UNC path. This is wrong, wrong, wrong. The copy won't work if you do this.

6. If you want to select another user profile, simply click the Change button,
   as labeled in Figure 12-47. A Choose User dialog box appears, which
   closely resembles the Add Users and Groups dialog box you've used so
   many times. Click the Show Users button, select the user account and
   click Add, and click OK. (You can even click the Search button here to do
   a domain-wide or LAN-wide search for the desired user account.)

7. Open the new profile folder located in the C:\WINWindows NT\PROFILES
   folder. (It's another folder named for the user.)

8. A file named Windows NTUSER.DAT is present in the folder. Rename the
   file as Windows NTUSER.MAN.

9. In the User Manager for Domains, make sure the user account is accessing
   the right path for the user profile. (In this case, it should be the
   C:\WINWindows NT\PROFILES type of path.)

10. Have the user log on to their system. Their account will make use of the new profile. If they open the System applet in Control Panel and view the User Profiles tab, their profile will still show up as Roaming.

That is how to create a mandatory roaming profile. You must do it one profile at a time.

A Final Word

A lot of ground has been covered in this chapter. Some vital server management tasks have been dealt with here. There's a lot more you can do to make your server's environment as airtight as possible, but the information conveyed here should give you a good running start towards that goal. You also have a good introduction to trust relationships and how they can help bind together a few domains into a cohesive whole.

But that User Environment Profile dialog box, now that's *really* confusing! Now you should be able to navigate its intricacies with aplomb and impress all your friends.

At this point, you're probably relieved to hear that only one chapter remains in this book. Chapter 13 contains a basic grab bag of topics that I had trouble fitting in anywhere else in the book, including working with logon scripts, exploring backup solutions under Windows NT, and creating a Backup Domain Controller and performing replication from the Primary Domain Controller to its backup.

Troubleshooting

When I try to define the trusting domain on a Primary Domain Controller, I receive a "Domain is the same as the current system" message.
You don't set the trusting domain on the server of the same name. Instead, you define it on the server that expects the server in question to "trust" it, which makes it the trusting server.

When I try to define a path for my user's home directory, I get an "Invalid Path" error message.
If you're creating a home directory on the server for a client user, then you must use the UNC name for the home directory. A C:\USERS\PAM or D:\USERS\PAM type of command will not work. Use the UNC path name as described earlier in this chapter. If you're setting up the user account to have home directory on their own machine, then you use a C:\PAMSFOLD path or something of that nature. A "local" home directory on the client doesn't have to be in a USERS folder. It can be any folder the user wants.

My users' home directory drive letters map to the USERS directory instead of their own private directory on the server! And some of my users' home directories show up in Network Neighborhood, cluttering up my server's window!
There's a specific reason for this. When you define your path to the home directory folders in User Manager, the home directories are not directly mapped by the server to their actual directory path. What happens is if you created a USERS folder and then created an EAP Home Directory folder for one of your users, you would expect to create a home directory path of:

\TEST_SERVER\USERS\EAP

when it really should be:

\TEST_SERVER\EAP

Illogical, yes, but it's true. Why?
The nature of home directories on Windows NT is that they're not designed very logically. Windows NT automatically looks for users' home directories in a specific place: the C:\USERS folder. If it finds them there, it promotes them to a top share level on the server across the network. Since each of the user profiles can map that home directory from the server to a client-local drive letter, that home directory folder is *promoted through the network* to a level equal to a normal shared hard disk or other share.

If you share the user's home directory folder in the normal way (right-click Sharing, click the Shared option), this user's personal folder will show up in Network Neighborhood, at the top level in the domain server's entry, along with any other drive shares and other shares that you may have provided. Unfortunately, you can't map those home directories to a drive letter and have a successful connection on the client unless you provide that share-level permission. But this results in clutter in the server's Network Neighborhood window.

If your directory permissions are correctly set, none of the home directories could be opened except the one for their particular user; it's just that it's a pain to scroll through all those meaningless folders. Figure 12-48 shows an example of what can happen when this whole process occurs.

Figure 12-48: What Happens If You Accidentally Share Home Directories Over the Network!

In an already crowded server window, six users' home directories are also displayed, which I've selected for easier viewing in the figure. Imagine what would happen if several hundred users were on the system and you did this! You'd never find anything. This phenomenon does reflect how home directories work when they're mapped to a local user's drive letter. They are *promoted*.

There's not much you can do about this arrangement, as noted earlier in this chapter. Also, make sure your To field in the User Profiles dialog box for your users' accounts in User Manager uses the path \\YOUR_SERVER_NAME_HERE\EAP or whatever user name is involved with each account. As described earlier in this chapter, this requires more work if you're building multiple home directories, but as Windows NT is currently designed, it's the only way to make them work *en masse*.

On a small network, consider using the NET USE command.

When my user logs on to their client workstation, they receive an error message saying "Your Roaming Profile is not available. The operating system is attempting to log you on with your local profile."
That's happening because the administrator accidentally entered the UNC Path for the User Profile Path to the WINWindows NT\PROFILES\USERNAME folder. This can be corrected in User Manager.

Instead of \\TEST_SERVER\WINNT\PROFILES\MYUSER, the user should enter C:\WINNT\PROFILES\MYUSER, and the client user account will use the roaming profile correctly.

Chapter 13

Typical Tasks You Need To Do

IN THIS CHAPTER

You'll find a number of useful odds and ends to help you meet emergencies and manage details of your client users' configurations in this chapter, including:

◆ Creating logon scripts and running Windows NT command-line networking statements

◆ Examining Windows NT's backup program

◆ Backing up the Registry

◆ Monitoring memory, disk throughput, and other system performance characteristics

◆ Using various strategies and tools for server maintenance

YOU'LL FIND THE only substantial discussion of scripting, DOS-type commands, and batch files in this chapter. In general, you're going to find that scripting is redundant, but it's a useful feature to have for troubleshooting and for small tasks that can't easily be handled by GUI-based applications, such as time synchronization.

Building Logon Scripts

I've already briefly touched upon logon scripts in Chapter 12. Here's where you can dig into them. As I've mentioned, logon scripts are analogous to Windows 95/Windows 3.1/MS-DOS batch files such as CONFIG.SYS and AUTOEXEC.BAT. What's really interesting about Windows NT logon scripts is that they can execute many Windows NT connectivity functions from the command prompt, using the same commands you've explored in other parts of this book, and many more.

Logon scripts are simply batch files for Windows NT. You write scripts using series of Windows NT command-line statements such as NET USE, NET TIME, and other commands that are described a bit later. Logon scripts are limited in their utility and in many situations completely unnecessary. They're a distinct advantage if you have a lot of MS-DOS/Windows 3.*x* systems on your network, or in the unlikely event that you're running a LANManager network and you want to preserve your scripts as you roll out Windows NT. (Windows NT's domain-based management system is actually derived in concept from LANManager.) In all the cases you'll see here, character-based scripting commands have GUI-based equivalents that are considerably less trouble to configure and use in the broader context of a department environment.

Logon scripts are always placed in the following Windows NT directory:

C:\WINWindows NT\SYSTEM32\REPL\IMPORT\SCRIPTS

TIP   The standard logon script always used by Windows NT is called LOGON.

By default, no logon scripts are created in this folder. You'll have to compose your own. The classic script that's typically used is simply titled LOGON. You can also call other batch files from LOGON, but you should always use LOGON as the starting point for your logon scripts. (The IMPORT and EXPORT directories are also used for another purpose, directory replication, which is discussed later in this chapter.)

Unlike Windows 95 and 16-bit Windows batch files, Windows NT batch files aren't placed in the root directory for either the server or any clients on the network that use logon scripts. All scripts live in the C:\WINNT\SYSTEM32\REPL\ IMPORT\SCRIPTS folder. Each is named for their respective client and can be specified in their User Profile Properties. When clients log in, a query is sent to the server, and the logon script is executed.

The System Policy Editor provides a setting to run your clients' logon scripts synchronously. This means that logon scripts will finish executing before their desktops come onscreen.

Using the NET Command

When you write logon scripts, it helps to have at least a basic grasp of some of the typical commands. Among the most prominent is the NET command, which provides a large number of command-line based networking functions for both logon scripts and command-prompt tasks.

The NET command is combined with a considerable collection of keywords to provide a wide range of character-based networking commands. To check the list, simply open a command prompt, type **NET**, and press Enter. Figure 13-1 shows you what you'll see.

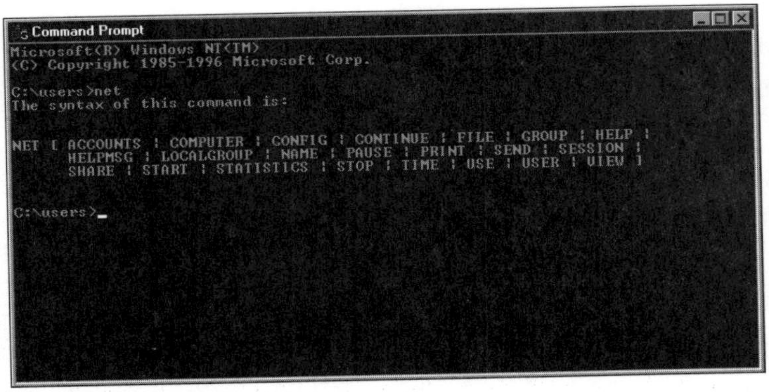

Figure 13-1: Listing the NET Command

The process of checking command syntax options goes a bit deeper but is still simple to perform. To check the syntax for any NET command, type the two-word combination and add a question mark. Figure 13-2 shows a sample query using the NET ACCOUNTS command.

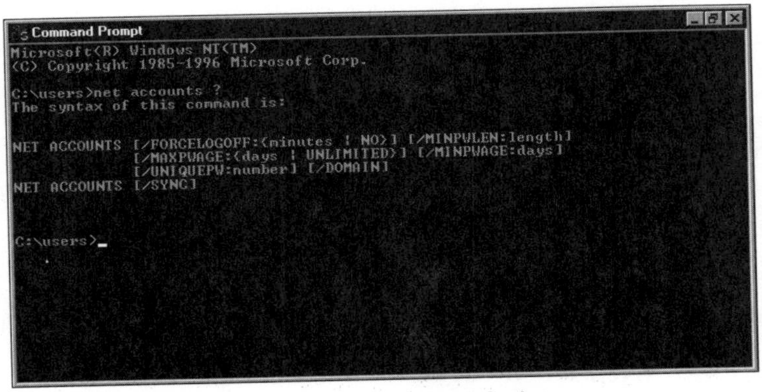

Figure 13-2: Listing Individual NET Command Options

Some NET commands are more useful than others. If you're a real fan of building networks, user accounts, and user groups by using command-line-options, the NET command is your baby. (The rest of us will just settle for getting work done.) Among commands useful for this purpose are NET USER, NET GROUP, NET ACCOUNTS, NET LOCALGROUP, and NET SHARE. Once your command-line based networking functions execute, their results will appear as normal GUI-based network elements, such as drive and directory shares, mapped drives, user accounts, enabled or disabled services, and other typical connectivity items.

Many Windows NT enthusiasts (some of them fellow Windows NT book authors) happily espouse using logon scripts to handle functions like this as often as possible. Why? Is it just command-line snobbery? The philosophy of this book is to assist the reader in actually getting things done. Every chapter so far in this book has been aimed at that goal. Mucking about with command-line settings and logon scripts may be nirvana to purists, but when you can do exactly the same function in 30 seconds using a GUI-based utility, as far as productivity goes, it isn't even a contest. The NET command features described here have their GUI-based equivalents in the User Manager, Server Manager, and various other Windows NT applications.

The following paragraphs introduce you to some of the key command-line capabilities of the NET command, some but not all of which are quite suitable for use in logon scripts. Wherever appropriate, I'll point out the location of GUI-based counterparts to these commands, so you can get an appreciation of just how much of the basic scripting methodology has been rendered somewhat redundant. Important command switches (phrases such as /DOMAIN or /ADD, that are denoted by the use of a forward slash) will also be pointed out.

ACCOUNTS

The NET ACCOUNTS command provides command-line control for any user account policy. (The GUI-based counterpart to this is in the User Manager; select Account from the Policies menu.) I haven't discussed the Policies feature of User Manager up to this point because most of its features are pretty obvious at a glance, and you had many more important things to deal with in this book. Figure 13-3 shows the User Manager's Account Policy feature.

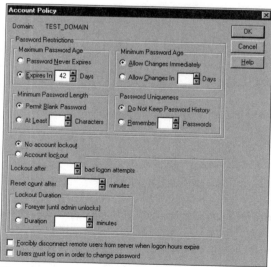

Figure 13-3: Checking User Account Policy Settings

This is different from the system policies described in Chapter 12; most settings govern password restrictions and capabilities, account lockouts after a certain amount of bad logon attempts and their duration, forcible disconnection of remote users after any defined logon hours are over, and other settings. Figure 13-4 shows the command-based equivalent.

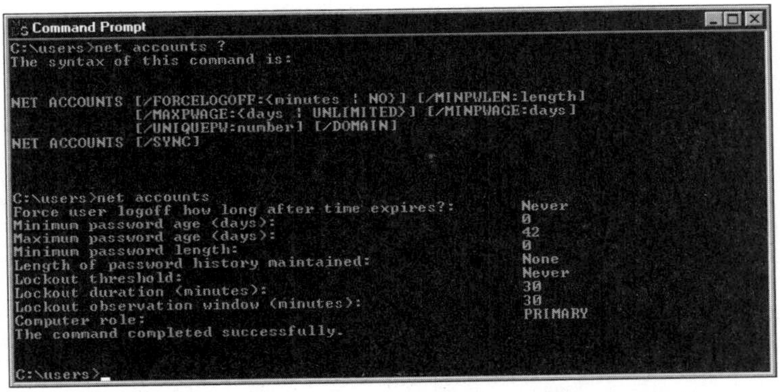

Figure 13-4: Viewing NET ACCOUNTS Switches and Current Settings

The NET ACCOUNTS command provides a huge number of options, listed in Table 13-1:

TABLE 13-1 NET ACCOUNTS COMMAND OPTIONS

Command Options	Function
/DOMAIN	This option can be executed in logon scripts on Windows NT workstations. It forces the NET command to be executed on the Primary Domain Controller. Since PDC operations are the default for NET commands in Windows NT Server, in most cases you won't need to use this option.
/FORCELOGOFF:(minutes|NO)	Sets the number of minutes before the account in question is automatically logged off the server. It's used when the account is restricted to logons during prescribed periods of time, such as an eight-to-five workday. Setting the command to NO allows the current logon to persist indefinitely

continued

TABLE 13-1 NET ACCOUNTS COMMAND OPTIONS *(Continued)*

Command Options	Function
	but prohibits subsequent logons by the same account. Also applies to expired accounts.
/LOCKOUTDUR:minutes	Defines the number of minutes that the user is locked out of the network after a certain number of unsuccessful logon attempts.
/LOCKOUTTHR:(attempts|NEVER)	Defines the number of unsuccessful logon attempts permitted to the account.
/MAXPWAGE:(days|UNLIMITED)	"Maximum Password Age" defines the duration of the account's password, in days.
/MINPWAGE:days	"Minimum Password Age" defines the minimum number of days permitted between password changes. This value can't be more than MAXPWAGE. The maximum value is 49710, which is far more than the average Windows NT client user's expected lifetime.
/MIPWLEN:characters	"Minimum Password Length" defines the minimum number of characters required in account passwords. Default is six characters, and the maximum is 14.
/UNIQUEPW:number of password changes	Sets the minimum number of password changes before a previous password can be reused in the account. The maximum value is eight. This feature prevents users from changing their password and then quickly changing it back to their accustomed value.
/SYNC	Synchronizes account databases with the Primary Domain Controller for the local domain. BDCs automatically synchronize over periods of time, but the SYNC option can be used to force an immediate synchronization operation.

The command-line options can be combined in a single command, such as

```
NET ACCOUNTS /MINPWLEN:8 /MAXPWAGE:120 /FORCELOGOFF:20 /LOCKOUTTHR:6
  /LOCKOUTDUR:240
```

Here, the minimum password length is eight characters, the maximum age of the password is 120 days, a forced logoff delay of 20 minutes is allowed so the users can save their work and close out any important tasks before the server logs them off, six unsuccessful logon attempts are allowed, and a lock-out duration of four hours is imposed if the user fails to log on properly after six attempts. Most of it is pretty simple.

NET ACCOUNTS's GUI counterpart is in User Manager.

USE

The NET USE command has a compelling use for home directories, which were discussed in detail in Chapter 12. You've already seen that Windows NT's User Manager isn't very well designed for automatically creating a batch of home directories and then insuring that all the user accounts use them properly. Chapter 12 provides a usable workaround for this problem. A simple version of the NET USE command offers another method.

On any client, you can issue the simple command in a logon script:

NET USE Z: /HOME

The /HOME switch instructs the client to map the user account's home directory to the specified drive letter — at least, in theory.

When this command executes, the workstation queries the server for the name and location of the home directory.

Unfortunately, the NET USE <drive letter>: /HOME command encounters the same issue that plagues home directories in the User Manager's User Environment Profiles dialog box: The home directory automatically mapped to the USERS directory, not to the user's own folder. As described in Chapter 12, you can use some tricks to force User Manager to map users' home directories to their proper folders and to any desired drive letter. When you do this, you have no need for the NET USE /HOME command, which does not allow for any further workarounds. It's just not as flexible.

NET USE's GUI counterpart is located in Windows NT's various disk browsing and file management utilities, such as File Manager and Explorer.

COMPUTER

The NET COMPUTER command is used to add a new computer or remove a computer as a participant in the Windows NT domain. This command can only be executed on Windows NT domain servers. This command's counterpart is located in the Server Manager, as the Add to Domain command in the Computer menu.

When you execute this command, the system in question should be connected to the network. The same restriction applies here: The added system must be a Windows NT computer, able to participate in domain security. The command itself is fairly simple; it's a matter of specifying the system's UNC name and using the /ADD or /DEL switches to add or delete the computer from the network. Here's an example:

```
NET COMPUTER \\laptop /ADD
```
or
```
NET COMPUTER \\laptop /DEL
```

Nothing to it. All you need to know is the computer's NetBIOS name, and you're all set.

The information conveyed by this command can also be located in the Server Manager.

CONFIG

Here's a NET command that you've seen before. NET CONFIG provides basic information about a server or workstation on the network, including its installed network card's MAC address. The command can be executed as NET CONFIG SERVER or NET CONFIG WKSTA. Each command conveys a slightly different set of information, but both commands provide the networked computer's NetBIOS name and the current user name, the MAC address of the networked device, and the domain to which the system belongs.

Windows NT Diagnostics conveys the same information as the NET CONFIG command.

USER

NET USER is employed to create brand-new user accounts that will automatically appear in the User Manager. This is separate and distinct from the NET ACCOUNTS command.

If you want to create a user in a hurry, try issuing a command similar to this:

```
NET USER Dinglesnort /DOMAIN /ADD
```

If you open up User Manager, you'll find the new user account "Dinglesnort" properly added to the list in User Manager for Domains. (Now delete it before your boss sees you've added a "Dinglesnort" user to the system.)

Note the /DOMAIN switch. This can be omitted if you're running a stand-alone server. The /ADD switch, obviously, enables the addition of the new account.

To remove a user account, issue a command similar to

```
NET USER Dinglesnort /DOMAIN /REMOVE
```

and the account is removed from the User Manager's database.

NET USER's functional equivalent can be found in the User Manager.

TIME

NET TIME, on the other hand, is a highly useful command for all your workstations. When you install this command in a logon script for all of your workstations, you can synchronize the time on all your connected clients to the time on your server. (Better make sure the time on your server is correct!) A good example of a NET TIME command is

```
NET TIME \\MAIN_SERVER /SET /YES
```

This command synchronizes the workstation's clock to that of the primary server in the domain, which is MAIN_SERVER in this example.

Running the NET TIME command is one good reason to define and use logon scripts for all your clients.

SHARE

The NET SHARE command provides a command-based method for sharing directories across the network and mapping them to preferred names. The basic syntax is

```
NET SHARE <sharename> = <drive:\directory path> /USERS:<number of
 accounts permitted> or /UNLIMITED
```

Possible examples include:

```
NET SHARE PIX = C:\SCREENCAPS /UNLIMITED
```

If you execute this command, a new share called PIX will be created in the user's Network Neighborhood from the server, using the SCREENCAPS directory off the root. The /UNLIMITED switch allows an unlimited number of users in the domain to access the share at once. This can be done from both workstations and servers.

If you want to limit the number of users that can have access at once, a possible command would be

```
NET SHARE PIX = C:\SCREENCAPS /USERS = 5
```

The USERS switch is used to define the maximum number of users that can access the shared directory. (This is not the same thing as the NET USERS command.)

GUI-based sharing features for directories can be found throughout the operating system as described in this book.

SEND

NET SEND is useful for sending messages automatically to your users from a logon script. Issuing this command from a batch file or a command prompt, you can send a dialog box bearing a message to any or all users. Sending a message to all your networked domain computers is easy:

```
NET SEND /DOMAIN Welcome to the machine.
```

The dialog box in Figure 13-5 indicates how using the /DOMAIN switch enables the local network client (a server in this figure) to broadcast a message across the entire domain.

Figure 13-5: Sending a Message

The /USERS switch enables you to send a message to all the networked workstation users:

```
NET SEND /USERS Welcome to the machine.
```

To send a message to an individual user, simply issue their name:

```
NET SEND Dinglesnort Welcome to the machine.
```

This is a highly useful test for network connections.

The GUI-based counterpart to this command can be found in the Server Manager, with its Send Message command.

SESSION

NET SESSION is a powerful command that lists current sessions in the server, provides a detailed list of a specific session, or disconnects sessions. Session types include shared files, printers, or other devices and resources that are being used by other computers across the network. Sessions can also be listed by individual computers on the network, to detect what resources are being used by any client.

Simply typing NET SESSION lists all current sessions in the local network.

To view the sessions for one system, enter the UNC name of the computer on the network:

```
NET SESSION \\MAIN_SERVER
```

The GUI-based equivalent of this command is located in Server Manager or the Server Control Panel.

START, STOP, PAUSE, CONTINUE

Here's a cluster of NET commands that are highly useful if you just can't keep your hands off that keyboard. NET START, NET STOP, NET PAUSE, and NET CONTINUE are primarily used for enabling, pausing, and ending Windows NT networking services. The services this set of commands supports include some of the key ones found in the Services tab of the Network applet, along with the host of low-level services underlying Windows NT's operations.

Instead of conveying a long boring list, you can get a sense of what these commands work on by simply typing NET START at a command prompt.

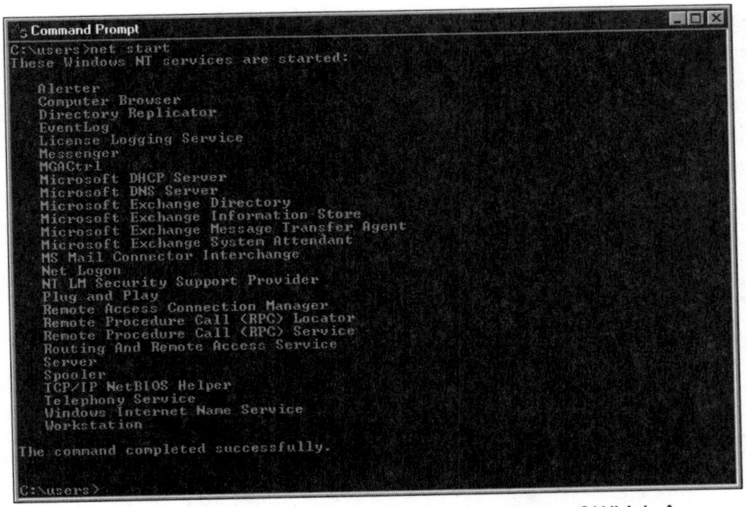

Figure 13-6: Services Listed in Command Prompt, Some of Which Are Available for Management Using NET START and NET STOP Commands

Any service listed by typing NET START can be affected by NET START or NET STOP commands. But you can't enter the entire name of a given service. You'll receive an error message if you try to do so. You'll have to think a little more creatively. Some services are difficult to figure out at all, and Command Prompt's Help is signally unhelpful in this area. Some services can't be worked with at all in this way. WINS, DNS, DHCP, Messaging, Browser, UPS, Workstation, and Server services can all be stopped and started by this method. So what's the point? Troubleshooting, for one. It's easy to issue a command such as

    NET PAUSE DNS

or

    NET PAUSE WINS

when you want to check your name resolution scheme. Once you've configured that type of service (which *must* be done in the GUI), issuing commands of this type can pause, stop, continue, or restart a service. This is a quick way to test how your services are working with one another in your TCP/IP configuration. Be aware that some services will take a bit of time to start up again.

Service names must be entered exactly as they appear in the Services control panel or in Server Manager. If a name has multiple words in it, such as "Microsoft DNS Server," enclose the service name in quote marks:

    NET PAUSE "Microsoft DNS Server"

PAUSE and CONTINUE are mirror images of one another. Some Windows NT Services can be paused without fully disabling the feature, including WINS, DNS, DHCP, Server, Workstation, and NetLogon. Pausing or Continuing also takes much less time to execute than a Start for many services.

The GUI-based equivalents can be found in the Services control panel, and in some cases the Server Manager.

GROUP AND LOCALGROUP

These commands are used for creating global groups and local groups, respectively, and for adding or deleting one or more user accounts from those groups. User accounts must already exist before they can be added to groups. Four options exist in common between both command types, as shown in Table 13-2.

TABLE 13-2 NET GROUP AND NET LOCALGROUP COMMAND OPTIONS

Command Options	Function
/ADD	Creates a new local group or global group, or adds existing user accounts to the named group.
/COMMENT:"comment text"	Used to add a 48-character comment field to the group.
/DELETE	Deletes, an existing local or global group, or removes, user accounts from the group.
/DOMAIN	This option can be executed in logon scripts or command prompts on Windows NT workstations. It forces the group-related command to be executed on the Primary Domain Controller.

Type the following command:

```
NET GROUP
```

and you'll receive a list of the global groups in the domain or the local system.

To create a new global group, the group name must be enclosed in quote marks and have the /ADD option applied:

```
NET GROUP "Everyday Users" /ADD
```

For local groups, the syntax is similar:

```
NET LOCALGROUP "Engineers" /ADD
```

Comments must also be provided in quotation marks:

```
NET GROUP "Everyday Users" /ADD /COMMENT:"Group for common daily
  users"
NET LOCALGROUP "Engineers" /ADD /COMMENT:"Group for circuit board
  engineers"
```

How do you add accounts to a group?

```
NET GROUP "Everyday Users" /ADD EAP RICHGRACE CAROL SHARONSTONE
NET LOCALGROUP "Engineers" /ADD EAP RICHGRACE CAROL SHARONSTONE
```

Caps are not required. Multiple-user accounts can be added with a single command. No quotation marks are required for account names. To delete accounts, simply substitute the /DELETE option.

Watch out for the /DELETE option: If you want to delete an account but forget to add the account name to the command before you press Enter, you'll accidentally delete the entire group!

Enabling Logon Scripts

We're not going to go into huge detail about the types of commands you can place in a logon script, for two reasons. First, when you look at the NET commands described, the process becomes pretty self-evident. Second, since every logon script-capable command has Windows NT GUI functional counterparts, the utility of logon scripts in Windows NT is somewhat limited. The best uses for them are to perform tasks such as synchronizing the time and date, executing special programs on startup, and testing services and connections.

So how do you set each client to use a logon script? Through the inevitable User Manager for Domains. Here's how:

1. Write a logon script.

2. Save it with the name LOGON.BAT in the C:\WINNT\SYSTEM32\REPL\IMPORT\SCRIPTS folder (the default path that Windows NT searches for executable logon scripts).

3. Open the User Manager.

4. Select the user account or accounts and press Enter. The User Properties dialog box appears.

5. Click the Profile button. The User Environment Profile dialog box appears, which you should be very familiar with after Chapter 12's painful introduction. It's shown in Figure 13-7.

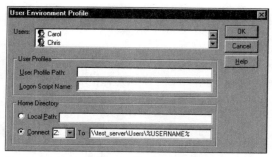

Figure 13-7: Preparing to Set Logon Script Paths

6. In the Logon Script Name field, type in the *name* of the logon script. Leave out the directory path; Windows NT automatically looks for it in its current path.

7. Click OK twice to commit your changes to the account.

If you select more than one account and follow the same steps, each account will use the LOGON.BAT file. You can also make batch files for each account, named accordingly and entered in each account's Profiles dialog box.

One final tip: When you create your logon scripts, make copies of the whole bunch and place them in the C:\WINNT\SYSTEM32\REPL\EXPORT\SCRIPTS directory. If you get into the habit of creating a lot of logon scripts for your users (which in many cases may not be necessary, as I've mentioned), you'll need a way to back them up efficiently. The best way is to use directory replication along with a Backup Domain Controller. That topic is the final one of this chapter and of this book.

Server Maintenance

Entire books can be (and are) written on server maintenance techniques. If you're working in an IS department, you're probably familiar with them. If you're running a network for a small business, you'll definitely need to know about some of the basic ins and outs of maintaining and tracking the operation of your Windows NT server. Windows NT provides a good set of free utilities that are automatically installed with the OS: the Event Viewer, Backup, Performance Monitor, and Windows NT Diagnostics.

Backing Up

Windows NT's backup utility is strictly functional and limited in device support. A huge number of different backup hardware solutions exist: magneto-optical, DAT tape, 1GB Jaz drives, CD-R and CD-RW, and many others. What backup devices does Windows NT's Backup utility directly support? 250MB IDE tape drives. Ouch! Some 4mm DAT SCSI tape devices are also supported. Fortunately, assuming you buy a tape drive that provides Windows NT drivers (a very dodgy proposition, even at this late date), you should be able to make Windows NT's Backup program automatically make use of that device. Upon startup, Backup attempts to detect whatever tape drive you presently have in your system. Unfortunately, Windows NT's list of drivers for tape devices is scanty. You can use the Tape Devices program in the Control Panel to load a new driver if it's available. Windows NT's Backup program is shown in Figure 3-8.

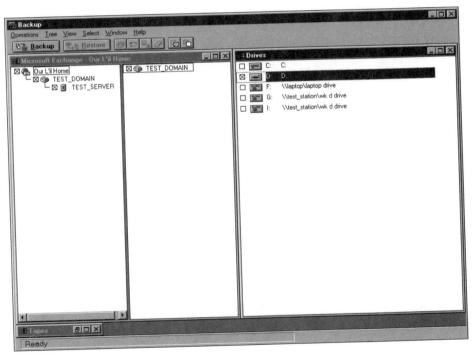

Figure 13-8: NT Backup

As with other Windows NT applications such as Server Manager, Backup is modified for use with Microsoft Exchange servers if that BackOffice application is installed in your network.

Backup works with both FAT and Windows NTFS disk volumes. Any network hard disk that's mapped to the Windows NT computer can automatically be backed up to a tape.

Anyone who has ever worked with a tape device on a PC will be familiar with the basic concepts and mechanisms underlying the Backup program. Backup allows you to create scheduled backups that will execute automatically at prescribed times. Unfortunately, any other backup-capable hardware is not at all supported. Here are some basic tips and techniques to keep in mind when you're considering backup solutions:

◆ Backups can be created as appended backups to existing sets. This is useful if a new application or service has been installed.

◆ If you've performed a large and complete system backup, you don't have to go through the whole process again every day. Differential backups maintain the existing backup set but also save only the changes that have occurred since the last backup was made.

◆ One process you'll rapidly grow to hate during the process of working with tape is the Verify operation. IDE tape drives of all sizes are notoriously difficult about verify operations, and often you'll receive errors even when the actual backup is perfectly good. It's also very time-consuming on slower tape drives. Do yourself another favor: bypass any IDE tape drive mechanism, no matter what compatibility is claimed or how good a deal it seems to be at the time.

Since any self-respecting Windows NT server has SCSI installed anyway (unless it's a very small workgroup server, and even then you're taking a risk), shop around for a good DAT drive. Although the mechanisms are still much more expensive than they should be, the media are dirt cheap and start at a bare minimum of 2GB. Start with a minimum 4GB DAT drive, especially on a good-sized network. DATs make it quite simple to back up entire networks economically and to maintain copious archives. Dollar for dollar, they're the best option for your money. Magneto-optical drives, and higher-capacity removables like the Iomega Jaz and SyQuest SyJet, are an option for local backups but not quite as practical for network-wide archiving operations. Local backups are also problematic because of the device support issue.

Backing Up and Restoring the Registry

The Registry is the central database of system information in your Windows machine. It's present in all versions of Windows beyond 3.x, and all versions work quite similarly. Key configurations for all aspects of your system reside here, including application settings.

Registry settings are divided into five *subtrees*, which are key configuration areas of the system. Their names and function are shown in Table 13-3.

TABLE 13-3 REGISTRY SETTINGS

Subtree Names	Function
HKEY_LOCAL_MACHINE	Most registry work is done in this subtree. It is the primary location for hardware information, software, and operating systems loaded on the computer.
HKEY_CLASSES_ROOT	Contains file associations (types of files, their suffixes, and the originating programs if any), and COM and OLE registration information.
HKEY_USER	Holds two user profiles, including a default profile for new user logons, and a profile associated with an existing user account. The profile is identified with a lengthy SID (Security ID) number.
HKEY_CURRENT_USER	Holds the currently active user profile.
HKEY_CURRENT_CONFIG	Current hardware configuration.

When you create or update Emergency floppy disks, you also back up the registry automatically. If you have servers whose configurations are being changed regularly, even in small ways, I strongly recommend keeping a rolling archive of Emergency disks, each of which represents a snapshot taken of the server, say a week apart from one another. Without consistently updated Emergency disks, you're robbing yourself of your simplest and most crucial weapon for coping with unexpected problems. There's no reason to hassle with backing up the Registry in any other fashion, except to make sure the Backup Local Registry check box is enabled in your Backup program.

One useful, Windows NT feature, the System Policy Editor, provides a reasonably efficient interface to many important areas of the system registry for client and server interface configuration. The System Policy Editor is discussed at length in Chapter 12.

Hard Disk Maintenance

Windows NT's basic Disk Administrator program offers solid if unspectacular capabilities for disk maintenance and management. Every major disk-related task in Windows NT offers its basic function in Disk Administrator, including the following:

♦ Formatting and partitioning of newly installed hard disks and removable drives of all descriptions

♦ Conversion of Windows NT hard disks from FAT to Windows NTFS

- ◆ Checking and isolation of bad sectors
- ◆ Building of basic disk mirroring, striping, volume sets, and RAID arrays

RAID-based disk management promotes a term called fault tolerance, which indicates that a particular method prevents data loss in case a hard disk fails. I describe each type of disk fault tolerance in the following paragraphs.

To use RAID techniques on your Windows NT server, you don't need to use a SCSI controller that has special, expensive built-in RAID capabilities. You don't even need to use SCSI hard disks! For some purposes, such as creating a mirror set, a pair of identically matched IDE hard disks will work fine. Windows NT implements RAID capabilities in software, obviating the need for extra hardware. Of course, having a higher-end SCSI controller that supports those features, and using SCSI hard disks for them, is certainly never going to hurt.

Volume sets are basically an Windows NT method of *disk spanning*, in which more than one partition of a hard disk or especially of several hard disks are combined to form one huge "super" partition. In some working environments, this can help performance, particularly if the volume contains a large database application. *Disk mirroring* is the process of taking two identically-sized disk partitions and using one as an exact, invisible duplicate of the other. If the front-line one goes down, the mirror steps in and takes over the prevailing job until the front-line device can be restored. For mirroring to work, the partitions must be exactly the same size. If you use two identically sized hard disks, mirroring is correspondingly much easier. Mirroring can be performed for a boot drive, and I highly recommend it. Performance isn't improved by using a mirror set, but safety certainly is. This type of fault tolerance is called RAID Level 1.

Disk striping is a case where you can select partitions on up to 32 hard disks to participate in a stripe set. It's a subtle form of disk spanning in which data is broken up across contiguous stripes on each successive disk. The first part of a large data file is written to one stripe of the first disk partition, then the first stripe of the second partition, and so on. Then, data continues to be written across the same stripe over each successive drive partition taking part in the stripe set. It's another method of load balancing across hard disks. For small workgroup servers not running a complex network or any serious groupware or database applications, disk striping is a bit esoteric, but it's a powerful tool in larger networks. This type of disk management is called RAIN Level 0.

Disk Administrator also supports stripe set with parity, which requires at least three available disk drives. A stripe set with parity functions similarly to a normal stripe set but allocates an entire disk to hold parity information for all the data in the stripe set. This enables fault tolerance on the stripe – if one disk goes bad (assuming it's not the parity drive), the system will continue to run and you won't lose any data. Normal stripe sets offer a big boost in performance; a stripe set with parity offers less performance because the parity reproduction requires more time. Both striping methods are more practical with SCSI disks because IDE has a limited capacity for disk drives compared to SCSI. This method of disk fault tolerance is called RAID Level 5. Stripe sets cannot be performed on boot disks.

In all cases, to create a stripe set, mirror set, or volume set, you can't use disk drives that are already partitioned and formatted. Simply install the hard disks into an existing system and run Windows NT. All drives must show up as "Free Space" in the Disk Administrator. Do not partition them! Select the drives/free space you want to use for your sets, select the appropriate menu option, and you're on your way.

Most of the processes involved in creating these arcane disk features are quite straightforward. According to Microsoft, you can use either SCSI or IDE for disk mirroring or striping.

Using the Event Viewer

The Event Viewer is a key troubleshooting tool. Located in the Administrative Tools group on the Start menu, the majority of its messages occur when you're starting up your Windows NT system. Figure 13-9 shows the Event Viewer, which is located in the Administrative Tools group for both Windows NT Server and Workstation.

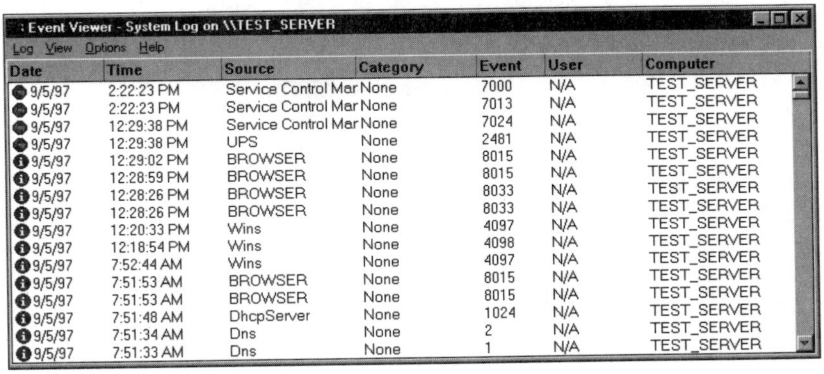

Date	Time	Source	Category	Event	User	Computer
9/5/97	2:22:23 PM	Service Control Mar	None	7000	N/A	TEST_SERVER
9/5/97	2:22:23 PM	Service Control Mar	None	7013	N/A	TEST_SERVER
9/5/97	12:29:38 PM	Service Control Mar	None	7024	N/A	TEST_SERVER
9/5/97	12:29:38 PM	UPS	None	2481	N/A	TEST_SERVER
9/5/97	12:29:02 PM	BROWSER	None	8015	N/A	TEST_SERVER
9/5/97	12:28:59 PM	BROWSER	None	8015	N/A	TEST_SERVER
9/5/97	12:28:26 PM	BROWSER	None	8033	N/A	TEST_SERVER
9/5/97	12:28:26 PM	BROWSER	None	8033	N/A	TEST_SERVER
9/5/97	12:20:33 PM	Wins	None	4097	N/A	TEST_SERVER
9/5/97	12:18:54 PM	Wins	None	4098	N/A	TEST_SERVER
9/5/97	7:52:44 AM	Wins	None	4097	N/A	TEST_SERVER
9/5/97	7:51:53 AM	BROWSER	None	8015	N/A	TEST_SERVER
9/5/97	7:51:53 AM	BROWSER	None	8015	N/A	TEST_SERVER
9/5/97	7:51:48 AM	DhcpServer	None	1024	N/A	TEST_SERVER
9/5/97	7:51:34 AM	Dns	None	2	N/A	TEST_SERVER
9/5/97	7:51:33 AM	Dns	None	1	N/A	TEST_SERVER

Figure 13-9: Running the Event Viewer

Events are typically split into Red, Yellow, and Blue categories. Red events indicate a service or network event has taken place that has failed. Double-clicking any event brings up a Detail window showing more information, as indicated in Figure 13-10.

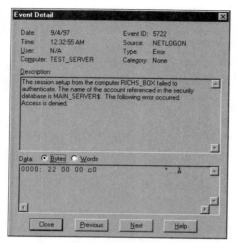

Figure 13-10: Checking Details of an Event

Events marked in yellow are usually warnings that something has occurred that could hamper normal network operation but is usually something that isn't catastrophic. On the other hand, blue is good. (It *is* good.) The Event Viewer also records good events, such as your services starting up the way they're supposed to. You want as many good events as you can get. It's a pretty elemental thing. Every major and minor network event, such as the initialization or failure of a service, a BDC receiving automatic updates from the Primary, clients logging on or failing to do so, and many other occurrences are recorded. You can save logs as separate files, and I strongly suggest you do so on a regular basis. Once you get a slight familiarity with the program, it will become one of your mainstays for monitoring the status of your network and its services.

Windows NT Hardware Tips

This section adds some important procedures to round out your preparation for everyday events in your Windows NT network. Among the useful tasks conveyed are the following:

◆ Enforcing consistency and caution with hardware drivers

◆ Building a Windows NT-formatting boot floppy

◆ Adding a second processor to a multiprocessor computer

◆ Checking and monitoring memory use and virtual memory

Everybody else says it, and I'll say the same thing: make sure to keep constant, up-to-date written records and logs of the systems on your network — particularly the servers. Every time you make a change to a system, log it in. Each system log should have a complete breakdown of its hardware configuration, including any hand-wired interrupt and I/O port settings (if any). Here's another place where uniformity of hardware choices for your clients can really pay off — in predictability.

Installing New Drivers

Chapter 1 discusses a huge selection of hardware issues that you'll have to deal with during the process of building and maintaining a Windows NT network. One issue I highlighted prominently is the necessity of making your network clients as consistent as possible in hardware. That was mentioned in the context of creating emergency boot floppies for servers and client computers. If you make sure that as many systems as possible use the same network cards, SCSI adapters, and video cards, you'll go a long way toward simplifying network client management. If you can go a level deeper by ensuring that the computers use the same motherboard manufacturer, or all come from a reliable system integrator like Gateway, Compaq, or Dell, you're even further ahead of the game.

The same rule applies after you have your systems up and running. Hardware manufacturers release new drivers on a frequent basis. Often those new drivers provide great improvements in performance, even if your Windows NT CD-ROM offers a driver for the involved device.

Without a doubt, the Internet is the best thing that ever happened to network integrators. You can download the newest bug fixes, motherboard BIOS updates, and driver revisions in five minutes using your Web browser. What previously took hours of busy signals trying to call a company's overloaded BBS is replaced with a simple point-and-click mechanism.

Use caution when deploying new drivers. BIOS updates are a particularly ticklish element in system updating. A good policy to follow is to have a test workstation available that contains a typical client hardware configuration. When you download new drivers, you can immediately test them out without harming any production systems. In many cases, new drivers may make matters worse or provide no tangible benefit. This issue is easier on small networks where you can pretty much control what goes on or trust your colleagues to do the right thing.

Laptops tend to be extremely difficult. Many laptop makers use an OEM implementation of Windows 95 or even Windows NT that does not lend itself to easy upgrading or even a standard installation process. Oftentimes, you're absolutely stuck with what you get pre-installed into your laptop. When you buy accessories for laptops and their traveling users, it pays to be extremely conservative. Even the most up-to-date laptops often use proprietary or third-party PC Card software utilities that offer limited PC Card device compatibility (as excellent as they are in other respects, Toshiba is an example of this problem). Although Windows NT is greatly unsuited for laptop use, many clients need it in the field. Buy laptop devices only from the most reputable and prominent manufacturers in the field—including Megahertz/US Robotics or 3Com for modems and network cards, Adaptec for SCSI controllers—and your laptop fleet will be easier to manage. And, be a fanatic about locating the latest software drivers for these devices.

Adding a Second Processor to a Multiprocessor System

Because dual-processor motherboards (for Pentiums, Pentium Pros, and Pentium IIs) are increasingly popular in the consumer market, this issue is worth taking a look at. By default, Windows NT doesn't automatically make use of a second processor. Turning off the system, plugging in the second chip (and hopefully setting your motherboard jumpers correctly), and firing the system back up again won't get it done. There are three ways to get around this:

◆ Simply build your system around a board with both processors.

◆ After belatedly buying the second chip, reinstall Windows NT from scratch so it loads the multiprocessing kernel automatically (which it will only do if it detects multiple CPUs).

◆ Buy Microsoft's Windows NT Server Resource Kit, which offers a special Uni- to Multiprocessor utility that allows you to upgrade your OS kernel on the fly. (If you bought the Resource Kit for no other reason, it's worth it for this alone.)

That's basically the size of it. If you're running Windows NT Server on any size network, you really should have the Resource Kit anyway. It carries detailed, intensive descriptions of all of Windows NT's most critical networking services, including DNS, DHCP, and WINS. The Kit also offers a huge CD-ROM library of special utilities for Windows NT that didn't make it into the release of the operating system, including a few others that I'll highlight here:

◆ **Timeserv.** A GUI-based program that uses your modem or the Internet to synchronize your server with the time set at any of several major time-setting locations—including the US Naval Observatory, the National Institute of Standards and Technology, and many other locations—and then synchronizes all the computers in your network to the same time.

◆ **CS Configuration Manager.** A comprehensive security configuration utility for Windows NT Server and Workstation. Every security function and characteristic of your system is managed here.

◆ **Process Viewer.** Process Viewer is a detailed viewer for pinpointing exactly how much memory is used by every single functioning process in your system.

- ◆ **IP Configuration.** A simple but handy little utility that provides a full account of the Internet Protocol Addressing configuration of your network adapter.

- ◆ **Quick Slice.** A dynamic viewer of time-slice processes for the tasks and services in your system.

- ◆ **Fault Tolerance Editor.** A program that expands upon the basic Fault Tolerance and RAID disk handling capabilities offered by Disk Administrator. A very impressive but somewhat risky little program that you shouldn't use unless you know exactly what you're doing.

Checking Memory Use and Setting Temp File Sizes

When it comes to running Windows NT, it's almost impossible to have too much memory. With memory prices now consistently at $5 per megabyte and less, there's no reason to stint on it. Every server you have should run at least 64MB, particularly if you're running a good collection of TCP/IP services on one system, or any BackOffice applications, such as Exchange or SQL Server.

One interesting point, which has been mentioned in many other places, is that some BackOffice applications can be dangerous when run on a Primary Domain Controller. SQL Server is a particular example. A Primary Domain Controller doesn't necessarily need as many resources in terms of memory and disk space as a server running key BackOffice or groupware applications. I strongly recommend breaking off those functions into separate machines if you plan to use them. Those programs can occupy so many processor clock cycles, and demand so much server interaction, that logging on and communicating over the network becomes prohibitively slow. SQL Server is particularly known as a memory and performance hog. A PDC doesn't have to be anywhere near the most powerful machine in your server farm. The most powerful resources need to be devoted to your groupware and BackOffice applications, and perhaps to your Web server if you plan to use one.

Windows NT provides an impressive utility called Performance Monitor. By far the most powerful way to monitor memory use, and any other aspect of your system's operating load, the Performance Monitor offers a huge list of resource monitoring capabilities. Figure 13-11 shows the PerfMon (which I'll call it from now on for brevity's sake) as it dynamically watches processor time occupation and memory use.

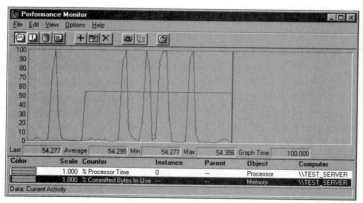

Figure 13-11: Performance Monitor, Showing Memory and
Processor Usage

At first, the program is a bit overwhelming. It's easy to add a resource or a characteristic of a resource for monitoring, but you have to be able to locate them.

If you plan to use PerfMon for tracking disk usage, the program does not automatically do so. Before you run the program for the first time, open up a command
line and run the following statement:

```
DISKPERF -Y
```

You'll have to execute this command only once. On every subsequent restart,
disk monitoring features will be enabled in PerfMon. Why do you need to do this?
It's a holdover from when people expected to run Windows NT on 386 or 486
machines. Monitoring disk throughput can occupy some system resources on slower
computers, but this is not an issue from lower-end Pentium machines on up. Run
this command before using PerfMon, and you'll never have to worry about it again.

PerfMon's key feature, Add to Chart, is located on the Edit menu. It's shown in
Figure 13-12.

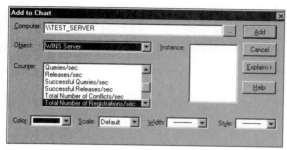

Figure 13-12: Adding Resources for Monitoring

You can monitor services as well as resources. The key part of the dialog box is the drop-down Objects list. A huge number of options are provided here, depending on how many BackOffice applications and services you have installed on your server. (Windows NT Workstation also provides a Performance Monitor program that works the same way but offers fewer Object types.) After you select an Object, you must then select a Counter type. The Counters are what provide chart displays.

Depending on the Object type, the Counter list can be very lengthy. (Disk monitoring, for example, provides a huge list.) You can monitor multithreading capabilities such as the number of context switches per second. Networking protocols such as NetBEUI, IP, and TCP are supported. To monitor memory levels, add two graphs: Available Bytes and Committed Bytes in Use. You can then watch memory levels fluctuate in real time as you open and close applications or as your users do so from across the network.

If you have multiple processors, PerfMon allows you to display a graph for each (called an *instance*) to monitor how much work each chip carries while the system operates. Once you start digging into this program, it rapidly becomes apparent that it's a computer geek's paradise. You can craft incredibly detailed (and crowded) PerfMons. On a busy server, you may want to have several instances of PerfMon running at once to watch different aspects of your system. It's great fun, and very useful as a daily management and troubleshooting tool, perhaps one of the best in Windows NT's collection of programs.

You can also use Windows NT's bundled Performance Monitor to check disk performance and activity. Windows NT uses a special temp file for disk caching and memory expansion. It's called Virtual Memory and is used as a supplement to installed RAM. The more RAM you have in your system, the less use Windows NT has to make of virtual memory to swap pages of program and data memory off the hard disk. You can define its settings by opening up the Control Panel, double-clicking the System icon, and selecting the Performance tab, as shown in Figure 13-13.

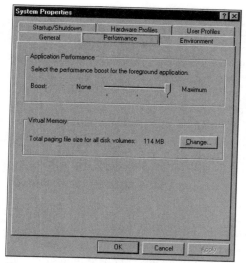

Figure 13-13: Viewing Virtual Memory Settings

Click the Change button to modify settings. No matter how much RAM you have, it's not a bad idea to leave at least some virtual memory. Even in memory-packed machines, you may run into situations where the system has to use virtual memory to compensate for handling huge demand or a big job. If this occurs and virtual memory isn't enabled, you will wind up with a system crash and some potentially very unpleasant consequences.

The rule of thumb for virtual memory is to multiply its value by double the amount of physical memory in your system. For example, if you have 128MB of memory in your computer, set virtual memory to 256MB.

Constructing a Windows NT Boot Floppy

Way back in Chapter 1, I described the process of building a DOS or Windows 95-based boot floppy for starting setup. Now you'll learn how to create a Windows NT-formatted, NT-executable boot floppy diskette. There are plenty of reasons for having boot floppies around, but Windows NT presents immediate difficulties regarding boot floppy construction. If you're running the Windows NTFS file system on your server or workstation, a DOS/Windows boot floppy isn't the right tool, because it won't even detect your NTFS-formatted hard drives.

You can create an NTFS boot floppy with all the right support files, and that's what this section is about. There are times when you're going to need it. Inevitably you'll encounter workstations and even servers that yield a "Missing Operating System" error at the very beginning of startup. Many Windows NT startup errors can be dealt with by having a Windows NT boot floppy, including the following:

◆ Corrupted boot sectors

◆ Corrupted Master Boot Record (MBR)

◆ Missing or corrupt Windows NTLDR or Windows NTDETECT.COM (This is what usually causes "Missing Operating System" errors, and it happens more often than you'd think.)

◆ Incorrect Windows NTBOOTDD.SYS disk driver

◆ Viruses

In situations like this, you'll thank yourself profusely for having the boot diskette around. It enables you to save or back up all your key data in case your boot track is suddenly lost on your hard disk. This problem happens much more often than is commonly understood. A hard disk manufacturer that has been reliable for years can suddenly release a batch of bad drives that blows away your boot track, rendering your system unusable unless you have a Windows NT boot diskette. This happens most frequently when manufacturers release a new line of higher-capacity hard disks, particularly in the IDE or Ultra-ATA area. Every single one of them does this from time to time. Having the diskette around, you'll always be able to recover from these annoying occurrences. As discussed in Chapter 1, regard disk manufacturers with a gimlet eye. Most drive makers produce very serviceable devices (including Western Digital, Quantum, Fujitsu, and Maxtor, all of which I've used in Windows NT systems), but all fall prey to this problem. Quality control seems to be a universal low-lying issue in the high-capacity drive market.

You won't be able to recover from or repair problems stemming from Blue Screen of Death errors, which occur after the basic boot process is started. In many cases, you'll have to use your Emergency Repair disk (you do have an updated Emergency Repair disk, don't you?) with the Windows NT Setup floppies. Fortunately, the boot track problem I've just described is much more common than catastrophic Blue Screen errors, at least in my experience.

Please note that a Windows NT boot floppy is a very different item from a Windows NT Emergency Repair disk. You can't boot from an Emergency Repair disk, and such a disk likely will not successfully repair a boot track problem. It is used for a different (but equally important) task.

When you decide to create a Windows NT boot floppy, ensure that you can locate the files that you need to copy. I favor doing two things before you start the process, particularly if you're less experienced. First, use the Find feature from the Start menu or from My Computer's shortcut menu to inspect your computer for the NTDETECT.COM, NTLDR, and BOOT.INI files. All are located on the root, and the Find feature will locate them. These files are crucial.

Second, Windows NTLDR and Windows NTDETECT are both hidden files. You won't be able to use the command prompt or Explorer to copy the files over unless you enable viewing of hidden files. Using the Find feature, you'll automatically locate hidden files and can drag them from the Find window to the floppy disk icon in My Computer to do a quick copy. Follow these steps:

1. Insert the Windows NT Setup Disk #1 into your floppy drive.

2. Open My Computer and right-click the floppy drive icon. From the shortcut menu, select Copy Disk and go through the process of copying the setup floppy. This automatically creates an Windows NTFS-formatted floppy, although it seems to take forever.

   If you just try to create a newly NTFS-formatted floppy, Windows NT only allows FAT-formatted floppy disks using the Format feature from the A shortcut menu, even though the system may be running Windows NTFS format on the hard drive.

3. Delete the entire contents of the newly-copied floppy disk. (You may notice that the floppy is automatically set to View All Files, thereby showing any files that are normally hidden on the Windows NT system.)

4. Copy the NTDETECT.COM and NTLDR files from the root of your system's hard disk to the floppy.

   The next step is very important.

5. Rename the NTLDR file to the exact name SETUPLDR.BIN. Don't leave out the suffix!

6. Copy the BOOT.INI file from the root of your hard disk to the floppy. Some authors recommend creating your own; in practice, the one running on your hard disk works just fine, and using it ensures that the correct settings are used on the boot floppy.

   These three files you've just copied will occupy about 180K of space between them.

   If you're running SCSI, you'll also have to follow this last step:

7. Copy the file NTBOOTDD.SYS from the root of the Windows NT system's boot disk to your floppy.

You won't need to perform Step 7 if you're not booting the Windows NT computer off a SCSI drive.

The BOOT.INI file *can* vary in its contents, primarily due to the type of hard disk you have installed in your system. Its entries are usually pretty uniform, and you can expect to see it read similar to the following:

```
[boot loader]
timeout=30
default=multi(0)disk(0)rdisk(0)partition(1)\WINNT
[operating systems]
multi(0)disk(0)rdisk(0)partition(1)\WINNT="Windows NT Server Version
  4.00"
```

```
multi(O)disk(O)rdisk(O)partition(1)\WINNT="Windows NT Server Version
 4.00 [VGA mode]"/basevideo /sos
```

There's no need to disturb the contents of your BOOT.INI file.

If you're running a SCSI hard disk subsystem and your system is booting from it, your BOOT.INI file will read as follows:

```
[boot loader]
timeout=30
default=scsi(O)disk(O)rdisk(O)partition(1)\WINNT
[operating systems]
scsi(O)disk(O)rdisk(O)partition(1)\WINNT="Windows NT Server Version
 4.00"
scsi(O)disk(O)rdisk(O)partition(1)\WINNT="Windows NT Server Version
 4.00 [VGA mode]"/basevideo /sos
```

The only significant difference is that the scsi(0) entry appears in several lines instead of multi(0). Again, it depends on what type of disk your system boots from. Copying your computer's BOOT.INI ensures the correct configuration.

When you're finished, you'll have a boot floppy that effectively allows you to bypass any corrupted boot files on the hard disk and start your system back up. The familiar multiboot screen appears as it normally does. If you still get Blue Screen errors, you'll have to run Setup and select the Emergency repair option when it appears. In that situation, the odds are about even as to whether the repair will work; still, the odds are better, and the rewards are a lot better than from just formatting the hard disk and running Setup again.

Please note that every Windows NT system on the network should have its own Emergency disk. It's easy to create it during setup, but you can also run the RDISK program from the computer's WINWindows NT directory by clicking the Start menu, selecting Run, and typing in **RDISK**. This is also the method you use to update emergency disks, which should be done regularly as I've mentioned elsewhere in this book. But nothing beats a good backup strategy, or at least a *consistent* backup strategy. I discussed that earlier in this chapter.

Building a Backup Domain Controller

Especially if you're just running a single-domain network, running a Backup Domain Controller is the surest way to ensure domain stability. Without a BDC, you're exposing yourself to serious danger even if you run a steady stream of backups.

A Backup Domain Controller allows you to do the following:

◆ Perform a complete server-based replication of your entire user account base

◆ Replicate selected directories to the backup domain server

◆ Promote a BDC to Primary Domain Controller status if a Primary fails, so that users can still connect to the network and work with network resources such as printers

Creating a Backup Domain Controller is quite simple. You simply run Windows NT Setup on the computer you've designated for that role, and when Windows NT Setup enters its GUI-based phase, name the computer properly. When Setup asks you for the Server Type, select Backup Domain Controller. After doing so, you'll install a number of components in the usual way, including network cards, protocols, and server components. Make sure, of course, that the right protocols are installed. Also, if your Primary is running TCP/IP with DHCP addressing, make sure to enable DHCP on the backup domain system.

When all that's done, Windows NT Server Setup will come back with a new screen stating, "You have requested that Windows NT create a Backup Domain Controller." At this point, you must supply the correct name for the domain in which the BDC will participate, along with the administrator name and password. (Make especially sure you get the password right.) After that, you'll go into the Finishing Setup phase.

Finally a window appears, titled "Replicating Account Information." This indicates that the BDC has successfully contacted the Primary and is downloading your user accounts and groups across the network. That's the very last step that occurs before you restart the computer. Setup is concluded.

The process is actually *very* slick. This is one of those areas that the Windows NT designers really nailed. When the BDC server comes back, open up the User Manager for Domains. The entire list of users, local, and global groups appears! The User Manager title bar even displays the correct domain. The two servers are joined at the hip. The servers also appear in the User Manager. BDC's are listed as "Windows NT 4.0 Backup" and PDC's as "Windows NT 4.0 Primary." No disks or directories are automatically shared in Network Neighborhood.

As you might expect, you'll discover that user accounts retain their home directory and user profile settings verbatim. Unfortunately, users' home directories aren't replicated along with their user accounts.

What's really interesting is that trust relationship settings are preserved on the Backup Domain Controller!

Once the BDC is set up, the Primary Domain Controller provides automatic replication. Every five minutes, the Primary examines its user accounts database to see if anything has changed — new accounts, new settings for an account, new groups, deletions, and so on. If any changes are discovered, those changes are sent as updates to the Backup Domain Controller without prompting from the administrator.

System Policies are not automatically replicated. Fortunately, this is easy to address, and I recommend doing so if you actively use them on the Primary. Here's a quick method for adding your PDC's System Policy to the BDC:

1. On the BDC, open the System Policy Editor.

2. From the File menu, select Open Policy. The Open Policy File dialog box appears.

3. Browse through the Open Policy File dialog box to Network Neighborhood, and open the NTCONFIG.POL file from the Primary Domain Controller's NETLOGON folder.

4. From the File menu, select Save As.

5. Browse through the Save As dialog box (it will automatically display the Primary's NETLOGON folder as its first level), locate the Backup Domain Controller, open it, and open its NETLOGON folder.

6. Save the Policy file by the same name. Alternatively, you can simply physically copy the file over by network or "sneakernet" with a floppy disk. Just make sure that the file winds up in the BDC's NETLOGON folder.

The Server Manager on your Primary Domain Controller contains two key features for working with your BDC, and they're both quite straightforward. They are both located on the Computer menu:

◆ **Promote to Primary Domain Controller.** When you select the BDC on your network and select this feature (preferably on the BDC in emergencies), you're notified that promoting the backup controller will close all client connections and any existing domain controller connections. In this event, it's likely that you're promoting the BDC for a reason: because the PDC has broken down.

◆ **Synchronize with Primary Domain Controller.** If you create new user accounts or groups on the Primary Domain Controller, you'll want to update, or synchronize, the account database with the Backup Domain Controller. This is quite easy to do. Selecting this option on either the Primary or the Backup simply displays a confirmation message asking if you want to make the change.

Figure 13-14 shows the Computer menu in Server Manager.

Shared Directories feature

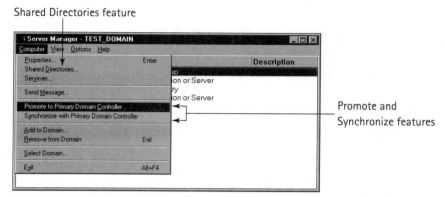

Figure 13-14: Using Server Manager to Handle BDC Management

Promote and
Synchronize features

Server Manager also allows you to browse shared resources on the BDC or PDC, by selecting the desired server, and choosing Shared Directories from the Computer menu, as Figure 13-15 illustrates.

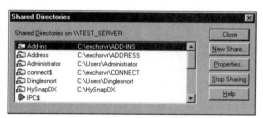

Figure 13-15: Server Manager Enables Management of BDC and PDC Share-level Permissions from One Place

Simply select a share and click Properties, and then click Permissions. You can then modify share-level permissions in the usual fashion.

When you've built your Backup Domain Controller (and by so doing, replicated your account database), you have another important, but somewhat more complicated, task ahead of you. If you use many logon scripts, directory replication allows you to duplicate entire directories of them from a Primary Domain Controller to a Backup, or to workstation clients as well. For this section, I'll describe how to replicate directories from a PDC to a BDC; the process for workstations is quite similar.

When you think about it, the concept of directory replication sounds great. Unfortunately, it's limited mainly to ensuring that logon script libraries on the server are fully updated on the Backup Domain Controller on a consistent basis. Replication is not a tool that you could use to, say, copy entire directories of sensitive user data, or office and groupware applications for mirroring on the backup controller. (The best way to achieve that is by using SCSI/RAID disk subsystems.) For the present version of Windows NT, directory replication is a useful but limited resource. Even Server Manager's online help for directory replication features, which is extensive and highly useful, conveys the impression that the feature can do more than it really is capable of performing.

Using Directory Replication

To enable replication, Windows NT offers a low-level directory replication service. You don't load it through the Network applet in Control Panel; instead, you either use the Control Panel's Services applet or the Server Manager. Both options are doable, but I'll use the Server Manager to keep things neat.

When directory replication processes occur, they're funneled through two directories that you'll already have some passing familiarity with:

◆ C:\WINWindows NT\SYSTEM32\REPL\IMPORT\

The standard place where your logon scripts live, in the SCRIPTS subdirectory

◆ C:\WINNT\SYSTEM32\REPL\EXPORT\

The directory from which your server exports the SCRIPTS subdirectory for replication on the other system. The contents of the IMPORT\SCRIPTS directory must be copied over to the EXPORTS\SCRIPTS subdirectory before replication can take place.

The domain user account that's employed to run directory replication (I prefer using the Administrator account) needs three key characteristics:

◆ Password Never Expires setting in the account

◆ Unlimited operating hours (set from the User Properties' Hours button)

◆ Membership in the Backup Operator domain group

You can also create a new account with only the required permissions to do replication, instead of using the Administrator account. I just prefer to keep things simple.

Import and export servers must also be defined. Windows NT workstations can only be configured as import servers. In the present example, a Primary Domain Controller will be configured as an export server, and a BDC will be set up for Import.

The first big step is to add the correct account to the Backup Operators group. This server group, though it's merely a local domain group, has some very special capabilities. Local accounts on the server have backup privileges. More important for the subject at hand, the Backup Operators group is uniquely enabled for handling directory replication. Follow these steps:

1. In User Manager for Domains on either the BDC or the PDC, double-click the Administrator account.

2. Click the Groups button.

3. Add the Backup Operators group to the list of groups for which the account is a member, and click OK.

Now you must start the directory replication service on the domain server and enable the user account for it. Follow these steps:

1. Open the Server Manager.

2. Select the PDC or BDC from the computer list.

3. From the Computer menu, select Services. The Services dialog box appears, as shown in Figure 13-16.

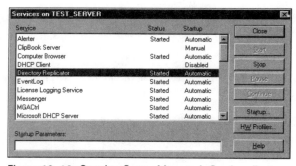

Figure 13–16: Opening Server Manager's Services Feature

4. Select Directory Replicator from the Services list and click Startup.

5. Select the Automatic option to enable the service upon bootup.

6. Select the This Account option.

7. Click the ellipsis button (...) and select the Administrator account that belongs to the Backup Operators group, as done in the previous section. (The account *must* be part of that group for this to work.)

   The next step is important.

8. Hand-enter the correct password for the account and confirm it. Figure 13-17 shows a sample result.

Figure 13-17: Enabling the Administrator Account for Directory Replication Services

9. Click OK. You'll receive a message indicating that the account has been successfully enabled for the service.

10. Follow Steps 1-9 for the Backup Domain Controller, and for any other computers participating in the replication process, if any. The same user account must be used in all cases.

So far, so good. Here's where the directory replication process starts to become a bit hairy. You need to enable the export system and the import system (the PDC and the BDC respectively, in our example). For this, you'll need to continue with Server Manager. Follow these steps:

1. In the Server Manager, double-click the Primary Domain Controller on the list (or, conversely, the server you wish to have as the exporting system). The Properties dialog box for the server appears, as shown in Figure 13-18.

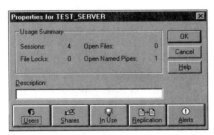

Figure 13-18: Continuing with Directory Replication Setup

2. Click the Replication button. The Directory Replication dialog box appears, as shown in Figure 13-19.

Default path values are correct
Manage (Export) button

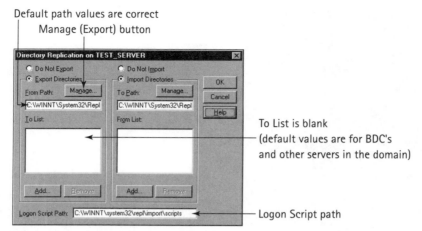

To List is blank
(default values are for BDC's
and other servers in the domain)

Logon Script path

Figure 13-19: Setting up Directory Replication
on the Exporting Machine

As the dialog's defaults are set, the exporting server (the PDC you're currently using) will automatically export from the C:\WINNT\SYSTEM32\REPL\EXPORT\SCRIPTS path described earlier. To obtain further proof of this, click the Manage button under the automatically enabled Export Directories option. The Manage Exported Directories dialog box appears. This is where directories and sub-folders are defined for export to the BDC and other importing systems, as shown in Figure 13-20.

SCRIPTS folder shows
up here automatically

Add button allows adding of
more subdirectories for export

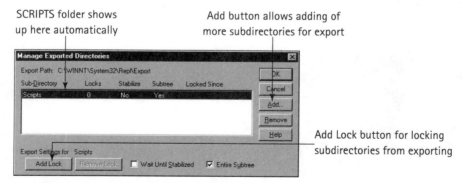

Add Lock button for locking
subdirectories from exporting

Figure 13-20: Default Exported Directories for Directory
Replication

You can see how the SCRIPTS folder, where your copies of your logon scripts have hopefully already been placed, has automatically been added here. Three features need to be briefly explained. The Add Lock button allows you to select a folder and prevent it from being exported. The Add button simply allows you to add another subfolder to the Export list — *if* it is already present in that pesky C:\WINNT\SYSTEM32\REPL\EXPORT path, basically as a parallel folder to the SCRIPTS directory. The Add feature does not provide for browsing to add just any folder you want here. It can't be done.

This is pretty useless, unless you go to a huge amount of trouble to create a bunch of new folders in that path and copy or move all your key files. That is almost pointless, since you can just use the LAN connection to make copies of key directories from the PDC to the BDC. Unfortunately, automatic updating isn't easily done in that case unless you set up an automated script to run at a specific time or times each day. If you organize all your key data files around a special folder in this path, then the process becomes more feasible. Neither task is especially difficult, but definitely not germane to the immediate topic.

3. If you should have another directory to add, do so here, keeping the previous restrictions in mind. If not, click OK.

4. The replication feature also shows blank To lists. The Add buttons allow you to add other domain servers, Windows NT workstations, or entire domains to either the export or the import list. By default, replication is done to all importing systems in the local domain.

5. Select the Do Not Import option. This prevents directory replication to this computer. It does not prevent replication *from* the computer. Click OK. Click OK again and the replication service is started.

6. Go to the Backup Domain Controller or other domain system doing the replication Import.

7. Open Server Manager and double-click the BDC listing. Its Properties dialog box appears.

8. Click the Replication button. The Directory Replication dialog box appears, the same as shown in Figure 13-19.

9. Select the Do Not Export function.

10. Finally, click OK. Replication is then performed and completed.

Generally, I think this feature is a bit overblown considering just what it's supposed to do. It's extremely simple to just write a batch file to perform an automated directory refresh each day or each hour without going through these gyrations. However, since this is basically an automated system, once you go through this process all your logon scripts are automatically replicated on all the domain systems that have Import privileges. It's easy to exclude systems or domains from the process or to include them. Since I take the distinctly unfashionable position of declaring logon scripts to be largely useless in Windows NT except for specialized tasks, I also find directory replication to be a bit underwhelming in its overall utility. It's more trouble than it's worth. Others may disagree.

Here's one argument: if directory replication is such a great thing, why can't it be made to perform user home directory replication without funneling everything through the required path? How about directories containing huge collections of data files?

By the way, the same replication feature can be found in the Control Panel. Double-click the Server icon, click the Replication button, and there it is.

When you build your Backup Domain Controller, you're doing so because you want a fail-safe mechanism for your network. After your user accounts are replicated, along with the logon scripts should that be necessary, you may still have some work to do. Namely, any key applications that may happen to reside on the PDC can probably be set up on the BDC as well. Vital home directory rosters should definitely be copied as well, along with any crucial data directories. Make sure the original path is preserved in all cases!

If and when your PDC fails, go to your BDC and promote it. Open the Server Manager, select the BDC, and select Promote to Primary Domain Controller from the Computer menu. Then go fix your computer.

A Final Word

That essentially wraps up this book. If you've plowed through every chapter, or even most of them, you now possess a thorough working knowledge of LAN-making with Windows NT 4.0. The intent of this book is to convey what most books in its field have failed to do consistently: provide clear-cut, reliable procedures for actual networking tasks, spanning nearly the entire gamut of things that you can do with Windows NT. When something in the OS comes up short in the features department, I haven't hesitated to say so. In the last few chapters, in particular, many more peripheral server features are somewhat less capable in their features than they really should be (the System Policy Editor is just one example). All in all, however, Windows NT 4.0's depth of networking features and its considerable accessibility are two powerful reasons for its accelerating acceptance in the networking market. It's been a privilege to guide you through this most utilitarian of network operating systems, and I wish you the best of luck in your future endeavors.

Appendix A

Final Networking Issues

You'll find a lot of basic information provided here, much of which either didn't fit or didn't have a place in the earlier chapters of this book.

Businesses really can't get along without networking, and even home users with a small business are handicapped if they don't have some kind of connection to the outside world, even if it's just through a 28.8 Kbps modem connection. This appendix is meant to fill in some of the conceptual gaps and provide some of the basic foundation knowledge for building a network in your office. You encounter many confusing terms here, and all of them are explained when they appear. Among the topics discussed in this appendix are

◆ An introduction and brief history of the Internet

◆ The various types of network media and what you may see in the future

◆ Windows NT's place in the networking software market

◆ A glance at the future of Windows NT

IT'S REALLY a grab-bag. One area I've discussed quite a bit in this book is the Internet. I've concentrated on applications within Windows NT, but it may be valuable to provide the larger context — what the Internet is and how this incomprehensibly huge network came into being. The following section provides a thumbnail sketch of its origins.

Introducing the Internet

A few decades ago, the Department of Defense decided it might be a good idea to build a communications system that would allow major government, academic, and military installations to share computing power. At the time, supercomputers, mainframes, and minicomputers were the stars of the computing industry. The Advanced Research Project Agency (ARPA) took seven years to design the first beginnings of the Internet, then called ARPAnet. In 1969 the first four hosts of the Internet were brought online, including Stanford, UCLA, UC Santa Barbara (go, Banana Slugs!), and the University of Utah. From the start the idea caught on among academics, but in an unexpected way. The plan was to use the ARPAnet to share supercomputing power among institutions that needed it, but those pesky professors discovered the wonders of e-mail instead. No one had ever seen anything like it, and new hosts across academia clamored to get on.

As the network expanded, a governing board had to be set up to manage the rapidly growing system. The serendipitously named *InterNetworking Working Group* (something like the Department of Redundancy Department) appeared, with the now-famous Vint Cerf as the first chairman. Over the next several years the network grew further and gradually shifted away from its academic/defense exclusivity. By 1976 Queen Elizabeth had been introduced to the wonders of e-mail. A pair of Duke University students invented the Usenet newsgroup system in 1979. Still one of the most popular applications on the Internet, the Usenet is democracy in action (sometimes a little too much so, perhaps), with anyone who possesses a modem being able to weigh in with their two cents on any conceivable subject on the Net.

Meanwhile, the ARPAnet continued to grow and included more than 200 host systems by 1981. Also, Mark Andreesen was nine years old.

Vint Cerf pops up again here because he is a key member of the team that created the TCP/IP networking protocol, which has played such a prominent role in the applied networking tasks in this book. The process took five years, from 1982 to 1987. When finished, TCP/IP became the common communications protocol for all computers on ARPAnet. It represented a huge advance in general computing and networking, although its effects took several years to affect the industry. Now TCP/IP dominates the networking business, and for good reason. TCP/IP is a highly logical, extensible, and flexible networking protocol that has been demonstrated to have the widest possible range of connectivity applications. At the same time, the term *Internet* was coined to describe the metastasizing network, and that new term crept into the lexicon.

Meanwhile, computing power underwent explosive growth in the hands of companies and private individuals, and the Internet began accepting host systems from non-academic sources. Suddenly millions of people discovered electronic mail, mostly within private networks such as CompuServe and MCI Mail. The Internet was still a well-kept secret to the bulk of computer users. Everything on the Internet was text-based, which limited its popular appeal to users who had a direct business or academic interest in its operation, or to a growing minority of pranksters, cheaters, and intensely curious spectators who were dubbed *hackers*. Serious incidents occurred involving software pranks and actual espionage, but generally the problem was (and still is) a creation of the mass media. Most people in computing or in the larger society still had no interest in the Internet.

Ultimately, hypertext was the solution.

The concept of hypertext has been around for decades. Invented by Ted Nelson in the late 1960s, hypertext allows creative links between different types of data objects (text, pictures, sounds, executable software, and music) from a large central database. Links can be made between items of different types, such as a text snippet like "The Rolling Stones' Jumpin' Jack Flash" and a sound recording of their little song. When the user clicks the text snippet, the recording actually plays. Nelson's idea was about 25 years ahead of its time. Although hypertext found its way into consumer applications such as Apple's HyperCard, true mass acceptance had to wait through the early '90s.

Users from the general public could actually use the Internet by this time, but the process was still frustrating and difficult, particularly in initial setup. Beginning Internet users had to know how to set up the TCP/IP protocol and configure each software utility, including FTP, Telnet, and e-mail. The Internet needed a visual stimulus to pull more people into the system and force software companies to build commercial products to make the Internet more accessible. Hypertext was the key and, unfortunately, Nelson wasn't able to exploit it. It was left to a wet-behind-the-ears college student named Mark Andreesen, and a few of his cronies at the University of Illinois, to invent the next killer application — the Web browser.

Andreesen's Mosaic Web browser immediately showed promise as the software tool that could tie all the disparate strands of the Internet together and make them accessible to a mass audience — FTP, Usenet discussion groups, electronic mail, and a new class of information called Web pages. In a few short years, as tens of millions of users flooded onto the Internet, and millions of new servers became Internet hosts, Andreesen became one of the most famous people in the country. As a vice-president of the company he cofounded, Netscape, he's already reached heights most of us can only dream of. Still only in his mid-20s, Andreesen now faces the odd predicament of wondering what he can do for an encore.

The Internet is now entering its corporate phase, while big business embraces the Net as a wide-area networking tool and a new method of doing business. Much is still up in the air. No one has quite cracked two key problems: how to extract really big money from the new commercial opportunities on the Net, and how to do so safely amid an online culture that is frequently hostile to mercantilist strivings. That's where we are today.

The Internet is a new medium for communication and information exchange, on a scale unlike anything the world has ever seen. It piggybacks upon last century's technology (the copper-wire phone system), offering a glittering promise of the future while being desperately hampered by the limits of the system it depends upon. In this book the Internet can be used as a networking medium with both remote access and Virtual Private Networks. There are many other media. What are they?

Networking Media

When I use the term *networking medium*, I'm discussing the wiring used to physically connect computers together. Although there are numerous ways to connect systems (including serial cables, ATM, Fibre Channel, Fiber-optic IBM Token-Ring, and Ethernet), there's only one medium of any importance for your LAN connections:

Ethernet. Because Ethernet commands more than 80 percent of all installed networking connections (IDC and `www.Gibabit-Ethernet.org`, 1997) and all current network operating systems are compatible with it, I'll turn to Ethernet as the dominant standard. Ethernet offers better compatibility with management standards such as SNMP (Simple Network Management Protocol), greater reliability, broad operating system support, and an overwhelming acceptance of its defined standards compared to any other networking alternative.

Normally you run into two types of Ethernet network cabling: 10Base-T (Unshielded twisted pair, or UTP) and 10Base-2 (Coaxial cable). UTP/10Base-T is the most commonly used because of convenience. You don't need to attach terminators to the end of a 10Base-T network as you do with coax. Cabling schemes are more graceful because you can string 10Base-T cabling and connectors through office cubicles and walls with much greater ease than is possible with coax. You also have much greater possible cable lengths with 10Base-T. When you build a network using this cable medium, you must use *hubs* to connect cable segments to each other. In a small network, one end of each 10Base-T cable might be connected to a workstation, with the other end of each cable length running into the hub. Another separate cable segment also runs from the hub to the server. UTP cabling supports a standard half-duplex (in which data is transferred in one direction at a time) transfer rate of 10 Mbps, 20 Mbps if both ends are running full duplex (where data is transferred in both directions simultaneously; a telephone is another example of a full-duplex device). Many of the better networking cards support full duplex. Once again: To build a 10Base-T network, you must use hubs as the intermediate devices between connections. Direct 10Base-T connections between machines will not work.

Also called Fast Ethernet, 100Base-T physical cabling is quite similar to 10Base-T, except that it runs at 100 Mbps, or 200 Mbps at full duplex. When Fast Ethernet appeared, users found a large increase in speed combined with the same reliability for their normal Ethernet networks. It showed that Ethernet networking performance could be scaled up exponentially at reasonable cost. To run Fast Ethernet in your network, you have to replace all the 10Base-T hubs with special 100Base-T hubs, which run three or four times the cost of 10Base-T hubs. Any workstations or servers planning to use Fast Ethernet must also upgrade their NICs. The performance increase is well worth it. Although you won't see anything like 100 Mbps performance even under the best conditions, Fast Ethernet offers roughly a threefold increase in transfer speed over standard 10Base-T.

Alternatives abound, but most are either too new to have widespread acceptance or have matured too slowly to be competitive. Among the latter are Fibre Channel, FDDI, and ATM. Fibre Channel uses fiber optic cable as the medium for transferring data among computers or as a high-speed disk controller system. It supports transfer rates ranging from 133 Mbps to 1.062 Gbps. UTP cable can also be used over short distances. As a network medium, Fibre Channel has yet to really catch on, and it is more commonly employed as an expensive alternative to SCSI, particularly in high-end multimedia development. Nevertheless, as a networking medium,

Fibre Channel is receiving new life by its inclusion in the new Gigabit Ethernet standard.

FDDI *(Fiber Distributed Data Interface)* is a 100 Mbps ANSI connection standard that uses fiber optic cable. It's frequently used as a backbone for wide-area networks and is a solid networking technology. FDDI actually supports numerous cable types, including UTP and fiber. Without getting too complicated, FDDI is considered a highly fault-tolerant networking standard that can withstand device or link failures on the network and generally continue to function.

Token-ring is a network configuration popularized by IBM, and it's actually been around since 1969. Unlike many networks that use a *star* topology, a token-ring is set up as a *ring* of computers that pass around a special data packet called a *token*. The token acts like an admissions ticket to the network, and computers attached to the network must capture the token in order to send a message or data. Only one token is allowed per network, which means that only one computer at a time can send messages, no matter how big the network. If the term *Token-Ring* is capitalized, it refers to a special networking protocol developed by IBM that is compatible with this networking scheme. At this point token-ring is basically obsolete and relegated to legacy IBM systems. It never really caught on in the larger market. Token-ring claims 12 million network nodes (Astral [www.astral.org/astrlwp1.html]), which sounds impressive until you realize that some 200 million PC-based networking nodes are in use. Most of these networking nodes are connected with Ethernet, and many millions more are on other platforms. Token-ring divides the remaining 15 percent of the networking connections market with the other alternatives: FDDI, ATM, and so on.

ATM, or *Asynchronous Transfer Mode,* is a widely talked-about but rarely used high-speed networking standard that most commonly offers a transfer rate of 155 Mbps but ranges from 25 to 622 Mbps. The biggest advantage of ATM is its data packet size, which is set up to be very small and maintained at one consistent size, regardless of the type of data. Because of this, ATM is well suited for networked multimedia applications such as video teleconferencing, ensuring that normal network traffic can still get through. Some newer ATM-related standards push the transfer rate up to 2.4 Gbps. One difficulty presented by ATM is its fixed-channel nature. Under TCP/IP, data packets can be routed over hundreds or thousands of different network paths to reach their destination. ATM requires a fixed path between two points. Another major problem holding ATM back is vendor incompatibility. No one has agreed on an overarching standard that enables all ATM switches and interfaces to communicate invisibly with each other. Some ATM backbones exist that form part of the underpinnings for the Internet, but use of ATM in corporate networks meets with slow progress and is in danger of being surpassed by upcoming rivals such as Gigabit Ethernet.

Using the same networking media as its predecessors, and leveraging many current networking technologies, Gigabit Ethernet is being presented as the next step up from 100 Mbps Ethernet. It offers the following characteristics:

◆ Provides half-duplex and full-duplex operation at speeds of 1000 Mbps/2000 Mbps

◆ Uses the 802.3 Ethernet frame format, as do Ethernet and Fast Ethernet

◆ Uses the CSMA/CD access method with support for one repeater per collision domain

◆ Uses fiber channel cable, fiber optic for longer distances, and the standard UTP (which will take longer to develop)

◆ Offers full backward compatibility with 10Base-T and 100Base-T technologies

As with its chief rivals, FDDI and ATM, Gigabit's role in networks of the future is not resolved; from all indications, its IEEE standard should be finished by the first quarter of 1998, and fully compliant product lines should appear immediately thereafter. It's hard to see how this alternative can lose. The new standard uses all the same technologies that everyone in the networking industry and in business is already familiar with. Legacy networks (Fast Ethernet as a *legacy* network?) are undisturbed and can be upgraded according to the user's time schedule. When Gigabit Ethernet first appears in standard-compliant hardware, the indications are that it will use Fibre Channel physical connections, which will be called 1000BASE-CX. The Fibre Channel standard is being tweaked in this context to support 1250 Gbps transfer rates, to account for the broadcast overhead and other communication's requirements for providing the full 1000 Gbps called for by the Gigabit Ethernet standard.

A future 1000Base-T physical connection using the common Category 5 UTP cabling will take a bit longer to develop. Hardware supporting Gigabit Ethernet will be minimally different from the devices you normally see: switches with high-performance backplanes, routers, uplink/downlink modules, network interface cards, and one new device called a buffered distributor. Similar to a hub, a distributor interconnects two or more network links running at 1 Gbps or faster, and functions as a repeater by forwarding every data packet to every connected device except the one originating the packet. It can also hold packets in a special dedicated memory buffer.

In the end, Ethernet is the prohibitive choice because of its integration with the desktop and server. Media like ATM are just as capable of handling the various types of data (text, video, graphics, and so on) on networks, but Ethernet is by far the most commonly supported, with no change in sight. On the other hand, big changes are happening in the networking and server operating system market.

Windows NT's Role in the Networking Market

Presently, three operating system competitors dominate the enterprise networking market: Novell NetWare, UNIX (primarily Sun, HP, and IBM), and Microsoft Windows NT. In this derby, Windows NT is the fair-haired boy coming up fast on the outside. UNIX and Novell are the longtime competitors glancing over their shoulders.

As I've noted in earlier chapters of this book, Novell practically invented the local-area network. NetWare is still the prohibitive favorite for vast numbers of networking customers. Unfortunately, Novell lost a lot of momentum. Due to badly conceived software, company acquisitions, and other management follies, Novell became a poster boy for what happens when a successful company loses its focus. After two CEO changes and wrenching reorganizations designed mainly to shed the ill-considered corporate buyouts of the recent past, Novell is now lean and mean again but is in desperate straits. NetWare 4.11 is now titled IntranetWare, even though TCP/IP is not the operating system's native networking protocol, and most of its Internet/intranet-related services are widely considered as patches that are not truly integrated into the operating system.

Sun (and its other UNIX competitors) maintains an unassailable position in the high-end server market. There is no way that the Wintel marketing machine can presently match the better UNIX houses' capability to service tens of thousands of clients at a time, run cross-country transaction processing systems, and provide truly huge scalability. At the same time, no UNIX competitor can even pretend to approach the lower-end, local-area networking market, now largely dominated by Novell and Microsoft. Although Sun now offers a $695 Solaris for Intranets package designed specifically to compete in that space, it remains to be seen whether anyone will even notice, other than hard-core UNIX partisans.

In enterprise networks, the key term is *scalability*. It refers to a network operating system's capability to add additional servers to a network for consistent increases in traffic capacity. Another major consideration is the capability to maintain network operation if any one server in the main managing group, which is called a *cluster*, happens to go down. (This feature is called *fail-over* capability.) In this area, there's still no doubt that UNIX is the king of scalability. Debates rage about Windows NT's effectiveness in large enterprise networks. Computer and business publications offer several compelling arguments to counter Microsoft's scalability claims.

First, there's no doubt that Windows NT is not as reliable as the front-line UNIX systems on which many corporations run. Although Windows NT represents a great improvement in reliability in the PC realm, it still has a long way to go before it can go head-to-head with UNIX in terms of reliability. Anecdotal stories abound describing UNIX mainframes and minicomputers that haven't been restarted for months or even years at a time. This can never happen with Windows NT because of its PC-centric nature, with its use of Dynamic Link Libraries (DLLs), several generations of legacy application software, and corresponding generations of legacy PC hardware.

Scalability is also unquestionably a problem with Windows NT 4.0, notwithstanding Microsoft's "Scalability Day" media blitz in May 1997. Because of NT 4.0's domain/trust relationship scheme, any large enterprise network becomes a rat's nest of unmanageable connections, and any true hierarchical network organization is a chimera. An additional irony is that at the outset of Microsoft's Scalability Day showing, its entire demonstration network had to be restarted due to what Microsoft claimed to be "hardware problems." (*Upside Magazine*, "The Taste Test," November 1997, p. 100.) At best, Microsoft will be able to offer four-way fail-over scalability with its Wolfpack upgrade for Windows NT 4.0. Windows NT 5.0 is also expected to max out at four-way. Given Microsoft's record at delivering solid, functional networking tools as upgrades (note Routing and RAS and the Exchange 5.0 updates), Wolfpack will probably work quite well and extend the NT 4.0 capabilities.

Another problem Windows NT presents in larger networks is its lack of real integration with Windows 95. The process of including Windows 95 clients in general Windows NT security tasks such as profiles and system policies is more a process of coercion than integration. Many companies have ignored Windows 95 altogether, to Microsoft's chagrin (but with little apparent effect on Microsoft's bottom line). Now, that bypassing of Windows 95 seems prescient.

None of this is to say that Windows NT 4.0 is a bad product. Far from it. Otherwise I wouldn't have written this book. The main point here is that Windows NT is not all things to all people in the networking arena. It's an excellent solution for small- to medium-size businesses. Comparing Windows NT Server 4.0 to its previous releases (versions 3.1, 3.5, and 3.51), its drastic improvements in performance, ease of use, and reliability stand stark in relief. Windows NT 4.0 is the first mature version of the operating system that companies can realistically consider for their business network. If Windows NT 5.0 achieves a similar quantum jump in its own capabilities, Microsoft will have pulled off perhaps the greatest feat of software engineering in computing history.

In the end, what is Microsoft's, and Windows NT's, most powerful selling point? It's the same point this entire book has made: price/performance and ease of configuration for small- and medium-size networks. In that area, NT goes head-to-head with NetWare and is presently undermining Novell's position in the market. At present, NT is far more accessible for small businesses that need to build a LAN or add to an existing one. The battle is by no means finished, because NetWare still holds approximately 50 percent of the local-area networking market. Many in the business hope that Novell is finally out of its death spiral and ready to make a comeback. If they don't, Microsoft will continue its inexorable march to take over the LAN market.

Windows NT's Future

Now that you've plowed through all the topics in *Windows NT 4.0 Connectivity Guide*, it's time for a foretaste of the future. Windows NT 5.0 represents a major upgrade, one that's intended to be more competitive in the large enterprise than NT 4.0. Among NT Server 5.0's expected improvements are the following:

◆ The aforementioned Active Directory, which introduces a new feature called *Namespace*, which contains the network's organizational scheme and defines methods for naming, accessing, and creating directory objects.

◆ Windows NT 5.0 will directly support LDAP 3.0 for directory access, indicating at least the possibility that other network operating systems supporting LDAP will be able to communicate with and query Windows NT directories in the future. This is a wise decision by Microsoft, enabling NT to become a real player in the enterprise market, where other directories dominate.

◆ Because of Active Directory, DNS will be Windows NT's main name resolution scheme, both inside and outside the network. NetBIOS name resolution schemes such as WINS will no longer be required but will still be supported for backward compatibility with older NT 4.0 network servers. Partially because of this, TCP/IP will be the NT 5.0 default protocol.

◆ Windows NT 5.0 will support four-way fail-over server clustering — a true version of scalability that was mentioned earlier. While still far short of several UNIX platforms in this area, four-way fail-over server clustering represents a major jump forward for NT in some enterprise networks.

◆ Trust relationships, NT's method for linking domains, will be retained but significantly enhanced by allowing *transitive trusts*, in which domains can be linked to others through an intermediate domain. Explicit trust relationships won't be required for complex interdomain access, simplifying larger domain network design. As an example, if Domain A has an explicit trust relationship with Domain B, and Domain B has an explicit trust with Domain C, Domains A and C can also recognize each other using a *transitive trust* without the additional overhead another explicit trust requires.

◆ Windows NT 5.0 will completely change its security structure, moving from the LAN Manager-based system in NT 4.0 to a new Kerberos-based security system. Windows NT 5.0 maintains backward security compatibility, and third-party security systems can still be implemented. *Kerberos* is a term that no one ever seems to define in the technology press, so here it is: It's a security scheme developed at the Massachusetts Institute of Technology that enables two clients to exchange private information on an otherwise open network. It does this using a system of "keys," called *tickets*. A unique ticket is assigned to every client user that connects to the network and is part of the user's account on the server. The ticket is then added to any message to identify its sender. This method supposedly prevents eavesdropping while ensuring that every user message proves its identity to the receiving end. It's more commonly used in UNIX systems and in services such as FTP, but with NT that's about to change. The interesting thing is that thin clients (terminal screens, as discussed earlier) cannot use this type of security. It will be interesting to see how Microsoft deals with this issue. One possible side effect is that using Kerberos security may improve NT's interconnectivity with UNIX systems.

◆ Within large NT networks, a new feature called *multimaster replication* allows multiple domain controllers (each of which controls its own domain, such as ISDEPARTMENT or ACCOUNTING, and so on) to retain a complete copy of the master directory. This allows for better distributed administration.

◆ Windows NT domains can be included in a hierarchical structure that bears some resemblance to an NDS tree (discussed in Chapter 7 of this book) but bears a closer resemblance to the DNS organization methods. Using this hierarchy, one domain can be labeled as a *parent* domain to other NT server domains. These subordinate domains then can actually control other subordinate domains. Using NT's revamped domain system, you should be able to have the best of both worlds: a familiar navigation system, and a better and simpler arrangement for your organization.

◆ A new Zero Administration Windows (ZAW) feature allows you to *publish* applications from a server to individual domains or workgroup units, allowing only certain groups to have access to a particular application. (Recent betas did not allow for individual user subscriptions, so granularity of application assignments is still a question.)

◆ Hardware support for Plug and Play.

◆ Full adoption of the Windows Driver Model, also supposedly provided by Windows 98, which ensures that one hardware driver for a device will run on either platform.

◆ Increased symmetric multiprocessing scalability (as distinct from server scalability).

◆ Support for a new Microsoft Installer, which will track every entry on a user's Registry and manage critical Dynamic Link Library dependencies, which is Windows' Achilles heel in general system management. This support provides a step towards alleviating the disastrous DLL problems encountered by Windows applications on the desktop and on the network. Applications will have to be certified to work with Microsoft Installer to be considered fully compliant with Windows 98 and Windows NT 5.0.

I've already mentioned Windows NT 5.0's Active Directory in earlier chapters of this book. You'll also note how TCP/IP is much more heavily emphasized in the next version, along with DNS. Now that you've read this book, you'll not only know and understand how TCP/IP works in Windows NT, but you'll be able to absorb the shift towards those two feature areas. The complexity of the trust relationship system also appears to be coming in for some relief, while retaining some of the ease of use and familiarity from the previous version.

Some Final Networking Tips

Although this book offers a huge collection of Windows NT networking tips and techniques, it seems important to give you as much knowledge as possible, even at the last minute as new information comes over my transom. The reason for this is that some new Windows NT-related computer publications are growing in popularity and circulation, and every time I pick up one of them, I learn new things. I've also discovered many things on my own since I finished writing the main body of this book, and I decided to pass this knowledge on to you as an extra added attraction.

Thin, lean, and fat clients

You need to keep some guidelines in mind when you build your network. One major criterion is the *type of client* you're planning to use in your network. The topic is becoming important in the networking world, especially with the advent of the NC (*network computer*) and so-called Java Terminals. Presently, both of these devices are more pregnant with possibility than they are established, useful products, but they've already had a major impact on Microsoft's avowed networking strategies. To understand the basic organization of your network, you also need to understand the differences between three different types of network clients — *thin*, *lean*, and *fat* — and how the client type influences the type of server you need.

There's a simple reason why *thin* and *lean* clients are important: ease of network maintenance. If you've read through part or all of this book, you'll have a good idea what I mean. That's also why so much time has been spent on home directories, the System Policy Editor, and user profiles in the final chapters of this book.

All three of those NT features, tied together, enable the network manager to create a LAN that's easier to manage and maintain, regardless of what kind of client you're using. Even with these tools, client hardware types can also make a big difference.

Here's a rule of thumb: the thinner the clients, the fatter the server. A thin client is simply a dumb terminal with a screen and keyboard, providing only a physical connection to the network. All applications are run off the server, and screen updates are sent from the server to the terminal monitor. No local disks or even a microprocessor or local RAM are provided on the client. The quality of the terminal screen can be almost anything from simple VGA grayscale to a 17- or 21-inch monitor.

On the server end you need a maxed-out system because it carries the entire processing and data-handling load for the entire network. After combing through a half-dozen networking and computing magazines, the general consensus is that a quad-processor Pentium Pro system with 512MB of RAM is the best server arrangement for a thin-client network. Using such a computer, you can support several hundred thin-client terminals (up to perhaps 600). This type of server is usually referred to as a *multi-user* system. All the intelligence is built into the server, and all calculations and screen redraws are centered there. The calculation load is huge.

Windows NT 4.0 doesn't directly support thin terminals, and it isn't inherently a multi-user operating system. In fact, Microsoft is working on an after-market solution called Hydra that retrofits NT 4.0 to support thin clients. Until Hydra appears, multi-user NT servers are stuck at version 3.51, which is made multi-user-capable by third-party software from Citrix Systems called WinFrame. (Citrix is also working on a Windows NT 4.0 version. They've also licensed their software to Microsoft, upon which Hydra is based.)

Thin clients offer the highest degree of control to the administrator. Users can save files to only their home directories on the server and cannot load software or new drivers into the system, and each client interacts with the system as a single-user load. Applications are run directly off the server, and no local storage is provided. Thin clients really aren't even computers, much less a Windows-based client.

Lean clients provide more local computing capabilities, including a CPU and RAM. Applications are run on the client system. Performance becomes more of an issue, because the CPU and RAM in the client affect the responsiveness of the application. As an example, Network PCs are defined as having actual PCI slots, a built-in network interface card, and a minimum of 16MB of RAM. Lean clients thus become vulnerable to the same endless hardware upgrade cycles so familiar to every PC user. Lean clients do bear many resemblances to thin ones. They're designed to allow continued central control of application code, data, user profiles, and security information. NetPCs must provide configuration locking features to avert changes by the end user. Because of their enhanced processing capabilities, lean clients also provide a major advantage: the server doesn't require the same level of processing power, or can apply the same power to a larger collection of clients. More clients can thus be serviced by the same quad-Pentium Pro server I mentioned earlier. NetPCs and Network Computers (NCs) are considered to be lean clients because they contain their own processing hardware. Lean clients don't necessarily have to run Windows natively, but in the context of Windows NT that's what you can expect to see (at least when actual products exist).

The irony is that if some of Microsoft's and Intel's management initiatives bear fruit, fat clients will be able to provide the same management capabilities as lean clients, thus rendering the latter less attractive (which might be deliberate). Among those initiatives by Microsoft are the Zero Administration Kit (ZAK, which just trips lightly off the tongue), Desktop Management Interface (DMI), and Intel's Wired for Management (WFM). WFM is interesting because it provides for remote system booting and configuration across the network for drives, buses and communications ports, and numerous other features in hardware. Future capabilities include Microsoft's ZAW (Zero Administration Windows) and a more interesting WBEM (Web-Based Enterprise Management). How much of this will bear fruit and how much of it is just *son et lumiere* remains to be seen. It all does translate into one thing: greater value for the Wintel network user. Even if half of these new management features wind up never being realized, network managers will finally receive some of the improvements they've been clamoring for since accepting Wintel's sweaty embrace.

Fat clients are simply normal, pumped-up PCs and laptops with a connection to the network. For fat clients, a relatively small server environment is sufficient, handling basic file and print sharing services, and the general domain services I've described throughout this book. Correspondingly, the Quad Pentium Pro server described earlier can handle a large number of clients, because applications are almost never run off the server. But by their nature, fat clients are the most difficult and expensive type of client to maintain. The Windows NT 4.0 user profiles, system policies, and other features were created to help managers increase their control over fat clients in the network. Despite many annoying glitches, many of which are detailed in this book, those features actually do a pretty good job. Unfortunately, full integration of Windows systems with NT Server's management features is really limited to NT Workstation clients. Even Windows 95 clients are limited in their ability to accept server management directives. (Windows 98 clients may make some strides in this area.)

For present Windows NT 4.0 users, the tools you've seen in Chapter 12 are a bit clunky but do provide some means to keep more effective control over your network. Much initial work is needed to build your home directories and define your system policies and profiles. After you finish building, the process becomes easier and network growth is fairly easy to accommodate. With the information I've provided in this book, those tasks are shown to be reasonably useful for basic management of fat clients on the Windows NT network, but there is a long way to go.

How many servers?

Typically, Windows NT networks tend to spread their networking functions over several different servers. As alluded to in Chapter 11, demanding tasks such as Microsoft Exchange, SQL Server, and other BackOffice applications should be isolated on their own server machines for best performance. The general trend in Windows NT networks seems to be that the more servers you have in each domain, the better. Any individual domain can have multiple servers, each of which handles one or two key network functions.

Exchange is a good example. It's a notorious memory hog. I've already discussed Exchange 4.0 and 5.0 earlier in this book. Except in the smallest networks, it's impractical to run Exchange on anything except dedicated over a bare-bones Windows NT Server installation. An even newer version of Exchange Server, version 5.5, is available as an upgrade to version 5.0. The upgrade removes Exchange's 16GB disk space limit and fixes numerous bugs in the previous release. Fail-over support is now built into the package, as is support for LDAP 3.0, which anticipates the eventual release of Windows NT 5.0 but won't offer much to current users. A new chat service is built in (based on Internet Relay Chat), which should enhance Exchange's collaboration capabilities. Unfortunately, the *one function per server* issue doesn't go away. Server farms are the norm in NT networking, especially when you're dealing with larger networks.

Tips for WINS servers

Chapter 3 describes the process of setting up and operating a WINS server, and it discusses the basics of how WINS operates. Although the typical statement for Windows NT networking is "The more servers, the better," WINS servers can't be applied in this fashion. If you're running a WINS server in your network and have a decent number of clients (say 50 to 100 or more), you can benefit from the additional security offered by a backup WINS server within your domain. When you set up WINS servers, you're provided with Primary and Secondary WINS Server address entry boxes (TCP/IP Properties, WINS Address tab). Windows NT workstations have the same ability to access secondary WINS servers. The Secondary WINS Server is where you can set up your WINS name resolution database for replication in case things go down on the primary. In fact, a Backup Domain Controller is a good candidate for this procedure. I won't go into intense detail about this topic; if you've read and applied Chapter 3 of this book, the information here will be quite simple.

A WINS server doesn't replicate automatically. You must set it to be a Push part-ner to the backup WINS server, and the backup WINS server must be set up to be a Pull partner with the Primary WINS server. This is actually quite easy to do. Just open the WINS Manager and select Replication Partners from the Server menu. The Replication Partners dialog box appears, as shown in Figure A-1.

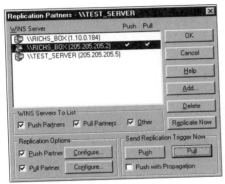

Figure A-1: Replicating a WINS Server
to a Backup

All the key features for WINS server replication are provided here. You may have to issue the IP address for your secondary WINS server in this dialog box. After you issue the IP address, you can select it from the WINS server list and enable the Push Partners and Pull Partners check boxes as desired.

If a secondary WINS server is set up to be a Pull partner, which is required for replication, the server from which the secondary WINS server is intended to *pull* the WINS name server database must also be set up as a *push* partner. The two set-tings are complementary and must be set up for replication to work. Under most circumstances, a Push partner setting for the back WINS server isn't necessary and can actually damage your existing installation.

If your primary server goes down, rebuild it and set it up as a Pull partner to the secondary, set up the secondary as a Push partner, and thus restore your entire WINS database to get that part of your TCP/IP network back up and running. The process is not too difficult, and the WINS Manager provides useful online help for every aspect of WINS replication.

WINS servers also present a major compatibility issue. Under Windows NT Server, WINS won't usually work properly on a multihomed system running two or more network interface cards. If you find yourself needing to do this, Microsoft also recommends that the server running WINS should not be a DHCP client. In Windows NT 5.0, WINS will be heavily deemphasized in favor of DNS. Fortunately, NT 5.0 will be backward-compatible, so any older servers can be maintained.

Improving Network Performance

Here's one related issue that enjoys hearty debate: How many routers and subnets do you need to build the most efficient network? You'll recall that Chapter 3 discusses the topic of subnets and how they're broken out of larger groupings of IP addresses, so I won't repeat that information here. Here's another rule of thumb: The more routers and subnets you have in your network, the more complicated and inefficient it tends to become.

Broadcast Storms and Routing

Broadcast storms are a common problem in TCP/IP-based networks. The more clients you have on any network segment, the higher the odds that you'll run into broadcast storms. It happens on the Internet all the time. What are broadcast storms? Because TCP/IP is a broadcast-based protocol, every time a client makes a request over the network, the network sends out a broadcast and waits for a response from the "other end." The more clients and servers you have doing this, the more bandwidth is taken up on the network by those broadcasts. Beyond a certain point, you have a broadcast storm that prevents efficient data exchange between systems. Two good methods for cutting down on this problem are to use a faster network (Fast Ethernet, for example) or use more routers to separate parts of your network from one another. Routers often function as filters to remove broadcast traffic from other parts of the LAN. They are expensive, and they do impose other penalties, but broadcast storms are about the worst thing that can happen on a busy LAN besides a main server crash.

Routers and bridges provide highly useful networking tools for larger networks, but they impose overhead. Sometimes you have no choice but to rely on routing. One way to cut down on routing hardware, at least in small department-level networks, is to immediately install and use the Windows NT Routing and RAS upgrade on a multihomed server. Unfortunately, you might have to keep a close eye on that system if it's running WINS. But routing drastically drives up the cost and complexity of your network. There may be many cases where a small workgroup can get along just fine with 10Base-T or 100Base-T hubs instead of using routers and the required subnets. Give it some thought when you design your network.

Another obvious dictum is to get as much RAM as you can. With memory costs dipping below $3 per megabyte for some configurations, there's never been a better time to max out the RAM on your server.

Also consider Virtual Private Networks. This is not an area where you necessarily get a performance boost; what you do get is a drastic decrease in remote operating costs: in some applications an 80 percent cost decrease. How is this possible?

To begin with, Microsoft actually led the creation of the PPTP (Point-to-Point Tunneling Protocol), which is what makes Virtual Private Networks possible over the Internet. Because Windows NT offers the first serious implementation of PPTP, by reading this book you have already acquired a key tool for the future.

If your office is or will be running a leased high-speed communications line, you should run, not walk, over to the nearest Internet terminal and look up Virtual Private Network information. In its September 22, 1997, issue, *InfoWorld* ran a solid comparison of four different Virtual Private Network system providers and found that all four could save their customers breathtaking amounts of money (*InfoWorld*, "Virtual Private Network Solutions," September 22, 1997, p. 1). Of course, the systems discussed do represent a significant initial investment. The process of creating a basic VPN is actually quite cheap and easy, as you've seen in Chapter 10 of this book. If you have wide-area networking needs, creating a Virtual Private Network can save you huge money over setting up leased lines for your offices.

Memory is an interesting issue. No matter how much RAM you have in your server, Windows NT insists on using a special Paging file to swap application and operating system data back and forth between disk and memory. The Paging file is used as virtual memory to contain the overflow of data and ensure that plenty of memory remains available for all the applications you run. Unfortunately, disk swapping slows things down, and virtual memory is inherently much slower than RAM. To ensure that your virtual memory has the least possible impact on performance, open the Control Panel and double-click the System applet. Click the Performance tab. In the Virtual Memory section of the Performance tab, click the Change button. Set the Initial and Maximum sizes for the paging file to the same value, and don't skimp on the size of the paging file. A good rule of thumb is to use at least twice as much disk space for a paging file as you have RAM in your system. The smaller your RAM footprint, the larger your paging file needs to be. If you do have a relatively small RAM installation (64MB or less), accept the Windows NT paging file defaults and leave it at that.

Another highly useful tip (*Windows NT Magazine*, "NT Performance," September 1997, p. 132-3.) is to set aside a special FAT-formatted (not NTFS) disk partition as your paging file, and set the paging file size to the size of that partition. If you're running a relatively small network, you can actually dispense with the paging file altogether. You should eliminate the paging file only on systems that have a huge amount of RAM, systems you know will not use all of the RAM when running all your applications and while fully functioning on the network. To check your expected highest RAM footprint, run all your typical application and server services during peak time, open the Windows NT Task Manager, and click the Performance tab. Check the Peak value in the Commit Charge section, as shown in Figure A-2.

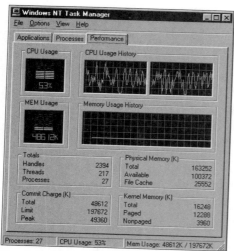

Figure A-2: Checking Current Memory Use
in Your Server

In Figure A-2, the Physical Memory section shows a total of 163MB of memory and 100MB free. The Peak Commit Charge value is 49360K, which means that much memory overhead is not being used on the current system. To make more use of installed memory, open the Registry Editor (REGEDT32.EXE) and locate the registry key called HKEY_LOCAL_MACHINE\SYSTEM\CurrentControlSet\Control\Session Manager\Memory Management. As you can see in Figure A-3, the hierarchical level brings up a set of memory management settings, the most important of which for your needs is the DisablePagingExecutive setting, second from the top.

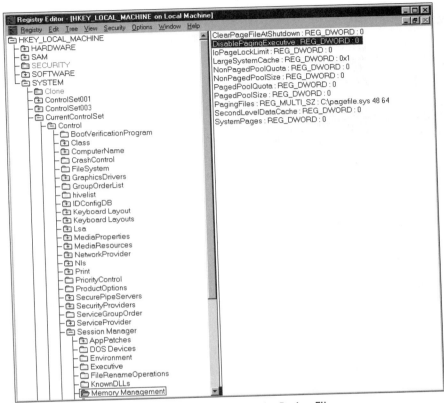

Figure A-3: Setting Virtual Memory for Disabling the Paging File

Change the DisablePagingExecutive setting to 1 from its default of 0. Save your changes and restart the system. If your computer has lots of memory, this will actually boost performance. If not, performance will definitely suffer, particularly in production environments. The DisablePagingExecutive setting is not a setting to mess around with during working hours.

What Is Networking and Why Do We Need it?

In this final section I want to offer a "fictional" account of the one company left in this entire country that doesn't have a local-area network. It's a litany of difficulties that can ensue when your workplace doesn't recognize the real need for basic networking in a small office. Have compassion for the Amalgamated Widgets of this world. Then go out and try to sell to them.

Mr. John Smith
Company President
Amagamated Widgets, Inc.

Dear Sir:

Enclosed in this document is the proposal you requested regarding why I feel it's important for our company to have a network.

I believe that building and installing a network would benefit us greatly in these terms:

◆ Increased productivity

◆ Better use of resources

◆ Accommodate growth for the future

Consider the situation we have now:

◆ Seven PCs

◆ Three Pentiums running Windows 95

◆ Four 486-based systems, all running Windows 3.11, scattered throughout the office

◆ Three Macintoshes (all in Graphics Department)

◆ Two laser printers

　　◆ One on the main office floor

　　◆ One Postscript-capable laser printer in the Graphics department, networked to two of the Macs

At the present time, none of our PCs are networked, and our Macintoshes are connected together by AppleTalk.

What is occurring in our office now?

To print something, an employee must copy the file onto a floppy disk, walk over to the person connected to the actual printer, and ask that person to print the document. This has many damaging effects on our company. First, the employee wanting to print has his or her workflow completely interrupted by the copy-walk routine. Second, the employee being asked to print the file is also having his or her workflow interrupted. Even if that person can attend to his or her colleagues' requests immediately (which, as I've seen, is rarely the case), the entire process means that two entire employees' valuable working time, which you're paying for, is lost for a minimum of five minutes. Consider that this happens to each person in our little group at least twice a day.

And what happens if the document is too big to fit on a floppy disk? You can understand why this presents a severe problem.

The whole situation, when you combine all these different factors, contributes to a sense of powerlessness on the part of the employees. They can't get their work done without constant interruptions; they can't be productive and must constantly bother other employees for jobs that they could easily perform themselves given the right resources.

Buying computers for all the employees in your company is a progressive step in the right direction. Now, to boost the productivity of your employees and eliminate waste, you need to take the next step.

If you merely consider the seven people using PCs, you can easily see that well over an hour of man-time per day is lost, at a bare minimum, just to print a simple document. Your average pay is roughly $12 per hour. (Don't bother asking how I know that. I'm the accountant, remember?) The process of copying files back and forth between computers is another tremendous time-waster.

Consider the rough average of 210 work days per year and multiply that by just this tiny, easily quantifiable example:

$12 * 210 = $2,520

That is one month's wages thrown down the drain. Consider how much it would cost to install our network:

Windows NT Server software with 10-user license	$750
Seven 10Base-T 16-bit ISA network cards	$49 each
10Base-T network hub	$150
One 600-watt Uninterruptible Power Supply for the server	$400
Our Macs already have 10Base-T built in, so no investment is needed there	
Total:	Approx. $1,800 (incl. tax)

Add a solid server machine with 128MB of RAM, which I've costed out at approximately $3,000, and the total startup hardware cost is less than $5,000. The initial hardware and software investment is minimal.

The cost of creating and installing the network is a bit more considerable. Nothing in this world of business comes for free, as I'm sure you're aware.

You can go in two directions:

1. Hire an expensive consultant who may or may not be able to get the job done in the prescribed period of time.

The advantages are:

- The skills that the consultant brings to the table
- Limited training and installation hassles
- Possible maintenance and support contact

The disadvantages are:

- Lengthy shopping time to locate the right consultant
- Very high cost
- Lack of accountability

2. Take the process in-house.

The advantages are:

- Accountability
- Cuts down on costs (which are exorbitant given the present situation)

The disadvantages are:

- Hourly cost of existing employee
- Who installs it?
- Who manages the network once it's installed?

I will manage the ongoing network, as I've discussed. When the system is up and running, it's largely self-sustaining. Why?

- Windows NT combines exceptional networking power with great accessibility.
- Windows NT is the first major network operating system to provide both of these attributes.
- It even allows us to integrate our Macintoshes into the larger network and share the same printing services

You don't need a Ph.D. in computer science to install and run Windows NT. Computing experience is a must, however. If you want to perform the installation in-house, we'll need the best possible reference we can buy — one that combines accessibility, attention to detail, and a broad coverage of specific networking tasks. We have such a resource, which largely eliminates the need to even hire a consultant. I'm one of the most computer-literate people in our company, and after reading *Windows NT 4.0 Connectivity Guide*, the new book published by IDG Books Worldwide, Inc., I can install and maintain our entire network without a huge cost in time from other projects.

There goes our consultant.

Basic networking tasks are rather simple in Windows NT. Unfortunately, that's not the picture you get from most of the technology press. With decent networking hardware and the proper knowledge conveyed by *Windows NT 4.0 Connectivity Guide*, you can build a complete 10-station LAN in two days using Windows NT. This book even tells you exactly what kind of hardware you need to make sure things get up and running properly! Why don't we hear more about this? In all likelihood, if consultants and the trade press were a little more honest about it, they might worry about their customers wondering why they're paying such exorbitant fees for their services. If our network were much larger, I'd recommend hiring a consultant in any case. If we planned to set up a Web host, I'd recommend the same thing. If we eventually do so, at least you'll have someone on hand who can check on things and know what's going on.

In many cases, even with the use of Windows NT, consultants can be a real asset. I submit that for our current purposes it isn't necessary. Our users are not a terribly demanding bunch; they just want something that will run properly and save them time. We don't have a huge network, and we don't plan to create a Web presence at present; we just need to boost our productivity.

We may even find other uses for our network. Wouldn't you like to be able to use your laptop to connect to the network when you're on the road? Out of the box, Windows NT allows you to do that.

Our PC users will be able to share files with our Mac users without running floppies back and forth. We can even pull the high-quality Postscript printer out of the Mac section and set it up for sharing across the entire network. Even our Windows 3.*x* users will be able to take advantage of new network resources.

We can have our network up and running this week. I urge you to authorize this with all possible speed.

Sincerely,

Jack Smith

Appendix B

What's on the CD-ROM

In this appendix you'll find a description of the contents of this book's companion CD-ROM. After the name and maker of each product you'll see the CD-ROM directory in which the installation software is located. The example drive letter in the path names is E, but your assigned drive letter to your CD-ROM drive may be different, so bear that in mind.

Please see the Installation Instructions at the back of the book for general instructions on how to install the software.

BEI UltraBac 4.1

(E:\UltraBac\SETUP.EXE)

This handy backup software program allows you to use any backup medium you want — Jaz, Zip, or SyQuest drives; hard disk drives; or any tape drive available and installed on your system. BEI is even kind enough to provide an Uninstall program that actually works. The evaluation version expires after one month. Its user interface is a little sparse, but it gets the job done without too much fuss. I use this program to back up my Windows NT Server hard disks to a networked Jaz drive. It's worth a look. An extensive Word help document is contained in the Ub41hlp.doc file.

Executive Software's Diskeeper Lite

(E:\DISKEEPER\SETUP.EXE)

This freeware package is a simple but detailed hard disk defragger program for Windows NT. It has no time limit placed on it, and you can use it on Windows NT Server or Workstation. It's an extremely handy and impressive little utility. The program's hard disk analysis takes a minute but gives you a direct assessment ("This disk is badly fragmented. We strongly recommend you defragment it NOW, before your system slows to a crawl."). It's very cool, and it's free. I like this one a lot. Whenever it gives you an analysis, it bugs you to upgrade to one of the commercial products, but that's understandable. To top it off, a version of Diskeeper is being built into Windows NT 5.0.

Bluecurve's Dynameasure

(E:\DYNAMEASURE\DYNADEMO.EXE)

Bluecurve™, Inc. is a leading developer of Active Measurement™ capacity and reliability management software for Windows NT. The Dynameasure family of software is intended to give hard performance data to IT professionals to help them establish a reliable and predictable distributed IT infrastructure. Dynameasure version 1.5 is a demo version of their flagship package.

Dynameasure is essentially a performance benchmark that uses so-called Active Measurement techniques to provide graduated, meaningful stress testing for a network infrastructure. It uses sample database files, which the user is expected to provide. Those sample files can be generated from SQL Server, Informix, Oracle, and other major database apps.

To begin setting up the Dynameasure demo program, double-click the dynademo icon. WinZip's self-extraction dialog box appears, showing a default directory of C:\DYNAINST where it will automatically place the extracted files for the demo software. You can also choose to run WinZip, assuming it's installed in your system, but I recommend accepting the default. After the files are extracted, double-click the Setup icon to install the demo.

Maximized Software's TcpSpeed v. 1.01

(E:\TCPSPEED\TS101.EXE)

TcpSpeed is a simple program that monitors the TCP/IP connection on your network. It requires the Visual Basic runtime library file VBRUN300.EXE, which is bundled with the software on this disk.

Kane Security Analyst (KSA)

(E:\KSA\Setup.exe)

KSA is a highly useful security auditing tool for performing quick checks of your network's security. Not only does it attempt to find the weak points in your network, it also makes suggestions on how to deal with them. You have the ability to check overall domain security, login violations, excessive rights to particular accounts, audit policy compliance, and Registry security settings with an interactive Registry assessment feature. You can even run a password-cracking test. Many more features are provided here than I can possibly list. The program bears a passing resemblance to Microsoft's C2 utility provided with the Windows NT Server

Please call Sunbelt Software at (888) NT UTILS for a license key to install the software.

Administrator's Kit. But it goes far beyond that. It ties together many busy-work management jobs together in one place, so you don't have to burrow through a half-dozen or more NT utilities to do many of the same tasks. Beware: This is a *big* program. The version on this disk is licensed to run on one NT Server and/or one NT Workstation.

You may need a license key to install this software. Please call Sunbelt Software at (888) NT UTILS for a key.

Kane Security Monitor (KSM)

(E:\KSM3\Setup.exe)

KSM is a security monitoring program that offers a huge collection of associated features, including (from Sunbelt Software's Web site):

◆ Automatically identifies security violations

◆ Uncovers security break-ins before they occur

◆ Identifies password guessers, curious users, file browsers, compromised user IDs, password-cracking attempts, network doorknob attacks, privileged ID abuse, data flooding, packet browsing, and more

◆ Focuses on sensitive users, workstations, and files

◆ Minimizes setup time by using a built-in, time-saving, self-populating database of expert security information

◆ Automatically alerts security officers, auditors, or LAN administrators about unauthorized access

◆ Integrates seamlessly with the Kane Security Analyst

Both KSM and KSA are designed for enterprise networks but can be tested and run on a single workstation or server using the evaluation software on this CD. KSM is also a big program, requiring a four-hour download on a 28.8 Kbps modem. Be glad I gave it to you here so that *you* don't have to download it!

SuperDisk-NT

(E:\SuperDisk-NT\Setup.bat)

SuperDisk-NT is a RAM disk program for Windows NT that enables you to devote a maximum of 512MB of system RAM to a special RAM disk. The RAM disk can be shared across the network and supports both FAT and NTFS. Very nice!
    Call Sunbelt Software at (888) NT UTILS for a license key to run the software.

SuperCache-NT

(E:\SuperCache-NT\Setup.bat)

SuperCache enables you to designate amounts of physical memory as cache RAM for your disk controller. Some SCSI disk controllers provide memory caching; this piece of software emulates this capability in system RAM. Whenever the system reads a piece of data more than once, the information is returned to the processor at full memory speeds without accessing the disk. The vendor claims between a 500 percent to 2,000 percent increase in performance over standard non-cached hard disks. Although I have doubts about the veracity of these claims, any improvement is always welcome in the NT environment. I *strongly* recommend being careful with your installation of this program; do not immediately install it in a working pro- duction server. Run tests with it in other systems to get familiar with its character- istics. When you're satisfied that SuperCache-NT offers what you're looking for (and who doesn't want faster disk performance?), try installing it in a network server that you're in the process of bringing up. Track your process carefully, as well as the system's behavior before and after you run the software. As far as I know, the software is bulletproof if you follow a few simple rules; network server environments are sensitive and precious enough that you can't afford to take chances.
    Most of what follows is taken from Sunbelt Software's Web site at http://www.sunbelt-software.com/scache.htm.
    First, do not install the SuperCache program on your main System Partition or the hard disk partition containing your paging file (the virtual memory in your system). Although SuperCache can be used to cache the system partition, the soft- ware itself must be installed on another hard disk. Bear this in mind.
    The program has a rough *20 percent rule*. If possible, you should reserve 20 per- cent of the size of the partition that you will be caching as free memory. Here's an example:

Caching 200MB of disk/reserve 20MB as FREE memory for apps on the server.

Caching 2GB of disk/reserve 200MB as FREE memory for apps on the server.

Follow these steps to install SuperCache:

1. Open a DOS window and cd to **A:\intel** if you are running on an Intel PC, or cd to **A:\alpha** if you are running on a Digital Alpha system.

2. Type **setup.bat**. You're asked to accept the terms of the EEC License Agreement. If you accept, the kit files are copied to the system directories on your system.

3. Still in the DOS window, type **ScConfig**. Unless you have licensed SuperCache-NT previously, you're prompted for a license key. Enter the key code (available by calling Sunbelt Software at (888) NT UTILS). You can also force ScConfig to prompt for a license key by invoking it with the "-l" switch, such as **ScConfig -l**.

4. When prompted, enter the drive letter of the disk you want to cache. Enter the drive letter as letter + :. For example, type **D:** to indicate you want to use the D drive.

5. When prompted, type **y** or **n** to indicate whether you want to use the Lazy Write feature. Lazy Write improves performance for write I/O. EEC Systems, Inc. recommends that you use this option with an uninterruptable power supply.

6. When prompted, type **y** or **n** to indicate whether you want SuperCache-NT to start running at the next reboot. Type **n** for no when you want to stop using SuperCache-NT.

7. The software now shows your configuration selections. If you want to change anything, type **n** for no when prompted, and you will be given the opportunity to reenter new settings.

8. If enabled, SuperCache-NT starts at the next system reboot.

Electronic Version of This Book

(E:\Book)

The CD-ROM contains an Acrobat PDF version of this book. You need to install the Acrobat Reader to access the electronic book. The Acrobat Reader can be found in E:\Acrobat Reader\ar32e301.exe.

PerfMan 1.3 (Performance Manager)

(E:\PERFMAN\PERFMAN.EXE)

PerfMan is yet another capacity-planning program. It uses a Collector mechanism to cull performance measurements from a variety of machines in your system, summarize the data, and send it to a separate Analyst program. The key program in the PerfMan set is its Server Admin program. When you install the program, a new menu appears in your Start menu. For a quick and useful introduction to PerfMan, I strongly recommend reading the Quick Start Instructions document from that menu. For a thorough test of the program, you probably want to run it for a couple of days to get a good data sample.

PerfMan installs its entire application in one directory, so you have little trouble removing it if it isn't what you want. This is good, because this program is in serious need of a user interface overhaul. Its dialog boxes are far too busy and cluttered to be useful to even advanced users, and it bears many marks of being an unrevised Windows NT 3.51 program. It's also a 30-day evaluation program that doesn't offer the ability to easily run performance-monitoring functions. It's worth a look, but I don't recommend it unless you're prepared to be very persistent.

Trusted Enterprise Manager 2.0

(E:\TEMeval\TEMSETUP.EXE)

This one is huge. Essentially, Trusted Enterprise Manager is a replacement for the User Manager in Windows NT. Its intended use is as a heavy-duty account management and security maintenance application. The version bundled in this CD-ROM functions normally for up to 10 clients but is really designed for much larger networks. Three modules comprise the TEM suite: TEM service, the TEM Administrator, and the TEM client. High-level Windows NT domain administrators are meant to use TEM Administrator to delegate and manage user account authority, through global groups, to lower-level remote administrators, who are dubbed trusted managers. This doesn't sound like a big deal, until you try to do this in a large, fully-trusted multiple-master domain setup like the ones discussed at the end of this book. The TEM client is used by those trusted managers to perform their lower-level account management functions, monitored consistently by the TEM Server. This is actually a pretty impressive product and is worth a look.

Fortress-NT

(E:\FORTRESS\Setup.exe)

This is a relatively small but useful utility that acts like a "beat cop" for your network. You'll often wind up with idle user accounts more or less permanently connected to the network. Fortress-NT basically tells those vagrant accounts, "All right, move along, get outta here." It offers control of workstation logons in addition to domain logons, logging the user off from the workstation as well as the domain. An Idle Logout screen saver logs the user off after a prescribed period of inactivity.

LAN Licenser

(E:\LAN Licenser\Setup.exe)

ABC LAN Licenser is a hard-core management program whose primary mission is to maintain and govern the software licenses on your network. Compatible with Microsoft BackOffice and basically any multi-user software program on your network, LAN Licenser's features are extremely broad in scope. It provides license balancing, an attempt to make sure that individual seat licenses are available for any program whenever a user on the network needs one. It also monitors idle times for open license instances and requests that the user log off the application to free the license for others' use. LAN Licenser can even govern how and when users can run various programs in the operating system, such as games. Individual license instances can be brokered to machines that are frequently off the network, such as laptops. Check this out if you find yourself in a situation where your company allocates only so many seat licenses for applications on your server, and you need some method to monitor their activity.

Call **(888) NT UTILS** for a license key to run the software.

OfficeCab 2.0

(E:\OfficeCab\Offcab.exe)

OfficeCab 2.0 is an Office Cabinet document manager that may be useful to heavy users of Microsoft Office. It also provides a more graceful Find File feature than the native Find in the Windows Start menu. The program is fully functional shareware.

QMaster

(E:\QMaster\Nt.bak\Setup.exe)

QMaster is a print management and batch output program that can be used as a substitute for Windows NT's Print Manager, particularly in systems in which you manage dozens of printers on the network. It handles more sophisticated print queues and load balancing, and it can dynamically set task execution according to computer speed and CPU loads and other criteria. Download the documentation from http://www.sunbelt-software.com/qmaster.htm.

Make sure to install QMaster from the Nt.bak directory (not the NT directory).

Various other programs

(E:\VARIOUS)

Numerous other Windows NT utilities can be found in the VARIOUS folder on the CD-ROM. For more information about Remotely Possible, XLNT, and Administrator Assistant Plus, go to http://www.sunbelt-software.com. For information about the Somarsoft products DumpEvt, DumpReg, and Regedit, go to http://www.somarsoft.com. To learn more about TweakBIOS, point your browser to http://miro.pair.com/tweakbios/tweak15g.exe. For information about Observer and Analyst/Probe, go to the Network Instruments website at http://www.networkinstruments.com. Finally, for more information about the Emwac utilities, point your browser to http://www.emwac.ed.ac.uk/html/toolchst.htm.

Note that to run RegEdit, you may need to install VB40032.DLL, available in the vb40032 folder. For XLN9, please call Sunbelt Software at (888) NT UTILS to obtain a license key.

Glossary

address scope A set of IP addresses set aside for management by a DHCP service.

AGP (Accelerated Graphics Port) A new standard developed by Intel to take the video display functions off the PCI bus (where a flourishing market for accelerated video cards has existed for several years) and yoke it directly to the main system bus and main memory. The dedicated AGP connection runs at 66 MHz, double the PCI bus speed, and is available only on the newest Pentium II systems.

AppleTalk Apple's broadcast-based, routable networking protocol for Macintoshes, which Windows NT also supports.

AppleTalk Zone The primary organizational unit in AppleTalk networks, in which each *Zone* can contain up to 256 networked devices. Zones have a simple numbering scheme and are similar to workgroups on the PC.

AV-capable A type of SCSI hard disk that uses a high spin rate (usually 7,200 rpm). The AV stands for Audio/Video, and it denotes a hard disk capable of handling sound and video recording in real time with minimal dropped frames or skips in multi-track audio recording.

BDC (Backup Domain Controller) Used in Windows NT to provide a fail-safe backup for the Primary Domain Controller.

bindery The directory organization used in NetWare 3.*x*.

binding The process of making more than one communications device use the same addressing scheme. As an example, if you use a modem to connect to a LAN using TCP/IP, the modem is *bound* to the IP address originally assigned to the networking card in the system, and the network treats both types of connections the same way.

broadcast-based protocol A networking protocol that relies on broadcasting messages across the entire network and waiting for responses from clients that match the request made. Broadcasting is a heavy-traffic and inefficient method of network communication, but many systems use it, including AppleTalk and NetBEUI.

C-Class A set of 255 contiguous IP addresses.

DAT (digital audio tape) Magnetic tape that sequentially stores data. Capacity varies from 2GB to 24GB, depending on the compression scheme. DAT offers three recording formats: DDS, which handles up to 4GB; DDS-2, which stores up to 8GB; and DDS-3, which can handle up to 24GB.

disk striping Using multiple disks to share contiguous data. When disks are striped, each disk has a sequential series of sectors allocated for its stripe, and each of the other disks has a corresponding stripe in the same position. More stripes are written in sequence until all the disks are filled. Then data is written sequentially along the stripes. Thus, a file can span several disks.

default gateway The IP address in your subnet occupied by your router. This provides the subnet's communications *gateway* to the outside networks.

DHCP (Dynamic Host Configuration Protocol) A Windows NT networking feature that assigns IP addresses to network clients using a server-defined *scope* of IP addresses.

DHCP agent A Windows NT feature that enables DHCP addressing requests to be sent through routers on a TCP/IP network. Required because DHCP is not compatible with routing.

DIMM (Double In-line Memory Module) A newer memory package similar to SIMMs but offering a different form factor and more flexibility for configuring systems. DIMMs place arrays of memory chips on a small board with two rows of I/O contacts. They have 168 pins and transfer data at 64 bits. Used in many newer PCs and Macintoshes.

disk mirroring The practice of using two identically sized disk partitions (or physical disks, which is even more preferable) to *mirror* each other's complete directory contents. This not only provides automatic data backup but also ensures that if one disk or partition fails, the mirror steps in and resumes system operation.

disk spanning The practice of using more than one disk for a single partition.

disk striping Writing data continuously across multiple drives, in a track-to-track sequence.

domain The basic organizational unit for Windows NT networks. A domain provides comprehensive self-contained security features, resource sharing, and the ability to divide up different server functions among separate machines (a separate WINS server, separate Exchange server, and so on).

DNS (Domain Name Service) A networking standard that allows computer names across any size of TCP/IP network to be resolved to IP addresses.

DNS Zone A set of IP addresses pre-defined or pre-assigned to specific network entities, such as organizations or servers.

DRAM (Dynamic Random Access Memory) The most common form of computer memory. The term *Dynamic* refers to the fact that the memory's contents are not permanent but are erased by program actions or by shutting down or resetting the computer.

EDO (Enhanced Data Out) A type of memory common and popular in Pentium and Pentium Pro-class PCs. Provides up to 25 percent faster access to data than standard DRAM, and is common in faster Pentium-class machines.

EIDE (Enhanced IDE) A high-density, high-speed hard disk connector standard that enables multi-gigabyte IDE hard drives for less money, and provides support for tape drives and CD-ROM devices.

FAT (file allocation table) A 16-bit standard file system used on most PCs, including MS-DOS and Windows computers.

FAT-32 A long-overdue but poorly implemented upgrade to FAT, introduced in an OEM-distributed revision of Windows 95, that offers smaller file cluster sizes. Not compatible with Windows NT. Highly difficult to work with in general, and best postponed until Windows 98.

group A collection of user accounts gathered together to provide uniform access rights to network resources.

GSNW (Gateway Services for NetWare)

IETF (Internet Engineering Task Force)

IP address A 12-digit address, each digit of which uses decimal code (0-9). Every three digits of the address are separated by a period, and each of the three-digit values has a maximum value of 255. (This is also called *dotted-quad notation*.) IP addressing is used in TCP/IP networks. An IP address can be used by only one specific client. If two systems attempt to use the same IP address, an addressing conflict results. This occurs on the Internet or on WANs as easily as in a LAN.

IP (Internet Protocol) Defines the addressing scheme used throughout every TCP/IP network.

IPv6 The upcoming new version of IP, which mandates a much larger address space and numerous other enhancements to the TCP/IP networking standard. Directly supported by Windows NT 5.0 but not by NT 4.0, which may receive a software patch or service pack providing this capability.

IPX/SPX The native networking protocol for Novell NetWare. Also supported by Windows NT. Unlike NetBEUI, IPX is a routable protocol, which makes it suitable for larger networks.

ISDN (Integrated Services Digital Network) A high-speed digital line widely used in businesses and homes, which operates at speeds of up to 128 Kbps. ISDN can also split its bandwidth into two separate 64K channels, one of which can be used to carry voice and analog modem transmissions across the same digital line as the other 64 kilobit connection.

ISP (Internet service provider) A company that provides dial-up access to the Internet.

LAN (local-area network)

LDAP (Lightweight Directory Access Protocol) A new standard that allows client access to directory trees (such as Novell NDS or Microsoft's upcoming Active Directory) across the Internet. LDAP promises to allow cross-platform access to directory structures, thereby, at least in theory, allowing Windows NT 5.0 to access and modify NDS directory trees and vice versa.

Level I cache A small bank of extremely high-speed memory built directly into the microprocessor and which runs at the same speed as the processor. A Level I cache is used for caching series of instructions for the fastest possible execution. Level 1 memory size ranges from between 4K to 64K, depending on the processor.

Level II cache A somewhat larger bank of memory (usually 256K or 512K in PCs) used as a *buffer* between the processor's Level 1 memory and main memory. Intel's Pentium Pro microprocessor builds the Level II cache into the chip package, enhancing speed.

MAC address The unique 12-digit hexadecimal address code hard-wired into every network interface card (NIC) in the computer business. Only one card can have any individual MAC address.

MCNE Master Certified Novell Engineer.

MMX By some accounts it means *Matrix Math Extensions*. By other accounts this acronym is essentially meaningless. Created by Intel, MMX is built into its latest generation of microprocessors, including the Pentium MMX and the Pentium II. Commonly called *Multimedia Extensions,* that term is in fact incorrect. MMX represents the first major enhancement to the *x*86 processor instruction set since the introduction of the 80386. MMX contains a set of 57 new mathematical instructions also commonly used to accelerate the definition of computing elements such as graphics drawing, audio, and other PC-based data.

MSCE Microsoft Certified Engineer.

multihomed server A server with multiple network connections that can be routed through the server between each network segment. A server with a modem used for Remote Access and a single network card is a multihomed system, as are computers with more than one network card.

NDS (Novell Directory Services) A elegant centralized database containing information about all users on the network. NDS organizes itself in a hierarchical tree form, with the root level at the top.

NetBEUI A native protocol for Microsoft LAN Manager, and also directly supported by Windows NT. NetBEUI is a fast and simple, but non-routable, protocol best suited for small networks.

NIC (network interface card) The device that connects your system to a local-area network.

NOS (network operating system) Includes software such as Windows NT, Novell NetWare, Sun Solaris, and others.

NTFS (NT File System) The file system natively used by Windows NT.

PDC (Primary Domain Controller) Used as the main security and user account management system for the network.

PPTP (Point-to-Point Tunneling Protocol) See also Virtual Private Network.

RAS (Remote Access Service)

registry The central configuration database for Windows NT Server, Windows NT Workstation, and Windows 95 computers. Contains many key settings for system startup, system configuration and screen settings, user identification and preferences, and application file relationships, among other things.

replication In Windows NT, the process of reproducing users' logon script directories to a Backup Domain Controller.

router An electronic device used to connect subnets to larger networks, or to route data from one LAN to another LAN locally or over a WAN (wide-area network).

scalability Although this term can have several meanings, in our context it means *the scalability of the processor* – how many processors can run in parallel in the same system without expensive bridging circuitry. The term scalability also indicates the capacity of the network operating system (NOS) to service larger numbers of clients.

SCSI (Small Computer Systems Interface) A parallel-type general-use interface standard that supports multiple devices on a single high-speed bus. Numerous flavors are available. Windows NT requires a minimum of SCSI-II for efficient operation.

SDRAM (Synchronous DRAM) A memory architecture of the future, SDRAM supports up to 100 MHz bus speeds and more efficient memory access by the processor. SDRAM is standard Dynamic RAM with added synchronous control logic. Data addressing and controlling signals can be synchronized with the system clock, providing significant boosts in performance.

SIMM (Single In-line Memory Module) A common physical package for computer memory. SIMMs are so-called because they have a single row of I/O contacts.

SNMP (Simple Network Management Protocol) A basic low-level software mechanism for monitoring and managing network characteristics and performance.

stand-alone server For Windows NT, a server not set up as a domain of any kind. Typically, stand-alone servers are set up to service workgroups and do not use or participate in domain security. Consequently, many key networking and security features are disabled in stand-alone servers.

subnet A set of contiguous IP addresses broken out from a larger set, such as a C-class or B-class, from the Internet. The subnet is then assigned to a set of client computers, and its network traffic is routed to the larger network as needed.

subnet mask A 12-digit value that indicates to the server how many IP addresses (and therefore how many clients) can participate in a subnet. The subnet mask tells the computer how large the subnet is. Subnet mask values are limited in size to 4, 8, 16, 32, and 64 IP addresses for practical applications.

T1 A telecommunications standard that transfers data at 1.544 Mbps. T1 lines can be split up into multiple 64 kilobit channels called DS0's or into segments called Fractional T1's.

TCP (Transfer Control Protocol)

TCP/IP The core networking protocol for the Internet, and a rapidly growing option for enterprise networks. TCP/IP uses a 12-digit numerical addressing scheme (soon to be expanded to 18 digits) for every connectivity device on the network, including clients, servers and routers.

trust relationship The Windows NT-based process of establishing communications and resource sharing between different domain servers. Windows NT domains cannot automatically communicate, and trust relationships are Windows NT's mechanism for doing so.

Ultra–DMA Similar to Enhanced IDE; supports another new generation of high-capacity IDE hard disk devices with faster throughput capabilities. Theoretically capable of 33 Mbps throughput, but rarely achieves this in practice.

UNC (Universal Naming Convention) A directory path definition standard that allows the inclusion of NetBIOS computer names and their shared drives in the path.

user rights A Windows NT mechanism for defining how a user account interacts with the client system, the network, and the server. User rights contain a large number of different privileges, some or all of which may be included for the account depending on its type. An Administrator account has a much larger list of user rights privileges than a typical user account.

WAN (wide-area network) WANs allow networking connections between company buildings across the street or worldwide, and typically use high-speed connections such as frame relay or T1.

WINS (Windows Internet Name Service) A Windows-internal NetBIOS name service that resolves IP addresses to computer names inside Windows-only networks. Frequently used to complement name resolution services in larger networks, such as DNS. WINS can also be used over the Internet but presents huge security holes in that context, and it is *not* recommended that you do so.

workgroup A collection of client computers on a network. In a peer-to-peer network, a workgroup is the highest level of organization.

VGA (Video Graphics Array) The base standard for PC video displays, which defines a screen resolution of 640 x 480 pixels at 16 colors or 4-bit color depth. Current PCs go far beyond this standard for their displays.

VPN (Virtual Private Network) The practice of using a TCP/IP-based Internet connection as the underpinning for a second, *virtual* connection to a LAN, called a *tunnel*. The tunnel creates a secure local-area network connection from the client to the server, and requires the IP address from the server-side Internet connection.

Index

C

cabling, network, 15
cache
   DNS, 118-119, 132
   microprocessor, 5-6
   user profiles, 472-473
CACHE.DNS file, 119, 132
callback types, RAS, 319-320
Capture Printer Port, option, 254
CD-ROM, 14
   initialization, 45
   Windows NT 4.0, 19
Change Access Rights dialog box, 234
Change access type, 56
Chip Merchant Web site, 10
chip sets, 8-9
CHKDSK, 25, 44
Chooser, 170, 185-186, 188, 196-197
   System 8, 198-199
Class C network, 104-109
Client for Microsoft Networks, 85-87
Client Services for NetWare
   NetWare 3.12, 302-304
   NetWare 4.11, 279-281, 282, 289
command prompt commands, 143-149. *See also specific commands*
   accessing NetWare drive, 276-277
   checking MAC addresses, 123
   IPCONFIG, 149
   NBTSTAT, 145-148
   NET, 148-149
   NET USE, 466-467
   NETSTAT, 147-148
   Ping, 143-145
   TRACERT, 143
Compaq, 8
ComputerWorld Web site, 315
CONFIG.SYS, 45, 479
configuration utility
   CSNW, 280-281, 304
   GSNW, 270-275, 296-300

Configure Gateway dialog box, 272-275, 298-299
Configure Port Usage dialog box, 29-30, 39
configuring. *See* installing; *specific programs*
Connect dialog box, 438
Connect Network Drive dialog box, 160-162
Connect To box, 93
Control Panel. *See specific applications*
Copy To dialog box, 475
Create Scope dialog box, 134-136
Create Volume dialog box, 180-181, 184
CS Configuration Manager, 500
Cyrix processors, 5, 7

D

DAT (Digital Audio Tape) drives, 14, 494
default gateway address, 105, 108, 127, 382
deleting network clients, 148
Dell, 8
Demand-Dial Interface, 372, 373
DEVICE= statements, 45
DHCP (Dynamic Host Control Protocol), 36, 121-123
   installation on NT server, 133-136
   RAS, 338-340
   troubleshooting, 153, 343-344
   Windows 95 client, 150
DHCP Manager, 122
   Scope options, 137-141
   subnet masks, 134-135
DHCP Relay Agent service, 121, 124
Dial-Up-Networking (DUN)
   applet, 94-96
   configuring for Internet, 349-354
   MS Exchange, 398-403
   RAS for TCP/IP, 331-336
   RAS with NetBEUI, 322-328
   VPN connection, 365-370
Dialin Information dialog box, 94-95, 320
dialin permissions, 66
Diamond Web site, 18

(continued)

my2cents.idgbooks.com

Register This Book — And Win!

Visit **http://my2cents.idgbooks.com** to register this book and we'll automatically enter you in our monthly prize giveaway. It's also your opportunity to give us feedback: let us know what you thought of this book and how you would like to see other topics covered.

Discover IDG Books Online!

The IDG Books Online Web site is your online resource for tackling technology — at home and at the office.

Ten Productive and Career-Enhancing Things You Can Do at www.idgbooks.com

1. Nab source code for your own programming projects.

2. Download software.

3. Read Web exclusives: special articles and book excerpts by IDG Books Worldwide authors.

4. Take advantage of resources to help you advance your career as a Novell or Microsoft professional.

5. Buy IDG Books Worldwide titles or find a convenient bookstore that carries them.

6. Register your book and win a prize.

7. Chat live online with authors.

8. Sign up for regular e-mail updates about our latest books.

9. Suggest a book you'd like to read or write.

10. Give us your 2¢ about our books and about our Web site.

Not on the Web yet? It's easy to get started with *Discover the Internet*, at local retailers everywhere.

IDG BOOKS WORLDWIDE, INC. END–USER LICENSE AGREEMENT

4. <u>Restrictions on Use of Individual Programs</u>. You must follow the individual requirements and restrictions detailed for each individual program on the CD-ROM Installation Instructions page of this Book. These limitations are contained in the individual license agreements recorded on the CD-ROM. These restrictions include a requirement that after using the program for the period of time specified in its text, the user must pay a registration fee or discontinue use. By opening the Software packet(s), you will be agreeing to abide by the licenses and restrictions for these individual programs. None of the material on this disc or listed in this Book may ever be distributed, in original or modified form, for commercial purposes.

5. <u>Limited Warranty</u>.

(a) IDGB warrants that the Software and CD-ROM are free from defects in materials and workmanship under normal use for a period of sixty (60) days from the date of purchase of this Book. If IDGB receives notification within the warranty period of defects in materials or workmanship, IDGB will replace the defective CD-ROM.

(b) IDGB AND THE AUTHOR OF THE BOOK DISCLAIM ALL OTHER WARRANTIES, EXPRESS OR IMPLIED, INCLUDING WITHOUT LIMITATION IMPLIED WARRANTIES OF MERCHANTABILITY AND FITNESS FOR A PARTICULAR PURPOSE, WITH RESPECT TO THE SOFTWARE, THE PROGRAMS, THE SOURCE CODE CONTAINED THEREIN, AND/OR THE TECHNIQUES DESCRIBED IN THIS BOOK. IDGB DOES NOT WARRANT THAT THE FUNCTIONS CONTAINED IN THE SOFTWARE WILL MEET YOUR REQUIREMENTS OR THAT THE OPERATION OF THE SOFTWARE WILL BE ERROR FREE.

This limited warranty gives you specific legal rights, and you may have other rights that vary from jurisdiction to jurisdiction.

6. <u>Remedies</u>.

(a) IDGB's entire liability and your exclusive remedy for defects in materials and workmanship shall be limited to replacement of the Software, which is returned to IDGB at the address set forth below with a copy of your receipt. This Limited Warranty is void if failure of the Software has resulted from accident, abuse, or misapplication. Any replacement Software will be warranted for the remainder of the original warranty period or thirty (30) days, whichever is longer.

(b) In no event shall IDGB or the author be liable for any damages whatsoever (including without limitation damages for loss of business profits, business interruption, loss of business information, or any other pecuniary loss) arising out of the use of or inability to use the Book or the Software, even if IDGB has been advised of the possibility of such damages.

(c) Because some jurisdictions do not allow the exclusion or limitation of liability for consequential or incidental damages, the above limitation or exclusion may not apply to you.

7. <u>**U.S. Government Restricted Rights**</u>. Use, duplication, or disclosure of the Software by the U.S. Government is subject to restrictions stated in paragraph (c) (1) (ii) of the Rights in Technical Data and Computer Software clause of DFARS 252.227-7013, and in subparagraphs (a) through (d) of the Commercial Computer—Restricted Rights clause at FAR 52.227-19, and in similar clauses in the NASA FAR supplement, when applicable.

8. <u>General</u>. This Agreement constitutes the entire understanding of the parties and revokes and supersedes all prior agreements, oral or written, between them, and may not be modified or amended except in a writing signed by both parties hereto which specifically refers to this Agreement. This Agreement shall take precedence over any other documents that may be in conflict herewith. If any one or more provisions contained in this Agreement are held by any court or tribunal to be invalid, illegal or, otherwise unenforceable, each and every other provision shall remain in full force and effect.

CD-ROM Installation Instructions

The CD-ROM for this book contains a number of software programs, as well as an electronic version of the book. Follow these steps to install the software on the CD-ROM:

1. Appendix B, "What's on the CD-ROM" lists each program's path name under the title of each program.

2. Navigate to the applicable folder on the CD-ROM.

3. Most programs contain a file called setup.exe that will lead you through the setup procedure when double-clicked. Some programs have a self-extracting executable file, which will simply install all of the necessary files for you.

To view the electronic Acrobat PDF version of the book, you need to have the Acrobat Reader installed. The Acrobat Reader can be found in the Acrobat Reader folder on the CD-ROM. Double-click ar32e301.exe and Acrobat Reader will extract itself to your hard drive.

The Acrobat PDF version of the book is located in the Book folder on the CD-ROM.

See Appendix B, "What's on the CD-ROM," for more information about the programs on the CD-ROM.